EXPOSITORY THOUGHTS ON THE GOSPELS

Vol. 3: Luke

By
J.C. Ryle

www.gideonhousebooks.com

Expository Thoughts on the Gospels: Luke

J.C. Ryle

© 2016 Gideon House Books

Published by:
Gideon House Books
2137 Ash Grove Way
Dallas, TX 75228
www.gideonhousebooks.com

Typesetting & Cover Design: Josh Pritchard

ISBN-13: 978-1-943133-29-1

Also from Gideon House Books

Sovereign Grace by D.L. Moody

God's Light in Dark Clouds by Theodore Cuyler

A Church in the House by Matthew Henry

Indwelling Sin in Believers by John Owen

Secret Power by D.L. Moody

Thoughts for Young Men by J.C. Ryle

The Divine Liturgy of St. John Chrysostom

A Study on Dispensationalism by A.W. Pink

Prevailing Prayer: What Hinders It by D.L. Moody

The Duty of Pastors by John Owen

The Expulsive Power of a New Affection by Thomas Chalmers

According to Promise by Charles Spurgeon

The Resurrection: A Symposium by Charles Spurgeon

The Acceptable Sacrifice by John Bunyan

Find these titles and more at
www.gideonhousebooks.com

Contents

Preface 7

Luke 1 9
Luke 2 37
Luke 3 55
Luke 4 68
Luke 5 81
Luke 6 97
Luke 7 118
Luke 8 137
Luke 9 161
Luke 10 189
Luke 11 211
Luke 12 237
Luke 13 261
Luke 14 279
Luke 15 292
Luke 16 302
Luke 17 312
Luke 18 326
Luke 19 345
Luke 20 358
Luke 21 373
Luke 22 391
Luke 23 416
Luke 24 434

Preface

The volume now in the reader's hands, is a continuation of the "Expository Thoughts on the Gospels," of which two volumes have been already published.

The general design of the work has been so fully explained in the preface to the volume on Matthew, that it seems needless to say anything further on the subject. I will only remark that I have steadily adhered to the threefold object, which I proposed to myself, when I first began. I have endeavored to produce something which may meet the needs of heads of families in conducting family prayers—of district visitors in reading to the sick and unlearned—and of private students of the Bible who have neither large libraries nor much leisure. These three classes I have constantly kept in view. Their needs have been continually before my eyes. Whatever would be unsuitable to them I have diligently tried to avoid.

I now send forth this volume with an earnest prayer, that the Holy Spirit may bless it, and that God may be pleased to use it for His own glory and the benefit of many souls. My chief desire in all my writings, is to exalt the Lord Jesus Christ and make Him beautiful and glorious in the eyes of men; and to promote the increase of repentance, faith, and holiness upon earth. If this shall be the result of this volume, the labor that it has cost me will be more than repaid.

I have a strong conviction that we need more reverent, deep-searching study of the Scripture in the present day. Most of Christians see nothing beyond the surface of the Bible when they read it. We need a more clear knowledge of Christ, as a living Person, a living Priest, a living Physician, a living Friend, a living Advocate at the right hand of God, and a living Savior soon about to come again. Most of Christians know little of Christianity but its skeleton of doctrines. I desire never to forget these two things. If I can do anything to make Christ and the Bible more honorable in these latter days, I shall be truly thankful and content.

Chapter 1

Forasmuch as many have taken in hand to draw up a narrative concerning those matters which have been fulfilled among us, even as they delivered them unto us, who from the beginning were eyewitnesses and ministers of the word, it seemed good to me also, having traced the course of all things accurately from the first, to write unto thee in order, most excellent Theophilus; that thou mightest know the certainty concerning the things wherein thou wast instructed.

The Gospel of Luke, which we now begin, contains many precious things which are not recorded in the other three Gospels. Such, for instance, are the histories of Zachariah and Elizabeth, the angel's announcement to the Virgin Mary—and, to speak generally, the whole contents of the first two chapters. Such, again, are the narratives of the conversion of Zaccheus and of the penitent thief—the walk to Emmaus, and the famous parables of the Pharisee and Tax-collector, the rich man and Lazarus, and the Prodigal Son. These are portions of Scripture for which every well-instructed Christian feels peculiarly thankful. And for these we are indebted to the Gospel of Luke.

The short preface which we have now read is a peculiar feature of Luke's Gospel. But we shall find, on examination, that it is full of most useful instruction.

In the first place, Luke gives us a short, but valuable, sketch of the nature of a Gospel. He calls it, "a declaration of those things which are most surely believed among us." It is a narrative of facts about Jesus Christ.

Christianity is a religion built upon facts. Let us never lose sight of this. It came before mankind at first in this shape. The first preachers did not go up and down the world, proclaiming an elaborate, artificial system of abstruse doctrines and deep principles. They made it their first business to tell men great plain facts. They went about telling a sin-laden world, that the Son of God had come down to earth, and lived for us, and died for us, and risen again. The Gospel, at its first publication, was far more simple than many make it now. It was neither more nor less than the history of Christ.

Let us aim at greater simplicity in our own personal religion. Let Christ and His Person be the sun of our system, and let the main desire of our souls be to live the life of faith in Him, and daily know Him better. This was Paul's Christianity. "To me to live is Christ." (Philipp. 1:21.)

In the second place, Luke draws a beautiful picture of the true position of the apostles in the early church. He calls them, "eye-witnesses and servants of the word."

There is an instructive humility in this expression. There is an utter absence of that man-exalting tone which has so often crept into the Church. Luke gives the apostles no flattering titles. He affords not the slightest excuse to those who speak of them with idolatrous veneration, because of their office and nearness to our Lord.

He describes them as "eye-witnesses." They told men what they had seen with their own eyes, and heard with their own ears. (1 John 1:1.) He describes them as "servants of the word." They were servants of the word of the Gospel. They were men who counted it their highest privilege to carry about, as messengers, the tidings of God's love to a sinful world, and to tell the story of the cross.

Well would it have been for the Church and the world, if Christian ministers had never laid claim to higher dignity and honor than the apostles claimed for themselves. It is a mournful fact, that ordained men have constantly exalted themselves and their office to a most unscriptural position. It is a no less mournful fact, that people have constantly helped forward the evil, by a lazy acceptance of the demands of priest-craft, and by contenting themselves with a mere vicarious religion. There have been faults on both sides. Let us remember this, and be on our guard.

In the third place, Luke describes his own qualifications for the work of writing a Gospel. He says that he "had perfect understanding of all things from the very first."

It would be mere waste of time to inquire from what source Luke obtained the information which he has given us in his Gospel. We have no good reason for supposing that he saw our Lord work miracles, or heard Him teach. To say that he obtained his information from the Virgin Mary, or any of the apostles, is mere conjecture and speculation. Enough for us to know that Luke wrote by inspiration of God. Unquestionably he did not neglect the ordinary means of getting knowledge. But the Holy Spirit guided him, no less than all other writers of the Bible, in his choice of matter. The Holy Spirit supplied him with thoughts, arrangement, sentences, and even words. And the result is, that what Luke wrote is not to be read as the "word of man," but the "word of God." (1 Thess. 2:13.)

Let us carefully hold fast the great doctrine of the plenary inspiration of every word of the Bible. Let us never allow that any writer of the Old or New Testament could make even the slightest verbal mistake or error, when, writing as he was "moved by the Holy Spirit." (2 Peter 1:21.) Let it be a settled principle with us in reading the Bible, that when we cannot understand a passage, or reconcile it with some other passage, the fault is not in the Book, but in ourselves. The adoption of this principle will place our feet upon a rock. To give it up is to stand upon a quicksand, and to fill our minds with endless uncertainties and doubts.

Finally, Luke informs us of one main object he had in view in writing his Gospel. It was that Theophilus "might know the certainty of those things wherein he had been instructed."

There is no encouragement here for those who place confidence in unwritten traditions, and the voice of the church. Luke knew well the weakness of man's memory, and the readiness with which a history alters its shape both by additions and alterations, when it depends only on word of mouth and report. What therefore does he do? He takes care to "write."

There is no encouragement here for those who are opposed to the spread of religious knowledge, and talk of ignorance, as the "mother of devotion." Luke does not wish his friend to remain in doubt on any matter of his faith. He tells him that he wants him to "know the certainty of those things wherein he had been instructed."

Let us close the passage with thankfulness for the Bible. Let us bless God daily that we are not left dependent on man's traditions, and need not be led astray by ministers' mistakes. We have a written volume, which is "able to make us wise unto salvation, through faith which is in Christ Jesus." (2 Tim. 3:15.)

Let us begin Luke's Gospel with an earnest desire to know more ourselves of the truth as it is in Jesus, and with a hearty determination to do what in us lies to spread the knowledge of that truth throughout the world.

LUKE 1:5-12

THE BIRTH OF JOHN THE BAPTIST FORETOLD

There was in the days of Herod, king of Judaea, a certain priest named Zacharias, of the course of Abijah: and he had a wife of the daughters of Aaron, and her name was Elisabeth. And they were both righteous before God, walking in all the commandments and ordinances of the Lord blameless. And they had no child, because that Elisabeth was barren, and they both were now well stricken in years. Now it came to pass, while he executed the priest's office before God in the order of his course, according to the custom of the priest's office, his lot was to enter into the temple of the Lord and burn incense. And the whole multitude of the people were praying without at the hour of incense. And there appeared unto him an angel of the Lord standing on the right side of altar of incense. And Zacharias was troubled when he saw him, and fear fell upon him.

The first event recorded in Luke's Gospel, is the sudden appearance of an angel to a Jewish priest, named Zachariah. The angel announces to him that a son is about to be born to him, by a miraculous interposition, and that this son is to be the forerunner of the long-promised Messiah. The word of God had plainly foretold that when Messiah came, someone would go before him to prepare his way. (Malachi 3:1.) The wisdom of God provided that when this forerunner appeared, he would be born in the family of a priest.

We can form very little idea, at this period of the world, of the immense importance of this angel's announcement. To the mind of a pious Jew, it must have been glad tidings of great joy. It was the first communication from God to Israel since the days of Malachi. It broke the long silence of four hundred years. It told the believing Israelite that the prophetic weeks of Daniel were at length fulfilled, (Dan. 9:25,)—that God's choicest promise was at length going to be accomplished—and that "the seed" was about to appear in whom all the nations of the earth should be blessed. (Gen. 22:18.) We must place ourselves in imagination in the position of Zachariah, in order to give the verses before us their due weight.

Let us mark, for one thing, in this passage, the high testimony which is borne to the character of Zachariah and Elizabeth. We are told that they were "both righteous before God," and that "they walked in all the commandments and ordinances of the Lord blameless."

It matters little whether we interpret this "righteousness" as that which is imputed to all believers for their justification, or that which is wrought inwardly in believers by the operation of the Holy Spirit, for their sanctification. The two sorts of righteousness are never disjoined. There are none justified who are not sanctified, and there are none sanctified who are not justified. Suffice it for us to know that Zachariah and Elizabeth had grace when grace was very rare, and kept all the burdensome observances of the ceremonial law with devout conscientiousness, when few Israelites cared for them excepting in name and form.

The main thing that concerns us all, is the example which this holy pair hold up to Christians. Let us all strive to serve God faithfully, and live fully up to our light, even as they did. Let us not forget the plain words of Scripture, "He that does righteousness is righteous." (1 John 3:7.) Happy are those Christian families in which it can be reported that both husband and wife are "righteous," and exercise themselves to have a conscience void of offence toward God and toward men. (Acts 24:16.)

Let us mark, for another thing, in this passage, the heavy trial which God was pleased to lay on Zachariah and Elizabeth. We are told that "they had no child." The full force of these words can hardly be understood by a modern Christian. To an ancient Jew they would convey the idea of a very weighty affliction. To be childless was one of the bitterest of sorrows. (1 Sam. 1:10.)

The grace of God exempts no one from trouble. "Righteous" as this holy priest and his wife were, they had a "crook in their lot." Let us remember this, if we serve Christ, and let us count trial no strange thing. Let us rather believe that a hand of perfect wisdom is measuring out all our portion, and that when God chastises us, it is to make us "partakers of his holiness." (Heb. 12:10.) If afflictions drive us nearer to Christ, the Bible, and prayer, they are positive blessings. We may not think so now. But we shall think so when we wake up in another world.

Let us mark, for another thing, in this passage, the means by which God announced the coming birth of John the Baptist. We are told that "an ANGEL of the Lord appeared to Zachariah."

The ministry of angels is undoubtedly a deep subject. Nowhere in the Bible do we find such frequent mention of them, as in the period of our Lord's earthly ministry. At no time do we read of so many appearances of angels, as about the time of our Lord's incarnation and entrance into the world. The meaning of this circumstance is sufficiently clear. It was meant to teach the church that Messiah was no angel, but the Lord of angels, as well as of men. Angels announced His coming. Angels proclaimed His birth. Angels rejoiced at his appearing. And by so doing they made it plain that He who came to die for sinners, was not one of themselves, but one far above them, the King of kings and Lord of lords.

One thing, at all events, about angels, we must never forget. They take a deep interest in the work of Christ, and the salvation which Christ has provided. They sang high praise when the Son of God came down to make peace by His own blood between God and man. They rejoice when sinners repent, and sons are born again to our Father in heaven. They delight to minister to those who shall be heirs of salvation. Let us strive to be like them, while we are upon earth—to be of their mind, and to share their joys. This is the way to be in tune for heaven. It is written of those who enter in there, that they shall be "as the angels." (Mark 12:25.)

Let us mark, lastly, in this passage, the effect which the appearance of an angel produced on the mind of Zachariah. We are told that he "was troubled, and fear fell upon him."

The experience of this righteous man here, tallies exactly with that of other saints under similar circumstances. Moses at the burning bush, and Daniel at the river of Hiddekel—the women at the sepulcher, and John at the isle of Patmos—all showed like fear to that of Zachariah. Like him, when they saw visions of things belonging to another world, they trembled and were afraid.

How are we to account for this fear? To that question there is only one answer. It arises from our inward sense of weakness, guilt, and corruption. The vision of an inhabitant of heaven reminds us forcibly of our own imperfection, and of our natural unfitness to stand before God. If angels are so great and terrible, what must the Lord of angels be?

Let us bless God, that we have a mighty Mediator between God and man, the man Christ Jesus. Believing on Him, we may draw near to God with boldness, and look forward to the day of judgment without fear. When the mighty angels shall go forth to gather together God's elect, the elect will have no cause to be afraid. To them the angels are fellow-servants and friends. (Rev. 22:9.)

Let us tremble when we think of the terror of the wicked at the last day. If even the righteous are troubled by a sudden vision of friendly spirits, where will the ungodly appear, when the angels come forth to gather them like tares for the burning? The fears of the saints are groundless, and endure but for a little season. The fears of the lost, when once aroused, will prove well-grounded, and will endure for evermore.

LUKE 1:13-17

But the angel said unto him, Fear not, Zacharias: because thy supplication is heard, and thy wife Elisabeth shall bear thee a son, and thou shalt call his name John. And thou shalt have joy and gladness; and many shall rejoice at his birth. For he shall be great in the sight of the Lord, and he shall drink no wine nor strong drink; and he shall be filled with the Holy Spirit, even from his mother's womb. And many of the children of Israel shall he turn unto the Lord their God. And he shall go before his face in the spirit and power of Elijah, to turn the hearts of the fathers to the children, and the disobedient to walk in the wisdom of the just; to make ready for the Lord a people prepared for him.

We have, in these verses, the words of the angel who appeared to Zachariah. They are words full of deep spiritual instruction.

We learn here, for one thing, that prayers are not necessarily rejected because the answer is long delayed. Zachariah, no doubt, had often prayed for the blessing of children, and, to all appearance, had prayed in vain. At his advanced time of life, he had probably long ceased to mention the subject before God, and had given up all hope of being a father. Yet the very first words of the angel show plainly that the bygone prayers of Zachariah had not been forgotten—"Your prayer is heard—your wife Elizabeth shall bear you a son."

We shall do well to remember this fact, whenever we kneel down to pray. We must beware of hastily concluding that our supplications are useless, and specially in the matter of intercessory prayer in behalf of others. It is not for us to prescribe either the time or the way in which our requests are to be answered. He who knows best the time for people to be born, knows also the time for them to be born again. Let us rather "continue in prayer," "watch unto prayer," "pray always, and not faint." "Delay of answer," says an old divine, "must not discourage our faith. It may be, God has long granted, before we shall know of His grant."

We learn, in the second place, that no children cause such true joy, as those who have the grace of God. It was a child about to be filled with the

Holy Spirit, to whose father it was said, "You shall have joy and gladness; and many shall rejoice at his birth."

Grace is the principal portion that we should desire for our children. It is a thousand times better for them than beauty, riches, honors, rank, or high connections. Until they have grace we never know what they may do. They may make us weary of our life, and bring down our grey hairs with sorrow to the grave. When they are converted, and not until then, they are provided for, both for time and eternity. "A wise son makes a glad father." (Prov. 10:1.) Whatever we seek for our sons and daughters, let us first seek that they may have a place in the covenant, and a name in the book of life.

We learn, in the third place, the nature of true greatness. The angel describes it, when he tells Zachariah that his son "shall be great in the sight of the Lord."

The measure of greatness which is common among men is utterly false and deceptive. Princes and potentates, conquerors and leaders of armies, statesmen and philosophers, artists and authors—these are the kind of men whom the world calls "great." Such greatness is not recognized among the angels of God. Those who do great things for God, they reckon great. Those who do little for God, they reckon little. They measure and value every man according to the position in which he is likely to stand at the last day.

Let us not be ashamed to make the angels of God our example in this matter. Let us seek for ourselves and our children that true greatness which will be owned and recognized in another world. It is a greatness which is within the reach of all—of the poor as well as the rich—of the servant as well as of the master. It does not depend on power or patronage, on money or on friends. It is the free gift of God to all who seek it at the Lord Jesus Christ's hands. It is the portion of all who hear Christ's voice and follow Him—who fight Christ's battle and do Christ's work in the world. Such may receive little honor in this life. But great shall be their reward at the last day.

We learn, in the fourth place, that children are never too young to receive the grace of God. Zachariah is informed that his son "shall be filled with the Holy Spirit, even from his mother's womb."

There is no greater mistake than to suppose that infants, by reason of their tender age, are incapable of being operated upon by the Holy Spirit. The manner of His work upon a little child's heart, is undoubtedly mysterious and incomprehensible. But so also are all His works upon the sons of men. Let us beware of limiting God's power and compassion. He is a merciful God. With Him nothing is impossible.

Let us remember these things in connection with the subject of infant baptism. It is a feeble objection to say that infants ought not to be baptized, because they cannot repent and believe. If an infant can be filled with the Holy Spirit, he is surely not unworthy to be admitted into the visible church. Let us remember these things specially in the training of young children. We should always deal with them as responsible to God. We should never allow ourselves to suppose that they are too young to have any religion. Of course we must be reasonable in our expectations. We must not look for evidences of grace, unsuitable to their age and capacities. But we must never forget that the heart which is not too young to sin, is also not too young to be filled with the grace of God.

We learn, in the last place, from these verses, the character of a really great and successful minister of God. The picture is set before us in a striking manner by the angel's description of John the Baptist. He is one who will "turn hearts"—turn them from ignorance to knowledge, from carelessness to thoughtfulness, from sin to God. He is one who will "go before the Lord"—he will delight in nothing so much as being the messenger and herald of Jesus Christ. He is one who "will make ready a people for the Lord." He will strive to gather out of the world a company of believers, who will be ready to meet the Lord in the day of His appearing.

For such ministers let us pray night and day. They are the true pillars of a Church, the true salt of the earth, the true light of the world. Happy is that Church, and happy is that nation, which has many such men. Without such men, learning, titles, endowments, and splendid buildings, will keep no Church alive. Souls will not be saved—good will not be done—Christ will not be glorified, excepting by men full of the Holy Spirit.

LUKE 1:18-25

And Zacharias said unto the angel, Whereby shall I know this? for I am an old man, and my wife well stricken in years. And the angel answering said unto him, I am Gabriel, that stand in the presence of God; and I was sent to speak unto thee, and to bring thee these good tidings. And behold, thou shalt be silent and not able to speak, until the day that these things shall come to pass, because thou believedst not my words, which shall be fulfilled in their season. And the people were waiting for Zacharias, and they marvelled while he tarried in the temple. And when he came out, he could not speak unto them: and they perceived that he had seen a vision in the temple: and he continued making signs unto them, and remained dumb. And it came to pass, when the days of his ministration were fulfilled, he departed unto his house. And after these days Elisabeth his wife conceived; and she hid herself five months, saying, Thus hath the Lord done unto me in the days wherein he looked upon me, to take away my reproach among men.

We see in this passage, the power of unbelief in a good man. Righteous and holy as Zachariah was, the announcement of the angel appears to him incredible. He cannot think it possible that an old man like himself should have a son. "How shall I know this?" he says, "for I am an old man, and my wife well along in years."

A well-instructed Jew, like Zachariah, ought not to have raised such a question. No doubt he was well acquainted with the Old Testament Scriptures. He ought to have remembered the wonderful births of Isaac, and Samson, and Samuel in old times. He ought to have remembered that what God has done once, He can do again, and that with Him nothing is impossible. But he forgot all this. He thought of nothing but the arguments of mere human reason and sense. And it often happens in religious matters, that where reason begins, faith ends.

Let us learn in wisdom from the fault of Zachariah. It is a fault to which God's people in every age have been sadly liable. The histories of Abraham, and Isaac, and Moses, and Hezekiah, and Jehoshaphat, will all show us that a true believer may sometimes be overtaken by unbelief. It is one of the first corruptions which came into man's heart in the day of the fall, when Eve believed the devil rather than God. It is one of the most deep-rooted sins by which a saint is plagued, and from which he is never entirely freed until he dies. Let us pray daily, "Lord increase my faith." Let us not doubt that when God says a thing, that thing shall be fulfilled.

We see furthermore, in these verses, the privilege and portion of God's angels. They carry messages to God's Church. They enjoy God's immediate presence. The heavenly messenger who appears to Zachariah, rebukes his unbelief by telling him who he is—"I am Gabriel, who stands in the presence of God—and am sent to speak unto you."

The name "Gabriel" would doubtless fill the mind of Zachariah with humiliation and self-abasement. He would remember it was that same Gabriel, who 490 years before had brought to Daniel the prophecy of the seventy weeks, and had told him how Messiah should be cut off. (Dan. 9:26.) He would doubtless contrast his own sad unbelief, when peaceably ministering as a priest in God's temple, with the faith of holy Daniel when dwelling a captive at Babylon, while the temple at Jerusalem was in ruins. Zachariah learned a lesson that day which he never forgot.

The account which Gabriel gives of his own office, should raise in our minds great searchings of heart. This mighty spirit, far greater in power and intelligence than we are, counts it his highest honor to "stand in God's presence" and do His will. Let our aims and desires be in the same direction. Let us strive so to live, that we may one day stand with boldness before the throne of God, and serve Him day and night in His temple. The way to this high and holy position is open before us. Christ has consecrated it for us by the offering of His own body and blood. May we endeavor to walk in it during the short time of this present life, that so we may stand in our lot with God's elect angels in the endless ages of eternity. (Dan. 12:13.)

We see, finally, in this passage, how exceeding sinful is the sin of unbelief in the sight of God. The doubts and questionings of Zachariah brought down upon him a heavy chastisement. "You shall be silent," says the angel, "and not able to speak, because you believe not my words." It was a chastisement peculiarly suitable to the offence. The tongue that was not ready to speak the language of believing praise was struck speechless. It was a chastisement of long continuance. For nine long months at least, Zachariah was condemned to silence, and was daily reminded, that by unbelief he had offended God.

Few sins appear to be so peculiarly provoking to God as the sin of unbelief. None certainly have called down such heavy judgments on men. It is a practical denial of God's Almighty power, to doubt whether He can do a thing, when He undertakes to do it. It is giving the lie to God to doubt whether He means to do a thing, when He has plainly promised that it shall be done. The forty years wanderings of Israel in the wilderness, should never be forgotten by professing Christians. The words of Paul are very solemn—"They could not enter in because of unbelief." (Heb. 3:19.)

Let us watch and pray daily against this soul-ruining sin. Concessions to it rob believers of their inward peace—weaken their hands in the day of battle—bring clouds over their hopes—make their chariot wheels drive heavily. According to the degree of our faith will be our enjoyment of Christ's salvation—our patience in the day of trial—our victory over the world. Unbelief, in short, is the true cause of a thousand spiritual diseases, and once allowed to nestle in our hearts, will eat as does a canker. "If you will not believe, you shall not be established." (Isaiah 7:9.) In all that respects the pardon of our sins, and the acceptance of our souls—the duties of our peculiar station and the trials of our daily life, let it be a settled maxim in our religion, to trust every word of God implicitly, and to beware of unbelief.

LUKE 1:26-33
THE BIRTH OF JESUS FORETOLD

Now in the sixth month the angel Gabriel was sent from God unto a city of Galilee, named Nazareth, to a virgin betrothed to a man whose name was Joseph, of the house of David; and the virgin's name was Mary. And he came in unto her, and said, Hail, thou that art highly favored, the Lord is with thee. But she was greatly troubled at the saying, and cast in her mind what manner of salutation this might be. And the angel said unto her, Fear not, Mary: for thou hast found favor with God. And behold, thou shalt conceive in thy womb, and bring forth a son, and shalt call his name JESUS. He shall be great, and shall be called the Son of the Most High: and the Lord God shall give unto him the throne of his father David: and he shall reign over the house of Jacob forever; and of his kingdom there shall be no end.

We have, in these verses, the announcement of the most marvelous event that ever happened in this world—the incarnation and birth of our Lord Jesus Christ. It is a passage which we should always read with mingled wonder, love and praise.

We should notice, in the first place, the lowly and unassuming manner in which the Savior of mankind came among us. The angel who announced His advent, was sent to an obscure town of Galilee, named Nazareth. The woman who was honored to be our Lord's mother, was evidently in a humble position of life. Both in her station and her dwelling-place, there was an utter absence of what the world calls "greatness."

We need not hesitate to conclude, that there was a wise providence in all this arrangement. The Almighty counsel, which orders all things in heaven and earth, could just as easily have appointed Jerusalem to be the place of Mary's residence as Nazareth, or could as easily have chosen the daughter of some rich scribe to be our Lord's mother, as a poor woman. But it seemed good that it should not be so. The first advent of Messiah was to be an advent of humiliation. That humiliation was to begin even from the time of His conception and birth.

Let us beware of despising poverty in others, and of being ashamed of it if God lays it upon ourselves. The condition of life which Jesus voluntarily chose, ought always to be regarded with holy reverence. The common tendency of the day to bow down before rich men, and make an idol of money, ought to be carefully resisted and discouraged. The example of our Lord is a sufficient answer to a thousand groveling maxims about wealth, which pass current among men. "Though He was rich, yet for our sakes He became poor." (2 Cor. 8:9.)

Let us admire the amazing condescension of the Son of God. The Heir of all things not only took our nature upon Him, but took it in the most humbling form in which it could have been assumed. It would have been condescension to come on earth as a king and reign. It was a miracle of mercy passing our comprehension to come on earth as a poor man, to be despised, and suffer, and die. Let His love constrain us to live not to ourselves, but to Him. Let His example daily bring home to our conscience the precept of Scripture—"Mind not high things, but condescend to men of low estate." (Rom. 12:16.)

We should notice, in the second place, the high privilege of the Virgin Mary. The language which the angel Gabriel addresses to her is very remarkable. He calls her "highly favored." He tells her that "the Lord is with her." He says to her, "Blessed are you among women."

It is a well-known fact, that the Roman Catholic Church pays an honor to the Virgin Mary, hardly inferior to that which it pays to her blessed Son. She is formally declared by the Roman Catholic Church to have been "conceived without sin." She is held up to Roman Catholics as an object of worship, and prayed to as a mediator between God and man, no less powerful than Christ Himself. For all this, be it remembered, there is not the slightest warrant in Scripture. There is no warrant in the verses before us now. There is no warrant in any other part of God's word.

But while we say this, we must in fairness admit, that no woman was ever so highly honored as the mother of our Lord. It is evident that one woman only out of the countless millions of the human race, could be the means whereby God could be "manifest in the flesh," and the Virgin Mary had the mighty privilege of being that one. By one woman, sin and death were brought into the world at the beginning. By the child-bearing of one woman, life and immortality were brought to light when Christ was born. No wonder that this one woman was called "highly favored" and "blessed."

One thing in connection with this subject should never be forgotten by Christians. There is a relationship to Christ within reach of us all—a relationship far nearer than that of flesh and blood—a relationship which belongs to all who repent and believe. "Whoever shall do the will of God," says Jesus, "the same is my brother, and sister, and mother." "Blessed is the womb that bare you," was the saying of a woman one day. But what was the reply? "Yes! rather blessed are those who hear the word of God and keep it." (Mark 3:35; Luke 11:27.)

We should notice, finally, in these verses, the glorious account of our Lord Jesus Christ, which the angel gives to Mary. Every part of the account is full of deep meaning, and deserves close attention.

Jesus "shall be great," says Gabriel. Of His greatness we know something already. He has brought in a great salvation. He has shown Himself a Prophet greater than Moses. He is a great High Priest. And He shall be greater still when He shall be owned as a King.

Jesus "shall be called the Son of the Highest," says Gabriel. He was so before He came into the world. Equal to the Father in all things, He was from all eternity the Son of God. But He was to be known and acknowledged as such by the Church. The Messiah was to be recognized and worshiped as nothing less than very God.

"The Lord God shall give unto Him the throne of his father David," says Gabriel, "and He shall reign over the house of Jacob forever." The literal fulfillment of this part of the promise is yet to come. Israel is yet to be gathered. The Jews are yet to be restored to their own land, and to look to Him whom they once pierced, as their King and their God. Though the accomplishment of this prediction tarry, we may confidently wait for it. It shall surely come one day and not tarry. (Hab. 2:3.)

Finally, says Gabriel, "Of the kingdom of Jesus there shall be no end." Before His glorious kingdom, the empires of this world shall one day go down and pass away. Like Nineveh, and Babylon, and Tyre, and Carthage, they shall all come to nothing one day, and the saints of the most high shall take the kingdom. Before Jesus, every knee shall one day bow, and every tongue confess that He is Lord. His kingdom alone shall prove an everlasting kingdom, and His dominion that which shall not pass away. (Dan. 7:14, 27.)

The true Christian should often dwell on this glorious promise and take comfort in its contents. He has no cause to be ashamed of his Master. Poor and despised as he may often be for the Gospel's sake, he may feel assured that he is on the conquering side. The kingdoms of this world shall yet become the kingdoms of Christ. Yet a little time and He that shall come will come, and will not tarry. (Heb. 10:37.) For that blessed day let us patiently wait, and watch, and pray. Now is the time for carrying the cross, and for fellowship with Christ's sufferings. The day draws near when Christ shall take His great power and reign; and when all who have served Him faithfully shall exchange a cross for a crown.

LUKE 1:34-38

And Mary said unto the angel, How shall this be, seeing I know not a man? And the angel answered and said unto her, The Holy Spirit shall come upon thee, and the power of the Most High shall overshadow thee: wherefore also the holy thing which is begotten shall be called the Son of God. And behold, Elisabeth thy kinswoman, she also hath conceived a son in her old age; and this is the sixth month with her that was called barren. For no word from God shall be void of power. And Mary said, Behold, the handmaid of the Lord; be it unto me according to thy word. And the angel departed from her.

Let us mark, in these verses, the reverent and discreet manner in which the angel Gabriel speaks of the great mystery of Christ's incarnation. In reply to the question of the Virgin "How shall this be?" he uses these remarkable words—"The Holy Spirit shall come upon you, and the power of the Highest shall overshadow you."

We shall do well to follow the example of the angel in all our reflections on this deep subject. Let us ever regard it with holy reverence, and abstain from those improper and unprofitable speculations upon it, in which some have unhappily indulged. Enough for us to know that "the Word was made flesh," and that when the Son of God came into the world, a real "body was prepared for Him," so that He "took part of our flesh and blood," and was "made of a woman." (John 1:14; Heb. 10:5; Heb. 2:14; Gal. 4:4.) Here we must stop. The manner in which all this was effected is wisely hidden from us. If we attempt to pry beyond this point, we shall but darken counsel by words without knowledge, and rush in where angels fear to tread. In a religion which really comes down from heaven there must needs be mysteries. Of such mysteries in Christianity, the incarnation is one.

Let us mark, in the second place, the prominent place assigned to the Holy Spirit in the great mystery of the incarnation. We find it written, "The Holy Spirit shall come upon you."

An intelligent reader of the Bible will probably not fail to remember, that the honor here given to the Spirit is in precise harmony with the teaching of Scripture in other places. In every step of the great work of man's redemption, we shall find special mention of the work of the Holy Spirit. Did Jesus die to make atonement for our sins? It is written that "through the eternal Spirit He offered himself without spot to God." (Heb. 9:14.) Did He rise again for our justification? It is written that He "was quickened by the Spirit." (1 Peter 3:18.) Does He supply His disciples with comfort between the time of His first and second advent? It is written that the Comforter, whom He promised to send is "the Spirit of truth." (John 14:17.)

Let us take heed that we give the Holy Spirit the same place in our personal religion, which we find Him occupying in God's word. Let us remember, that all that believers have, and are, and enjoy under the Gospel, they owe to the inward teaching of the Holy Spirit. The work of each of the three Persons of the Trinity is equally and entirely needful to the salvation of every saved soul. The ELECTION of God the Father, the REDEMPTION of God the Son, and the SANCTIFICATION of God the Spirit, ought never to be separated in our Christianity.

Let us mark, in the third place, the mighty principle which the angel Gabriel lays down to silence all objections about the incarnation. "With God nothing shall be impossible."

A hearty reception of this great principle is of immense importance to our own inward peace. Questions and doubts will often arise in men's minds about many subjects in religion. They are the natural result of our fallen estate of soul. Our faith at the best is very feeble. Our knowledge at its highest is clouded with much infirmity. And among many antidotes to a doubting, anxious, questioning state of mind, few will be found more useful than that before us now—a thorough conviction of the almighty power of God. With Him who called the world into being and formed it out of nothing, everything is possible. Nothing is too hard for the Lord.

There is no sin too black and bad to be pardoned. The blood of Christ cleanses from all sin. There is no heart too hard and wicked to be changed. The heart of stone can be made a heart of flesh. There is no work too hard for a believer to do. We may do all things through Christ strengthening us. There is no trial too hard to be borne. The grace of God is sufficient for us. There is no promise too great to be fulfilled. Christ's words never pass away, and what He has promised He is able to perform. There is no difficulty too great for a believer to overcome. When God is for us who shall be against us? The mountain shall become a plain. Let principles like these be continually before our minds. The angel's receipt is an invaluable remedy.

Faith never rests so calmly and peacefully as when it lays its head on the pillow of God's omnipotence.

Let us mark, in the last place, the meek and ready acquiescence of the Virgin Mary in God's revealed will concerning her. She says to the angel, "Behold the handmaid of the Lord; be it unto me according to your word."

There is far more of admirable grace in this answer than at first sight appears. A moment's reflection will show us, that it was no light matter to become the mother of our Lord in this unheard of and mysterious way. It brought with it, no doubt, at a distant period great honor; but it brought with it for the present no small danger to Mary's reputation, and no small trial to Mary's faith. All this danger and trial the holy Virgin was willing and ready to risk. She asks no further questions. She raises no further objections. She accepts the honor laid upon her with all its attendant perils and inconveniences. "Behold," she says, "the handmaid of the Lord."

Let us seek in our daily practical Christianity to exercise the same blessed spirit of faith which we see here in the Virgin Mary. Let us be willing to go anywhere, and do anything, and be anything, whatever be the present and immediate inconvenience, so long as God's will is clear and the path of duty is plain. The words of good Bishop Hall on this passage are worth remembering.

"All disputations with God after His will is known, arise from infidelity. There is not a more noble proof of faith than to captivate all the powers of our understanding and will to our Creator, and without any questionings to go blindfold where He will lead us."

LUKE 1:39-45

MARY VISITS ELIZABETH

And Mary arose in these days and went into the hill country with haste, into a city of Judah; and entered into the house of Zacharias and saluted Elisabeth. And it came to pass, when Elisabeth heard the salutation of Mary, the babe leaped in her womb; and Elisabeth was filled with the Holy Spirit; and she lifted up her voice with a loud cry, and said, Blessed art thou among women, and blessed is the fruit of thy womb. And whence is this to me, that the mother of my Lord should come unto me? For behold, when the voice of thy salutation came into mine ears, the babe leaped in my womb for joy. And blessed is she that believed; for there shall be a fulfilment of the things which have been spoken to her from the Lord.

We should observe in this passage, the benefit of fellowship and communion between believers. We read of a visit paid by the Virgin Mary to her cousin Elizabeth. We are told in a striking manner how the hearts of both these holy women were cheered, and their minds lifted up by this interview. Without this visit, Elizabeth might never have been so filled with the Holy Spirit, as we are here told she was; and Mary might never have uttered that song of praise which is now known all over the Church of Christ. The words of an old divine are deep and true—"Happiness communicated doubles itself. Grief grows greater by concealing—joy by expression."

We should always regard communion with other believers as an eminent means of grace. It is a refreshing break in our journey along the narrow way to exchange experience with our fellow travelers. It helps us insensibly and it helps them, and so is a mutual gain. It is the nearest approach that we can make on earth to the joy of heaven. "As iron sharpens iron, so does the countenance of a man his friend." We need reminding of this. The subject does not receive sufficient attention, and the souls of believers suffer in consequence. There are many who fear the Lord and think upon His name, and yet forget to speak often one to another. (Malachi 3:16.) First let us seek the face of God. Then let us seek the face of God's friends. If we did this more, and were more careful about the company we keep, we would oftener know what it is to feel filled with the Holy Spirit.

We should observe in this passage, the clear spiritual knowledge which appears in the language of Elizabeth. She uses an expression about the Virgin Mary which shows that she herself was deeply taught of God. She calls her "the mother of my Lord."

Those words "my Lord" are so familiar to our ears, that we miss the fullness of their meaning. At the time they were spoken they implied far more than we are apt to suppose. They were nothing less than a distinct declaration that the child who was to be born of the Virgin Mary was the long promised Messiah, the "Lord" of whom David in spirit had prophesied, the Christ of God. Viewed in this light, the expression is a wonderful example of faith. It is a confession worthy to be placed by the side of that of Peter, when he said to Jesus, "You are the Christ."

Let us remember the deep meaning of the words, "the Lord," and beware of using them lightly and carelessly. Let us consider that they rightly apply to none but Him who was crucified for our sins on Calvary. Let the recollection of this fact invest the words with a holy reverence, and make us careful how we let them fall from our lips. There are two texts connected with the expression which should often come to our minds. In one it is written, "No man can say that Jesus is the Lord but by the Holy Spirit." In the other it is written, "Every tongue shall confess that Jesus Christ is Lord, to the glory of God the Father." (1 Cor. 12:3. Philipp. 2:11.)

Finally, we should observe in these verses, the high praise which Elizabeth bestows upon the grace of faith. "Blessed," she says, "is she who has believed that what the Lord has said to her will be accomplished!" We need not wonder that this holy woman should thus commend faith. No doubt she was well acquainted with the Old Testament Scriptures. She knew the great things that faith had done. What is the whole history of God's saints in every age but a record of men and women who obtained a good report by faith? What is the simple story of all from Abel downwards but a narrative of redeemed sinners who believed, and so were blessed? By faith they embraced promises. By faith they lived. By faith they walked. By faith they endured hardships. By faith they looked to an unseen Savior, and good things yet to come. By faith they battled with the world, the flesh, and the devil. By faith they overcame, and got safely home. Of this goodly company the Virgin Mary was proving herself one. No wonder that Elizabeth said, "Blessed is she who has believed that what the Lord has said to her will be accomplished!"

Do we know anything of this precious faith? This, after all, is the question that concerns us. Do we know anything of the faith of God's elect, the faith which is the working of God? (Titus 1:2. Col. ii. 12.) Let us never rest until we know it by experience. Once knowing it, let us never cease to pray that our faith may grow exceedingly. Better a thousand times be rich in faith than rich in gold. Gold will be worthless in the unseen world to which we are all traveling. Faith will be owned in that world before God the Father and the holy angels. When the great white throne is set, and the books are opened, when the dead are called from their graves, and receiving their final sentence, the value of faith will at length be fully known. Men will learn then, if they never learned before, how true are the words, "Blessed are those who believed."

LUKE 1:46-56

MARY'S SONG

And Mary said, My soul doth magnify the Lord, And my spirit hath rejoiced in God my Saviour. For he hath looked upon the low estate of his handmaid: For behold, from henceforth all generations shall call me blessed. For he that is mighty hath done to me great things; And holy is his name. And his mercy is unto generations and generations On them that fear him. He hath showed strength with his arm; He hath scattered the proud in the imagination of their heart. He hath put down princes from their thrones, And hath exalted them of low degree. The hungry he hath filled with good things; And the rich he hath sent empty away. He hath given help to Israel his servant, That he might remember mercy (As he spake unto our fathers) Toward Abraham and his seed for ever. And Mary abode with her about three months, and returned unto her house.

These verses contain the Virgin Mary's famous hymn of praise, in the prospect of becoming the "mother of our Lord." Next to the Lord's Prayer, perhaps, few passages of Scripture are better known than this. Wherever the Church of England Prayer-book is used, this hymn forms part of the evening service. And we need not wonder that the compilers of that Prayer-book gave it so prominent a place. No words can express more aptly the praise for redeeming mercy which ought to form part of the public worship of every branch of Christ's Church.

Let us mark, firstly, the full acquaintance with Scripture which this hymn exhibits. We are reminded as we read it, of many expressions in the book of Psalms. Above all, we are reminded of the song of Hannah, in the book of Samuel. (1 Sam. 2) It is evident that the memory of the Blessed Virgin was stored with Scripture. She was familiar, whether by hearing or by reading, with the Old Testament. And so, when out of the abundance of her heart her mouth spoke, she gave vent to her feelings in Scriptural language. Moved by the Holy Spirit to break forth into praise, she chooses language which the Holy Spirit had already consecrated and used.

Let us strive, every year we live, to become more deeply acquainted with Scripture. Let us study it, search into it, dig into it, meditate on it, until it dwell in us richly. (Coloss. 3:16.) In particular, let us labor to make ourselves familiar with those parts of the Bible which, like the book of Psalms, describe the experience of the saints of old. We shall find it most helpful to us in all our approaches to God. It will supply us with the best and most suitable language both for the expression of our needs and thanksgivings. Such knowledge of the Bible can doubtless never be attained without regular, daily study. But the time spent on such study is never misspent. It will bear fruit after many days.

Let us mark, secondly, in this hymn of praise, the Virgin Mary's deep humility. She who was chosen of God to the high honor of being Messiah's mother, speaks of her own "low estate," and acknowledges her need of a "Savior." She does not let fall a word to show that she regarded herself as a sinless, "immaculate" person. On the contrary, she uses the language of one who has been taught by the grace of God to feel her own sins, and so far from being able to save others, requires a Savior for her own soul. We may safely affirm that none would be more forward to reprove the honor paid by the Romish Church to the Virgin Mary, than the Virgin Mary herself.

Let us copy this holy humility of our Lord's mother, while we steadfastly refuse to regard her as a mediator, or to pray to her. Like her, let us be lowly in our own eyes, and think little of ourselves. Humility is the highest grace that can adorn the Christian character. It is a true saying of an old divine, that "a man has just so much Christianity as he has humility." It is the grace, which of all is most suiting to human nature. Above all, it is the grace which is within the reach of every converted person. All are not rich. All are not learned. All are not highly gifted. All are not preachers. But all children of God may be clothed with humility.

Let us mark, thirdly, the lively thankfulness of the Virgin Mary. It stands out prominently in all the early part of her hymn. Her "soul magnifies the Lord." Her "spirit rejoices in God." "All generations shall call her blessed." "Great things have been done for her." We can scarcely enter into the full extent of feelings which a holy Jewess would experience on finding herself in Mary's position. But we should try to recollect them as we read her repeated expressions of praise.

We too shall do well to walk in Mary's steps in this matter, and cultivate a thankful spirit. It has ever been a mark of God's most distinguished saints in every age. David, in the Old Testament, and Paul, in the New, are remarkable for their thankfulness. We seldom read much of their writings without finding them blessing and praising God. Let us rise from our beds every morning with a deep conviction that we are debtors, and that every day we have more mercies than we deserve. Let us look around us every week, as we travel through the world, and see whether we have not much to thank God for. If our hearts are in the right place, we shall never find any difficulty in building an Ebenezer. Well would it be if our prayers and supplications were more mingled with thanksgiving. (1 Sam. 7:12. Phil. 4:6.)

Let us mark, fourthly, the experimental acquaintance with God's former dealings with His people, which the Virgin Mary possessed. She speaks of God as One whose "mercy is on those who fear Him"—as One who "scatters the proud, and puts down the mighty, and sends the rich empty away"—as

One who "exalts them of low degree, and fills the hungry with good things." She spoke, no doubt, in recollection of Old Testament history. She remembered how Israel's God had put down Pharaoh, and the Canaanites, and the Philistines, and Sennacherib, and Haman, and Belshazzar. She remembered how He had exalted Joseph and Moses, and Samuel, and David, and Esther, and Daniel, and never allowed His chosen people to be completely destroyed. And in all God's dealings with herself, in placing honor upon a poor woman of Nazareth—in raising up Messiah in such a dry ground as the Jewish nation seemed to have become—she traced the handiwork of Israel's covenant God.

The true Christian should always give close attention to Bible history, and the lives of individual saints. Let us often examine the "footsteps of the flock." (Cant. 1:8.) Such study throws light on God's mode of dealing with His people. He is of one mind. What He does for them, and to them, in time past, He is likely to do in time to come. Such study will teach us what to expect, check unwarrantable expectations, and encourage us when cast down. Happy is that man whose mind is well stored with such knowledge. It will make him patient and hopeful.

Let us mark, lastly, the firm grasp which the Virgin Mary had of Bible promises. She ends her hymn of praise by declaring that God has "blessed Israel in remembrance of His mercy," and that He has done "as He spoke to our fathers, to Abraham and his seed forever." These words show clearly that she remembered the old promise made to Abraham, "In you shall all nations of the earth be blessed." And it is evident that in the approaching birth of her Son she regarded this promise as about to be fulfilled.

Let us learn from this holy woman's example, to lay firm hold on Bible promises. It is of the deepest importance to our peace to do so. Promises are, in fact, the manna that we should daily eat, and the water that we should daily drink, as we travel through the wilderness of this world. We see not yet all things put under us. We see not Christ, and heaven, and the book of life and the mansions prepared for us. We walk by faith, and this faith leans on promises. But on those promises we may lean confidently. They will bear all the weight we can lay on them. We shall find one day, like the Virgin Mary, that God keeps His word, and that what He has spoken, so He will always in due time perform.

LUKE 1:57-66

THE BIRTH OF JOHN THE BAPTIST

Now Elisabeth's time was fulfilled that she should be delivered; and she brought forth a son. And her neighbors and her kinsfolk heard that the Lord had magnified his mercy towards her; and they rejoiced with her. And it came to pass on the eighth day, that they came to circumcise the child; and they would have called him Zacharias, after the name of the father. And his mother answered and said, Not so; but he shall be called John. And they said unto her, There is none of thy kindred that is called by this name. And they made signs to his father, what he would have him called. And he asked for a writing tablet, and wrote, saying, His name is John. And they marvelled all. And his mouth was opened immediately, and his tongue loosed, and he spake, blessing God. And fear came on all that dwelt round about them: and all these sayings were noised abroad throughout all the hill country of Judaea. And all that heard them laid them up in their heart, saying, What then shall this child be? For the hand of the Lord was with him.

We have in this passage the history of a birth, the birth of a burning and shining light in the Church, the forerunner of Christ Himself—John the Baptist. The language in which the Holy Spirit describes the event is well worthy of remark. It is written that "The Lord showed great mercy to Elizabeth." There was mercy in bringing her safely through her time of trial. There was mercy in making her the mother of a living child. Happy are those family circles, whose births are viewed in this light—as especial instances of "the mercy" of the Lord.

We see in the conduct of Elizabeth's neighbors and cousins, a striking example of the kindness we owe to one another. It is written that "They rejoiced with her." How much more happiness there would be in this evil world, if conduct like that of Elizabeth's relations was more common! Sympathy in one another's joys and sorrows costs little, and yet is a grace of most mighty power. Like the oil on the wheels of some large engine, it may seem a trifling and unimportant thing, yet in reality it has an immense influence on the comfort and well-working of the whole machine of society. A kind word of congratulation or consolation is seldom forgotten. The heart that is warmed by good tidings, or chilled by affliction, is peculiarly susceptible, and sympathy to such a heart is often more precious than gold.

The servant of Christ will do well to remember this grace. It seems "a little one," and amid the din of controversy, and the battle about mighty doctrines, we are sadly apt to overlook it. Yet it is one of those pins of the tabernacle which we must not leave in the wilderness. It is one of those ornaments of the Christian character which make it beautiful in the eyes of men. Let us not forget that it is enforced upon us by a special precept—"Rejoice with those who do rejoice, and weep with those who weep." (Rom. 12:15.) The practice of it seems to bring down a special blessing. The Jews who came to comfort Mary and Martha at Bethany, saw the greatest miracle that Jesus ever worked. Above all, it is commended to us by the most perfect example. Our Lord was ready both to go to a marriage feast, and to weep at a grave. (John 2, John 11) Let us be ever ready to go and do likewise.

We see in the conduct of Zachariah in this passage, a striking example of the benefit of affliction. He resists the wishes of his relations to call his new-born son after his own name. He clings firmly to the name "John," by which the angel Gabriel had commanded him to be called. He shows that his nine months' dumbness had not been inflicted on him in vain. He is no longer faithless, but believing. He now believes every word that Gabriel had spoken to him, and every word of his message shall be obeyed.

We need not doubt that the past nine months had been a most profitable time to the soul of Zachariah. He had learned, probably, more about his own heart, and about God, than he ever knew before. His conduct shows it. Correction had proved instruction. He was ashamed of his unbelief. Like Job, he could say, "I have heard of you by the hearing of the ear, but now my eye sees you." Like Hezekiah, when the Lord left him, he had found out what was in his heart. (Job 42:5. 2 Chron. 32:31.)

Let us take heed that affliction does us good, as it did to Zachariah. We cannot escape trouble in a sin-laden world. Man is born to trouble, as the sparks fly upwards. (Job 5:7.) But in the time of our trouble, let us make earnest prayer that we may "hear the rod and who has appointed it," that we may learn wisdom by the rod, and not harden our hearts against God. "Sanctified afflictions," says an old divine, "are spiritual promotions." The sorrow that humbles us, and drives us nearer to God, is a blessing, and a downright gain. No case is more hopeless than that of the man who, in time of affliction turns his back upon God. There is a dreadful mark set against one of the kings of Judah—"In his time of trouble King Ahaz became even more unfaithful to the Lord." (2 Chron. 28:22.)

We see in the early history of John Baptist the nature of the blessing that we should desire for all young children. We read that "the hand of the Lord was with him."

We are not told distinctly what these words mean. We are left to gather their meaning from the promise that went before John before his birth, and the life that John lived all his days. But we need not doubt that the hand of the Lord was with John to sanctify and renew his heart—to teach and fit him for his office—to strengthen him for all his work as the forerunner of the Lamb of God-to encourage him in all his bold denunciation of men's sins—and to comfort him in his last hours, when he was beheaded in prison. We know that he was filled with the Holy Spirit from his mother's womb. We need not doubt that from his earliest years the grace of the Holy Spirit appeared in his ways. In his boyhood as well as in his manhood the constraining power of a mighty principle from above appeared in him. That power was the "hand of the Lord."

This is the portion that we ought to seek for our children. It is the best portion, the happiest portion, the only portion that can never be lost, and will endure beyond the grave. It is good to have over them "the hand" of teachers and instructors; but it is better still to have "the hand of the Lord." We may be thankful if they obtain the patronage of the great and the rich. But we ought to care far more for their obtaining the favor of God. The hand of the Lord is a thousand times better than the hand of Herod. The one is weak, foolish, and uncertain; caressing today and beheading tomorrow. The other is almighty, all-wise, and unchangeable. Where it holds it holds for evermore. Let us bless God that the Lord never changes. What He was in John the Baptist's day, He is now. What He did for the son of Zachariah, He can do for our boys and girls. But He waits to be entreated. If we would have the hand of the Lord with our children, we must diligently seek it.

LUKE 1:67-80

ZACHARIAH'S SONG

And his father Zacharias was filled with the Holy Spirit, and prophesied, saying, Blessed be the Lord, the God of Israel; For he hath visited and wrought redemption for his people, And hath raised up a horn of salvation for us In the house of his servant David (As he spake by the mouth of his holy prophets that have been from of old), Salvation from our enemies, and from the hand of all that hate us; To show mercy towards, our fathers, And to remember his holy covenant; The oath which he spake unto Abraham our father, To grant unto us that we being delivered out of the hand of our enemies Should serve him without fear, In holiness and righteousness before him all our days. Yea and thou, child, shalt be called the prophet of the Most High: For thou shalt go before the face of the Lord to make ready his ways; To give knowledge of salvation unto his people In the remission of their sins, Because of the tender mercy of our God, Whereby the dayspring from on high shall visit us, To shine upon them that sit in darkness and the shadow of death; To guide our feet into the way of peace. And the child grew, and waxed strong in spirit, and was in the deserts till the day of his showing unto Israel.

Another hymn of praise demands our attention in these verses. We have read the thanksgiving of Mary, the mother of our Lord. Let us now read the thanksgiving of Zachariah, the father of John the Baptist. We have heard what praises the first advent of Christ drew from the Virgin of the house of David. Let us now hear what praise it draws from an aged priest.

We should notice, firstly, the deep thankfulness of a Jewish believer's heart in the prospect of Messiah's appearing. Praise is the first word that falls from the mouth of Zachariah as soon as his speechlessness is removed, and his tongue restored. He begins with the same expression with which Paul begins several of his epistles—"Blessed be the Lord."

At this period of the world we can hardly understand the depth of this good man's feelings. We must imagine ourselves in his position. We must fancy ourselves seeing the fulfillment of the oldest promise in the Old Testament-the promise of a Savior, and beholding the accomplishment of this promise brought near to our own door. We must try to realize what a dim and imperfect view men had of the Gospel before Christ actually appeared, and the shadows and types passed away. Then perhaps we may have some idea of the feelings of Zachariah when he cried out, "Blessed be the Lord."

It may be feared that Christians have very low and inadequate conceptions of their amazing privileges in living under the full light of the Gospel. We have probably a very faint idea of the comparative dimness and twilight of the Jewish dispensation. We have a very feeble notion of what a church must have been before the incarnation of Christ. Let us open our eyes to the extent of our obligations. Let us learn from the example of Zachariah, to be more thankful.

We should notice, secondly, in this hymn of praise, how much emphasis Zachariah lays on God's fulfillment of His promises. He declares that God has "visited and redeemed his people," speaking of it in the manner of the prophets as a thing already accomplished, because sure to take place. He goes on to proclaim the instrument of this redemption—"a horn of salvation"—a strong Savior of the house of David. And then he adds that all this is done, "as He spoke by the mouth of His holy prophet, to perform the mercy promised, to remember His holy covenant, and the oath which He swore to our father Abraham."

It is clear that the souls of Old Testament believers fed much on God's promises. They were obliged to walk by faith far more than we are. They knew nothing of the great facts which we know about Christ's life, and death, and resurrection. They looked forward to redemption as a thing hoped for, but not yet seen—and their only warrant for their hope was God's covenanted word. Their faith may well put us to shame. So far from disparaging Old Testament believers, as some are disposed to do, we ought to marvel that they were what they were.

Let us learn to rest on promises and embrace them as Zachariah did. Let us not doubt that every word of God about His people concerning things future, shall as surely be fulfilled as every word about them has been fulfilled concerning things past. Their safety is secured by promise. The world, the flesh, and the devil, shall never prevail against any believer. Their acquittal at the last day is secured by promise. They shall not come into condemnation, but shall be presented spotless before the Father's throne. Their final glory is secured by promise. Their Savior shall come again the second time, as surely as He came the first—to gather His saints together and to give them a crown of righteousness. Let us be persuaded of these promises. Let us embrace them and not let them go. They will never fail us. God's word is never broken. He is not a man that He should lie. We have a seal on every promise which Zachariah never saw. We have the seal of Christ's blood to assure us, that what God has promised God will perform.

We should notice, thirdly, in this hymn, what clear views of Christ's kingdom Zachariah possessed. He speaks of being "saved and delivered from the hands of enemies," as if he had in view a temporal kingdom and a temporal deliverer from Gentile power. But he does not stop here. He declares that the kingdom of Messiah, is a kingdom in which His people are to "serve Him without fear, in holiness and righteousness before Him." This kingdom, he proclaimed, was drawing near. Prophets had long foretold that it would one day be set up. In the birth of his son John the Baptist, and the near approach of Christ, Zachariah saw this kingdom close at hand.

The foundation of this kingdom of Messiah was laid by the preaching of the Gospel. From that time the Lord Jesus has been continually gathering out subjects from an evil world. The full completion of the kingdom is an event yet to come. The saints of the Most High shall one day have entire dominion. The little stone of the Gospel-kingdom shall yet fill the whole earth. But whether in its incomplete or complete state, the subjects of the kingdom are always of one character. They "serve God without fear." They serve God in "holiness and righteousness."

Let us give all diligence to belong to this kingdom. Small as it seems now, it will be great and glorious one day. The men and women who have served God in "holiness and righteousness" shall one day see all things put under them. Every enemy shall be subdued, and they shall reign forever in that new heaven and earth, wherein dwells righteousness.

We should notice, finally, what clear views of doctrine Zachariah enjoyed. He ends his hymn of praise by addressing his infant son John the Baptist. He foretells that he shall "go before the face" of Messiah, and "give knowledge of the salvation" that He is about to bring in—a salvation which is all of grace and mercy—a salvation of which the leading privileges are "remission of sins," "light," and "peace."

Let us end the chapter by examining what we know of these three glorious privileges. Do we know anything of pardon? Have we turned from darkness to light? Have we tasted peace with God? These, after all, are the realities of Christianity. These are the things, without which church-membership and sacraments save no one's soul. Let us never rest until we are experimentally acquainted with them. Mercy and grace have provided them. Mercy and grace will give them to all who call on Christ's name. Let us never rest until the Spirit witnesses with our spirit that our sins are forgiven us, that we have passed from darkness to light, and that we are actually walking in the narrow way, the way of peace.

Chapter 2

Now it came to pass in those days, there went out a decree from Caesar Augustus, that all the world should be enrolled. This was the first enrolment made when Quirinius was governor of Syria. And all went to enroll themselves, everyone to his own city. And Joseph also went up from Galilee, out of the city of Nazareth, into Judaea, to the city of David, which is called Bethlehem, because he was of the house and family of David; to enroll himself with Mary, who was betrothed to him, being great with child. And it came to pass, while they were there, the days were fulfilled that she should be delivered. And she brought forth her firstborn son; and she wrapped him in swaddling clothes, and laid him in a manger, because there was no room for them in the inn.

We have, in these verses, the story of a birth—the birth of the incarnate Son of God, the Lord Jesus Christ. Every birth of a living child is a marvelous event. It brings into being a soul that will never die. But never since the world began was a birth so marvelous as the birth of Christ. In itself it was a miracle—"God was manifest in the flesh." (1 Tim. 3:16.) The blessings it brought into the world were unspeakable—it opened to man the door of everlasting life.

In reading these verses, let us first notice the TIMES when Christ was born. It was in the days when Augustus, the first Roman emperor, made "a decree that all the world should be taxed."

The wisdom of God appears in this simple fact. The scepter was practically departing from Judah. (Gen. 49:10.) The Jews were coming under the dominion and taxation of a foreign power. Strangers were beginning to rule over them. They had no longer a really independent government of their own. The "due time" had come for the promised Messiah to appear. Augustus taxes "the world," and at once Christ is born.

It was a time peculiarly suitable for the introduction of Christ's Gospel. The whole civilized earth was at length governed by one master. (Dan. 2:40.) There was nothing to prevent the preacher of a new faith going from city to city, and country to country. The princes and priests of the heathen world had been weighed in the balances and found lacking. Egypt, and Assyria, and Babylon, and Persia, and Greece, and Rome, had all successively proved that "the world by wisdom knew not God." (1 Cor. 1:21.) Notwithstanding their mighty conquerors, and poets, and historians, and architects, and philosophers, the kingdoms of the world were full of dark idolatry. It was indeed "due time" for God to interpose from heaven, and send down an almighty Savior. It was "due time" for Christ to be born. (Rom. 5:6.)

Let us ever rest our souls on the thought, that times are in God's hand. (Psalm 31:15.) He knows the best season for sending help to His church, and new light to the world. Let us beware of giving way to over anxiety about the course of events around us, as if we knew better than the King of kings what time relief should come. "Cease, Philip, to try to govern the world," was a frequent saying of Luther to an anxious friend. It was a saying full of wisdom.

Let us notice, secondly, the PLACE where Christ was born. It was not at Nazareth of Galilee, where His mother, the Virgin Mary, lived. The prophet Micah had foretold that the event was to take place at Bethlehem. (Micah 5:2.) And so it came to pass. At Bethlehem Christ was born.

The overruling providence of God appears in this simple fact. He orders all things in heaven and earth. He turns the hearts of kings wherever He will. He overruled the time when Augustus decreed the taxing. He directed the enforcement of the decree in such a way, that Mary must needs be at Bethlehem when "the time came for the baby to be born." Little did the haughty Roman emperor, and his officer Cyrenius, think that they were only instruments in the hand of the God of Israel, and were only carrying out the eternal purposes of the King of kings. Little did they think that they were helping to lay the foundation of a kingdom, before which the empires of this world would all go down one day, and Roman idolatry pass away. The words of Isaiah, upon a like occasion, should be remembered, "He means not so, neither does his heart think so." (Isaiah 10:7.)

The heart of a believer should take comfort in the recollection of God's providential government of the world. A true Christian should never be greatly moved or disturbed by the conduct of the rulers of the earth. He should see with the eye of faith a hand overruling all that they do to the praise and glory of God. He should regard every king and potentate—an Augustus, a Cyrenius, a Darius, a Cyrus, a Sennacherib—as a creature who, with all his power, can do nothing but what God allows, and nothing which is not carrying out God's will. And when the rulers of this world "set themselves against the Lord," he should take comfort in the words of Solomon, "There is one higher than they." (Eccles. 5:8.)

Let us notice, lastly, the MANNER in which Christ was born. He was not born under the roof of His mother's house, but in a strange place, and at an "inn." When born, He was not laid in a carefully prepared cradle. He was "laid in a manger (that is, a feeding trough for the cattle), because there was no room in the inn."

We see here the grace and condescension of Christ. Had He come to save mankind with royal majesty, surrounded by His Father's angels, it would have been an act of undeserved mercy. Had He chosen to dwell in a palace, with power and great authority, we should have had reason enough to wonder. But to become poor as the very poorest of mankind, and lowly as the very lowliest—this is a love that passes knowledge. It is unspeakable and unsearchable. Never let us forget that through this humiliation Jesus has purchased for us a title to glory. Through His life of suffering, as well as His death, He has obtained eternal redemption for us. All through His life He was poor for our sakes, from the hour of His birth to the hour of His death. And through His poverty we are made rich. (2 Cor. 8:9.)

Let us beware of despising the poor, because of their poverty. Their condition is one which the Son of God has sanctified and honored, by taking it voluntarily on Himself. God is no respecter of people. He looks at the hearts of men, and not at their incomes. Let us never be ashamed of the affliction of poverty, if God thinks fit to lay it upon us. To be godless and covetous is disgraceful, but it is no disgrace to be poor. A lowly dwelling place, and coarse food, and a hard bed, are not pleasing to flesh and blood. But they are the portion which the Lord Jesus Himself willingly accepted from the day of His entrance into the world. Wealth ruins far more souls than poverty. When the love of money begins to creep over us, let us think of the manger at Bethlehem, and of Him who was laid in it. Such thoughts may deliver us from much harm.

LUKE 2:8-20

THE SHEPHERDS AND THE ANGELS

And there were shepherds in the same country abiding in the field, and keep-ing watch by night over their flock. And an angel of the Lord stood by them, and the glory of the Lord shone round about them: and they were sore afraid. And the angel said unto them, Be not afraid; for behold, I bring you good tidings of great joy which shall be to all the people: for there is born to you this day in the city of David a Saviour, who is Christ the Lord. And this is the sign unto you: Ye shall find a babe wrapped in swaddling clothes, and lying in a manger. And suddenly there was with the angel a multitude of the heavenly host praising God, and saying, Glory to God in the highest, And on earth peace among men in whom he is well pleased. And it came to pass, when the angels went away from them into heaven, the shepherds said one to another, Let us now go even unto Bethlehem, and see this thing that is come to pass, which the Lord hath made known unto us. And they came with haste, and found both Mary and Joseph, and the babe lying in the manger. And when they saw it, they made known concerning the saying which was spoken to them about this child. And all that heard it wondered at the things which were spoken unto them by the shepherds. But Mary kept all these sayings, pondering them in her heart. And the shepherds returned, glorifying and praising God for all the things that they had heard and seen, even as it was spoken unto them.

We read, in these verses, how the birth of the Lord Jesus was first an-nounced to the children of men. The birth of a king's son is generally made an occasion of public reveling and rejoicing. The announcement of the birth of the Prince of Peace was made privately, at midnight, and without anything of worldly pomp and ostentation.

Let us mark who they were to whom the tidings first came that Christ was born. They were "shepherds abiding in the field near Bethlehem, keeping watch over their flocks by night." To shepherds—not to priests and rulers—to shepherds—not to Scribes and Pharisees, an angel appeared, proclaiming, "unto you is born this day a Savior, who is Christ the Lord."

The saying of James should come into our mind, as we read these words-"Has not God chosen the poor of this world, rich in faith and heirs of the kingdom, which he has promised to those who love him." (James 2:5.) The lack of money debars no one from spiritual privileges. The things of God's kingdom are often hidden from the great and noble, and revealed to the poor. The busy labor of the hands need not prevent a man being favored with special communion with God. Moses was keeping sheep, Gideon was threshing wheat, Elisha was ploughing, when they were each honored by direct calls and revelations from God. Let us resist the suggestion of Satan, that religion is not for the working man. The weak of the world are often called before the mighty. The last are often first, and the first last.

Let us mark, secondly, the language used by the angel in announcing Christ's birth to the shepherds. He said, "I bring you good tidings of great joy, which shall be to all people."

We need not wonder at these words. The spiritual darkness which had covered the earth for four thousand years, was about to be rolled away. The way to pardon and peace with God was about to be thrown open to all mankind. The head of Satan was about to be crushed. Liberty was about to be proclaimed to the captives, and recovering of sight to the blind. The mighty truth was about to be proclaimed that God could be just, and yet, for Christ's sake, justify the ungodly. Salvation was no longer to be seen through types and figures, but openly, and face to face. The knowledge of God was no longer to be confined to the Jews, but to be offered to the whole Gentile world. The days of heathenism were numbered. The first stone of God's kingdom was about to be set up. If this was not "good tidings," there never were tidings that deserved the name.

Let us mark, thirdly, who they were that first praised God, when Christ was born. They were ANGELS, and not men—angels who had never sinned, and needed no Savior—angels who had not fallen, and required no redeemer, and no atoning blood. The first hymn to the honor of "God manifest in the flesh," was sung by "a multitude of the heavenly host."

Let us note this fact. It is full of deep spiritual lessons. It shows us what good servants the angels are. All that their heavenly Master does pleases and interests them. It shows us what clear knowledge they have. They know what misery sin has brought into creation. They know the blessedness of heaven, and the privilege of an open door into it. Above all, it shows us the deep love and compassion which the angels feel towards poor lost man. They rejoice in the glorious prospect of many souls being saved, and many brands plucked from the burning.

Let us strive to be more like-minded with the angels. Our spiritual ignorance and deadness appear most painfully in our inability to enter into the joy which we see them here expressing. Surely if we hope to dwell with them forever in heaven, we ought to share something of their feelings while we are here upon earth. Let us seek a more deep sense of the sinfulness and misery of sin, and then we shall have a more deep sense of thankfulness for redemption.

Let us mark, fourthly, the hymn of praise which the heavenly host sung in the hearing of the shepherds. They said, "Glory to God in the highest, and on earth peace, good will towards men."

These famous words are variously interpreted. Man is by nature so dull in spiritual things, that it seems as if he cannot understand a sentence of heavenly language when he hears it. Yet a meaning may be drawn from the words which is free from any objection, and is not only good sense, but excellent theology, "Glory to God in the highest!" the song begins. Now is come the highest degree of glory to God, by the appearing of His Son Jesus Christ in the world. He by His life and death on the cross will glorify God's attributes—justice, holiness, mercy, and wisdom—as they never were glorified before. Creation glorified God, but not so much as redemption.

"Peace on earth!" the song goes on. Now is come to earth the peace of God which passes all understanding—the perfect peace between a holy God and sinful man, which Christ was to purchase with His own blood—the peace which is offered freely to all mankind—the peace which, once admitted into the heart, makes men live at peace one with another, and will one day overspread the whole world.

"Good will towards men!" the song concludes. Now is come the time when God's kindness and good will towards guilty man is to be fully made known. His power was seen in creation. His justice was seen in the flood. But His mercy remained to be fully revealed by the appearing and atonement of Jesus Christ.

Such was the purport of the angels' song. Happy are they that can enter into its meaning, and with their hearts subscribe to its contents. The man who hopes to dwell in heaven, should have some experimental acquaintance with the language of its inhabitants.

Let us mark, before we leave the passage, the prompt obedience to the heavenly vision displayed by the shepherds. We see in them no doubts, or questionings, or hesitation. Strange and improbable as the tidings might seem, they at once act upon them. They went to Bethlehem in haste. They found everything exactly as it had been told them. Their simple faith received a rich reward. They had the mighty privilege of being the first of all mankind, after Mary and Joseph, who saw with believing eyes the new-born Messiah. They soon returned, "glorifying and praising God" for what they had seen.

May our spirit be like theirs! May we ever believe implicitly, act promptly, and wait for nothing, when the path of duty is clear! So doing, we shall have a reward like that of the shepherds. The journey that is begun in faith, will generally end in praise.

LUKE 2:21-24
JESUS PRESENTED IN THE TEMPLE

And when eight days were fulfilled for circumcising him, his name was called JESUS, which was so called by the angel before he was conceived in the womb. And when the days of their purification according to the law of Moses were fulfilled, they brought him up to Jerusalem, to present him to the Lord (as it is written in the law of the Lord, Every male that openeth the womb shall be called holy to the Lord), and to offer a sacrifice according to that which is said in the law of the Lord, A pair of turtledoves, or two young pigeons.

The first point which demands our attention in this passage, is the obedience which our Lord rendered, as an infant, to the Jewish law. We read of His being circumcised on the eighth day. It is the earliest fact which is recorded in His history.

It is a mere waste of time to speculate, as some have done, about the reason why our Lord submitted to circumcision. We know that "in Him was no sin," either original or actual. (1 John 3:5.) His being circumcised was not meant in the least as an acknowledgment that there was any tendency to corruption in His heart. It was not a confession of inclination to evil, and of need of grace to mortify the deeds of His body. All this should be carefully borne in mind.

Let it suffice us to remember that our Lord's circumcision was a public testimony to Israel, that according to the flesh He was a Jew, made of a Jewish woman, and "made under the law." (Galat. 4:4.) Without it He would not have fulfilled the law's requirements. Without it He could not have been recognized as the son of David, and the seed of Abraham.

Let us remember, furthermore, that circumcision was absolutely necessary before our Lord could be heard as a teacher in Israel. Without it he would have had no place in any lawful Jewish assembly, and no right to any Jewish ordinance. Without it He would have been regarded by all Jews as nothing better than an uncircumcised Gentile, and an apostate from the faith of the fathers.

Let our Lord's submission to an ordinance which He did not need for Himself, be a lesson to us in our daily life. Let us endure much, rather than increase the offence of the Gospel, or hinder in any way the cause of God. The words of Paul deserve frequent pondering—"Though I be free from all men, yet have I made myself servant unto all, that I might gain the more, and unto the Jews I became as a Jew, that I might gain the Jews—to those who are under the law, as under the law, that I might gain those who are under the law." "I am made all things to all men, that I might by all means save some." (1 Cor. 9:19-22.) The man who wrote these words walked very closely in the footsteps of His crucified Master.

The second point which demands our attention in this passage, is the name by which our Lord was called, by God's special command. "Eight days later, when the baby was circumcised, he was named JESUS, the name given him by the angel even before he was conceived." The word Jesus means simply "Savior." It is the same word as "Joshua" in the Old Testament. Very striking and instructive is the selection of this name. The Son of God came down from heaven to be not only the Savior, but the King, the Lawgiver, the Prophet, the Priest, the Judge of fallen man. Had He chosen any one of these titles, He would only have chosen that which was His own. But He passed by them all. He selects a name which speaks of mercy, grace, help, and deliverance for a lost world. It is as a deliverer and Redeemer that He desires principally to be known.

Let us often ask ourselves what our own hearts know of the Son of God. Is He our Jesus, our Savior? This is the question on which our salvation turns. Let it not content us to know Christ as One who wrought mighty miracles, and spoke as never man spoke; or to know Him as One who is very God, and will one day judge the world. Let us see that we know Him experimentally, as our Deliverer from the guilt and power of sin, and our Redeemer from Satan's bondage. Let us strive to be able to say, "This is my Friend—I was dead, and He gave me life—I was a prisoner, and He set me free." Precious indeed is this name of Jesus to all true believers! It is "as ointment poured forth." (Cant. 1:3.) It restores them when conscience-troubled. It comforts them when cast down. It smooths their pillows in sickness. It supports them in the hour of death. "The name of the Lord is a strong tower; the righteous runs into it, and is safe." (Prov. 18:10.)

The last point which demands our attention in this passage, is the poor and humble condition of our Lord's mother, the Virgin Mary. This is a fact which, at first sight, may not stand out clearly in the form of these verses. But a reference to the twelfth chapter of Leviticus will at once make it plain. There we shall see, that the offering which Mary made was specially appointed to be made by poor people—"If she is not able to bring a lamb, then she shall bring two turtle-doves, or two young pigeons." In short, her offering was a public declaration that she was poor. (Lev. 12:6.)

Poverty, it is manifest, was our Lord's portion upon earth, from the days of His earliest infancy. He was nursed and tended as a babe, by a poor woman. He passed the first thirty years of His life on earth, under the roof of a poor man. We need not doubt that He ate a poor man's food, and wore a poor man's apparel, and worked a poor man's work, and shared in all a poor man's troubles. Such condescension is truly marvelous. Such an example of humility passes man's understanding.

Facts like these ought often to be laid to heart by poor people. They would help to silence murmuring and complaining, and go far to reconcile them to their hard lot. The simple fact that Jesus was born of a poor woman, and lived all his life on earth among poor people, ought to silence the common argument that "religion is not for the poor." Above all it ought to encourage every poor believer in all his approaches to the throne of grace in prayer. Let him remember in all his prayers that his mighty Mediator in heaven is accustomed to poverty, and knows by experience the heart of a poor man. Well would it be for the world if working men could only see that Christ is the true poor man's friend!

LUKE 2:25-35

THE PROPHECY OF SIMEON

And behold, there was a man in Jerusalem whose name was Simeon; and this man was righteous and devout, looking for the consolation of Israel: and the Holy Spirit was upon him. And it had been revealed unto him by the Holy Spirit, that he should not see death, before he had seen the Lord's Christ. And he came in the Spirit into the temple: and when the parents brought in the child Jesus, that they might do concerning him after the custom of the law, then he received him into his arms, and blessed God, and said, Now lettest thou thy servant depart, Lord, According to thy word, in peace; For mine eyes have seen thy salvation, Which thou hast prepared before the face of all peoples; A light for revelation to the Gentiles, And the glory of thy people Israel. And his father and his mother were marvelling at the things which were spoken concerning him; and Simeon blessed them, and said unto Mary his mother, Behold, this child is set for the falling and the rising of many in Israel; and for a sign which is spoken against; yea and a sword shall pierce through thine own soul; that thoughts out of many hearts may be revealed.

We have in these verses the history of one whose name is nowhere else mentioned in the New Testament, "a just and devout man" named Simeon. We know nothing of his life before or after the time when Christ was born. We are only told that he came by the Spirit into the temple, when the child Jesus was brought there by His mother, and that he "took him up in his arms and blessed God "in words which are now well-known all over the world.

We see, in the case of Simeon, how God has a believing people even in the worst of places, and in the darkest times. Religion was at a very low ebb in Israel when Christ was born. The faith of Abraham was spoiled by the doctrines of Pharisees and Sadducees. The fine gold had become deplorably dim. Yet even then we find in the midst of Jerusalem a man "just and devout"-a man "upon whom is the Holy Spirit."

It is a cheering thought that God never leaves Himself entirely without a witness. Small as His believing church may sometimes be, the gates of hell shall never completely prevail against it. The true church may be driven into the wilderness, and be a scattered little flock, but it never dies. There was a Lot in Sodom and an Obadiah in Ahab's household, a Daniel in Babylon and a Jeremiah in Zedekiah's court; and in the last days of the Jewish Church, when its iniquity was almost full, there were godly people, like Simeon, even in Jerusalem.

True Christians, in every age, should remember this and take comfort. It is a truth which they are apt to forget, and in consequence to give way to despondency. "I alone am left," said Elijah, "and they seek my life to take it away." But what said the answer of God to him, "Yet have I reserved seven thousand in Israel." (1 Kings 19:14, 18.) Let us learn to be more hopeful. Let us believe that grace can live and flourish, even in the most unfavorable circumstances. There are more Simeons in the world than we suppose.

We see in the song of Simeon how completely a believer can be delivered from the fear of death. "Lord," says old Simeon, "now let you your servant depart in peace." He speaks like one for whom the grave has lost its terrors, and the world its charms. He desires to be released from the miseries of this pilgrim-state of existence, and to be allowed to go home. He is willing to be "absent from the body and present with the Lord." He speaks as one who knows where he is going when he departs this life, and cares not how soon he goes. The change with him will be a change for the better, and he desires that his change may come.

What is it that can enable a mortal man to use such language as this? What can deliver us from that "fear of death" to which so many are in bondage? What can take the sting of death away? There is but one answer to such questions. Nothing but strong faith can do it. Faith laying firm hold on an unseen Savior, faith resting on the promises of an unseen God—faith, and faith only, can enable a man to look death in the face, and say, "I depart in peace." It is not enough to be weary of pain, and sickness, and ready to submit to anything for the sake of a 'hopeful change'. It is not enough to feel indifferent to the world, when we have no more strength to mingle in its business, or enjoy its pleasures. We must have something more than this, if we desire to depart in real peace. We must have faith like old Simeon's, even that faith which is the gift of God. Without such faith we may die quietly, and there may seem "no bands in our death." (Psalm 73:4.) But, dying without such faith, we shall never find ourselves at home, when we wake up in another world.

We see, furthermore, in the song of Simeon, what clear views of Christ's work and office some Jewish believers attained, even before the Gospel was preached. We find this good old man speaking of Jesus as "the salvation which God had prepared"—as "a light to enlighten the Gentiles, and the glory of his people Israel." Well would it have been for the letter-learned Scribes and Pharisees of Simeon's time, if they had sat at his feet, and listened to his word.

Christ was indeed "a light to enlighten the Gentiles." Without Him they were sunk in gross darkness and superstition. They knew not the way of life. They worshiped the works of their own hands. Their wisest philosophers were utterly ignorant in spiritual things. "Professing themselves to be wise they became fools." (Rom. 1:22.) The Gospel of Christ was like sun-rise to Greece and Rome, and the whole heathen world. The light which it let in on men's minds on the subject of religion, was as great as the change from night to day.

Christ was indeed "the glory of Israel." The descent from Abraham—the covenants—the promises—the law of Moses—the divinely ordered Temple service—all these were mighty privileges. But all were as nothing compared to the mighty fact, that out of Israel was born the Savior of the world. This was to be the highest honor of the Jewish nation, that the mother of Christ was a Jewish woman, and that the blood of One "made of the seed of David, according to the flesh," was to make atonement for the sin of mankind. (Rom. 1:3.)

The words of old Simeon, let us remember, will yet receive a fuller accomplishment. The "light" which he saw by faith, as he held the child Jesus in his arms, shall yet shine so brightly that all the nations of the Gentile world shall see it. The "glory" of that Jesus whom Israel crucified, shall one day be revealed so clearly to the scattered Jews, that they shall look on Him whom they pierced, and repent, and be converted. The day shall come when the veil shall be taken from the heart of Israel, and all shall "glory in the Lord." (Isaiah. 45:25.) For that day let us wait, and watch, and pray. If Christ be the light and glory of our souls, that day cannot come too soon.

We see, lastly, in this passage, a striking account of the RESULTS which would follow when Jesus Christ and His Gospel came into the world. Every word of old Simeon on this subject deserves private meditation. The whole forms a prophecy which is being daily fulfilled.

Christ was to be "a sign spoken against." He was to be a mark for all the fiery darts of the wicked one. He was to be "despised and rejected of men." He and His people were to be a "city set upon a hill," assailed on every side, and hated by all sorts of enemies. And so it proved. Men who agreed in nothing else have agreed in hating Christ. From the very first, thousands have been persecutors and unbelievers. Christ was to be the occasion of "the fall of many in Israel." He was to be a stone of stumbling and rock of offence to many proud and self-righteous Jews, who would reject Him and perish in their sins. And so it proved. To multitudes among them Christ crucified was a stumbling-block, and His Gospel "a savor of death." (1 Cor. 1:23; 2 Cor. 2:16.)

Christ was to be the occasion of "rising again to many in Israel." He was to prove the Savior of many who, at one time, rejected, blasphemed, and reviled Him, but afterwards repented and believed. And so it proved. When the thousands who crucified Him repented, and Saul who persecuted Him was converted, there was nothing less than a rising again from the dead.

Christ was to be the occasion of "the thoughts of many hearts being revealed." His Gospel was to bring to light the real characters of many people. The enmity to God of some—the inward weariness and hunger of others, would be discovered by the preaching of the cross. It would show what men really were. And so it proved. The Acts of the Apostles, in almost every chapter, bear testimony that in this, as in every other item of his prophecy, old Simeon spoke truth.

And now what do we think of Christ? This is the question that ought to occupy our minds. What thoughts does He call forth in our hearts? This is the inquiry which ought to receive our attention. Are we for Him, or are we against Him? Do we love Him, or do we neglect Him? Do we stumble at His doctrine, or do we find it life from the dead? Let us never rest until these questions are satisfactorily answered.

LUKE 2:36-40

THE ADORATION OF ANNA

And there was one Anna, a prophetess, the daughter of Phanuel, of the tribe of Asher (she was of a great age, having lived with a husband seven years from her virginity, and she had been a widow even unto fourscore and four years), who departed not from the temple, worshipping with fastings and supplications night and day. And coming up at that very hour she gave thanks unto God, and spake of him to all them that were looking for the redemption of Jerusalem. And when they had accomplished all things that were according to the law of the Lord, they returned into Galilee, to their own city Nazareth. And the child grew, and waxed strong, filled with wisdom: and the grace of God was upon him.

The verses we have now read introduce us to a servant of God whose name is nowhere else mentioned in the New Testament. The history of Anna, like that of Simeon, is related only by Luke. The wisdom of God ordained that a woman as well as a man should testify to the fact that Messiah was born. In the mouth of two witnesses it was established that Malachi's prophecy was fulfilled, and the messenger of the covenant had suddenly come to the Temple. (Malachi 3:1.)

Let us observe, in these verses, the character of a holy woman before the establishment of Christ's Gospel. The facts recorded about Anna are few and simple. But we shall find them full of instruction.

Anna was a woman of irreproachable character. After a married life of only seven years' duration, she had spent eighty-four years as a lone widow. The trials, desolation, and temptation of such a condition were probably very great. But Anna by grace overcame them all. She answered to the description given by Paul. She was "a widow indeed." (1 Tim. 5:5.)

Anna was a woman who loved God's house. "She departed not from the temple." She regarded it as the place where God especially dwelt, and toward which every pious Jew in foreign lands, like Daniel, loved to direct his prayers. "Nearer to God, nearer to God," was the desire of her heart, and she felt that she was never so near as within the walls which contained the ark, the altar, and the holy of holies. She could enter into David's words, "my soul longs, yes, even faints for the courts of the Lord." (Psalm 84:2.)

Anna was a woman of great self-denial. She "served God with fastings night and day." She was continually crucifying the flesh and keeping it in subjection by voluntary abstemiousness. Being fully persuaded in her own mind that the practice was helpful to her soul, she spared no pains to keep it up.

Anna was a woman of much prayer. She "served God with prayer night and day." She was continually communing with him, as her best Friend, about the things that concerned her own peace. She was never weary of pleading with Him on behalf of others, and, above all, for the fulfillment of His promises of Messiah.

Anna was a woman who held communion with other saints. So soon as she had seen Jesus, she "spoke of Him" to others whom she knew in Jerusalem, and with whom she was evidently on friendly terms. There was a bond of union between her and all who enjoyed the same hope. They were servants of the same Master; and travelers to the same home.

And Anna received a rich reward for all her diligence in God's service, before she left the world. She was allowed to see Him who had been so long promised, and for whose coming she had so often prayed. Her faith was at last changed to sight, and her hope to certainty. The joy of this holy woman must indeed have been "unspeakable and full of glory." (1 Peter 1:8.)

It would be well for all Christian women to ponder the character of Anna, and learn wisdom from it. The times, no doubt, are greatly changed. The social duties of the Christian are very different from those of the Jewish believer at Jerusalem. All are not placed by God in the condition of widows. But still, after every deduction, there remains much in Anna's history which is worthy of imitation. When we read of her consistency, and holiness, and prayerfulness, and self-denial, we cannot but wish that many daughters of the Christian Church would strive to be like her.

Let us observe, secondly, in these verses, the description given of saints in Jerusalem in the time when Jesus was born. They were people "who looked for redemption."

Faith, we shall always find, is the universal character of God's elect. These men and women here described, dwelling in the midst of a wicked city, walked by faith, and not by sight. They were not carried away by the flood of worldliness, formality, and self-righteousness around them. They were not infected by the carnal expectations of a mere worldly Messiah, in which most Jews indulged. They lived in the faith of patriarchs and prophets, that the coming Redeemer would bring in holiness and righteousness, and that His principal victory would be over sin and the devil. For such a Redeemer they waited patiently. For such a victory they earnestly longed.

Let us learn a lesson from these good people. If they, with so few helps and so many discouragements, lived such a life of faith, how much more ought we with a finished Bible and a full Gospel. Let us strive, like them, to walk by faith and look forward. The second advent of Christ is yet to come. The complete "redemption" of this earth from sin, and Satan, and the curse, is yet to take place. Let us declare plainly by our lives and conduct, that for this second advent we look and long. We may be sure that the highest style of Christianity even now, is to "wait for redemption," and to love the Lord's appearing. (Rom. 8:23; 2 Tim. 4:8.)

Let us observe, lastly, in these verses, what clear proof we have that the Lord Jesus was really and truly man, as well as God. We read, that when Mary and Joseph returned to their own city Nazareth, "the child GREW and became strong."

There is, doubtless, much that is deeply mysterious in the Person of the Lord Jesus. How the same Person could be at once perfect God and perfect man, is a point that necessarily passes our understanding. In what manner and measure, and in what proportion at the early part of His life, that divine knowledge which He doubtless possessed, was exercised, we cannot possibly explain. It is a lofty truth. We cannot attain unto it.

One thing, however, is perfectly clear, and we shall do well to lay firm hold upon it. Our Lord partook of everything that belongs to man's nature, sin only excepted. As man He was born an infant. As man He grew from infancy to boyhood. As man He yearly increased in bodily strength and mental power, during His passage from boyhood to full age. Of all the sinless conditions of man's body, its first feebleness, its after growth, its regular progress to maturity, He was in the fullest sense a partaker. We must rest satisfied with knowing this. To pry beyond is useless. To know this clearly is of much importance. A absence of settled knowledge of it has led to many wild heresies.

One comfortable practical lesson stands out on the face of this truth, which ought never to be overlooked. Our Lord is able to sympathize with man in every stage of man's existence, from the cradle to the grave. He knows by experience the nature and temperament of—the child, the boy, and the young man. He has stood in their place. He has occupied their position. He knows their hearts. Let us never forget this in dealing with young people about their souls. Let us tell them confidently, that there is One in heaven at the right hand of God, who is exactly suited to be their Friend. He who died on the cross was once a boy Himself, and feels a special interest in boys and girls, as well as in grown up people.

LUKE 2:41-52

JESUS AND HIS PARENTS AT THE PASSOVER

And his parents went every year to Jerusalem at the feast of the passover. And when he was twelve years old, they went up after the custom of the feast; and when they had fulfilled the days, as they were returning, the boy Jesus tarried behind in Jerusalem; and his parents knew it not; but supposing him to be in the company, they went a day's journey; and they sought for him among their kinsfolk and acquaintance: and when they found him not, they returned to Jerusalem, seeking for him. And it came to pass, after three days they found him in the temple, sitting in the midst of the teachers, both hearing them, and asking them questions: and all that heard him were amazed at his understanding and his answers. And when they saw him, they were astonished; and his mother said unto him, Son, why hast thou thus dealt with us? behold, thy father and I sought thee sorrowing. And he said unto them, How is it that ye sought me? knew ye not that I must be in my Father's house? And they understood not the saying which he spake unto them. And he went down with them, and came to Nazareth; and he was subject unto them: and his mother kept all these sayings in her heart. And Jesus advanced in wisdom and stature, and in favor with God and men.

These verses should always be deeply interesting to a reader of the Bible. They record the only facts which we know about our Lord Jesus Christ during the first thirty years of His life on earth, after His infancy. How many things a Christian would like to know about the events of those thirty years, and the daily history of the house at Nazareth! But we need not doubt that there is wisdom in the silence of Scripture on the subject. If it had been good for us to know more, more would have been revealed.

Let us first, draw from the passage a lesson for all married people. We have it in the conduct of Joseph and Mary, here described. We are told that "they went to Jerusalem every year, at the feast of the passover." They regularly honored God's appointed ordinances and they honored them together. The distance from Nazareth to Jerusalem was great. The journey, to poor people without any means of conveyance, was, doubtless, troublesome and fatiguing. To leave house and home for some two weeks was no slight expense. But God had given Israel a command, and Joseph and Mary strictly obeyed it. God had appointed an ordinance for their spiritual good, and they regularly kept it. And all that they did concerning the passover they did together. When they went up to the feast, they always went up side by side.

So ought it to be with all Christian husbands and wives. They ought to help one another in spiritual things, and to encourage one another in the service of God. Marriage, unquestionably, is not a sacrament, as the Romish Church vainly asserts. But marriage is a state of life which has the greatest effect on the souls of those who enter into it. It helps them upwards or downwards. It leads them nearer to heaven or nearer to hell. We all depend much on the company we keep. Our characters are insensibly molded by those with whom we pass our time. To none does this apply so much as to married people. Husbands and wives are continually doing either good or harm to one another's souls.

Let all who are married, or think of being married, ponder these things well. Let them take example from the conduct of Joseph and Mary, and resolve to do likewise. Let them pray together, and read the Bible together, and go to the house of God together, and talk to one another about spiritual matters. Above all, let them beware of throwing obstacles and discouragements in one another's way about means of grace. Blessed are those husbands who say to their wives as Elkanah did to Hannah, "Do all that is in your heart." Happy are those wives who say to their husbands as Leah and Rachel did to Jacob, "Whatever God has said unto you, do." (1 Sam. 1:23; Gen. 31:16.)

Let us, secondly, draw from the passage, an example for all young people. We have it in the conduct of our Lord Jesus Christ, when He was left by Himself in Jerusalem at the age of twelve years. For four days He was out of sight of Mary and Joseph. For three days they "sought him sorrowing," not knowing what had befallen Him. Who can imagine the anxiety of such a mother at losing such a child? And where did they find Him at last? Not idling His time away, or getting into mischief, as many boys of twelve years old do. Not in vain and unprofitable company. "They found him in the temple of God-sitting in the midst" of the Jewish teachers, "hearing" what they had to say, and "asking questions" about things He wished to be explained.

So ought it to be with the younger members of Christian families. They ought to be steady and trustworthy behind the backs of their parents, as well as before their faces. They ought to seek the company of the wise and prudent, and to use every opportunity of getting spiritual knowledge, before the cares of life come on them, and while their memories are fresh and strong.

Let Christian boys and girls ponder these things well, and take example from the conduct of Jesus at the age of only twelve years. Let them remember, that if they are old enough to do wrong, they are also old enough to do right; and that if able to read story-books and to talk, they are also able to read their Bibles and pray. Let them remember, that they are accountable to God, even while they are yet young, and that it is written that God "heard the voice of a BOY." (Gen. 21:17.) Happy indeed are those families in which the children "seek the Lord early," and cost their parents no tears. Happy are those parents who can say of their boys and girls, when absent from them, "I can trust my children that they will not wilfully run into sin."

Let us, in the last place, draw from this passage, an example for all true Christians. We have it in the solemn words which our Lord addressed to His mother Mary, when she said to Him, "Son, why have you dealt with us thus?" "Know you not," was the reply, "that I must be about my father's business?" A mild reproof was evidently implied in that reply. It was meant to remind His mother that He was no common person, and had come into the world to do no common work. It was a hint that she was insensibly forgetting that He had come into the world in no ordinary way, and that she could not expect Him to be ever dwelling quietly at Nazareth. It was a solemn remembrancer that, as God, He had a Father in heaven, and that this heavenly Father's work demanded His first attention.

The expression is one that ought to sink down deeply into the hearts of all Christ's people. It should supply them with a mark at which they should aim in daily life, and a test by which they should try their habits and conversation. It should quicken them when they begin to be slothful. It should check them when they feel inclined to go back to the world. "Are we about our Father's business? Are we walking in the steps of Jesus Christ?" Such questions will often prove very humbling, and make us ashamed of ourselves. But such questions are eminently useful to our souls. Never is a Church in so healthy a condition as when its believing members aim high, and strive in all things to be like Christ.

Chapter 3

THE MINISTRY OF JOHN THE BAPTIST

Now in the fifteenth year of the reign of Tiberius Caesar, Pontius Pilate being governor of Judaea, and Herod being tetrarch of Galilee, and his brother Philip tetrarch of the region of Ituraea and Trachonitis, and Lysanias tetrarch of Abilene, in the highpriesthood of Annas and Caiaphas, the word of God came unto John the son of Zacharias in the wilderness. And he came into all the region round about the Jordan, preaching the baptism of repentance unto remission of sins; as it is written in the book of the words of Isaiah the prophet, The voice of one crying in the wilderness, Make ye ready the way of the Lord, Make his paths straight. Every valley shall be filled, And every mountain and hill shall be brought low; And the crooked shall become straight, And the rough ways smooth; And all flesh shall see the salvation of God.

These verses describe the beginning of the Gospel of Christ. It began with the preaching of John the Baptist. The Jews could never say, that when Messiah came, He came without notice or preparation. He graciously sent a mighty forerunner before His face, by whose ministry the attention of the whole nation was awakened.

Let us notice first, in this passage, the wickedness of the times when Christ's Gospel was brought into the world. The opening verses of the chapter tell us the names of some who were rulers and governors in the earth, when the ministry of John the Baptist began. It is a melancholy list, and full of instruction. There is hardly a name in it which is not infamous for wickedness. Tiberius, and Pontius Pilate, and Herod, and his brother, and Annas, and Caiaphas, were men of whom we know little or nothing but evil. The earth seemed given into the hands of the wicked. (Job 9:24.) When such were the rulers, what must the people have been? Such was the state of things when Christ's forerunner was commissioned to begin preaching. Such were the times when the first foundation of Christ's church was brought out and laid. We may truly say, that God's ways are not our ways.

Let us learn never to despair about the cause of God's truth, however black and unfavorable its prospects may appear. At the very time when things seem hopeless, God may be preparing a mighty deliverance. At the very season when Satan's kingdom seems to be triumphing, the "little stone, cut without hands," may be on the point of crushing it to pieces. The darkest hour of the night is often that which just precedes the day.

Let us beware of slacking our hands from any work of God, because of the wickedness of the times, or the number and power of our adversaries. "He that observes the wind shall not sow, and he that regards the clouds shall not reap." (Eccles. 11:4.) Let us work on, and believe that help will come from heaven, when it is most needed. In the very hour when a Roman emperor, and ignorant priests, seemed to have everything at their feet, the Lamb of God was about to come forth from Nazareth, and set up the beginnings of His kingdom. What He has done once, He can do again. In a moment He can turn His church's midnight into the blaze of noon day.

Let us notice, secondly, in this passage, the account which Luke gives of the calling of John the Baptist into the ministry. We are told that "the word of God came to John, the son of Zachariah." He received a special call from God to begin preaching and baptizing. A message from heaven was sent to his heart, and under the impulse of that message, he undertook his marvelous work.

There is something in this account which throws great light on the office of all ministers of the Gospel. It is an office which no man has a right to take up, unless he has an inward call from God, as well as an outward call from man. Visions and revelations from heaven, of course we have no right to expect. Fanatical claims to special gifts of the Spirit must always be checked and discouraged. But an inward call a man must have, before he puts his hand to the work of the ministry. The word of God must "come to him," as really and truly as it came to John the Baptist, before he undertakes to "come to the word." In short, he must be able to profess with a good conscience, that he is "inwardly moved by the Holy Spirit" to take upon him the office of a minister. The man who cannot say this, when he comes forward to be ordained, is committing a great sin, and running without being sent.

Let it be a part of our daily prayers, that our churches may have no ministers excepting those who are really called of God. An unconverted minister is an injury and burden to a church. How can a man speak of truths which he has never tasted? How can he testify of a Savior whom he has never seen by faith, and never laid hold on for his own soul? The pastor after God's own heart, is a man to whom the Word of God has come. He runs confidently and speaks boldly, because he has been sent.

Let us notice, lastly, in this passage, the close connection between true repentance and forgiveness. We are told that John the Baptist came "preaching the baptism of repentance for the remission of sins." The plain meaning of this expression is, that John preached the necessity of being baptized, in token of repentance, and that he told his hearers that except they repented of sin, their sins would not be forgiven.

We must carefully bear in mind that no repentance can make atonement for sin. The blood of Christ, and nothing else, can wash away sin from man's soul. No quantity of repentance can ever justify us in the sight of God. "We are accounted righteous before God, only for the sake of our Lord Jesus Christ, by faith, and not for our own works or deservings." It is of the utmost importance to understand this clearly. The trouble that men bring upon their souls, by misunderstanding this subject, is more than can be expressed.

But while we say all this, we must carefully remember that without repentance no soul was ever yet saved. We must know our sins, mourn over them, forsake them, abhor them, or else we shall never enter the kingdom of heaven. There is nothing meritorious in this. It forms no part whatever of the price of our redemption. Our salvation is all of grace, from first to last. But the great fact still remains, that saved souls are always penitent souls, and that saving faith in Christ, and true repentance toward God, are never found asunder. This is a mighty truth, and one that ought never to be forgotten.

Do we ourselves repent? This, after all, is the question which most nearly concerns us. Have we been convinced of sin by the Holy Spirit? Have we fled to Jesus for deliverance from the wrath to come? Do we know anything of a broken and contrite heart, and a thorough hatred of sin? Can we say, "I repent," as well as "I believe?" If not, let us not delude our minds with the idea that our sins are yet forgiven. It is written, "Except you repent, you shall all likewise perish." (Luke 13:3.)

LUKE 3:7-14

He said therefore to the multitudes that went out to be baptized of him, Ye offspring of vipers, who warned you to flee from the wrath to come? Bring forth therefore fruits worthy of repentance, and begin not to say within yourselves, We have Abraham to our father: for I say unto you, that God is able of these stones to raise up children unto Abraham. And even now the axe also lieth at the root of the trees: every tree therefore that bringeth not forth good fruit is hewn down, and cast into the fire. And the multitudes asked him, saying, What then must we do? And he answered and said unto them, He that hath two coats, let him impart to him that hath none; and he that hath food, let him do likewise. And there came also publicans to be baptized, and they said unto him, Teacher, what must we do? And he said unto them, Extort no more than that which is appointed you. And soldiers also asked him, saying, And we, what must we do? And he said unto them, Extort from no man by violence, neither accuse any one wrongfully; and be content with your wages.

We have, in these verses, a specimen of John the Baptist's ministry. It is a portion of Scripture which should always be specially interesting to a Christian mind. The immense effect which John produced on the Jews, however temporary, is evident, from many expressions in the Gospels. The remarkable testimony which our Lord bore to John, as "a prophet greater than any born of woman," is well-known to all Bible readers. WHAT THEN WAS THE CHARACTER OF JOHN'S MINISTRY? This is the question to which the chapter before us supplies a practical answer.

We should first mark the holy boldness with which John addresses the multitudes who came to his baptism. He speaks to them as "a generation of vipers." He saw the rottenness and hypocrisy of the profession that the crowd around him were making, and uses language descriptive of their case. His head was not turned by popularity. He cared not who was offended by his words. The spiritual disease of those before him was desperate, and of long standing, and he knew that desperate diseases need strong remedies.

Well would it be for the Church of Christ, if it possessed more plain-speaking ministers, like John the Baptist, in these latter days. A morbid dislike to strong language—an excessive fear of giving offence—a constant flinching from directness and plain speaking, are, unhappily, too much the characteristics of the modern Christian pulpit. Uncharitable language is no doubt always to be deprecated. But there is no charity in flattering unconverted people, by abstaining from any mention of their vices, or in applying smooth epithets to damnable sins. There are two texts which are too much forgotten by Christian preachers. In one it is written, "Woe unto you when all men shall speak well of you." In the other it is written, "Obviously, I'm not trying to be a people pleaser! No, I am trying to please God. If I were still trying to please people, I would not be Christ's servant." (Luke 6:26; Gal. 1:10.)

We should mark, secondly, how plainly John speaks to his hearers about hell and danger. He tells them that there is a "wrath to come." He speaks of "the ax" of God's judgments, and of unfruitful trees being cast into "the fire."

The subject of HELL is always offensive to human nature. The minister who dwells much upon it, must expect to find himself regarded as barbaric, violent, unfeeling, and narrow-minded. Men love to hear "smooth things," and to be told of peace, and not of danger. (Isaiah. 30:10.) But the subject is one that ought not to be kept back, if we desire to do good to souls. It is one that our Lord Jesus Christ brought forward frequently in His public teachings. That loving Savior, who spoke so graciously of the way to heaven, has also used the plainest language about the way to hell.

Let us beware of being wise above that which is written, and more charitable than Scripture itself. Let the language of John the Baptist be deeply engraved in our hearts. Let us never be ashamed to avow our firm belief, that there is a "wrath to come" for the impenitent, and that it is possible for a man to be lost as well as to be saved. To be silent on the subject is dreadful treachery to men's souls. It only encourages them to persevere in wickedness, and fosters in their minds the devil's old delusion, "You shall not surely die." That minister is surely our best friend who tells us honestly of danger, and warns us, like John the Baptist, to "flee from the wrath to come." Never will a man flee until he sees there is real cause to be afraid. Never will he seek heaven until be is convinced that there is risk of his falling into hell. The religion in which there is no mention of hell, is not the religion of John the Baptist, and of our Lord Jesus, and His apostles.

We should mark, thirdly, how John exposes the uselessness of a repentance which is not accompanied by fruits in the life. He said to the multitude, who came to be baptized, "Bring forth fruit worthy of repentance." He tells those who "Every tree which brings not forth good fruit is hewn down, and cast into the fire."

This is a truth which should always occupy a prominent place in our Christianity. It can never be impressed on our minds too strongly, that religious talking and profession are utterly worthless, without religious doing and practice. It is vain to say with our lips that we repent, if we do not at the same time repent in our lives. It is more than vain. It will gradually sear our consciences, and harden our hearts. To say that we are sorry for our sins is mere hypocrisy, unless we show that we are really sorry for them, by giving them up. Doing is the very life of repentance. Tell us not merely what a man says in religion. Tell us rather what he does. "The talk of the lips," says Solomon, "tends only to poverty." (Prov. 14:23.)

We should mark, fourthly, what a blow John strikes at the common notion, that connection with godly people can save our souls. "Do not begin to say to yourselves," he tells the Jews, "we have Abraham to our Father; for I say unto you that God is able of these stones to raise up children unto Abraham."

The strong hold that this notion has obtained on the heart of man, in every part of the world, is an affecting proof of our fallen and corrupt condition. Thousands have always been found, in every age of the church, who have believed that connection with godly men made them acceptable in the sight of God. Thousands have lived and died in the blind delusion, that because they were allied to holy people by ties of blood or church-membership, they might themselves hope to be saved.

Let it be a settled principle with us, that saving religion is a PERSONAL thing. It is a business between each man's own soul and Christ. It will profit us nothing at the last day, to have belonged to the Church of Luther, or Calvin, or Cranmer, or Knox, or Owen, or Wesley, or Whitfield. Had we the faith of these holy men? Did we believe as they believed, and strive to live as they lived, and to follow Christ as they followed Him? These will be the only points on which our salvation will turn. It will save no man to have had Abraham's blood in his veins, if he did not possess Abraham's faith and do Abraham's works.

We should remark, lastly, in this passage, the searching test of sincerity which John applied to the consciences of the various classes who came to his baptism. He bade each man who made a profession of repentance, to begin by breaking off from those sins which specially beset him. The selfish multitude must show common charity to each other. The publicans must "exact no more than their due." The soldiers must "do violence to no man, and be content with their wages." He did not mean that, by so doing, they would atone for their sins, and make their peace with God. But he did mean that, by so doing, they would prove their repentance to be sincere.

Let us leave the passage with a deep conviction of the wisdom of this mode of dealing with souls, and specially with the souls of those who are beginning to make a profession of religion. Above all, let us see here the right way to prove our own hearts. It must not content us to cry out against sins to which, by natural temperament, we are not inclined, while we deal gently with other sins of a different character. Let us find out our own peculiar corruptions. Let us know our own besetting sins. Against them let us direct our principal efforts. With these let us wage unceasing war. Let the rich break off from the rich man's sins, and the poor from the sins of the poor. Let the young man give up the sins of youth, and the old man the sins of old age. This is the first step towards proving that we are in earnest, when we first begin to feel about our souls. Are we real? Are we sincere? Then let us begin by looking at home, and looking within.

LUKE 3:15-20

And as the people were in expectation, and all men reasoned in their hearts concerning John, whether haply he were the Christ; John answered, saying unto them all, I indeed baptize you with water; but there cometh he that is mightier than I, the latchet of whose shoes I am not worthy to unloose: he shall baptize you in the Holy Spirit and in fire: whose fan is in his hand, thoroughly to cleanse his threshing-floor, and to gather the wheat into his garner; but the chaff he will burn up with unquenchable fire. With many other exhortations therefore preached he good tidings unto the people; but Herod the tetrarch, being reproved by him for Herodias his brother's wife, and for all the evil things which Herod had done, added this also to them all, that he shut up John in prison.

We learn, firstly, from these verses, that one effect of a faithful ministry is to set men thinking. We read concerning John the Baptist's hearers, that "the people were in expectation, and all men mused in their hearts of John, whether he were the Christ, or not."

The cause of true religion has gained a giant step in a parish, or congregation, or family, when people begin to think. Thoughtlessness about spiritual things is one great feature of unconverted men. It cannot be said, in many cases, that they either like the Gospel, or dislike it. But they do not give it a place in their thoughts. They never "consider." (Isaiah 1:3.)

Let us always thank God when we see a spirit of reflection on religious subjects coming over the mind of an unconverted man. Thinking and deliberation are the high road to conversion. The truth of Christ has nothing to fear from sober examination. We invite inquiry. We desire to have its claims fully investigated. We know that its fitness to supply every need of man's heart and conscience is not appreciated in many cases, simply because it is not known. Thinking, no doubt, is not faith and repentance. But it is always a hopeful symptom. When hearers of the Gospel begin to "muse in their hearts," we ought to bless God and take courage.

We learn, secondly, from these verses, that a faithful minister will always exalt Christ. We read that when John saw the state of mind in which his hearers were, he told them of a coming One far mightier than himself. He refused the honor which he saw the people ready to give him, and referred them to Him who had the "winnowing fork in his hand,"—the Lamb of God, the Messiah.

Conduct like this will always be the characteristic of a true "man of God." He will never allow anything to be credited to him, or his office, which belongs to his divine Master. He will say like Paul, "we preach not ourselves, but Christ Jesus, the Lord, and ourselves your servants for Jesus' sake." (2 Cor. 4:5.) To commend Christ dying, and rising again for the ungodly—to make known Christ's love and power to save sinners, this will be the main object of his ministry. "He must increase but I must decrease," will be a ruling principle in all his preaching. He will be content that his own name be forgotten, so long as Christ crucified is exalted.

Would we know whether a minister is sound in the faith, and deserving of our confidence as a teacher? We have only to ask a simple question, Where is Christ in his teaching? Would we know whether we ourselves are receiving benefit from the preaching we attend? Let us ask whether its effect is to magnify Christ in our esteem? A minister who is really doing us good will make us think more of Jesus every year we live.

We learn, thirdly, from these verses, the essential difference between the Lord Jesus and even the best and holiest of His ministers. We have it in the solemn words of John the Baptist—"I indeed baptize you with water—He shall baptize you with the Holy Spirit."

Man, when ordained, can administer the outward ordinances of Christianity, with a prayerful hope, that God will graciously bless the means which he has Himself appointed. But man cannot read the hearts of those to whom he ministers. He can preach the Gospel faithfully to their ears, but he cannot make them receive it into their consciences. He can apply baptismal water to their foreheads, but he cannot cleanse their inward nature. He can give the bread and wine of the Lord's Supper into their hands, but he cannot enable them to eat Christ's body and blood by faith. Up to a certain point he can go, but he can go no further. No ordination, however solemnly conferred, can give man power to change the heart. Christ, the great Head of the Church, can alone do this by the power of the Holy Spirit. It is His peculiar office to do it, and it is an office which He has delegated to no child of man.

May we never rest until we have tasted by experience the power of Christ's grace upon our souls! We have been baptized with water. But have we also been baptized with the Holy Spirit? Our names are in the baptismal register. But are they also in the Lamb's book of life? We are members of the visible Church. But are we also members of that mystical body of which Christ alone is the Head? All these are privileges which Christ alone bestows, and for which all who would be saved must make personal application to Him. Man cannot give them. They are treasures laid up in Christ's hand. From Him we must seek them by faith and prayer, and believing we shall not seek in vain.

We learn, fourthly, in these verses, the change that Christ will work in his visible church at his second appearing. We read in the figurative words of His forerunner, "that he will thoroughly purge his floor, and gather the wheat into his garner; but the chaff he will burn with fire unquenchable."

The visible Church is now a 'mixed' body. Believers and unbelievers, holy and unholy, converted and unconverted, are now mingled in every congregation, and often sit side by side. It passes the power of man to separate them. False profession is often so like true; and grace is often so weak and feeble, that, in many cases, the right discernment of character is an impossibility. The wheat and the chaff will continue together until the Lord returns.

But there will be a dreadful separation at the last day The unerring judgment of the King of kings shall at length divide the wheat from the chaff, and divide them for evermore. The righteous shall be gathered into a place of happiness and safety. The wicked shall be cast down to shame and everlasting contempt. In the great sifting day, every one shall go to his own place.

May we often look forward to that day, and judge ourselves, that we be not judged of the Lord. May we give all diligence to make our calling and election sure, and to know that we are God's "wheat." A mistake in the day that the floor is "purged," will be a mistake that is irretrievable.

We learn, lastly, from these verses, that the reward of God's servants is often not in this world. Luke closes his account of John the Baptist's ministry, by telling us of his imprisonment by Herod. The end of that imprisonment we know from other parts of the New Testament. It led at last to John being beheaded.

All true servants of Christ must be content to wait for their wages. Their best things are yet to come. They must count it no strange thing, if they meet with hard treatment from man. The world that persecuted Christ will never hesitate, to persecute Christians. "Marvel not if the world hate you." (1 John 3:13.)

But let us take comfort in the thought that the great Master has laid up in heaven for His people such things as pass man's understanding. The blood that His saints have shed in His name will all be reckoned for one day. The tears that often flow so freely in consequence of the unkindness of the wicked, will one day be wiped from all faces. And when John the Baptist, and all who have suffered for the truth are at last gathered together, they will find it true that heaven makes amends for all.

LUKE 3:21-38

THE BAPTISM AND GENEALOGY OF JESUS

Now it came to pass, when all the people were baptized, that, Jesus also having been baptized, and praying, the heaven was opened, and the Holy Spirit descended in a bodily form, as a dove, upon him, and a voice came out of heaven, Thou art my beloved Son; in thee I am well pleased. And Jesus himself, when he began to teach, was about thirty years of age, being the son (as was supposed) of Joseph, the son of Heli, the son of Matthat, the son of Levi, the son of Melchi, the son of Jannai, the son of Joseph, the son of Mattathias, the son of Amos, the son of Nahum, the son of Esli, the son of Naggai, the son of Maath, the son of Mattathias, the son of Semein, the son of Josech, the son of Joda, the son of Joanan, the son of Rhesa, the son of Zerubbabel, the son of Shealtiel, the son of Neri, the son of Melchi, the son of Addi, the son of Cosam, the son of Elmadam, the son of Er, the son of Jesus, the son of Eliezer, the son of Jorim, the son of Matthat, the son of Levi, the son of Symeon, the son of Judas, the son of Joseph, the son of Jonam, the son of Eliakim, the son of Melea, the son of Menna, the son of Mattatha, the son of Nathan, the son of David, the son of Jesse, the son of Obed, the son of Boaz, the son of Salmon, the son of Nahshon, the son of Amminadab, the son of Arni, the son of Hezron, the son of Perez, the son of Judah, the son of Jacob, the son of Isaac, the son of Abraham, the son of Terah, the son of Nahor, the son of Serug, the son of Reu, the son of Peleg, the son of Eber, the son of Shelah the son of Cainan, the son of Arphaxad, the son of Shem, the son of Noah, the son of Lamech, the son of Methuselah, the son of Enoch, the son of Jared, the son of Mahalaleel, the son of Cainan, the son of Enos, the son of Seth, the son of Adam, the son of God.

We see in the passage before us, the high honor the Lord Jesus has put on baptism. We find that among others who came to John the Baptist, the Savior of the world came, and was "baptized."

An ordinance which the Son of God was pleased to use, and afterwards to appoint for the use of His whole Church, ought always to be held in peculiar reverence by His people. Baptism cannot be a thing of slight importance, if Christ Himself was baptized. The use of baptism would never have been enjoined on the Church of Christ, if it had been a mere outward form, incapable of conveying any blessing.

It is hardly necessary to say that errors of every sort and description abound on the subject of baptism. Some make an idol of it, and exalt it far above the place assigned to it in the Bible. Some degrade it and dishonor it, and seem almost to forget that it was ordained by Christ Himself. Some limit the use of it so narrowly that they will baptize none unless they are grown up, and can give full proof of their conversion. Some invest the baptismal water with such magic power, that they would like missionaries to go into heathen lands and baptize all people, old and young indiscriminately, and believe that however ignorant the heathen may be, baptism must do them good. On no subject, perhaps, in religion, have Christians more need to pray for a right judgment and a sound mind.

Let it suffice us to hold firmly the general principle, that baptism was graciously intended by our Lord to be a help to His Church, and "a means of grace," and that, when rightly and worthily used, we may confidently look upon it for a blessing. But let us never forget that the grace of God is not tied to any sacrament, and that we may be baptized with water, without being baptized with the Holy Spirit.

We see, secondly, in this passage, the close connection that ought to exist between the administration of baptism and prayer. We are specially told by Luke, that when our Lord was baptized He was also "praying."

We need not doubt that there is a great lesson in this fact, and one that the Church of Christ has too much overlooked. We are meant to learn that the baptism which God blesses must be a baptism accompanied by prayer. The sprinkling of water is not sufficient. The use of the name of the blessed Trinity is not enough. The form of the sacrament alone conveys no grace. There must be something else beside all this. There must be "the prayer of faith." A baptism without prayer, it may be confidently asserted, is a baptism on which we have no right to expect God's blessing.

Why is it that the sacrament of baptism appears to bear so little fruit? How is it that thousands are every year baptized, and never give the slightest proof of having received benefit from it? The answer to these questions is short and simple. In the vast majority of baptisms there is no prayer except the prayer of the officiating minister. Parents bring their children to the font, without the slightest sense of what they are doing. Sponsors stand up and answer for the child, in evident ignorance of the nature of the ordinance they are attending, and as a mere matter of form. What possible reason have we for expecting such baptisms to be blessed by God? None! none at all! Such baptisms may well be barren of results. They are not baptisms according to the mind of Christ. Let us pray that the eyes of Christians on this important subject may be opened. It is one on which there is great need of change.

We see, thirdly, in these verses, a remarkable proof of the doctrine of the Trinity. We have all the Three Persons of the Godhead spoken of, as cooperating and acting at one time. God the Son begins the mighty work of His earthly ministry, by being baptized. God the Father solemnly accredits Him as the appointed Mediator, by a voice from heaven. God the Holy Spirit descends "in a bodily shape like a dove" upon our Lord, and by so doing declares that this is He to whom "the Father gives the Spirit without measure." (John 3:34.)

There is something deeply instructive, and deeply comforting in this revelation of the blessed Trinity, at this particular season of our Lord's earthly ministry. It shows us how mighty and powerful is the agency that is employed in the great business of our redemption. It is the common work of God the Father, God the Son, and God the Holy Spirit. All Three Persons in the Godhead are equally concerned in the deliverance of our souls from hell. The thought should cheer us, when disturbed and cast down. The thought should hearten and encourage us, when weary of the conflict with the world, the flesh, and the devil. The enemies of our souls are mighty, but the Friends of our souls are mightier still. The whole power of the triune Jehovah is engaged upon our side. "A three-fold cord is not easily broken." (Eccles. 4:12.)

We see, fourthly, in these verses, a marvelous proclamation of our Lord's office as Mediator between God and man. A voice was heard from heaven at His baptism, "which said, You are my beloved Son; in you I am well pleased." There is but One who could say this. It was the voice of God the Father.

These solemn words no doubt contain much that is deeply mysterious. One thing however about them is abundantly clear. They are a divine declaration, that our Lord Jesus Christ is the promised Redeemer, whom God from the beginning undertook to send into the world, and that with His incarnation, sacrifice, and substitution for man, God the Father is satisfied and well pleased—In Him, He regards the claim of His holy law as fully discharged. Through Him, He is willing to receive poor sinful man to mercy, and to remember his sins no more.

Let all true Christians rest their souls on these words, and draw from them daily consolation. Our sins and shortcomings are many and great. In ourselves we can see no good thing. But if we believe in Jesus, the Father sees nothing in us that He cannot abundantly pardon. He regards us as the members of His own dear Son, and, for His Son's sake, He is well pleased.

We see, lastly, in these verses, what a frail and dying creature is man. We read at the end of the chapter a long list of names, containing the genealogy of the family in which our Lord was born, traced up through David and Abraham to Adam. How little we know of many of the seventy-five people, whose names are here recorded! They all had their joys and sorrows, their hopes and fears, their cares and troubles, their schemes and plans, like any of ourselves. But they have all passed away from the earth, and gone to their own place. And so will it be with us. We too are passing away, and shall soon be gone.

Forever let us bless God, that in a dying world we are able to turn to a living Savior, "I am he," says Jesus, "who lives and was dead, and behold I am alive for evermore." "I am the resurrection and the life," (Rev. 1:18; John 11:25.) Let our main care be, to be one with Christ and Christ with us. Joined to the Lord Jesus by faith we shall rise again to live for evermore. The second death shall have no power over us. "Because I live," says Christ, "you shall live also." (John 14:19.)

Chapter 4

LUKE 4:1-13

THE TEMPTATION OF JESUS

And Jesus, full of the Holy Spirit, returned from the Jordan, and was led in the Spirit in the wilderness during forty days, being tempted of the devil. And he did eat nothing in those days: and when they were completed, he hungered. And the devil said unto him, if thou art the Son of God, command this stone that it become bread. And Jesus answered unto him, It is written, Man shall not live by bread alone. And he led him up, and showed him all the kingdoms of the world in a moment of time. And the devil said unto him, To thee will I give all this authority, and the glory of them: for it hath been delivered unto me; and to whomsoever I will I give it. If thou therefore wilt worship before me, it shall all be thine. And Jesus answered and said unto him, It is written, Thou shalt worship the Lord thy God, and him only shalt thou serve. And he led him to Jerusalem, and set him on the pinnacle of the temple, and said unto him, If thou art the Son of God, cast thyself down from hence: for it is written, He shall give his angels charge concerning thee, to guard thee: and, On their hands they shall bear thee up, Lest haply thou dash thy foot against a stone. And Jesus answering said unto him, It is said, Thou shalt not make trial of the Lord thy God. And when the devil had completed every temptation, he departed from him for a season.

The first event recorded in our Lord's history, after His baptism, is His temptation by the devil. From a season of honor and glory he passed immediately to a season of conflict and suffering. First came the testimony of God the Father, "You are my beloved Son." Then came the sneering suggestion of Satan, "If you are the Son of God." The portion of Christ will often prove the portion of Christians. From great privilege to great trial there will often be but a step.

Let us first mark in this passage, the power and unwearied malice of the devil.

That old serpent who tempted Adam to sin in Paradise, was not afraid to assault the second Adam, the Son of God. Whether he understood that Jesus was "God manifest in the flesh" may perhaps be doubted. But that he saw in Jesus One who had come into the world to overthrow his kingdom, is clear and plain. He had seen what happened at our Lord's baptism. He had heard the marvelous words from heaven. He felt that the great Friend of man was come, and that his own dominion was in peril. The Redeemer had come. The prison door was about to be thrown open. The lawful captives were about to be set free. All this, we need not doubt, Satan saw, and resolved to fight for his own. The prince of this world would not give way to the Prince of peace without a mighty struggle. He had overcome the first Adam in the garden of Eden—why should he not overcome the second Adam in the wilderness? He had spoiled man once of Paradise—why should he not spoil him of the kingdom of God.

Let it never surprise us, if we are tempted by the devil. Let us rather expect it, as a matter of course, if we are living members of Christ. The Master's lot will be the lot of His disciples. That mighty spirit who did not fear to attack Jesus himself, is still going about as a roaring lion, seeking whom he may devour. That murderer and liar who vexed Job, and overthrew David and Peter, still lives, and is not yet bound. If he cannot rob us of heaven, he will at any rate make our journey there painful. If he cannot destroy our souls, he will at least bruise our heels. (Gen. 3:15.) Let us beware of despising him, or thinking lightly of his power. Let us rather put on the whole armor of God, and cry to the strong for strength. "Resist the devil and he will flee from you." (James 4:7.)

Let us mark, secondly, our Lord Jesus Christ's ability to sympathize with those who are tempted. This is a truth that stands out prominently in this passage. Jesus has been really and literally tempted Himself.

It was proper that He who came "to destroy the works of the devil," should begin His own work by a special conflict with Satan. It was proper that the great Shepherd and bishop of souls should be fitted for His earthly ministry by strong temptation, as well as by the word of God and prayer. But above all, it was proper that the great High Priest and advocate of sinners should be one who has had personal experience of conflict, and has known what it is to be in the fire. And this was the case with Jesus, It is written that He suffered being tempted." (Heb. 2:18.) How much He suffered, we cannot tell. But that His pure and spotless nature did suffer intensely, we may be sure.

Let all true Christians take comfort in the thought that they have a Friend in heaven, who can be touched with the feeling of their infirmities. (Heb. 4:15.) When they pour out their hearts before the throne of grace, and groan under the burden that daily harasses them, there is One making intercession who knows their sorrows. Let us take courage. The Lord Jesus is not an "austere man." He knows what we mean when we complain of temptation, and is both able and willing to give us help.

Let us mark, thirdly, the exceeding subtlety of our great spiritual enemy, the devil. Three times we see him assaulting our Lord, and trying to draw Him into sin. Each assault showed the hand of a master in the art of temptation. Each assault was the work of one acquainted by long experience with every weak point in human nature. Each deserves an attentive study.

Satan's first device was to persuade our Lord to DISTRUST HIS FATHER'S PROVIDENTIAL CARE. He comes to Him, when weak and exhausted with forty days' hunger, and suggests to Him to work a miracle, in order to gratify a carnal appetite. Why should He wait any longer? Why should the Son of God sit still and starve? Why not "command this stone to become bread?"

Satan's second device was to persuade our Lord to GRASP AT WORLDLY POWER BY UNLAWFUL MEANS. He takes Him to the top of a mountain and shows Him "all the kingdoms of the world in a moment of time." All these he promises to give Him, if He will but "fall down and worship him." The concession was small. The promise was large. Why not by a little momentary act, obtain an enormous gain?

Satan's last device was to persuade our Lord to an act of PRESUMPTION. He takes Him to a pinnacle of the temple and suggests to Him to "cast Himself down." By so doing he would give public proof that He was one sent by God. In so doing He might even depend on being kept from harm. Was there not a text of Scripture, which specially applied to the Son of God, in such a position? Was it not written that "angels should bear Him up?"

On each of these three temptations it would be easy to write much. Let it be sufficient to remind ourselves, that we see in them the three favorite weapons of the devil. UNBELIEF, WORLDLINESS, and PRESUMPTION are three grand engines which he is ever working against the soul of man, and by which he is ever enticing him to do what God forbids, and to run into sin. Let us remember this, and be on our guard. The acts that Satan suggests to us to do, are often in appearance trifling and unimportant. But the principle involved in each of these little acts, we may be sure, is nothing short of rebellion against God. Let us not be ignorant of Satan's devices.

Let us mark lastly, the manner in which our Lord resisted Satan's temptations. Three times we see Him foiling and baffling the great enemy who assaulted Him. He does not yield a hair's breadth to him. He does not give him a moment's advantage. Three times we see Him using the same weapon, in reply to his temptations—"the sword of the Spirit, which is the word of God." (Ephes. 6:17.) He who was "full of the Holy Spirit," was yet not ashamed to make the Holy Scripture His weapon of defense, and His rule of action.

Let us learn from this single fact, if we learn nothing else from this wondrous history, the high authority of the Bible, and the immense value of a knowledge of its contents. Let us read it, search into it, pray over it, diligently, perseveringly, unweariedly. Let us strive to be so thoroughly acquainted with its pages, that its text may abide in our memories, and stand ready at our right hand in the day of need. Let us be able to appeal from every perversion and false interpretation of its meaning, to those thousand plain passages, which are written as it were with a sunbeam. The Bible is indeed a sword, but we must take heed that we know it well, if we would use it with effect.

LUKE 4:14-22

JESUS IN THE SYNAGOGUE AT NAZARETH

And Jesus returned in the power of the Spirit into Galilee: and a fame went out concerning him through all the region round about. And he taught in their synagogues, being glorified of all. And he came to Nazareth, where he had been brought up: and he entered, as his custom was, into the synagogue on the sabbath day, and stood up to read. And there was delivered unto him the book of the prophet Isaiah. And he opened the book, and found the place where it was written, The Spirit of the Lord is upon me, Because he anointed me to preach good tidings to the poor: He hath sent me to proclaim release to the captives, And recovering of sight to the blind, To set at liberty them that are bruised, To proclaim the acceptable year of the Lord. And he closed the book, and gave it back to the attendant, and sat down: and the eyes of all in the synagogue were fastened on him. And he began to say unto them, To-day hath this scripture been fulfilled in your ears. And all bare him witness, and wondered at the words of grace which proceeded out of his mouth: and they said, Is not this Joseph's son?

These verses relate events which are only recorded in the Gospel of Luke. They describe the first visit which our Lord paid, after entering on His public ministry, to the city of Nazareth, where He had been brought up. Taken together with the two verses which immediately follow, they furnish an awfully striking proof, that "the carnal mind is enmity against God." (Rom. 8:7.)

We should observe, in these verses, what marked honor our Lord Jesus Christ gave to public means of grace. We are told that "He went into the synagogue of Nazareth on the Sabbath day, and stood up to read" the Scriptures. In the days when our Lord was on earth, the Scribes and Pharisees were the chief teachers of the Jews. We can hardly suppose that a Jewish synagogue enjoyed much of the Spirit's presence and blessing under such teaching. Yet even then we find our Lord visiting a synagogue, and reading and preaching in it. It was the place where His Father's day and word were publicly recognized, and, as such, He thought it good to do it honor.

We need not doubt that there is a practical lesson for us in this part of our Lord's conduct. He would have us know that we are not lightly to forsake any assembly of worshipers, which professes to respect the name, the day, and the book of God. There may be many things in such an assembly which might be done better. There may be a deficiency of fullness, clearness, and distinctness in the doctrine preached. There may be a lack of unction and devoutness in the manner in which the worship is conducted. But so long as no positive error is taught, and there is no choice between worshiping with such an assembly, and having no public worship at all, it becomes a Christian to think much before he stays away. If there be but two or three in the congregation who meet in the name of Jesus, there is a special blessing promised. But there is no like blessing promised to him who tarries alone at home.

We should observe, for another thing, in these verses, what a striking account our Lord gave to the congregation at Nazareth, of His own office and ministry. We are told that He chose a passage from the book of Isaiah, in which the prophet foretold the nature of the work Messiah was to do when He came into the world. He read how it was foretold that He would "preach the Gospel to the poor"—how He would be sent to "heal the broken hearted"—how He would "preach deliverance to the captives, sight to the blind, and liberty to the bruised"—and how He would "proclaim that a year of jubilee to all the world had come." And when our Lord had read this prophecy, He told the listening crowd around Him, that He Himself was the Messiah of whom these words were written, and that in Him and in His Gospel the marvelous figures of the passage were about to be fulfilled.

We may well believe that there was a deep meaning in our Lord's selection of this special passage of Isaiah. He desired to impress on His Jewish hearers, the true character of the Messiah, whom He knew all Israel were then expecting. He well knew that they were looking for a mere temporal king, who would deliver them from Roman dominion, and make them once more, foremost among the nations. Such expectations, He would have them understand, were premature and wrong. Messiah's kingdom at His first coming was to be a spiritual kingdom over hearts. His victories were not to be over worldly enemies, but over sin. His redemption was not to be from the power of Rome, but from the power of the devil and the world. It was in this way, and in no other way at present, that they must expect to see the words of Isaiah fulfilled.

Let us take care that we know for ourselves in what light we ought chiefly to regard Christ. It is right and good to reverence Him as very God. It is well to know Him as Head over all things—the mighty Prophet—the Judge of all—the King of kings. But we must not rest here, if we hope to be saved. We must know Jesus as the Friend of the poor in spirit, the Physician of the diseased heart, the deliverer of the soul in bondage. These are the principal offices He came on earth to fulfill. It is in this light we must learn to know Him, and to know Him by inward experience, as well as by the hearing of the ear. Without such knowledge we shall die in our sins.

We should observe, finally, what an instructive example we have in these verses of the manner in which religious teaching is often heard. We are told that when our Lord had finished His sermon at Nazareth, His hearers "bore Him witness, and wondered at the gracious words which proceeded out of His mouth." They could not find any flaw in the exposition of Scripture they had heard. They could not deny the beauty of the well-chosen language to which they had listened. "Never man spoke like this man." But their hearts were utterly unmoved and unaffected. They were even full of envy and enmity against the Preacher. In short, there seems to have been no effect produced on them, except a little temporary feeling of admiration.

It is vain to conceal from ourselves that there are thousands of people in Christian churches, in little better state of mind than our Lord's hearers at Nazareth. There are thousands who listen regularly to the preaching of the Gospel, and admire it while they listen. They do not dispute the truth of what they hear. They even feel a kind of intellectual pleasure in hearing a good and powerful sermon. But their religion never goes beyond this point. Their sermon-hearing does not prevent them living a life of thoughtlessness, worldliness, and sin.

Let us often examine ourselves on this important point. Let us see what practical effect is produced on our hearts and lives by the preaching which we profess to like. Does it lead us to true repentance towards God, and lively faith towards our Lord Jesus Christ? Does it excite us to weekly efforts to cease from sin, and to resist the devil? These are the fruits which sermons ought to produce, if they are really doing us good. Without such fruit, a mere barren admiration is utterly worthless. It is no proof of grace. It will save no soul.

LUKE 4:22-32

And all bare him witness, and wondered at the words of grace which proceeded out of his mouth: and they said, Is not this Joseph's son? And he said unto them, Doubtless ye will say unto me this parable, Physician, heal thyself: whatsoever we have heard done at Capernaum, do also here in thine own country. And he said, Verily I say unto you, No prophet is acceptable in his own country. But of a truth I say unto you, There were many widows in Israel in the days of Elijah, when the heaven was shut up three years and six months, when there came a great famine over all the land; and unto none of them was Elijah sent, but only to Zarephath, in the land of Sidon, unto a woman that was a widow. And there were many lepers in Israel in the time of Elisha the prophet; and none of them was cleansed, but only Naaman the Syrian. And they were all filled with wrath in the synagogue, as they heard these things; and they rose up, and cast him forth out of the city, and led him unto the brow of the hill whereon their city was built, that they might throw him down headlong. But he passing through the midst of them went his way.

And he came down to Capernaum, a city of Galilee. And he was teaching them on the sabbath day: and they were astonished at his teaching; for his word was with authority.

Three great lessons stand out on the face of this passage. Each deserves the close attention of all who desire spiritual wisdom.

We learn for one thing, how apt men are to despise the highest privileges, when they are familiar with them. We see it in the conduct of the men of

Nazareth when they had heard the Lord Jesus preach. They could find no fault in His sermon. They could point to no inconsistency in His past life. But because the preacher had dwelt among them thirty years, and His face, and voice, and appearance were familiar to them, they would not receive His doctrine. They said to one another, "Is not this Joseph's son?" Is it possible that one so well-known as this man can be the Christ? And they drew from our Lord's lips the solemn saying, "No prophet is accepted in his own country."

We shall do well to remember this lesson in the matter of ordinances and means of grace. We are always in danger of undervaluing them, when we have them in abundance. We are apt to think lightly of the privilege of an open Bible, a preached Gospel, and the liberty of meeting together for public worship. We grow up in the midst of these things, and are accustomed to have them without trouble. And the consequence is that we often hold them very cheap, and underrate the extent of our mercies. Let us take heed to our own spirit in the use of sacred things. Often as we may read the Bible, let us never read it without deep reverence. Often as we hear the name of Christ, let us never forget that He is the One Mediator, in whom is life. Even the manna that came down from heaven was at length scorned by Israel, as "light bread." (Num. 21:5.) It is an evil day with our souls, when Christ is in the midst of us, and yet, because of our familiarity with His name, is lightly esteemed.

We learn, for another thing, how bitterly human nature dislikes the doctrine of the sovereignty of God. We see this in the conduct of the men of Nazareth, when our Lord reminded those who God was under no obligation to work miracles among them. Were there not many widows in Israel in the days of Elijah? No doubt there were. Yet to none of them was the prophet sent. All were passed over in favor of a GENTILE widow at Zarephath. Were there not many lepers in Israel in the days of Elisha? No doubt there were. Yet to none of them was the privilege of healing granted. Naaman the SYRIAN was the only one who was cleansed. Such doctrine as this was intolerable to the men of Nazareth. It wounded their pride and self-conceit. It taught those who God was no man's debtor, and that if they themselves were passed over in the distribution of His mercies, they had no right to find fault. They could not bear it. They were "filled with wrath." They thrust our Lord out of their city, and had it not been for an exercise of miraculous power on His part, they would doubtless have put Him to a violent death.

Of all the doctrines of the Bible none is so offensive to human nature as the doctrine of God's sovereignty. To be told that God is great, and just, and holy, and pure, man can bear. But to be told that "He has mercy on whom He will have mercy"—that He "gives no account of His matters," that it is "not of him that wills, nor of him that runs, but of God that shows mercy"—these are truths that natural man cannot stand. They often call forth all his enmity against God, and fill him with wrath. Nothing, in short, will make him submit to them but the humbling teaching of the Holy Spirit.

Let us settle it in our minds that, whether we like it or not, the sovereignty of God is a doctrine clearly revealed in the Bible, and a fact clearly to be seen in the world. Upon no other principle can we ever explain why some members of a family are converted, and others live and die in sin—why some quarters of the earth are enlightened by Christianity, and others remain buried in heathenism. One account only can be given of all this. All is ordered by the sovereign hand of God. Let us pray for humility in respect of this deep teaching. Let us remember that our life is but a vapor, and that our best knowledge compared to that of God is unmixed folly. Let us be thankful for such light as we enjoy ourselves, and use it diligently while we have it. And let us not doubt that at the last day the whole world shall be convinced, that He who now "gives no account of His matters" has done all things well.

We learn, lastly, from this passage, how diligently we ought to persevere in well doing, notwithstanding discouragements. We are doubtless meant to draw this lesson from the conduct of our Lord, after His rejection at Nazareth. Not moved by the treatment He received, He patiently works on. Thrust out of one place, He passes on to another. Cast forth from Nazareth He comes to Capernaum, and there "teaches on the Sabbath days."

Such ought to be the conduct of all the people of Christ. Whatever the work they are called to do, they should patiently continue in it, and not give up for lack of success. Whether preachers, or teachers, or visitors, or missionaries, they must labor on and not faint. There is often more stirring in the hearts and consciences of people than those who teach and preach to them are at all aware of. There is preparatory work to be done in many a part of God's vineyard, which is just as needful as any other work, though not so agreeable to flesh and blood. There must be sowers as well as reapers. There must be some to break up the ground and pick out the stones, as well as some to gather in the harvest. Let each labor on in his own place. The day comes when each shall be rewarded according to his work. The very discouragements we meet with enable us to show the world that there are such things as faith and patience. When men see us working on, in spite of treatment like that which Jesus received at Nazareth, it makes them think.

It convinces those who, at all events, we are persuaded that we have truth on our side.

LUKE 4:33-44

JESUS DRIVES OUT AN EVIL
SPIRIT, AND HEALS MANY

And in the synagogue there was a man, that had a spirit of an unclean demon; and he cried out with a loud voice, Ah! what have we to do with thee, Jesus thou Nazarene? art thou come to destroy us? I know thee who thou art, the Holy One of God. And Jesus rebuked him, saying, Hold thy peace, and come out of him. And when the demon had thrown him down in the midst, he came out of him, having done him no hurt. And amazement came upon all, and they spake together, one with another, saying, What is this word? for with authority and power he commandeth the unclean spirits, and they come out. And there went forth a rumor concerning him into every place of the region round about. And he rose up from the synagogue, and entered into the house of Simon. And Simon's wife's mother was holden with a great fever; and they besought him for her. And he stood over her, and rebuked the fever; and it left her: and immediately she rose up and ministered unto them. And when the sun was setting, all they that had any sick with divers diseases brought them unto him; and he laid his hands on every one of them, and healed them. And demons also came out from many, crying out, and saying, Thou art the Son of God. And rebuking them, he suffered them not to speak, because they knew that he was the Christ. And when it was day, he came out and went into a desert place: and the multitudes sought after him, and came unto him, and would have stayed him, that he should not go from them. But he said unto them, I must preach the good tidings of the kingdom of God to the other cities also: for therefore was I sent. And he was preaching in the synagogues of Galilee.

We should notice, in this passage, the clear religious knowledge possessed by the devil and his agents. Twice in these verses we have proof of this. "I know you who you are, the holy one of God," was the language of an unclean devil in one case. "You are Christ the son of God," was the language of many devils in another. Yet this knowledge was a knowledge unaccompanied by faith, or hope, or charity. Those who possessed it were miserable fallen beings, full of bitter hatred both against God and man.

Let us beware of an unsanctified knowledge of Christianity. It is a dangerous possession, but a fearfully common one in these latter days. We may know the Bible intellectually, and have no doubt about the truth of its contents. We may have our memories well stored with its leading texts, and be able to talk glibly about its leading doctrines. And all this time the Bible may have no influence over our hearts, and wills, and consciences. We may, in reality, be nothing better than the devils.

Let it never content us to know religion with our heads only. We may go on all our lives saying, "I know that, and I know that," and sink at last into hell, with the words upon our lips. Let us see that our knowledge bears fruit in our lives. Does our knowledge of sin make us hate it? Does our knowledge of Christ make us trust and love Him? Does our knowledge of God's will make us strive to do it? Does our knowledge of the fruits of the Spirit make us labor to show them in our daily behavior? Knowledge of this kind is really profitable. Any other religious knowledge will only add to our condemnation at the last day.

We should notice, secondly, in this passage, the almighty power of our Lord Jesus Christ. We see sicknesses and devils alike yielding to His command. He rebukes unclean spirits, and they come forth from the unhappy people whom they had possessed. He rebukes a fever, and lays his hands on sick people, and at once their diseases depart, and the sick are healed.

We cannot fail to observe many similar cases in the four Gospels. They occur so frequently that we are apt to read them with a thoughtless eye, and forget the mighty lesson which each one is meant to convey. They are all intended to fasten in our minds the great truth that Christ is the appointed Healer of every evil which sin has brought into the world. Christ is the true antidote and remedy for all the soul-ruining mischief which Satan has wrought on mankind. Christ is the universal physician to whom all the children of Adam must repair, if they would be made whole. In Him is life, and health, and liberty. This is the grand doctrine which every miracle of mercy in the Gospel is ordained and appointed to teach. Each is a plain witness to that mighty fact, which lies at the very foundation of the Gospel. The ability of Christ to supply to the uttermost every need of human nature, is the very corner-stone of Christianity. Christ, in one word, is "all." (Coloss. 3:11.) Let the study of every miracle help to engrave this truth deeply on our hearts.

We should notice, thirdly, in these verses, our Lord's practice of occasional retirement from public notice into some solitary place. We read, that after healing many that were sick and casting out many devils, "he departed and went into a desert place." His object in so doing is shown by comparison with other places in the Gospels. He went aside from His work for a season, to hold communion with His Father in heaven, and to pray. Holy and sinless as his human nature was, it was a nature kept sinless in the regular use of means of grace, and not in the neglect of them.

There is an example here which all who desire to grow in grace and walk closely with God would do well to follow. We must make time for private meditation, and for being alone with God. It must not content us to pray daily and read the Scriptures, to hear the Gospel regularly and to receive the Lord's Supper. All this is well. But something more is needed. We should set apart special seasons for solitary self-examination and meditation on the things of God. How often in a year this practice should be attempted each Christian must judge for himself. But that the practice is most desirable seems clear both from Scripture and experience.

We live in hurrying, bustling times. The excitement of daily business and constant engagements keeps many men in a perpetual whirl, and entails great peril on souls. The neglect of this habit of withdrawing occasionally from worldly business is the probable cause of many an inconsistency or backsliding which brings scandal on the cause of Christ. The more work we have to do the more we ought to imitate our Master. If He, in the midst of His abundant labors, found time to retire from the world occasionally, how much more may we? If the Master found the practice necessary, it must surely be a thousand times more necessary for His disciples.

We ought to notice, lastly, in these verses, the declaration of our Lord as to one of the objects of His coming into the world. We read that He said, "I must preach the kingdom of God to other cities also—for therefore was I sent." An expression like this ought to silence forever the foolish remarks that are sometimes made against preaching. The mere fact that the eternal Son of God undertook the office of a preacher, should satisfy us that preaching is one of the most valuable means of grace. To speak of preaching, as some do, as a thing of less importance than reading public prayers or administering the sacraments, is, to say the least, to exhibit ignorance of Scripture. It is a striking circumstance in our Lord's history, that although He was almost incessantly preaching, we never read of His baptizing any person. The witness of John is distinct on this point—"Jesus baptized not." (John 4:2.)

Let us beware of despising preaching. In every age of the Church, it has been God's principal instrument for the awakening of sinners and the edifying of saints. The days when there has been little or no preaching have been days when there has been little or no good done in the Church. Let us hear sermons in a prayerful and reverent frame of mind, and remember that they are the principal engines which Christ Himself employed, when He was upon earth. Not least, let us pray daily for a continual supply of faithful preachers or God's word. According to the state of the pulpit will always be the state of a congregation and of a Church.

Chapter 5

*N*ow it came to pass, while the multitude pressed upon him and heard the word
*of God, that he was standing by the lake of Gennesaret; and he saw two boats
standing by the lake: but the fishermen had gone out of them, and were washing
their nets. And he entered into one of the boats, which was Simon's, and asked
him to put out a little from the land. And he sat down and taught the multitudes
out of the boat. And when he had left speaking, he said unto Simon, Put out into
the deep, and let down your nets for a draught. And Simon answered and said,
Master, we toiled all night, and took nothing: but at thy word I will let down the
nets. And when they had done this, they inclosed a great multitude of fishes; and
their nets were breaking; and they beckoned unto their partners in the other boat,
that they should come and help them. And they came, and filled both the boats, so
that they began to sink. But Simon Peter, when he saw it, fell down at Jesus' knees,
saying, Depart from me; for I am a sinful man, O Lord. For he was amazed, and
all that were with him, at the draught of the fishes which they had taken; and so
were also James and John, sons of Zebedee, who were partners with Simon. And
Jesus said unto Simon, Fear not; from henceforth thou shalt catch men. And when
they had brought their boats to land, they left all, and followed him.*

We have, in these verses, the history of what is commonly called the
miraculous catch of fish. It is a remarkable miracle on two accounts. For
one thing, it shows us our Lord's complete dominion over the animal creation. The fish of the sea are as much obedient to His will, as the frogs, and

flies, and lice, and locusts, in the plagues of Egypt. All are His servants, and all obey His commands. For another thing, there is a singular similarity between this miracle worked at the beginning of our Lord's ministry, and another which we find Him working after His resurrection, at the end of His ministry, recorded by John. (John 21) In both we read of a miraculous catch of fish. In both the Apostle Peter has a prominent place in the story. And in both there is, probably, a deep spiritual lesson, lying below the outward surface of the facts described.

We should observe, in this passage, our Lord Jesus Christ's unwearied readiness for every good work. Once more we find Him preaching to a people who "pressed upon Him to hear the word of God." And where does He preach? Not in any consecrated building, or place set apart for public worship, but in the open air—not in a pulpit constructed for a preacher's use, but in a fisherman's boat. Souls were waiting to be fed. Personal inconvenience was allowed no place in His consideration. God's work must not stand still.

The servants of Christ should learn a lesson from their Master's conduct on this occasion. We are not to wait until every little difficulty or obstacle is removed, before we put our hand to the plough, or go forth to sow the seed of the word. Convenient buildings may often be lacking for assembling a company of hearers. Convenient rooms may often not be found for gathering children to school. What, then, are we to do? Shall we sit still and do nothing? God forbid! If we cannot do all we want, let us do what we can. Let us work with such tools as we have. While we are lingering and delaying, souls are perishing. It is the slothful heart that is always looking at the hedge of thorns and the lion in the way. (Prov. 15:19; 22:13.) Where we are and as we are, in season of out of season, by one means or by another, by tongue or by pen, by speaking or by writing, let us strive to be ever working for God. But let us never stand still.

We should observe, secondly, in this passage, what encouragement our Lord gives to unquestioning obedience. We are told, that after preaching He bade Simon "launch out into the deep and let down his net for a catch." He receives an answer which exhibits in a striking manner the mind of a good servant. "Master," says Simon, "we have toiled all the night and have taken nothing-nevertheless, at your word I will let down the net." And what was the reward of this ready compliance with the Lord's commands? At once, we are told, "When they had done so, they caught such a large number of fish that their nets began to break."

We need not doubt that a practical lesson for all Christians is contained under these simple circumstances. We are meant to learn the blessing of immediate unhesitating obedience to every plain command of Christ. The path of duty may sometimes be hard and disagreeable. The wisdom of the course we propose to follow may not be apparent to the world. But none of these things must move us. We are not to confer with flesh and blood. We are to go straight forward when Jesus says, "go;" and do a thing boldly, unflinchingly, and decidedly, when Jesus says, "do it." We are to walk by faith and not by sight, and believe that what we don't see now to be right and reasonable, we shall see hereafter. So acting, we shall never find in the long run that we are losers. So acting, we shall find, sooner or, later, that we reap a great reward.

We should observe, thirdly, in this passage, how much a sense of God's presence abases man and makes him feel his sinfulness. We see this strikingly illustrated by Peter's words, when the miraculous draught convinced him that One greater than man was in his boat. We read that "he fell down at Jesus' knees, saying, depart from me; for I am a sinful man, O Lord."

In measuring these words of Peter, we must of course remember the time at which they were spoken. He was, at best, but a babe in grace, weak in faith, weak in experience, and weak in knowledge. At a later period in his life he would, doubtless, have said, "Abide with me," and not, "depart." But still, after every deduction of this kind, the words of Peter exactly express the first feelings of man when he is brought into anything like close contact with God. The sight of divine greatness and holiness makes him feel strongly his own littleness and sinfulness. Like Adam after the fall, his first thought is to hide himself. Like Israel under Sinai, the language of his heart is, "let not God speak with us, lest we die." (Exod. 20:19.)

Let us strive to know more and more, every year we live, our need of a mediator between ourselves and God. Let us seek more and more to realize that without a mediator our thoughts of God can never be comfortable, and the more clearly we see God the more uncomfortable we must feel. Above all, let us be thankful that we have in Jesus the very Mediator whose help our souls require, and that through Him we may draw near to God with boldness, and cast fear away. Out of Christ, God is a consuming fire. In Christ, He is a reconciled Father. Without Christ, the strictest moralist may well tremble, as he looks forward to his end. Through Christ, the chief of sinners may approach God with confidence, and feel perfect peace.

We should observe, lastly, in this passage, the mighty promise which Jesus holds out to Peter—"Fear not," He says, "from henceforth you shall catch men."

That promise, we may well believe, was not intended for Peter only but for all the Apostles—and not for all the Apostles only, but for all faithful ministers of the Gospel who walk in the Apostles' steps. It was spoken for their encouragement and consolation. It was intended to support them under that sense of weakness and unprofitableness by which they are sometimes almost overwhelmed. They certainly have a treasure in earthen vessels. (2 Cor. 4:7.) They are men of like passions with others. They find their own hearts weak and frail, like the hearts of any of their hearers. They are often tempted to give up in despair, and to leave off preaching. But here stands a promise, on which the great Head of the Church would have them daily lean—"Fear not, you shall catch men."

Let us pray daily for all ministers that they may be true successors of Peter and his brethren, that they may preach the same full and free Gospel which they preached, and live the same holy lives which they lived. These are the only ministers who will ever prove successful fishermen. To some of them God may give more honor, and to others less. But all true and faithful preachers of the Gospel have a right to believe that their labor shall not prove in vain. They may often preach the Word with many tears, and see no result of their labor. But God's word shall not return void. (Isaiah. 55:11.) The last day shall show that no work for God was ever thrown away. Every faithful fisherman shall find his Master's words made good—"You shall catch men."

LUKE 5:12-16

JESUS HEALS A LEPER

And it came to pass, while he was in one of the cities, behold, a man full of leprosy: and when he saw Jesus, he fell on his face, and besought him, saying, Lord, if thou wilt, thou canst make me clean. And he stretched forth his hand, and touched him, saying, I will; be thou made clean. And straightway the leprosy departed from him. And he charged him to tell no man: but go thy way, and show thyself to the priest, and offer for thy cleansing, according as Moses commanded, for a testimony unto them. But so much the more went abroad the report concerning him: and great multitudes came together to hear, and to be healed of their infirmities. But he withdrew himself in the deserts, and prayed.

We see in this passage, our Lord Jesus Christ's POWER over incurable diseases. "A man full of leprosy" applies to Him for relief, and is at once healed. This was a mighty miracle. Of all ills which can afflict the body of man, leprosy appears to be the most severe. It affects every part of the constitution at once. It brings sores and decay upon the skin, corruption into the blood, and rottenness into the bones. It is a living death, which no medicine can check or stop. Yet here we read of a leper being made well in a moment. It is but one touch from the hand of the Son of God, and the cure is effected. One single touch of that almighty hand! "And immediately the leprosy departed from him."

We have in this wonderful history a lively emblem of Christ's power to heal our souls. What are we all but spiritual lepers in the sight of God? Sin is the deadly sickness by which we are all affected. It has eaten into our vitals. It has infected all our faculties. Heart, conscience, mind, and will, all are diseased by sin. From the sole of our foot to the crown of our head, there is no soundness about us, but covered with wounds, and bruises, and putrefying sores. (Isaiah 1:6.) Such is the state in which we are born. Such is the state in which we naturally live. We are in one sense dead long before we are laid in the grave. Our bodies may be healthy and active, but our souls are by nature dead in trespasses and sins.

Who shall deliver us from this body of death? Let us thank God that Jesus Christ can. He is that divine Physician, who can make old things pass away and all things become new. In Him is life. He can wash us thoroughly from all the defilement of sin in His own blood. He can quicken us, and revive us by His own Spirit. He can cleanse our hearts, open the eyes of our understandings, renew our wills, and make us whole. Let this sink down deeply into our hearts. There is medicine to heal our sickness. If we are lost it is not because we cannot be saved. However corrupt our hearts, and however wicked our past lives, there is hope for us in the Gospel. There is no case of spiritual leprosy too hard for Christ.

We see, secondly, in this passage, our Lord Jesus Christ's WILLING-NESS to help those that are in need. The petition of the afflicted leper was a very touching one. "Lord," he said, "if you will, you can make me clean." The answer he received was singularly merciful and gracious. At once our Lord replies, "I will—be clean!"

Those two little words, "I will," deserve special notice. They are a deep mine, rich in comfort and encouragement to all laboring and heavy laden souls. They show us the mind of Christ towards sinners. They exhibit His infinite willingness to do good to the sons of men, and His readiness to show compassion. Let us always remember, that if men are not saved, it is not because Jesus is not willing to save them. He is not willing that any should perish, but that all should come to repentance. He would have all men to be saved and come to the knowledge of the truth. He has no pleasure in the death of him that dies. He would have gathered Jerusalem's children, as a hen gathers her chicks, if they would only have been gathered. He would, but they would not. The blame of the sinner's ruin must be borne by himself. It is his own will, and not Christ's will, if he is lost forever. It is a solemn saying of our Lord's, "You will not come unto me that you might have life." (2 Pet. 3:9; 1 Tim. 2:4; Ezek. 18:32; Matt. 23:37; John 5:40)

We see, thirdly, in this passage, what respect our Lord Jesus Christ paid to the ceremonial law of Moses. He bids the leper "go and show himself to the priest," according to the requirement in Leviticus, that he may be legally pronounced clean. He bids him offer an offering on the occasion of his doing so, "according as Moses commanded." Our Lord knew well that the ceremonies of the Mosaic law were only shadows and figures of good things to come, and had in themselves no inherent power. He knew well that the last days of the Levitical institutions were close at hand, and that they were soon to be laid aside forever. But so long as they were not abrogated He would have them respected. They were ordained by God Himself. They were pictures and lively emblems of the Gospel. They were not therefore to be lightly esteemed.

There is a lesson here for Christians, which we shall do well to remember. Let us take heed that we do not despise the ceremonial law, because its work is done. Let us beware of neglecting those parts of the Bible, which contain it, under the idea that the believer in the Gospel has nothing to do with them. It is true that the darkness is past, and the true light now shines. (1 John 2:8.) We have nothing to do now with altars, sacrifices, or priests. Those who wish to revive them are like men who light a candle at noon day. But true as this is, we must never forget that the ceremonial law is still full of instruction. It contains that same Gospel in the bud, which we now see in full flower. Rightly understood we shall always find it throwing strong light on the Gospel of Christ. The Bible reader who neglects to study it, will always find at least that by the neglect his soul has suffered damage.

We see, lastly, in this passage, our Lord Jesus Christ's diligence about private prayer. Although "great multitudes came together to hear, and to be healed by him of their infirmities," He still made time for secret devotion.

Holy and undefiled as He was He would not allow the demands of public business to prevent regular private communion with God. We are told that "He withdrew himself into the wilderness and prayed."

There is an example set before us here, which is much overlooked in these latter days. There are few professing Christians, it may be feared, who strive to imitate Christ in this matter of private devotion. There is abundance of hearing, and reading, and talking, and profession, and visiting, and almsgiving, and subscribing to societies, and teaching at schools. But is there, together with all this, a due proportion of private prayer? Are believing men and women sufficiently careful to be frequently alone with God? These are humbling and heart-searching questions. But we shall find it useful to give them an answer.

Why is it that there is so much apparent religious working, and yet so little result in positive conversions to God—so many sermons, and so few souls saved—so much machinery, and so little effect produced—so much running here and there, and yet so few brought to Christ? Why is all this? The reply is short and simple. There is not enough private prayer. The cause of Christ does not need less working, but it does need among the workers more praying. Let us each examine ourselves, and amend our ways. The most successful workmen in the Lord's vineyard, are those who are like their Master, often and much upon their knees.

LUKE 5:17-26

JESUS HEALS A PARALYTIC

And it came to pass on one of those days, that he was teaching; and there were Pharisees and doctors of the law sitting by, who were come out of every village of Galilee and Judaea and Jerusalem: and the power of the Lord was with him to heal. And behold, men bring on a bed a man that was palsied: and they sought to bring him in, and to lay him before him. And not finding by what way they might bring him in because of the multitude, they went up to the housetop, and let him down through the tiles with his couch into the midst before Jesus. And seeing their faith, he said, Man, thy sins are forgiven thee. And the scribes and the Pharisees began to reason, saying, Who is this that speaketh blasphemies? Who can forgive sins, but God alone? But Jesus perceiving their reasonings, answered and said unto them, Why reason ye in your hearts? Which is easier, to say, Thy sins are forgiven thee; or to say, Arise and walk? But that ye may know that the Son of man hath authority on earth to forgive sins (he said unto him that was palsied), I say unto thee, Arise, and take up thy couch, and go unto thy house. And immediately he rose up before them, and took up that whereon he lay, and departed to his house, glorifying God. And amazement took hold on all, and they glorified God; and they were filled with fear, saying, We have seen strange things to-day.

A threefold miracle demands our attention in these verses. At one and the same time, we see our Lord forgiving sins, reading men's thoughts, and healing a paralytic. He that could do such things, and do them with such perfect ease and authority, must indeed be very God. Power like this was never possessed by man.

Let us mark, firstly, in this passage, what pains men will take about an object when they are in earnest. The friends of a man, sick with the palsy, desired to bring him to Jesus that he might be cured. At first they were unable to do it, because of the crowd by which our Lord was surrounded. What, then, did they do? "They went upon the house-top, and let him down through the tiling, with his couch, into the midst before Jesus." At once their object was gained. Our Lord's attention was drawn to their sick friend, and he was healed. By pains, and labor, and perseverance, his friends succeeded in obtaining for him the mighty blessing of a complete cure.

The importance of pains and diligence, is a truth that meets our eyes on every side. In every calling, and vocation, and trade, we see that great effort is one prominent secret of success. It is not by luck or accident that men prosper, but by hard working. Fortunes are not made without trouble and attention, by bankers and merchants. Practice is not secured without diligence and study, by lawyers and physicians. The principle is one with which the children of this world are perfectly familiar. It is one of their favorite maxims, that there are "no gains without pains."

Let us thoroughly understand that pains and diligence are just as essential to the well-being and prosperity of our souls as of our bodies. In all our endeavors to draw near to God, in all our approaches to Christ, there ought to be the same determined earnestness which was shown by this sick man's friends. We must allow no difficulties to check us, and no obstacle to keep us back from anything which is really for our spiritual good. Specially must we bear this in mind in the matter of regularly reading the Bible, hearing the Gospel, keeping the Sabbath holy, and private prayer. On all these points we must beware of laziness and an excuse-making spirit. Necessity must be the mother of invention. If we cannot find means of keeping up these habits in one way, we must in another. But we must settle in our minds, that the thing shall be done. The health of our soul is at stake. Let the crowd of difficulties be what it may, we must get through it. If the children of this world take so much pains about a corruptible crown, we ought to take far more pains about one that is incorruptible.

Why is it that so many people take no pains in religion? How is it that they can never find time for praying, Bible reading and hearing the Gospel? What is the secret of their continual string of excuses for neglecting means of grace? How is it that the very same men who are full of zeal about money, business, pleasure, or politics, will take no trouble about their souls? The answer to these questions is short and simple. These men are not in earnest about salvation. They have no sense of spiritual disease. They have no consciousness of requiring a Spiritual Physician. They do not feel that their souls are in danger of dying eternally. They see no use in taking trouble about religion. In darkness like this thousands live and die. Happy indeed are they who have found out their peril, and count all things loss if they may only win Christ, and be found in Him!

Let us mark, secondly, the kindness and compassion of our Lord Jesus Christ. Twice in this passage we see Him speaking most graciously to the poor sufferer who was brought before Him. At first He addressed to him those marvelous and heart-cheering words, "Friend, your sins are forgiven." Afterwards He adds words, which in point of comfort, must have been second only to the blessing of forgiveness. "Arise," He says, "and take up your couch, and go into your house." First He assures him that his soul is healed. Then He tells him that his body is cured, and sends him away rejoicing.

Let us never forget this part of our Lord's character. Christ's loving-kindness to His people never changes, and never fails. It is a deep well of which no one ever found the bottom. It began from all eternity, before they were born. It chose, called, and quickened them when they were dead in trespasses and sins. It drew them to God and changed their character, and put a new will in their minds, and a new song in their mouths. It has borne with them in all their waywardness and shortcomings. It will never allow them to be separated from God. It will flow ever forward, like a mighty river, through the endless ages of eternity. Christ's love and mercy must be a sinner's plea when he first begins his journey. Christ's love and mercy will be his only plea when he crosses the dark river and enters home. Let us seek to know this love by inward experience, and prize it more. Let it constrain us more continually to live, not to ourselves, but to Him who died for us and rose again.

Let us mark, lastly, our Lord Jesus Christ's perfect knowledge of the thoughts of men. We read that when the Scribes and Pharisees began to reason secretly among themselves, and privately charge our Lord with blasphemy, He knew what they were about and put them to an open shame. It is written, that "He knew what they were thinking."

It should be a daily and habitual reflection with us that we can keep nothing secret from Christ. To Him apply the words of Paul, "all things are naked and opened to the eyes of him with whom we have to do." (Heb. 4:13.) To Him belong the solemn expressions of the 139th Psalm—the Psalm which every Christian should often study. There is not a word in our mouths, nor an imagination in our hearts, but Jesus knows it altogether. (Psalm 139:4.)

How many searchings of heart this mighty truth ought to awaken within us! Christ ever sees us! Christ always knows us! Christ daily reads and observes our acts, words and thoughts! The recollection of this should alarm the wicked and drive them from their sins! Their wickedness is not hidden, and will one day be fearfully exposed, except they repent. It should frighten hypocrites out of their hypocrisy. They may deceive man, but they are not deceiving Christ. It should quicken and comfort all sincere believers. They should remember that a loving Master is looking at them, and should do all as in His sight. Above all, they should feel that, however mocked and slandered by the world, they are fairly and justly measured by their Savior's eye. They can say, "You, Lord, who know all things, know that I love You." (John 21:17.)

LUKE 5:27-32

THE CALLING OF MATTHEW

And after these things he went forth, and beheld a publican, named Levi, sitting at the place of toll, and said unto him, Follow me. And he forsook all, and rose up and followed him. And Levi made him a great feast in his house: and there was a great multitude of publicans and of others that were sitting at meat with them. And the Pharisees and their scribes murmured against his disciples, saying, Why do ye eat and drink with the publicans and sinners? And Jesus answering said unto them, They that are in health have no need of a physician; but they that are sick. I am not come to call the righteous but sinners to repentance.

The verses we have now read, ought to be deeply interesting to everyone who knows the value of an immortal soul, and desires salvation. They describe the conversion and experience of one of Christ's earliest disciples. We also, are all by nature born in sin, and need conversion. Let us see what we know of the mighty change. Let us compare our own experience with that of the man whose case is here described, and by comparison learn wisdom.

We are taught, in this passage, the power of Christ's calling grace. We read that our Lord called a tax-collector named Levi to become one of His disciples. This man belonged to a class who were a very proverb for wicked-ness among the Jews. Yet even to him our Lord says, "Follow me." We read furthermore, that such mighty influence on Levi's heart accompanied our Lord's words, that although "sitting at his tax booth," when called, he at once "left all, rose up, followed" Christ, and became a disciple.

We must never despair of any one's salvation, so long as he lives, after reading a case like this. We must never say of anyone that he is too wicked, or too hardened, or too worldly to become a Christian. No sins are too many, or too bad, to be forgiven. No heart is too hard or too worldly to be changed. He who called Levi still lives, and is the same that He was 1800 years ago. With Christ nothing is impossible.

How is it with ourselves? This, after all, is the grand question. Are we waiting, and delaying, and hanging back, under the idea that the cross is too heavy, and that we can never serve Christ? Let us cast such thoughts away at once and forever. Let us believe that Christ can enable us by His Spirit to give up all, and come out from the world. Let us remember that He who called Levi never changes. Let us take up the cross boldly, and go forward.

We are taught, secondly, in this passage, that conversion is a cause of joy to a true believer. We read, that when Levi was converted, he made a "great feast in his own house." A feast is made for laughter and merriment. (Eccles. 10:19.) Levi regarded the change in himself as an occasion of rejoicing, and wished others to rejoice with him.

We can easily imagine that Levi's conversion was a cause of grief to his worldly friends. They saw him giving up a profitable calling, to follow a new teacher from Nazareth! They doubtless regarded his conduct as a grievous piece of folly, and an occasion for sorrow rather than joy. They only looked at his temporal losses by becoming a Christian. Of his spiritual gains they knew nothing. And there are many like them. There are aways thousands of people who, if they hear of a relation being converted, consider it rather a misfortune. Instead of rejoicing, they only shake their heads and mourn.

Let us, however, settle it in our minds that Levi did right to rejoice, and if we are converted, let us rejoice likewise. Nothing can happen to a man which ought to be such an occasion of joy, as his conversion. It is a far more important event than being married, or coming of age, or being made a nobleman, or receiving a great fortune. It is the birth of an immortal soul! It is the rescue of a sinner from hell! It is a passage from life to death! It is being made a king and priest for evermore! It is being provided for, both in time and eternity! It is adoption into the noblest and richest of all families, the family of God!

Let us not heed the opinion of the world in this matter. They speak evil of things which they know not. Let us, with Levi, consider every fresh conversion as a cause for great rejoicing. Never ought there to be such joy, gladness, and congratulation, as when our sons, or daughters, or brethren, or sisters, or friends, are born again and brought to Christ. The words of the prodigal's father should be remembered—"It was fit that we should make merry and be glad—for this your brother was dead, and is alive again; he was lost, and is found." (Luke 15:32.)

We are taught, thirdly, in this passage, that converted souls desire to promote the conversion of others. We are told that when Levi was converted, and had made a feast on the occasion, he invited "a great company of tax-collectors" to share it. Most probably these men were his old friends and companions. He knew well what their souls needed, for he had been one of them. He desired to make them acquainted with that Savior who had been merciful to himself. Having found mercy, he wanted them also to find it. Having been graciously delivered from the bondage of sin, he wished others also to be set free.

This feeling of Levi will always be the feeling of a true Christian. It may be safely asserted that there is no grace in the man who cares nothing about the salvation of his fellow men. The heart which is really taught by the Holy Spirit, will always be full of love, charity, and compassion. The soul which has been truly called of God, will earnestly desire that others may experience the same calling. A converted man will not wish to go to heaven alone.

How is it with ourselves in this matter? Do we know anything of Levi's spirit after his conversion? Do we strive in every way to make our friends and relatives acquainted with Christ? Do we say to others, as Moses to Hobab, "Come with us, and we will do you good?" (Num. 10:29.) Do we say as the Samaritan woman, "Come, see a man that told me all that ever I did?" Do we cry to our brethren as Andrew did to Simeon, "We have found the Christ?" These are very serious questions. They supply a most searching test of the real condition of our souls. Let us not shrink from applying it. There is not enough of a missionary spirit among Christians. It should not satisfy us to be safe ourselves. We ought also to try to do good to others. All cannot go to the heathen, but every believer should strive to be a missionary to his fellow men. Having received mercy, we should not hold our peace.

We are taught, lastly, in this passage, one of the chief objects of Christ's coming into the world. We have it in the well-known world, "I came not to call the righteous, but sinners to repentance."

This is that great lesson of the Gospel which, in one form or another, we find continually taught in the New Testament. It is one which we can never have too strongly impressed upon our minds. Such is our natural ignorance and self-righteousness in religion, that we are constantly losing sight of it. We need to be frequently reminded, that Jesus did not come merely as a teacher, but as the Savior of that which was utterly lost, and that those only can receive benefit from Him who will confess that they are ruined, bankrupt, hopeless, miserable sinners.

Let us use this mighty truth, if we never used it before. Are we sensible of our own wickedness and sinfulness? Do we feel that we are unworthy of anything but wrath and condemnation? Then let us understand that we are the very people for whose sake Jesus came into the world. If we feel ourselves righteous, Christ has nothing to say to us. But if we feel ourselves sinners, Christ calls us to repentance. Let not the call be made in vain.

Let us go on using this mighty truth, if we have used it in time past. Do we find our own hearts weak and deceitful? Do we often feel that "when we would do good, evil is present with us?" (Rom. 7:21.) It may be all true, but it must not prevent our resting on Christ. He "came in to the world to save sinners," and if we feel ourselves such, we have warrant for applying to, and trusting in Him to our life's end. One thing only let us never forget—Christ came to call us to repentance, and not to sanction our continuing in sin.

LUKE 5:33-39

FASTING

And they said unto him, The disciples of John fast often, and make supplications; likewise also the disciples of the Pharisees; but thine eat and drink. And Jesus said unto them, Can ye make the sons of the bride-chamber fast, while the bridegroom is with them? But the days will come; and when the bridegroom shall be taken away from them, then will they fast in those days. And he spake also a parable unto them: No man rendeth a piece from a new garment and putteth it

*upon an old garment; else he will rend the new, and also the piece from the new
will not agree with the old. And no man putteth new wine into old wine-skins;
else the new wine will burst the skins, and itself will be spilled, and the skins will
perish. But new wine must be put into fresh wine-skins. And no man having drunk
old wine desireth new; for he saith, The old is good.*

We should observe in these verses, that men may disagree on the lesser
points of religion, while they agree on its weightier matters. We have this
brought out in the alleged difference between the disciples of John the Baptist,
and the disciples of Christ. The question was put to our Lord, "Why do the
disciples of John fast often, and make prayers, and likewise the disciples of
the Pharisees, but yours eat and drink?"

We cannot suppose that there was any essential difference between the
doctrines held by these two parties of disciples. The teaching of John the
Baptist was doubtless clear and explicit upon all the main points necessary
to salvation. The man who could say of Jesus, "Behold the Lamb of God,
who takes away the sin of the world," was not likely to teach his followers
anything contrary to the Gospel. His teaching of course lacked the fullness
and perfection of his divine Master's teaching, but it is absurd to suppose
that it contradicted it. Nevertheless there were points of practice on which
his disciples differed from those of Christ. Agreeing, as they doubtless did,
about the necessity of repentance, and faith, and holiness, they disagreed
about such matters as fasting, eating, drinking, and manner of public devotion.
One in heart, and hope, and aim, as they were about the weightier matters of
inward religion, they were not entirely of one mind about outward matters.

We must make up our minds to see differences of this kind among Christians so long as the world stands. We may regret them much, because of the
handle they give to an ignorant and prejudiced world. But they will exist,
and are one of the many evidences of our fallen condition. About church
government, about the manner of conducting public worship, about fasts
and feasts, and saint's days, and ceremonials, Christians have never been
entirely of one mind, even from the days of the apostles. On all these points
the holiest and ablest servants of God have arrived at different conclusions.
Argument, reasoning, persuasion, persecution, have all alike proved unable
to produce unity.

Let us, however, bless God that there are many points on which all true
servants of God are thoroughly agreed. About sin and salvation, about repentance, and faith, and holiness, there is a mighty unity among all believers,
of every name, and nation, and people, and tongue. Let us make much of

these points in our own personal religion. These, after all, are the principal things which we shall think of in the hour of death, and the day of judgment. On other matters we must agree to differ. It will signify little at the last day what we thought about fasting, and eating, and drinking, and ceremonies. Did we repent, and bring forth fruits fit for repentance? Did we behold the Lamb of God by faith, and receive Him as our Savior? All, of every church, who are found right on these points, will be saved. All, of every church, who are found wrong on these points, will be lost for evermore.

We should observe, secondly, in these verses, the name by which our Lord Jesus Christ speaks of Himself. Twice He calls Himself "the Bridegroom."

The name "bridegroom," like every name applied to our Lord in the Bible, is full of instruction. It is a name peculiarly comforting and encouraging to all true Christians. It teaches the deep and tender love with which Jesus regards all sinners of mankind, who believe in Him. Weak, and unworthy, and shortcoming as they are in themselves, He feels towards them a tender affection, even as a husband does towards his wife. It teaches the close and intimate UNION, which exists between Jesus and believers. It is something far nearer than the union of king and subject, master and servant, teacher and scholar, shepherd and sheep. It is the closest of all unions, the union of husband and wife, the union of which it is written, "what God has joined together, let no man put asunder."

Above all, the name teaches that entire PARTICIPATION of all that Jesus is and has, which is the privilege of every believer. Just as the husband gives to his wife his name, makes her partaker of his property, home, and dignity, and undertakes all her debts and liabilities, so does Christ deal with all true Christians. He takes on Himself all their sins. He declares that they are a part of Himself, and that he who hurts them hurts Him. He gives them, even in this world, such good things as pass man's understanding. And He promises that in the next world they shall sit with Him on His throne, and go out from His presence no more.

If we know anything of true and saving religion, let us often rest our souls on this name and office of Christ. Let us remember daily, that the weakest of Christ's people are cared for with a tender care that passes knowledge, and that whoever hurts them is hurting the apple of Christ's eye. In this world we may be poor and contemptible, and laughed at because of our religion. But if we have faith, we are precious in the sight of Christ. The Bridegroom of our soul will one day plead our cause before the whole world.

We should observe, lastly, in these verses, how gently and tenderly Christ would have His people deal with young and inexperienced Christians. He teaches us this lesson by two parables, drawn from the affairs of daily life. He shows the folly of sewing "new cloth on an old garment," or of putting "new wine into old bottles." In like manner, He would have us know, there is a lack of harmony between a new dispensation and an old one. It is vain to expect those who have been trained and taught under one system, to become immediately used to another system. On the contrary, they must be led on by degrees, and taught as they are able to bear.

The lesson is one which all true Christians would do well to lay to heart, and none perhaps so much as Christian ministers and Christian parents. Forgetfulness of it often does much harm to the cause of truth. The hard judgments and unreasonable expectations of old disciples have often driven back and discouraged young beginners in the school of Christ.

Let us settle it in our minds, that grace must have a beginning in every believer's heart, and that we have no right to say a man has no grace, because it does not come to full ripeness at once. We do not expect a child to do the work of a full-grown man, though he may one day, if he lives long enough. We mast not expect a learner of Christianity to show the faith, and love, and knowledge of an old soldier of the cross. He may become by and bye a mighty champion of the truth. But at first we must give him time. There is great need of wisdom in dealing with young people about religion, and, generally speaking, with all young disciples. Kindness, and patience, and gentleness, are of the first importance. We must not try to pour in the new wine too quickly, or it will run over. We must take them by the hand and lead them on gently. We must beware of frightening, or hurrying them, or pressing them on too fast. If they have only got hold of the main principles of the Gospel, let us not set them down as godless, because of a few lesser matters. We must bear with much weakness and infirmity, and not expect to find old heads on young shoulders, or ripe Christian experience in those who are only babes. There was deep wisdom in Jacob's saying, "If men should over-drive them one day, all the flock will die." (Gen. 33:13.)

Chapter 6

LUKE 6:1-5

JESUS AND THE SABBATH

Now it came to pass on a sabbath, that he was going through the grainfields; and his disciples plucked the ears, and did eat, rubbing them in their hands. But certain of the Pharisees said, Why do ye that which it is not lawful to do on the sabbath day? And Jesus answering them said, Have ye not read even this, what David did, when he was hungry, he, and they that were with him; how he entered into the house of God, and took and ate the showbread, and gave also to them that were with him; which it is not lawful to eat save for the priests alone? And he said unto them, The Son of man is lord of the sabbath.

We should notice, in this passage, what excessive importance hypocrites attach to trifles. We are told that, "One Sabbath day as Jesus was walking through some grainfields, his disciples broke off heads of wheat, rubbed off the husks in their hands, and ate the grains." At once the hypocritical Pharisees found fault, and charged them with committing a sin. They said, "Why do you that which is not lawful to do on the Sabbath days?" The mere act of plucking the heads of wheat of course they did not find fault with. It was an action sanctioned by the Mosaic law. (Deut. 23:25.) The supposed fault with which they charged the disciples, was the breach of the fourth commandment. They had done work on the Sabbath, by taking and eating a handful of food.

This exaggerated zeal of the Pharisees about the Sabbath, we must remember, did not extend to other plain commandments of God. It is evident from many expressions in the Gospels, that these very men, who pretended such strictness on one little point, were more than lax and indifferent about other points of infinitely greater importance. While they stretched the commandment about the Sabbath beyond its true meaning, they openly trampled on the tenth commandment, and were notorious for covetousness. (Luke 16:14.) But this is precisely the character of the hypocrite. To use our Lord's illustration, in some things he makes fuss about straining out of his cup a gnat, while in other things he can swallow a camel. (Matt. 23:24.)

It is a bad symptom of any man's state of soul, when he begins to put the second things in religion in the first place, and the first things in the second, or the things ordained by man above the things ordained by God. Let us beware of falling into this state of mind. There is something sadly wrong in our spiritual condition, when the only thing we look at in others is their outward Christianity, and the principal question we ask is, whether they worship in our communion, and use our ceremonial, and serve God in our way.

Do they repent of sin? Do they believe on Christ? Are they living holy lives? These are the chief points to which our attention ought to be directed. The moment we begin to place anything in religion before these things, we are in danger of becoming as thorough Pharisees as the accusers of the disciples.

We should notice, secondly, in this passage, how graciously our Lord Jesus Christ pleaded the cause of His disciples, and defended them against their accusers. We are told that He answered the cavils of the Pharisees with arguments by which they were silenced, if not convinced. He did not leave His disciples to fight their battle alone. He came to their rescue, and spoke for them.

We have in this fact a cheering illustration of the work that Jesus is ever doing on behalf of His people. There is one, we read in the Bible, who is called "the accuser of the brethren, who accuses them day and night," even Satan, the prince of this world. (Rev. 12:10.) How many grounds of accusation we give him, by reason of our infirmity! How many charges he may justly lay against us before God! But let us thank God that believers "have an Advocate with the Father, Jesus Christ the righteous," who is ever maintaining the cause of His people in heaven, and continually making intercession for them. Let us take comfort in this cheering thought. Let us daily rest our souls on the recollection of our great Friend in heaven. Let our morning and evening prayer continually be, "Answer for me, answer for me, O Lord my God."

We should notice, lastly, in these verses, the clear light which our Lord Jesus Christ throws on the real requirements of the fourth commandment.

He tells the hypocritical Pharisees, who pretended to such strictness in their observance of the Sabbath, that the Sabbath was never intended to prevent works of necessity. He reminds them how David himself, when suffering from hunger, took and ate that show-bread, which ought only to be eaten by the priests, and how the act was evidently allowed of God, because it was an act of necessity. And He argues from David's case, that He who permitted His own temple rules to be infringed, in cases of necessity, would doubtless allow work to be done on His own Sabbath days, when it was work for which there was really a need.

We should weigh carefully the nature of our Lord Jesus Christ's teaching about the observance of the Sabbath, both here and in other places. We must not allow ourselves to be carried away by the common notion that the Sabbath is a mere Jewish ordinance, and that it was abolished and done away by Christ. There is not a single passage of the Gospels which proves this. In every case where we find our Lord speaking upon it, He speaks against the false views of it, which were taught by the Pharisees, but not against the day itself. He cleanses and purifies the fourth commandment from the man-made additions by which the Jews had defiled it, but never declares that it was not to bind Christians. He shows that the seventh day's rest was not meant to prevent works of necessity and mercy, but He says nothing to imply that it was to pass away, as a part of the ceremonial law.

We live in days when anything like strict Sabbath observance is loudly denounced, in some quarters, as a remnant of Jewish superstition. We are boldly told by some people, that to keep the Sabbath holy is legal, and that to enforce the fourth commandment on Christians, is going back to bondage. Let it suffice us to remember, when we hear such things, that assertions are not proofs, and that vague talk like this has no confirmation in the word of God. Let us settle it in our minds, that the fourth commandment has never been repealed by Christ, and that we have no more right to break the Sabbath day, under the Gospel, than we have to murder and to steal.

The architect who repairs a building, and restores it to its proper use, is not the destroyer of it, but the preserver. The Savior who redeemed the Sabbath from Jewish traditions, and so frequently explained its true meaning, ought never to be regarded as the enemy of the fourth commandment. On the contrary, He has "magnified it, and made it honorable."

Let us cling to our Sabbath, as the best safeguard of our Country's religion. Let us defend it against the assaults of ignorant and mistaken men, who would gladly turn the day of God into a day of business and pleasure. Above all, let us each strive to keep the day holy ourselves. Much of our spiritual prosperity depends, under God, on the manner in which we employ our Sundays.

LUKE 6:6-11

THE WITHERED HAND HEALED

And it came to pass on another sabbath, that he entered into the synagogue and taught: and there was a man there, and his right hand was withered. And the scribes and the Pharisees watched him, whether he would heal on the sabbath; that they might find how to accuse him. But he knew their thoughts; and he said to the man that had his hand withered, Rise up, and stand forth in the midst. And he arose and stood forth. And Jesus said unto them, I ask you, Is it lawful on the sabbath to do good, or to do harm? to save a life, or to destroy it? And he looked round about on them all, and said unto him, Stretch forth thy hand. And he did so: and his hand was restored. But they were filled with madness; and communed one with another what they might do to Jesus.

These verses contain another example of our Lord Jesus Christ's mode of dealing with the Sabbath question. Once more we find Him coming into collision with the vain traditions of the Pharisees, about the observance of the fourth commandment. Once more we find Him clearing the day of God from the rubbish of human traditions, and placing its requirements on the right foundation.

We are taught in these verses, the lawfulness of doing works of mercy on the Sabbath day. We read that before all the Scribes and Pharisees, our Lord healed a man with a withered hand on the Sabbath. He knew that these enemies of all righteousness were watching to see whether He would do it, in order that they might "find an accusation against Him." He boldly asserts the right of doing such works of mercy, even on the day when it is said, "you shall do no manner of work." He openly challenges them to show that such a work was contrary to the law. "I will ask you one thing," He says, "Is it lawful on the Sabbath to do good, or to do evil? to save life or to destroy?" To this question His enemies were unable to find an answer.

The principle here laid down, is one of wide application. The fourth commandment was never meant to be so interpreted, as to inflict injury on man's body. It was intended to admit of adaptation to that state of things which sin has brought into the world. It was not meant to forbid showing kindness on the Sabbath to the afflicted, or attending to the needs of the sick. We may drive in a carriage to minister comfort to the dying. We may stay away from public worship, in order to fetch a doctor, or be useful in a sick room. We may visit the fatherless and widow in trouble. We may preach, and teach, and instruct the ignorant. These are works of mercy. We may do them, and yet keep the Sabbath holy. They are not breaches of God's law.

One thing, however, we must carefully remember. We must take heed that we do not abuse the liberty which Christ has given us. It is in this direction that our danger chiefly lies in modern times. There is little risk of our committing the error of the Pharisees, and keeping the Sabbath more strictly than God intended. The thing to be feared is the general disposition to neglect the Sabbath, and to rob it of that honor which it ought to receive. Let us take heed to ourselves in this matter. Let us beware of making God's day a day for visiting, feasting, journeying, and pleasure parties. These are not works of necessity or mercy, whatever a self-willed and unbelieving world may say. The person who spends his Sundays in such ways as these, is sinning a great sin, and proving himself entirely unprepared for the great rest in heaven.

We are taught, secondly, in these verses, the perfect knowledge that our Lord Jesus Christ possesses of men's thoughts. We see this in the language used about Him, when the Scribes and Pharisees were watching Him. We read that "He knew their thoughts."

Expressions like this are among the many evidences of our Lord's divinity. It belongs to God only to read hearts. He who could discern the secret intents and imaginations of others, must have been more than man. No doubt He was man like ourselves in all things, sin only excepted. This we may freely grant to the Socinian, who denies the divinity of Christ. The texts the Socinian quotes, in proof of our Lord's manhood, are texts which we believe and hold as fully as himself. But there are other plain texts in Scripture which prove that our Lord was God as well as man. Of such texts the passage before us is one. It shows that Jesus was "God over all, blessed forever." (Rom. 9:5.)

Let the remembrance of our Lord's perfect knowledge always exercise a humbling influence upon our souls. How many vain thoughts, and worldly imaginations, pass through our minds every hour, which man's eye never see! What are our own thoughts at this moment? What have they been this very day, while we have been reading, or listening to this passage of Scripture? Would they bear public examination? Would we want others to know all that passes in our mind? These are serious questions, and deserve serious answers. Whatever we may think of them, it is a certain fact that Jesus Christ is hourly reading our hearts. Truly we ought to humble ourselves before Him, and cry daily, "Who can tell how often he offends?"—"Cleanse me from secret faults." "God be merciful to me a sinner!"

We are taught, lastly, in these verses, the nature of the first act of faith, when a soul is converted to God. The lesson is conveyed to us in a striking manner, by the history of the cure which is here described. We read that our Lord said to the man whose hand was withered, "Stretch forth your hand." The command, at first sight, seems unreasonable, because the man's obedience was apparently impossible. But the poor sufferer was not stopped by any doubts or reasonings of this kind. At once we read that he made the attempt to stretch forth his hand, and, in making it, was cured. He had faith enough to believe that He who bade him stretch forth his hand, was not mocking him, and ought to be obeyed. And it was precisely in this act of implicit obedience, that he received a blessing. "His hand was completely restored!"

Let us see in this simple history, the best answer to those doubts, and hesitations, and questionings, by which anxious inquirers often perplex themselves, in the matter of coming to Christ. "How can they believe?" they ask us—"How can they come to Christ? How can they lay hold on the hope set before them?" The best answer to all such inquiries, is to bid men do as he did who had the withered hand. Let them not stand still reasoning, but act. Let them not torment themselves with metaphysical speculations, but cast themselves, just as they are, on Jesus Christ. So doing, they will find their course made clear. How, or in what manner, we may not be able to explain. But we may boldly make the assertion, that in the act of striving to draw near to God, they shall find God drawing near to them, but that if they deliberately sit still, they must never expect to be saved.

LUKE 6:12-19

CHOOSING OF THE 12 APOSTLES

And it came to pass in these days, that he went out into the mountain to pray; and he continued all night in prayer to God. And when it was day, he called his disciples; and he chose from them twelve, whom also he named apostles: Simon, whom he also named Peter, and Andrew his brother, and James and John, and Philip and Bartholomew, and Matthew and Thomas, and James the son of Alphaeus, and Simon who was called the Zealot, and Judas the son of James, and Judas Iscariot, who became a traitor; and he came down with them, and stood on a level place, and a great multitude of his disciples, and a great number of the people from all Judaea and Jerusalem, and the sea coast of Tyre and Sidon, who came to hear him, and to be healed of their diseases; and they that were troubled with unclean spirits were healed. And all the multitude sought to touch him; for power came forth from him, and healed them all.

These verses describe the appointment of our Lord Jesus Christ's twelve apostles. That appointment was the beginning of the Christian ministry. It was the first ordination, and an ordination conducted by the Great Head of the Church Himself. Since the day when the events here recorded took place, there have been many thousand ordinations. Myriads of bishops, elders, and deacons have been called to the office of the ministry, and often with far more pomp and splendor than we read of here. But never was there so solemn an ordination as this. Never were men ordained who have done so much for the church and the world as these twelve apostles.

Let us observe, firstly, in these verses, that when our Lord ordained His first ministers, He did it after much prayer. We read that He "went out into a mountain to pray, and continued all night in prayer to God. And when it was day, He called unto Him His disciples, and of them He chose twelve, whom also He named apostles."

We need not doubt that there is a deep significance in this special mention of our Lord's praying upon this occasion. It was intended to be a perpetual lesson to the Church of Christ. It was meant to show the great importance of prayer and intercession on behalf of ministers, and particularly at the time of their ordination. Those to whom the responsible office of ordaining is committed, should pray that they may "lay hands suddenly on no man." Those who offer themselves for ordination, should pray that they may not take up work for which they are unfit, and not run without being sent. The lay members of the Church, not least, should pray that none may be ordained, but men who are inwardly moved by the Holy Spirit. Happy are those ordinations, in which all concerned have the mind that was in Christ, and come together in a prayerful spirit!

Do we desire to help forward the cause of pure and undefiled religion in the world? Then let us never forget to pray for ministers, and especially for young men about to enter the ministry. The progress of the Gospel, under God, will always depend much on the character and conduct of those who profess to preach it. An unconverted minister can never be expected to do good to souls. He cannot teach properly what he does not feel experimentally. From such men let us pray daily that the Church may be delivered. Converted ministers are God's special gift. Man cannot create them. If we would have good ministers, we must remember our Lord's example, and pray for them. Their work is heavy. Their responsibility is enormous. Their strength is small. Let us see that we support them, and hold up their hands by our prayers. In this, and in too many other cases, the words of James are often sadly applicable, "You have not, because you ask not." (James 4:2.) We do not ask God to raise up a constant supply of converted young men to fill our pulpits, and God chastises our neglect by withholding them.

Let us observe, secondly, how little we are told of the worldly position of the first ministers of the Christian Church. Four of them, we know, were fishermen. One of them, at least, was a tax-collector. Most of them, probably, were Galileans. Not one of them, so far as we can see from the New Testament, was great, or rich, or noble, or highly connected. Not one was a Pharisee, or Scribe, or Priest, or Ruler, or Elder among the people. All were, apparently, "unlearned and ignorant men." (Acts 4:13.) All were poor.

There is something deeply instructive in the fact which is now before us. It shows us that our Lord Jesus Christ's kingdom was entirely independent of help from this world. His Church was not built by might, or by power, but by the Spirit of the living God. (Zech. 4:6.) It supplies us with an unanswerable proof of the divine origin of Christianity. A religion which turned the world upside down, while its first preachers were all poor men, must needs have been from heaven. If the apostles had possessed money to give their hearers, or been followed by armies to frighten them, an infidel might well deny that there was anything astonishing in their success. But the poverty of our Lord's disciples cuts away such arguments from beneath the infidel's feet. With a doctrine most unpalatable to the natural heart—with nothing whatever to bribe or compel obedience—a few lowly Galileans shook the world, and changed the face of the Roman empire. One thing only can account for this. The Gospel of Christ, which these men proclaimed, was the truth of God.

Let us remember these things, if we ever strive to do any work for Christ, and beware of leaning on an arm of flesh. Let us watch against the secret inclination, which is natural to all, to look to money, or learning, or high patronage, or great men's support, for success. It we want to do good to souls, we must not look first to the powers of this world. We should begin where the Church of Christ began. We should seek pastors filled with the Holy Spirit.

Let us observe, lastly, in these verses, that one whom our Lord chose to be an apostle, was a false disciple and a traitor. That man was Judas Iscariot.

We cannot for a moment doubt, that in choosing Judas Iscariot, our Lord Jesus knew well what He was doing. He who could read hearts, certainly saw from the beginning that, notwithstanding his profession of piety, Judas was a graceless man, and would one day betray Him. Why then did He appoint him to be an apostle? The question is one which has perplexed many. Yet it admits of a satisfactory answer. Like everything which our Lord did, it was done advisedly, deliberately, and with deep wisdom. It conveyed lessons of high importance to the whole Church of Christ.

The choice of Judas was meant to teach ministers humility. They are not to suppose that ordination necessarily conveys grace, or that once ordained they cannot err. On the contrary, they are to remember, that one ordained by Christ Himself was a wretched hypocrite. Let the minister who thinks he stands, take heed lest he fall.

Again, the choice of Judas was meant to teach the lay-members of the Church, not to make idols of ministers. They are to esteem them highly in love for their work's sake, but they are not to bow down to them as infallible, and honor them with an unscriptural honor. They are to remember that ministers may be successors of Judas Iscariot, as well as of Peter and Paul. The name of Judas should be a standing warning to "cease from man." Let no man glory in men. (1 Cor. 3:21.)

Finally, our Lord's choice of Judas was meant to teach the whole church, that it must not expect to see a perfectly pure communion in the present state of things. The wheat and the tares—the good fish and the bad—will always be found side by side, until the Lord comes again. It is vain to look for perfection in visible churches. We shall never find it. A Judas was found even among the apostles. Converted and unconverted people will always be found mixed together in all congregations.

LUKE 6:20-26
BLESSINGS AND WOES

And he lifted up his eyes on his disciples, and said, Blessed are ye poor: for yours is the kingdom of God. Blessed are ye that hunger now: for ye shall be filled. Blessed are ye that weep now: for ye shall laugh. Blessed are ye, when men shall hate you, and when they shall separate you from their company, and reproach you, and cast out your name as evil, for the Son of man's sake. Rejoice in that day, and leap for joy: for behold, your reward is great in heaven; for in the same manner did their fathers unto the prophets. But woe unto you that are rich! for ye have received your consolation. Woe unto you, ye that are full now! for ye shall hunger. Woe unto you, ye that laugh now! for ye shall mourn and weep. Woe unto you, when all men shall speak well of you! for in the same manner did their fathers to the false prophets.

The discourse of our Lord, which we have now begun, resembles, in many respects, His well-known Sermon on the Mount. The resemblance, in fact, is so striking that many have concluded that Luke and Matthew are reporting one and the same discourse, and that Luke is giving us, in an abridged form, what Matthew reports at length. There seems no sufficient ground for this conclusion. The occasions on which the two discourses were delivered, were entirely different. Our Lord's repetition of the same great lesson, in almost the same words, on two different occasions, is nothing extraordinary. It is unreasonable to suppose that none of His mighty teachings were ever delivered more than once. In the present case, the repetition is very significant. It shows us the great and deep importance of the lessons which the two discourses contain.

Let us first notice in these verses, who are those whom the Lord Jesus pronounced BLESSED. The list is a remarkable and startling one. It singles out those who are "poor," and those who "hunger"—those who "weep," and those who are "hated" by man. These are the people to whom the great Head of the Church says, "Blessed are you!"

We must take good heed that we do not misunderstand our Lord's meaning, when we read these expressions. We must not for a moment suppose that the mere fact of being poor, and hungry, and sorrowful, and hated by man, will entitle any one to lay claim to an interest in Christ's blessing. The poverty here spoken of, is a poverty accompanied by grace. The need is a need entailed by faithful adherence to Jesus. The afflictions are the afflictions of the Gospel. The persecution is persecution for the Son of Man's sake. Such need, and poverty, and affliction, and persecution, were the inevitable consequences of faith in Christ, at the beginning of Christianity. Thousands had to give up everything in this world, because of their belief in Jesus. It was their case which Jesus had specially in view in this passage. He desired to supply them, and all who suffer like them for the Gospel's sake, with special comfort and consolation.

Let us notice, secondly, in these verses, who are those to whom our Lord addresses the solemn words, "WOE unto you." Once more we read expressions which at first sight seem most extraordinary. "Woe unto you that are rich! Woe unto you that are full! Woe unto you that laugh! Woe unto you when all men shall speak well of you!" Stronger and more cutting sayings than these cannot be found in the New Testament.

Here, however, no less than in the preceding verses, we must take care that we do not misapprehend our Lord's meaning. We are not to suppose that the possession of riches, and a rejoicing spirit, and the good word of man, are necessarily proofs that people are not Christ's disciples. Abraham and Job were rich. David and Paul had their seasons of rejoicing. Timothy was one who "had a good report from those that were outside." All these, we know, were true servants of God. All these were blessed in this life, and shall receive the blessing of the Lord in the day of His appearing.

Who then, are the people to whom our Lord says, "Woe unto you?" They are the men who refuse to seek treasure in heaven, because they love the good things of this world better, and will not give up their money, if need requires, for Christ's sake. They are the men who prefer the joys and so-called happiness of this world, to joy and peace in believing, and will not risk the loss of the one in order to gain the other. They are those who love the praise of man more than the praise of God, and will turn their backs on Christ, rather than not keep in with the world. These are the kind of men whom our Lord had in view when He pronounced the solemn words, "Woe, woe unto you." He knew well that there were thousands of such people among the Jews-thousands who, notwithstanding His miracles and sermons, would love the world better than Him. He knew well that there would always be thousands of such in His professing Church—thousands who, though convinced of the truth of the Gospel, would never give up anything for its sake. To all such He delivers a dreadful warning. "Woe, woe unto you!"

One mighty lesson stands out plainly on the face of these verses. May we all lay it to heart, and learn wisdom! That lesson is the utter contrariety between the mind of Christ, and the common opinions of mankind; the entire variance between the thoughts of Jesus, and the prevailing thoughts of the world. The conditions of life which the world reckons desirable, are the very conditions upon which the Lord pronounces "woes." Poverty, and hunger, and sorrow, and persecution, are the very things which man labors to avoid. Riches, and fullness, and merriment, and popularity, are precisely the things which men are always struggling to attain. When we have said all, in the way of qualifying, explaining, and limiting our Lord's words, there still remain two sweeping assertions, which flatly contradict the current doctrine of mankind. The state of life which our Lord blesses, the world cordially dislikes. The people to whom our Lord says, "woe unto you," are the very people whom the world admires, praises, and imitates. This is a dreadful fact. It ought to raise within us great searchings of heart.

Let us leave the whole passage with honest self-inquiry and self-examination. Let us ask ourselves what we think of the wonderful declarations that it contains. Can we subscribe to what our Lord says? Are we of one mind with Him? Do we really believe that poverty and persecution, endured for Christ's sake, are positive blessings? Do we really believe that riches and worldly enjoyments, and popularity among men, when sought for more than salvation, or preferred in the least to the praise of God, are a certain curse? Do we really think that the favor of Christ, with trouble and the world's ill word, is better worth having than money, and merriment, and a good name among men, without Christ?

These are most serious questions, and deserve a most serious answer. The passage before us is eminently one which tests the reality of our Christianity. The truths it contains, are truths which no unconverted man can love and receive. Happy are those who have found them truths by experience, and can say "amen" to all our Lord's declarations. Whatever men may please to think, those whom Jesus blesses are blessed, and those whom Jesus does not bless will be cast out for evermore.

LUKE 6:27-38

LOVE FOR ENEMIES

But I say unto you that hear, Love your enemies, do good to them that hate you, bless them that curse you, pray for them that despitefully use you. To him that smiteth thee on the one cheek offer also the other; and from him that taketh away thy cloak withhold not thy coat also. Give to everyone that asketh thee; and of him that taketh away thy goods ask them not again. And as ye would that men should do to you, do ye also to them likewise. And if ye love them that love you, what thank have ye? for even sinners love those that love them. And if ye do good to them that do good to you, what thank have ye? for even sinners do the same. And if ye lend to them of whom ye hope to receive, what thank have ye? even sinners lend to sinners, to receive again as much. But love your enemies, and do them good, and lend, never despairing; and your reward shall be great, and ye shall be sons of the Most High: for he is kind toward the unthankful and evil. Be ye merciful, even as your Father is merciful.

And judge not, and ye shall not be judged: and condemn not, and ye shall not be condemned: release, and ye shall be released: give, and it shall be given unto you; good measure, pressed down, shaken together, running over, shall they give into your bosom. For with what measure ye mete it shall be measured to you again.

The teaching of our Lord Jesus Christ, in these verses, is confined to one great subject. That subject is Christian love and charity. Charity, which is the grand characteristic of the Gospel—charity, which is the bond of perfectness-charity, without which a man is nothing in God's sight—charity is here fully expounded and strongly enforced. Well would it have been for the Church of Christ, if its Master's precept in this passage had been more carefully studied and more diligently observed!

In the first place, our Lord explains the nature and extent of Christian charity. The disciples might ask, WHOM are we to love? He bids them "love their enemies, do good to those who hate them, bless those who curse them, and pray for those who despitefully use them." Their love was to be like His own towards sinners—unselfish, and uninfluenced by any hope of return.

What was to be the MANNER of this love? the disciples might ask. It was to be self-sacrificing and self-denying. "Unto him that smites you on the one cheek offer also the other." "Him that takes away your cloak, forbid not to take your coat also." They were to give up much, and endure much, for the sake of showing kindness and avoiding strife. They were to forego even their rights, and submit to wrong, rather than awaken angry passions and create quarrels. In this they were to be like their Master, long-suffering, meek, and lowly of heart.

In the second place, our Lord lays down a golden principle for the settlement of doubtful cases. He knew well that there will always be occasions when the line of duty towards our neighbor is not clearly defined. He knew how much self-interest and private feelings will sometimes dim our perceptions of right and wrong. He supplies us with a precept for our guidance in all such cases, of infinite wisdom; a precept which even infidels have been compelled to admire. "As you would that men should do to you, you do also to them likewise." To do to others as they do to us, and return evil for evil, is the standard of the heathen. To behave to others as we should like others to behave to us, whatever their actual behavior may be, this should be the mark at which the Christian should aim. This is to walk in the steps of our blessed Savior. If He had dealt with the world as the world dealt with Him, we would all have been ruined forever in hell.

In the third place, our Lord points out to His disciples the necessity of their having a HIGHER STANDARD OF DUTY to their neighbor than the children of this world. He reminds them that to love those who love them, and do good to those who do good to them, and lend to those of whom they hope to receive, is to act no better than "the sinner" who knows nothing of the Gospel. The Christian must be altogether another style of man. His feelings of love, and his deeds of kindness, must be like his Master's—free and gratuitous. He must let men see that he loves others from higher principles than the ungodly do, and that his charity is not confined to those from whom he hopes to get something in return. Anybody can show kindness and charity, when he hopes to gain something by it. But such charity should never content a Christian. The man who is content with it, ought to remember that his practice does not rise an inch above the level of an old Roman or Greek idolater.

In the fourth place, our Lord shows His disciples that in discharging their duty to their neighbors, they should look to the example of God. If they called themselves "children of the Highest," they should consider that their Father is "kind to the unthankful and the evil," and they should learn from Him to be merciful, even as He is merciful. The extent of God's unacknowledged mercies to man can never be reckoned up. Every year he pours benefits on millions who do not honor the hand from which they come, or thank the Giver of them. Yet every year these benefits are continued. "Seed time and harvest, summer and winter, never cease." His mercy endures forever. His lovingkindness is unwearied. His compassions fail not. So ought it to be with all who profess themselves to be His children. Thanklessness and ingratitude should not make them slack their hands from works of love and mercy. Like their Father in heaven, they should never be tired of doing good.

In the last place, our Lord assures His disciples that the practice of the high standard of charity He recommends shall bring its own REWARD. "Judge not," He says, "and you shall not be judged—condemn not, and you shall not be condemned—forgive, and you shall be forgiven—give, and it shall be given unto you." And He concludes with the broad assertion, "With the same measure that you mete out, shall it be measured to you again." The general meaning of these words appears to be, that no man shall ever be a loser, in the long run, by deeds of self-denying charity, and patient patience love. At times he may seem to get nothing by his conduct. He may appear to reap nothing but ridicule, contempt, and injury. His kindness may sometimes tempt men to impose on him. His patience and forbearance may be abused. But at the last he will always be found a gainer—often, very often, a gainer in this life-certainly, most certainly, a gainer in the life to come.

Such is the teaching of our Lord Jesus Christ about charity. Few of His sayings are so deeply heart-searching as those we have now been considering. Few passages in the Bible are so truly humbling as these eleven verses.

How little of the style of charity which our Lord recommends is to be seen, either in the world or in the Church! How common is an angry, passionate spirit, a morbid sensitiveness about what is called honor, and a readiness to quarrel on the least occasion! How seldom we see men and women who love their enemies, and do good hoping for nothing again, and bless those that curse them, and are kind to the unthankful and evil! Truly we are reminded here of our Lord's words, "Narrow is the way which leads unto life, and few there be that find it." (Matt. 7:13.)

How happy the world would be, if Christ's precepts were strictly obeyed! The chief causes of half the sorrows of mankind, are selfishness, strife, unkindness, and lack of love. Never was there a greater mistake than to suppose that vital Christianity interferes with human happiness. It is not having too much religion, but too little, that makes people gloomy, wretched, and miserable. Wherever Christ is best known and obeyed, there will always be found most real joy and peace.

Would we know anything by experience of this blessed grace of charity? Then let us seek to be joined to Christ by faith, and to be taught and sanctified by His Spirit. We do not gather grapes of thorns, or figs of thistles. We cannot have flowers without roots, or fruit without trees. We cannot have the fruit of the Spirit, without vital union with Christ, and a new creation within. Such as are not born again can never really love in the manner that Christ enjoins.

LUKE 6:39-45

A TREE AND ITS FRUIT

And he spake also a parable unto them, Can the blind guide the blind? shall they not both fall into a pit? The disciple is not above his teacher: but every one when he is perfected shall be as his teacher. And why beholdest thou the mote that is in thy brother's eye, but considerest not the beam that is in thine own eye? Or how canst thou say to thy brother, Brother, let me cast out the mote that is in thine eye, when thou thyself beholdest not the beam that is in thine own eye? Thou hypocrite, cast out first the beam out of thine own eye, and then shalt thou see clearly to cast out the mote that is in thy brother's eye. For there is no good tree that bringeth forth corrupt fruit; nor again a corrupt tree that bringeth forth good fruit. For each tree is known by its own fruit. For of thorns men do not gather figs, nor of a bramble bush gather they grapes. The good man out of the good treasure of his heart bringeth forth that which is good; and the evil man out of the evil treasure bringeth forth that which is evil: for out of the abundance of the heart his mouth speaketh.

We learn, in the first place, from these verses, the great danger of listening to false religious teachers. Our Lord compares such teachers and their hearers to the blind leading the blind, and asks the reasonable question, "Shall they not both fall into the ditch?" He goes on to confirm the importance of His warning by declaring, that "the disciple is not above his master," and the scholar cannot be expected to know more than his teacher. If a man will hear unsound instruction, we cannot expect him to become otherwise than unsound in the faith himself.

The subject which our Lord brings before us here deserves far more attention than it generally receives. The amount of evil which unsound religious teaching has brought on the Church in every age is incalculable. The loss of souls which it has occasioned is fearful to contemplate. A teacher who does not know the way to heaven himself, is not likely to lead his hearers to heaven. The man who hears such a teacher runs a fearful risk himself of being lost eternally. "If the blind lead the blind both must fall into the ditch."

If we would escape the danger against which our Lord warns us, we must not neglect to prove the teaching that we hear by the holy Scriptures. We must not believe things merely because ministers say them. We must not suppose, as a matter of course, that ministers can make no mistakes. We must call to mind our Lord's words on another occasion, "Beware of false prophets." (Matt. 7:15.) We must remember the advice of Paul and John—"Prove all things." "Try the spirits whether they are of God." (1 Thess. 5:21; 1 John 4:1.) With the Bible in our hands, and the promise of guidance from the Holy Spirit to all who seek it, we shall be without excuse if our souls are led astray. The blindness of ministers is no excuse for the darkness of the people. The man who from indolence, or superstition, or affected humility, refuses to distrust the teaching of the minister whom he finds set over him, however unsound it may be, will at length share his minister's portion. If people will trust blind guides, they must not be surprised if they are led to the pit.

We learn, secondly, from these verses, that those who reprove the sins of others should strive to be of blameless life. Our Lord teaches us this lesson by a practical saying. He shows the unreasonableness of a man finding fault with "a speck," or trifling thing in a brother's eye, while he himself has "a beam," or some large and formidable object sticking in his own eye.

The lesson must doubtless be received with suitable and scriptural qualifications. If no man is to teach or preach to others, until he himself is faultless, there could be no teaching or preaching in the world. The erring would never be corrected, and the wicked would never be reproved. To put such a sense as this on our Lord's words, brings them into collision with other plain passages of Scripture.

The main object of our Lord Jesus appears to be to impress on ministers and teachers THE IMPORTANCE OF CONSISTENCY OF LIFE. The passage is a solemn warning not to contradict by our lives, what we have said with our lips. The office of the preacher will never command attention unless he practices what he preaches. Episcopal ordination, university degrees, high-sounding titles, a loud profession of doctrinal purity, will never procure respect for a minister's sermon, if his congregation sees him cleaving to ungodly habits.

But there is much here which we shall all do well to remember. The lesson is one which many besides ministers should seriously consider. All heads of families and masters of households, all parents, all teachers of schools, all tutors, all managers of young people—should often think of the "speck" and the "beam." All such should see in our Lord's words the mighty lesson, that nothing influences others so much as consistency. Let the lesson be treasured up and not forgotten.

We learn, lastly, from these verses, that there is only one satisfactory test of a man's religious character. That test is his conduct and conversation.

The words of our Lord on this subject are clear and unmistakable. He draws an illustration from a tree, and lays down the broad principle, "every tree is known by his own fruit." But our Lord does not stop here. He proceeds further to show that a man's conversation is one indication of his state of heart. "Of the abundance of the heart his mouth speaks." Both these sayings are deeply important. Both should be stored up among the leading maxims of our practical Christianity.

Let it be a settled principle in our religion that when a man brings forth no fruits of the Spirit, he has not the Holy Spirit within him. Let us resist as a deadly error the common idea, that all baptized people are born again, and that all members of the Church, as a matter of course, have the Holy Spirit. One simple question must be our rule. What fruit does a man bring forth? Does he repent? Does he believe with the heart on Jesus? Does he live a holy life? Does he overcome the world? Habits like these are what Scripture calls "fruit." When these "fruits" are lacking, it is profane to talk of a man having the Spirit of God within him.

Let it be a settled principle again in our religion, that when a man's general conversation is ungodly, his heart is graceless and unconverted. Let us not give way to the vulgar notion, that no one can know anything of the state of another's heart, and that although men are living wickedly, they have got good hearts at the bottom. Such notions are flatly contradictory to our Lord's teaching. Is the general tone of a man's communication carnal, worldly, irreligious, godless, or profane? Then let us understand that this is the state of his heart. When a man's tongue is extensively wrong, it is absurd, no less than unscriptural, to say that his heart is right.

Let us close this passage with solemn self-inquiry, and use it for the trial of our own state before God. What fruits are we bringing forth in our lives? Are they, or are they not, fruits of the Spirit? What kind of evidence do our words supply as to the state of our hearts? Do we talk like men whose hearts are "right in the sight of God?"—There is no evading the doctrine laid down by our Lord in this passage. Conduct is the grand test of character. Words are one great evidence of the condition of the heart.

LUKE 6:46-49

THE WISE AND THE FOOLISH BUILDERS

And why call ye me, Lord, Lord, and do not the things which I say? Every one that cometh unto me, and heareth my words, and doeth them, I will show you to whom he is like: he is like a man building a house, who digged and went deep, and laid a foundation upon the rock: and when a flood arose, the stream brake against that house, and could not shake it: because it had been well builded. But he that heareth, and doeth not, is like a man that built a house upon the earth without a foundation; against which the stream brake, and straightway it fell in; and the ruin of that house was great.

It has been said, with much truth, that no sermon should conclude without some personal application to the consciences of those who hear it. The passage before us is an example of this rule, and a confirmation of its correctness. It is a solemn and heart-searching conclusion of a most solemn discourse.

Let us mark, in these verses, what an old and common sin is profession without practice. It is written that our Lord said, "Why do you call me Lord, Lord, and do not the things which I say?" The Son of God Himself had many followers, who pretended to honor Him by calling Him Lord, but yielded no obedience to His commandments.

The evil which our Lord exposes here, has always existed in the Church of God. It was found six hundred years before our Lord's time, in the days of Ezekiel—"My people come to you, as they usually do, and sit before you to listen to your words, but they do not put them into practice. With their mouths they express devotion, but their hearts are greedy for unjust gain." (Ezek. 33:31.) It was found in the primitive Church of Christ, in the days of James. "Be doers of the word," he says, "and not hearers only, deceiving your own selves." (James 1:22.) It is a disease which has never ceased to prevail all over Christendom. It is a soul-ruining plague, which is continually sweeping away crowds of Gospel-hearers down the broad way to destruction. Open sin, and avowed unbelief, no doubt slay their thousands. But profession without practice slays its tens of thousands.

Let us settle it in our minds, that no sin is so foolish and unreasonable as the sin which Jesus here denounces. Common sense alone might tell us that the name and form of Christianity can profit us nothing, so long as we cleave to sin in our hearts, and live unchristian lives. Let it be a fixed principle in our religion, that obedience is the only sound evidence of saving faith, and that the talk of the lips is worse than useless, if it is not accompanied by sanctification of the life. The man in whose heart the Holy Spirit really dwells, will never be content to sit still, and do nothing to show his love to Christ.

Let us mark, secondly, in these verses, what a striking picture our Lord draws of the religion of the man who not only hears Christ's sayings, but DOES Christ's will. He compares him to one who "built a house, and dug deep, and laid the foundation on a rock."

Such a man's religion may cost him much. Like the house built on a rock, it may entail on him pains, labor, and self-denial. To lay aside pride and self-righteousness, to crucify the rebellious flesh, to put on the mind of Christ, to take up the cross daily, to count all things but loss for Christ's sake—all this may be hard work. But, like the house built on the rock, such religion will stand. The streams of affliction may beat violently upon it, and the floods of persecution dash fiercely against it, but it will not give way. The Christianity which combines good profession and good practice, is a building that will not fall.

Let us mark, lastly, in these verses, what a mournful picture our Lord draws of the religion of the man who hears Christ's sayings, but does not obey them. He compares him to one who, "without a foundation, built an house upon the earth."

Such a man's religion may look well for a season. An ignorant eye may detect no difference between the possessor of such a religion, and a true Christian. Both may worship in the same Church. Both may use the same ordinances. Both may profess the same faith. The outward appearance of the house built on the rock, and the house without any solid foundation, may be much the same. But the day of trial and affliction is the test which the religion of the mere outward professor cannot stand. When storm and tempest beat on the house which has no foundation, the walls which looked well in sunshine and fair weather, are sure to come to the ground. The Christianity which consists of merely hearing religion taught, without doing anything, is a building which must finally fall. Great indeed will be the ruin! There is no loss like the loss of a soul.

This passage of Scripture is one which ought to call up in our minds peculiarly solemn feelings. The pictures it presents, are pictures of things which are daily going on around us. On every side we shall see thousands building for eternity, on a mere outward profession of Christianity—striving to shelter their souls under false refuges—contenting themselves with a name to live, while they are dead, and with a form of godliness without the power. Few indeed are the builders upon rocks, and great is the ridicule and persecution which they have to endure! Many are the builders upon sand, and mighty are the disappointments and failures which are the only result of their work! Surely, if ever there was a proof that man is fallen and blind in spiritual things, it may be seen in the fact that the majority of every generation of baptized people, persist in building on sand.

What is the foundation on which we ourselves are building? This, after all, is the question that concerns our souls. Are we upon the rock, or are we upon the sand? We love perhaps to hear the Gospel. We approve of all its leading doctrines. We assent to all its statements of truth about Christ and the Holy Spirit, about justification and sanctification, about repentance and faith, about conversion and holiness, about the Bible and prayer. But what are we doing? What is the daily practical history of our lives, in public and private, in the family and in the world? Can it be said of us, that we not only hear Christ's sayings, but that we also do them?

The hour comes, and will soon be here, when questions like these must be asked and answered, whether we like them or not. The day of sorrow and bereavement, of sickness and death, will make it plain whether we are on the rock, or on the sand. Let us remember this betimes, and not trifle with our souls. Let us strive so to believe and so to live, so to hear Christ's voice and so to follow Him, that when the flood arises, and the streams beat over us, our house may stand and not fall.

Chapter 7

THE FAITH OF THE CENTURION

*A*fter he had ended all his sayings in the ears of the people, he entered into *Capernaum. And a certain centurion's servant, who was dear unto him, was sick and at the point of death. And when he heard concerning Jesus, he sent unto him elders of the Jews, asking him that he would come and save his servant. And they, when they came to Jesus, besought him earnestly, saying, He is worthy that thou shouldest do this for him; for he loveth our nation, and himself built us our synagogue. And Jesus went with them. And when he was now not far from the house, the centurion sent friends to him, saying unto him, Lord, trouble not thyself; for I am not worthy that thou shouldest come under my roof: wherefore neither thought I myself worthy to come unto thee: but say the word, and my servant shall be healed. For I also am a man set under authority, having under myself soldiers: and I say to this one, Go, and he goeth; and to another, Come, and he cometh; and to my servant, Do this, and he doeth it. And when Jesus heard these things, he marvelled at him, and turned and said unto the multitude that followed him, I say to you, I have not found so great faith, no, not in Israel. And they that were sent, returning to the house, found the servant whole.*

These verses describe the miraculous cure of a sick man. A centurion, or officer in the Roman army, applies to our Lord on behalf of his servant, and obtains what he requests. A greater miracle of healing than this, is nowhere recorded in the Gospels. Without even seeing the sufferer, without touch of hand or look of eye, our Lord restores health to a dying man by a single word. He speaks, and the sick man is cured. He commands, and the disease departs. We read of no prophet or apostle, who wrought miracles in this manner. We see here the finger of God!

We should notice in these verses the KINDNESS of the centurion. It is a part of his character which appears in three ways. We see it in his treatment of his servant. He cares for him tenderly when sick, and takes pains to have him restored to health. We see it again in his feeling towards the Jewish people. He did not despise them as other Gentiles commonly did. The elders of the Jews bear this strong testimony, "He loves our nation." We see it lastly in his liberal support of the Jewish place of worship at Capernaum. He did not love Israel "in word and tongue only, but in deed." The messengers he sent to our Lord supported their petition by saying, "He has built a synagogue for us."

Now where did the centurion learn this kindness? How can we account for one who was a heathen by birth, and a soldier by profession, showing such a spirit as this? Habits of mind like these were not likely to be gathered from heathen teaching, or promoted by the society of a Roman camp. Greek and Latin philosophy would not recommend them. Tribunes, consuls, prefects and emperors would not encourage them. There is but one account of the matter. The centurion was what he was "by the grace of God." The Spirit had opened the eyes of his understanding, and put a new heart within him. His knowledge of divine things no doubt was very dim. His religious views were probably built on a very imperfect acquaintance with the Old Testament Scriptures. But whatever light from above he had, it influenced his life, and one result of it was the kindness which is recorded in this passage.

Let us learn a lesson from the centurion's example. Let us, like him, show kindness to everyone with whom we have to do. Let us strive to have an eye ready to see, and a hand ready to help, and a heart ready to feel, and a will ready to do good to all. Let us be ready to weep with those who weep, and rejoice with those who rejoice. This is one way to recommend our religion, and make it beautiful before men. Kindness is a grace that all can understand. This is one way to be like our blessed Savior. If there is one feature in His character more notable than another, it is His unwearied kindness and love. This is one way to be happy in the world, and see good days. Kindness always brings its own reward. The kind person will seldom be without friends.

We should notice, secondly, in this passage, the HUMILITY of the centurion. It appears in his remarkable message to our Lord when He was not far from his house—"I am not worthy that you should enter under my roof—neither thought I myself worthy to come unto you." Such expressions are a striking contract to the language used by the elders of the Jews. "He is worthy," said they, "for whom you should do this." "I am not worthy," says the good centurion, "that you should enter under my roof."

Humility like this is one of the strongest evidences of the indwelling of the Spirit of God. We know nothing of humility by nature, for we are all born proud. To convince us of sin, to show us our own vileness and corruption, to put us in our right place, to make us lowly and self-abased—these are among the principal works which the Holy Spirit works in the soul of man. Few of our Lord's sayings are so often repeated as the one which closes the parable of the Pharisee and Tax-collector—"Every one that exalts himself shall be abased, and he that humbles himself shall be exalted." (Luke 18:14.) To have great gifts, and do great works for God, is not given to all believers. But all believers ought to strive to be clothed with humility.

We should notice, thirdly, in this passage, the centurion's FAITH. We have a beautiful example of it in the request that he made to our Lord—"Just say the word, and my servant shall be healed." He thinks it needless for our Lord to come to the place where his servant lay dying. He regards our Lord as one possessing authority over diseases, as complete as his own authority over his soldiers, or a Roman Emperor's authority over himself. He believes that a word of command from Jesus is sufficient to send sickness away. He asks to see no sign or wonder. He declares his confidence that Jesus is an almighty Master and King, and that diseases, like obedient servants, will at once depart at His orders.

Faith like this was indeed rare when the Lord Jesus was upon earth. "Show us a sign from heaven," was the demand of the sneering Pharisees. To see something sensational was the great desire of the multitudes who crowded after our Lord. No wonder that we read the remarkable words, "Jesus marveled at him," and said unto the people, "I have not found so great faith, no, not in Israel." None ought to have been so believing as the children of those who were led through the wilderness, and brought into the promised land. But the last was first and the first last. The faith of a Roman soldier proved stronger than that of the Jews.

Let us not forget to walk in the steps of this blessed spirit of faith which the centurion here exhibited. Our eyes do not yet behold the book of life. We see not our Savior pleading for us at God's right hand. But have we the word of Christ's promises? Then let us rest on it and fear nothing. Let us not doubt that every word that Christ has spoken shall be made good. The word of Christ is a sure foundation. He that leans upon it shall never be confounded. Believers shall all be found pardoned, justified, and glorified at the last day. "Jesus says so," and therefore it shall be done.

We should notice, finally, in these verses, the advantage of being connected with godly families. We need no clearer proof of this than the case of the centurion's servant. We see him cared for in sickness. We see him restored to health through his master's intercession. We see him brought under Christ's notice through his master's faith. Who can tell but the issue of the whole history, was the conversion and salvation of the man's soul? It was a happy day for that servant, when he first took service in such a household!

Well would it be for the Church, if the benefits of connection with the "household of faith," were more frequently remembered by professing Christians. Often, far too often, a Christian parent will hastily place his son in a position where his soul can get no good, for the sake of mere worldly advantage. Often, far too often, a Christian servant will seek a new place where religion is not valued, for the sake of a little more wages. These things ought not so to be. In all our moves, our first thought should be the interest of our souls. In all our settlements, our chief desire should be to be connected with godly people. In all our purposes and planning, for ourselves or our children, one question should ever be uppermost in our minds—"What shall it profit to gain the whole world, and lose our own souls?" Good situations, as they are called, are often godless situations, and ruin to all eternity those who take them.

LUKE 7:11-17

JESUS RAISES A WIDOW'S SON

And it came to pass soon afterwards, that he went to a city called Nain; and his disciples went with him, and a great multitude. Now when he drew near to the gate of the city, behold, there was carried out one that was dead, the only son of his mother, and she was a widow: and much people of the city was with her. And when the Lord saw her, he had compassion on her, and said unto her, Weep not. And he came nigh and touched the bier: and the bearers stood still. And he said, Young man, I say unto thee, Arise. And he that was dead sat up, and began to speak. And he gave him to his mother. And fear took hold on all: and they glorified God, saying, A great prophet is arisen among us: and, God hath visited his people. And this report went forth concerning him in the whole of Judaea, and all the region round about.

The wondrous event described in these verses, is only recorded in Luke's Gospel. It is one of the three great instances of our Lord restoring a dead person to life, and, like the raising of Lazarus and the ruler's daughter, is rightly regarded as one of the greatest miracles which He wrought on earth. In all three cases, we see an exercise of divine power. In each we see an indisputable proof that the Prince of Peace is stronger than the king of terrors, and that though death, the last enemy, is mighty, he is not as mighty as the sinner's Friend.

We learn from these verses, what sorrow SIN has brought into the world. We are told of a funeral at Nain. All funerals are mournful things, but it is difficult to imagine a funeral more mournful than the one here described. It was the funeral of a young man, and that young man the only son of his mother, and that mother a widow. There is not an item in the whole story, which is not full of misery. And all this misery, be it remembered, was brought into the world by sin. God did not create it at the beginning, when He made all things "very good." Sin is the cause of it all. "Sin entered into the world" when Adam fell, "and death by sin." (Rom. 5:12.)

Let us never forget this great truth. The world around us is full of sorrow. Sickness, and pain, and infirmity, and poverty, and labor, and trouble, abound on every side. From one end of the world to the other, the history of families is full of lamentation, and weeping, and mourning, and woe. And whence does it all come? Sin is the fountain and root to which all must be traced. There would neither have been tears, nor tares, nor illness, nor deaths, nor funerals in the earth, if there had been no sin. We must bear this state of things patiently. We cannot alter it. We may thank God that there is a remedy in the Gospel, and that this present life is not all. But in the meantime, let us lay the blame at the right door. Let us lay the blame on sin.

How much we ought to hate sin! Instead of loving it, cleaving to it, dallying with it, excusing it, playing with it, we ought to hate it with a deadly hatred. Sin is the great murderer, and thief, and pestilence, and nuisance of this world. Let us make no peace with it. Let us wage a ceaseless warfare against it. It is "the abominable thing which God hates." Happy is he who is of one mind with God, and can say, I "abhor that which is evil." (Rom. 12:9.)

We learn, secondly, from these verses, how deep is the COMPASSION of our Lord Jesus Christ's heart. We see this beautifully brought out in His behavior at this funeral in Nain. He meets the mournful procession, accompanying the young man to his grave, and is moved with compassion at the sight. He waits not to be applied to for help. His help appears to have been neither asked for nor expected. He saw the weeping mother, and knew well what her feelings must have been, for He had been born of a woman Himself. At once He addressed her with words alike startling and touching He "said unto her, Weep not." A few more seconds, and the meaning of His words became plain. The widow's son was restored to her alive. Her darkness was turned into light, and her sorrow into joy.

Our Lord Jesus Christ never changes. He is the same yesterday, today, and forever. His heart is still as compassionate as when He was upon earth. His sympathy with sufferers is still as strong. Let us bear this in mind, and take comfort in it. There is no friend or comforter who can be compared to Christ. In all our days of darkness, which must needs be many, let us first turn for consolation to Jesus the Son of God. He will never fail us, never disappoint us, never refuse to take interest in our sorrows. He lives, who made the widow's heart sing for joy in the gate of Nain. He lives, to receive all laboring and heavy-laden ones, if they will only come to Him by faith. He lives, to heal the broken-hearted, and be a Friend that sticks closer than a brother. And He lives to do greater things than these one day. He lives to come again to His people, that they may weep no more at all, and that all tears may be wiped from their eyes.

We learn, lastly, from these verses, the almighty POWER of our Lord Jesus Christ. We can ask no proof of this more striking than the miracle which we are now considering. He gives back life to a dead man with a few words. He speaks to a cold corpse, and at once it becomes a living person. In a moment, in the twinkling of an eye, the heart, the lungs, the brain, the senses, again resume their work and discharge their duty. "Young man," He cried, "I say unto you arise." That voice was a voice mighty in operation. At once "he that was dead sat up and began to speak."

Let us see in this mighty miracle a pledge of that solemn event, the general resurrection. That same Jesus who here raised one dead person, shall raise all mankind at the last day. "The hour comes in the which all that are in the grave shall hear his voice, and shall come forth; those who have done good unto the resurrection of life, and those who have done evil unto the resurrection of damnation." (John 5:28, 29.) When the trumpet sounds and Christ commands, there can be no refusal or escape. All must appear before His bar in their bodies. All shall be judged according to their works.

Let us see, furthermore, in this mighty miracle, a lively emblem of Christ's power to quicken the dead in sins. In Him is life. He quickens whom He will. (John 5:21.) He can raise to a new life souls that now seem dead in worldliness and sin. He can say to hearts that now appear corrupt and lifeless, "Arise to repentance, and live in the service of God." Let us never despair of any soul. Let us pray for our children, and faint not. Our young men and our young women may long seem traveling on the way to ruin. But let us pray on. Who can tell but He that met the funeral at the gates of Nain may yet meet our unconverted children, and say with almighty power, "Young man, arise!" With Christ nothing is impossible.

Let us leave the passage with a solemn recollection of those things which are yet to happen at the last day. We read that "there came a fear on all," at Nain, when the young man was raised. What then shall be the feelings of mankind when all the dead are raised at once? The unconverted man may well fear that day. He is not prepared to meet God. But the true Christian has nothing to fear. He may lay himself down and sleep peacefully in his grave. In Christ He is complete and safe, and when he rises again he shall see God's face in peace.

LUKE 7:18-23

JESUS AND JOHN THE BAPTIST

And the disciples of John told him of all these things.

And John calling unto him two of his disciples sent them to the Lord, saying, Art thou he that cometh, or look we for another? And when the men were come unto him, they said, John the Baptist hath sent us unto thee, saying, Art thou he that cometh, or look we for another? In that hour he cured many of diseases and plagues and evil spirits; and on many that were blind he bestowed sight. And he answered and said unto them, Go and tell John the things which ye have seen and heard; the blind receive their sight, the lame walk, the lepers are cleansed, and the deaf hear, the dead are raised up, the poor have good tidings preached to them. And blessed is he, whosoever shall find no occasion of stumbling in me.

The message which John the Baptist sent to our Lord, in these verses, is peculiarly instructing, when we consider the circumstances under which it was sent. John the Baptist was now a prisoner in the hands of Herod. "He heard in the prison the works of Christ." (Matt. 11:2.) His life was drawing to a close. His opportunities of active usefulness were ended. A long imprisonment, or a violent death, were the only prospects before him. Yet even in these dark days, we see this holy man maintaining his old ground, as a witness to Christ. He is the same man that he was when he cried, "Behold the Lamb of

God." To testify of Christ, was his continual work as a preacher at liberty. TO SEND MEN TO CHRIST, was one of his last works as a prisoner in chains.

We should mark, in these verses, the wise fore-thought which John exhibited about his disciples, before he left the world. He sent some of them to Jesus, with a message of inquiry—"Are you he that should come, or do we look for another?" He doubtless calculated that they would receive such an answer as would make an indelible impression on their minds. And he was right. They got an answer in deeds, as well as words, an answer which probably produced a deeper effect than any arguments which they could have heard from their master's lips.

We can easily imagine that John the Baptist must have felt much anxiety about the future course of his disciples. He knew their ignorance and weakness in the faith. He knew how natural it was for them to regard the disciples of Jesus with feelings of jealousy and envy. He knew how likely it was that petty party-spirit would creep in among them, and make them keep aloof from Christ when their own master was dead and gone. Against this unhappy state of things he makes provision, as far as possible, while he is yet alive. He sends some of them to Jesus, that they may see for themselves what kind of teacher He is, and not reject Him unseen and unheard. He takes care to supply them with the strongest evidence that our Lord was indeed the Messiah. Like his divine Master, having loved his disciples, he loved them to the end. And now, perceiving that he must soon leave them, he strives to leave them in the best of hands. He does his best to make them acquainted with Christ.

What an instructive lesson we have here for ministers, and parents, and heads of families—for all, in short, who have anything to do with the souls of others! We should endeavor, like John the Baptist, to provide for the future spiritual welfare of those we leave behind when we die. We should often remind those who we cannot always be with them. We should often urge them to beware of the broad way, when we are taken from them, and they are left alone in the world. We should spare no pains to make all, who in any way look up to us, acquainted with Christ. Happy are those ministers and parents, whose consciences can testify on their death-beds, that they have told their hearers and children to go to Jesus and follow Him!

We should mark, secondly, in these verses, the peculiar answer which the disciples of John received from our Lord. We are told that "in the same hour He cured many of their infirmities and plagues." And then, "He said unto them, Go your way, and tell John what things you have seen and heard."

He makes no formal declaration that he is the Messiah that was to come. He simply supplies the messengers with facts to repeat to their master, and sends them away. He knew well how John the Baptist would employ these facts. He would say to his disciples, "Behold in him who worked these miracles, the prophet greater than Moses. This is he whom you must hear and follow, when I am dead. This is indeed the Christ."

Our Lord's reply to John's disciples, contains a great practical lesson, which we shall do well to remember. It teaches us that the right way to test the value of Churches and ministers, is to examine the works they do for God, and the fruits they bring forth. Would we know whether a Church is true and trustworthy? Would we know whether a minister is really called of God, and sound in the faith? We must apply the old rule of Scripture, "You shall know them by their fruits." As Christ would be known by His works and doctrine, so must true Churches of Christ, and true ministers of Christ. When the dead in sin are not quickened, and the blind are not restored to sight, and the poor have no glad tidings proclaimed to them, we may generally suspect that Christ's presence is lacking. Where He is, He will be seen and heard. Where He is, there will not only be profession, forms, ceremonies, and a show of religion. There will be actual, visible work in hearts and lives.

We should mark, lastly, in these verses, the solemn warning which our Lord gave to John's disciples. He knew the danger in which they were. He knew that they were disposed to question His claim to be the Messiah, because of His lowly appearance. They saw no signs of a king about Him, no riches, no royal apparel, no guards, no courtiers, and no crown. They only saw a man, to all appearance poor as any one of themselves, attended by a few fishermen and publicans. Their pride rebelled at the idea of such an one as this being the Christ! It seemed incredible! There must be some mistake! Such thoughts as these, in all probability, passed through their minds. Our Lord read their hearts, and dismissed them with a searching caution. "Blessed," He said, "is he that is not offended in me."

The warning is one that is just as needful now as it was when it was delivered. So long as the world stands, Christ and His Gospel will be a stumbling-block to many. To hear that we are all lost and guilty sinners, and cannot save ourselves—to hear that we must give up our own righteousness, and trust in One who was crucified between two thieves—to hear that we must be content to enter heaven side by side with publicans and harlots, and to owe all our salvation to free grace, this is always offensive to the natural man. Our proud hearts do not like it. We are offended.

Let the caution of these verses sink down deeply into our memories. Let us take heed that we are not offended. Let us beware of being stumbled, either by the humbling doctrines of the Gospel, or the holy practice which it enjoins on those who receive it. Secret pride is one of the worst enemies of man. It will prove at last to have been the ruin of thousands of souls. Thousands will be found to have had the offer of salvation, but to have rejected it. They did not like the terms. They would not stoop to "enter in at the strait gate." They would not humbly come as sinners to the throne of grace. In a word, they were offended. And then will appear the deep meaning in our Lord's words, "Blessed is he who shall not be offended in me."

LUKE 7:24-30

JESUS' TESTIMONY TO JOHN THE BAPTIST

And when the messengers of John were departed, he began to say unto the multitudes concerning John, What went ye out into the wilderness to behold? a reed shaken with the wind? But what went ye out to see? a man clothed in soft raiment? Behold, they that are gorgeously apparelled, and live delicately, are in kings' courts. But what went ye out to see? a prophet? Yea, I say unto you, and much more than a prophet. This is he of whom it is written, Behold, I send my messenger before thy face, Who shall prepare thy way before thee. I say unto you, Among them that are born of women there is none greater than John: yet he that is but little in the kingdom of God is greater than he. And all the people when they heard, and the publicans, justified God, being baptized with the baptism of John. But the Pharisees and the lawyers rejected for themselves the counsel of God, being not baptized of him.

The first point that demands our notice in this passage, is the tender care which Jesus takes of the characters of His faithful servants. He defends the reputation of John the Baptist, as soon as his messengers were departed. He saw that the people around him were apt to think lightly of John, partly because he was in prison, partly because of the inquiry which his disciples had just brought. He pleads the cause of His absent friend in warm and strong language. He bids His hearers dismiss from their minds their unworthy doubts and suspicions about this holy man. He tells them that John was no wavering and unstable character, a mere reed shaken by the wind. He tells them that John was no mere courtier and hanger-on about king's palaces, though circumstances at the end of his ministry had brought him into connection with king Herod. He declares to them that John was "much more than a prophet," for he was a prophet who had been the subject of prophecy himself. And he winds up his testimony by the remarkable saying, that "among those that are born of woman there is not a greater prophet than John the Baptist."

There is something deeply touching in these sayings of our Lord on behalf of his absent servant. The position which John now occupied as Herod's prisoner was widely different from that which he occupied at the beginning of his ministry. At one time he was the best-known and most popular preacher of his day. There was a time when "there went out to him Jerusalem and all Judea—and were baptized in Jordan." (Matt. 3:5.) Now he was an obscure prisoner in Herod's hands, deserted, friendless, and with nothing before him but death. But the lack of man's favor is no proof that God is displeased. John the Baptist had one Friend who never failed him and never forsook him—a Friend whose kindness did not ebb and flow like John's popularity, but was always the same. That Friend was our Lord Jesus Christ.

There is comfort here for all believers who are suspected, slandered, and falsely accused. Few are the children of God who do not suffer in this way, at some time or other. The accuser of the brethren knows well that character is one of the points in which he can most easily wound a Christian. He knows well that slanders are easily called into existence, greedily received and propagated, and seldom entirely silenced. Lies and false reports are the chosen weapons by which he labors to injure the Christian's usefulness, and destroy his peace. But let all who are assaulted in their characters rest in the thought that they have an Advocate in heaven who knows their sorrows. That same Jesus who maintained the character of His imprisoned servant before a Jewish crowd, will never desert any of His people. The world may frown on them. Their names may be cast out as evil by man. But Jesus never changes, and will one day plead their cause before the whole world.

The second point which demands our attention in these verses is, the vast superiority of the privileges enjoyed by believers under the New Testament, compared to those of believers under the Old. This is a lesson which appears to be taught by one expression used by our Lord respecting John the Baptist. After commending his graces and gifts, He adds these remarkable words, "He that is least in the kingdom of God is greater than John."

Our Lord's meaning in using this expression appears to be simply this. He declares that the religious light of the least disciple who lived after His crucifixion and resurrection, would be far greater than that of John Baptist, who died before those mighty events took place. The weakest believing hearer of Paul would understand things, by the light of Christ's death on the cross, which John the Baptist could never have explained. Great as that holy man was in faith and courage, the humblest Christian would, in one sense, be greater than he. Greater in grace and works he certainly could not be. But beyond doubt he would be greater in privileges and knowledge.

Such an expression as this should teach all Christians to be deeply thankful for Christianity. We have probably very little idea of the wide difference between the religious knowledge of the best-instructed Old Testament believer and the knowledge of one familiar with the New Testament. We little know how many blessed truths of the Gospel were at one time seen through a glass darkly, which now appear to us plain as noon-day. Our very familiarity with the Gospel makes us blind to the extent of our privileges. We can hardly realize at this time how many glorious verities of our faith were brought out in their full proportions by Christ's death on the cross, and were never unveiled and understood until His blood was shed.

The hopes of John the Baptist and Paul were undoubtedly one and the same. Both were led by one Spirit. Both knew their sinfulness. Both trusted in the Lamb of God. But we cannot suppose that John could have given as full an account of the way of salvation as Paul. Both looked at the same object of faith. But one saw it afar off, and could only describe it generally. The other saw it close at hand, and could describe the reason of his hope particularly. Let us learn to be more thankful. The child who knows the story of the cross, possesses a key to religious knowledge which patriarchs and prophets never enjoyed.

The last point which demands our attention in these verses is, the solemn declaration which it makes about man's power to injure his own soul. We read that "The Pharisees and Scribes rejected the counsel of God against themselves." The meaning of these words appears to be simply this, that they rejected God's offer of salvation. They refused to avail themselves of the door of repentance which was offered to them by John the Baptist's preaching. In short they fulfilled to the very letter the words of Solomon—"You have set at nothing all my counsel and would have none of my reproof." (Prov. 1:25.)

That every man possesses a power to ruin himself forever in hell is a great foundation truth of Scripture, and a truth which ought to be continually before our minds. Impotent and weak as we all are for everything which is good, we are all naturally potent for that which is evil. By continued impenitence and unbelief, by persevering in the love and practice of sin, by pride, self-will, laziness, and determined love of the world, we may bring upon ourselves everlasting destruction. And if this takes place, we shall find that we have no one to blame but ourselves. God has "no pleasure in the death of him that dies." (Ezek. 18:32.) Christ is "willing to gather" men to His bosom, if they will only be gathered. (Matt. 23:37.) The fault will lie at man's own door. Those who are lost will find that they have "lost than own souls." (Mark 8:36.)

What are we doing ourselves? This is the chief question that the passage should suggest to our minds. Are we likely to be lost or saved? Are we in the way towards heaven or hell? Have we received into our hearts that Gospel which we hear? Do we really live by that Bible which we profess to believe? Or are we daily traveling towards the pit, and ruining our own souls? It is a painful thought that the Pharisees are not the only people who "reject the counsel of God." There are thousands of people called Christians who are continually doing the very same thing.

LUKE 7:31-35

JESUS EXPOSES THE UNREASONABLENESS OF UNBELIEF

Whereunto then shall I liken the men of this generation, and to what are they like? They are like unto children that sit in the marketplace, and call one to another; who say, We piped unto you, and ye did not dance; we wailed, and ye did not weep. For John the Baptist is come eating no bread nor drinking wine; and ye say, He hath a demon. The Son of man is come eating and drinking; and ye say, Behold, a gluttonous man, and a winebibber, a friend of publicans and sinners! And wisdom is justified of all her children.

We learn, in the first place, from these verses, that the hearts of unconverted men are often desperately perverse as well as wicked.

Our Lord brings out this lesson in a remarkable comparison, describing the generation of men among whom He lived while He was on earth. He compares them to children. He says, that children at play were not more wayward, perverse, and hard to please, than the Jews of His day. Nothing would satisfy them. They were always finding fault. Whatever ministry God employed among them, they took exception to it. Whatever messenger God sent among them, they were not pleased. First came John the Baptist, living a retired, ascetic, self-denying life. At once the Jews said, "he has a devil." After him the Son of Man came, eating and drinking, and adopting habits of social life like the ordinary run of men. At once the Jews accused Him of being "a gluttonous man, and a wine bibber." In short, it became evident that the Jews were determined to receive no message from God at all. Their pretended objections were only a cloak to cover over their hatred of God's truth. What they really disliked was, not so much God's ministers, as God Himself.

Perhaps we read this account with wonder and surprise. We think that never were men so wickedly unreasonable as these Jews were. But are we sure that their conduct is not continually repeated among Christians? Do we know that the same thing is continually going on around us at the present day? Strange as it may seem at first sight, the generation which will neither "dance" when their companions "pipe," nor "lament" when they "mourn," is only too numerous in the Church of Christ. Is it not a fact that many who strive to serve Christ faithfully, and walk closely with God, find their neighbors and relations always dissatisfied with their conduct? No matter how holy and consistent their lives may be, they are always thought wrong. If they withdraw entirely from the world, and live, like John the Baptist, a retired and ascetic life, the cry is raised that they are exclusive, narrow-minded, sour-spirited, and righteous overmuch. If, on the other hand, they go much into society, and endeavor as far as they can to take interest in their neighbor's pursuits, the remark is soon made that they are no better than other people, and have no more real religion than those who make no profession at all. Treatment like this is only too common. Few are the decided Christians who do not know it by bitter experience. The servants of God in every age, whatever they do, are blamed.

The plain truth is, that the natural heart of man hates God. The carnal mind is enmity against God It dislikes His law, His Gospel, and His people. It will always find some excuse for not believing and obeying. The doctrine of repentance is too strict for it! The doctrine of faith and grace is too easy for it! John the Baptist goes too much out of the world! Jesus Christ goes too much into the world! And so the heart of man excuses itself for sitting still in its sins. All this must not surprise us. We must make up our minds to find unconverted people as perverse, unreasonable, and hard to please as the Jews of our Lord's time.

We must give up the vain idea of trying to please everybody. The thing is impossible, and the attempt is mere waste of time. We must be content to walk in Christ's steps, and let the world say what it likes. Do what we will we shall never satisfy it, or silence its ill-natured remarks. It first found fault with John the Baptist, and then with his blessed Master. And it will go on caviling and finding fault with that Master's disciples, so long as one of them is left upon earth.

We learn, secondly, from these verses, that the wisdom of God's ways is always recognized and acknowledged by those who are wise-hearted.

This is a lesson which is taught in a sentence of somewhat obscure character-"Wisdom is justified by all her children." But it seems difficult to extract any other meaning from the words, by fair and consistent interpretation. The idea which our Lord desired to impress upon us appears to be, that though the vast majority of the Jews were hardened and unreasonable, there were some who were not—and that though multitudes saw no wisdom in the ministry of John the Baptist and Himself, there were a chosen few who did. Those few were the "children of wisdom." Those few, by their lives and obedience, declared their full conviction that God's ways of dealing with the Jews were wise and right, and that John the Baptist and the Lord Jesus were both worthy of all honor. In short, they "justified" God's wisdom; and so proved themselves truly wise.

This saying of our Lord about the generation among whom He lived, describes a state of things which will always be found in the Church of Christ. In spite of the cavils, sneers, objections, and unkind remarks with which the Gospel is received by the majority of mankind, there will always be some in every country who will assent to it, and obey it with delight. There will never be lacking a "little flock" which hears the voice of the Shepherd gladly, and counts all His ways right.

The children of this world may mock at the Gospel, and pour contempt on the lives of believers. They may count their practice madness, and see no wisdom nor beauty in their ways. But God will take care that He has a people in every age. There will be always some who will assert the perfect excellence of the doctrines and requirements of the Gospel, and will "justify the wisdom" of Him who sent it. And these, however much the world may despise them, are they whom Jesus calls wise. They are "wise unto salvation, through faith which is in Christ Jesus." (2 Tim. 3:15.)

Let us ask ourselves, as we leave this passage, whether we deserve to be called children of wisdom? Have we been taught by the Spirit to know the Lord Jesus Christ? Have the eyes of our understanding been opened? Have we the wisdom that comes from above? If we are truly wise, let us not be ashamed to confess our Master before men. Let us declare boldly that we approve the whole of His Gospel, all its doctrines and all its requirements. We may find few with us and many against us. The world may laugh at us, and count our wisdom no better than folly. But such laughter is but for a moment. The hour comes when the few who have confessed Christ, and justified His ways before men, shall be confessed and "justified" by Him before His Father and the angels.

LUKE 7:36-50

JESUS ANOINTED BY A SINFUL WOMAN

And one of the Pharisees desired him that he would eat with him. And he entered into the Pharisee's house, and sat down to meat. And behold, a woman who was in the city, a sinner; and when she knew that he was sitting at meat in the Pharisee's house, she brought an alabaster cruse of ointment, and standing behind at his feet, weeping, she began to wet his feet with her tears, and wiped them with the hair of her head, and kissed his feet, and anointed them with the ointment. Now when the Pharisee that had bidden him saw it, he spake within himself, saying, This man, if he were a prophet, would have perceived who and what manner of woman this is that toucheth him, that she is a sinner. And Jesus answering said unto him, Simon, I have somewhat to say unto thee. And he saith, Teacher, say on. A certain lender had two debtors: the one owed five hundred shillings, and the other fifty. When they had not wherewith to pay, he forgave them both. Which of them therefore will love him most? Simon answered and said, He, I suppose, to whom he forgave the most. And he said unto him, Thou hast rightly judged. And turning to the woman, he said unto Simon, Seest thou this woman? I entered into thy house, thou gavest me no water for my feet: but she hath wetted my feet with her tears, and wiped them with her hair. Thou gavest me no kiss: but she, since the time I came in, hath not ceased to kiss my feet. My head with oil thou didst not anoint: but she hath anointed my feet with ointment. Wherefore I say unto thee, Her sins, which are many, are forgiven; for she loved much: but to whom little is forgiven, the same loveth little. And he said unto her, Thy sins are forgiven. And they that sat at meat with him began to say within themselves, Who is this that even forgiveth sins? And he said unto the woman, Thy faith hath saved thee; go in peace.

The deeply interesting narrative contained in these verses, is only found in the Gospel of Luke. In order to see the full beauty of the story, we should read, in connection with it, the eleventh chapter of Matthew. We shall then discover the striking fact, that the woman whose conduct is here recorded, most likely owed her conversion to the well-known words, "Come unto me all you that labor and are heavy-laden, and I will give you rest." That wondrous invitation, in all human probability, was the saving of her soul, and gave her that sense of peace for which we see her so grateful. A full offer of free pardon is generally God's chosen instrument for bringing the chief of sinners to repentance.

We see in this passage that men may show some outward respect to Christ, and yet remain unconverted. The Pharisee before us is a case in point. He showed our Lord Jesus Christ more respect than many did. He even "desired Him that He would eat with him." Yet all this time he was profoundly ignorant of the nature of Christ's Gospel. His proud heart secretly revolted at the sight of a poor contrite sinner being allowed to wash our Lord's feet. And even the hospitality he showed appears to have been cold and niggardly. Our Lord Himself says, "You gave me no water for my feet; you gave me no kiss; my head with oil you did not anoint." In short, in all that the Pharisee did, there was one great defect. There was outward civility, but there was no heart-love.

We shall do well to remember the case of this Pharisee. It is quite possible to have a decent form of religion, and yet to know nothing of the Gospel of Christ—to treat Christianity with respect, and yet to be utterly blind about its cardinal doctrines—to behave with great correctness and propriety at Church, and yet to hate justification by faith, and salvation by grace, with a deadly hatred. Do we really feel affection toward the Lord Jesus? Can we say, "Lord, you know all things, you know that I love you?" Have we cordially embraced His whole Gospel? Are we willing to enter heaven side by side with the chief of sinners, and to owe all our hopes to free grace? These are questions which we ought to consider. If we cannot answer them satisfactorily, we are in no respect better than Simon the Pharisee; and our Lord might say to us, "I have something to tell you."

We see, in the next place, in this passage, that grateful love is the secret of doing much for Christ. The penitent woman, in the story before us, showed far more honor to our Lord than the Pharisee had done. She "stood at His feet behind Him weeping." She "washed His feet with tears." She "wiped them with the hair of her head." She "kissed His feet, and anointed them with costly ointment." No stronger proofs of reverence and respect could she have given, and the secret of her giving such proofs, was love. She loved our Lord, and she thought nothing too much to do for Him. She felt deeply grateful to our Lord, and she thought no mark of gratitude too costly to bestow on Him.

More "doing" for Christ is the universal demand of all the Churches. It is the one point on which all are agreed. All desire to see among Christians, more good works, more self-denial, more practical obedience to Christ's commands. But what will produce these things? Nothing, nothing but love. There never will be more done for Christ until there is more hearty love to Christ Himself. The fear of punishment, the desire of reward, the sense of duty, are all useful arguments, in their way, to persuade men to holiness. But they are all weak and powerless, until a man loves Christ. Once let that mighty principle get hold of a man, and you will see his whole life changed.

Let us never forget this. However much the world may sneer at "feelings" in religion, and however false or unhealthy religious feelings may sometimes be, the great truth still remains behind, that feeling is the secret of doing. The heart must be engaged for Christ, or the hands will soon hang down. The affections must be enlisted into His service, or our obedience will soon stand still. It will always be the loving workman who will do most in the Lord's vineyard.

We see, lastly, in this passage, that a sense of having our sins forgiven is the mainspring and life-blood of love to Christ. This, beyond doubt, was the lesson which our Lord wished Simon the Pharisee to learn, when He told him the story of the two debtors. "One owed his creditor five hundred pence, and the other fifty." Both had "nothing to pay," and both were forgiven freely. And then came the searching question—"Which of them will love him most?" Here was the true explanation, our Lord told Simon, of the deep love which the penitent woman before Him had displayed. Her many tears, her deep affection, her public reverence, her action in anointing His feet, were all traceable to one cause. She had been much forgiven, and so she loved much.

Her love was the effect of her forgiveness—not the cause—the consequence of her forgiveness, not the condition, the result of her forgiveness, not the reason—the fruit of her forgiveness, not the root. Would the Pharisee know why this woman showed so much love? It was because she felt much forgiven. Would he know why he himself had shown his guest so little love? It was because he felt under no obligation—had no consciousness of having obtained forgiveness—had no sense of debt to Christ.

Forever let the mighty principle laid down by our Lord in this passage, abide in our memories, and sink down into our hearts. It is one of the great cornerstones of the whole Gospel. It is one of the master-keys to unlock the secrets of the kingdom of God. The only way to make men holy, is to teach and preach free and full forgiveness through Jesus Christ. The secret of being holy ourselves, is to know and feel that Christ has pardoned our sins. Peace with God is the only root that will bear the fruit of holiness.

Forgiveness must go before sanctification. We shall do nothing until we are reconciled to God. This is the first step in religion. We must work from life, and not for life. Our best works before we are justified are little better than SPLENDID SINS. We must live by faith in the Son of God, and then, and not until then, we shall walk in His ways. The heart which has experienced the pardoning love of Christ, is the heart which loves Christ, and strives to glorify Him.

Let us leave the passage with a deep sense of our Lord Jesus Christ's amazing mercy and compassion to the chief of sinners. Let us see in his kindness to the woman, of whom we have been reading, an encouragement to any one, however bad he may be, to come to Him for pardon and forgiveness. That word of His shall never be broken, "Him that comes unto me I will in no wise cast out." Never, never need any one despair of salvation, if he will only come to Christ.

Let us ask ourselves, in conclusion, What we are doing for Christ's glory? What kind of lives are we living? What proof are we making of our love to Him which loved us, and died for our sins? These are serious questions. If we cannot answer them satisfactorily, we may well doubt whether we are forgiven. The hope of forgiveness which is not accompanied by love in the life is no hope at all. The man whose sins are really cleansed away will always show by his ways that he loves the Savior who cleansed them.

Chapter 8

*A*nd it came to pass soon afterwards, that he went about through cities and villages, preaching and bringing the good tidings of the kingdom of God, and with him the twelve, and certain women who had been healed of evil spirits and infirmities: Mary that was called Magdalene, from whom seven demons had gone out, and Joanna the wife of Chuzas Herod's steward, and Susanna, and many others, who ministered unto them of their substance.

Let us mark, in these verses, our Lord Jesus Christ's unwearied diligence in doing good. We read that "He went throughout every city and village, preaching and proclaiming the good news of the kingdom of God." We know the reception that He met with in many places. We know that while some believed, many believed not. But man's unbelief did not move our Lord, or hinder His working. He was always "about His Father's business." Short as His earthly ministry was in point of duration, it was long when we consider the work that it comprised.

Let the diligence of Christ be an example to all Christians. Let us follow in His steps, however far we may come short of His perfection. Like Him, let us labor to do good in our day and generation, and to leave the world a better world than we found it. It is not for nothing that the Scripture says expressly—"He that abides in him ought himself also so to walk even as he walked." (1 John 2:6.)

Time is undoubtedly short. But much is to be done with time, if it is well economized and properly arranged. Few have an idea how much can be done in twelve hours, if men will stick to their business and avoid idleness and frivolity. Then let us, like our Lord, be diligent, and "redeem the time."

Time is undoubtedly short. But it is the only season in which Christians can do any active work of mercy. In the world to come there will be no ignorant to instruct, no mourners to comfort, no spiritual darkness to enlighten, no distress to relieve, no sorrow to make less. Whatever work we do of this kind must be done on this side of the grave. Let us awake to a sense of our individual responsibility. Souls are perishing, and time is flying! Let us resolve, by God's grace, to do something for God's glory before we die. Once more let us remember our Lord's example, and, like Him, be diligent and "redeem the time."

Let us mark, secondly, in these verses, the power of the grace of God, and the constraining influence of the love of Christ. We read that among those who followed our Lord in his journeyings, were "certain women who had been healed of evil spirits and infirmities."

We can well imagine that the difficulties these holy women had to face in becoming Christ's disciples were neither few nor small. They had their full share of the contempt and scorn which was poured on all followers of Jesus by the Scribes and Pharisees. They had, besides, many a trial from the hard speeches and hard usage which any Jewish woman who thought for herself about religion would probably have to undergo. But none of these things moved them. Grateful for mercies received at our Lord's hands, they were willing to endure much for His sake. Strengthened inwardly, by the renewing power of the Holy Spirit, they were enabled to cleave to Jesus and not give way. And nobly they did cleave to Him to the very end!

It was not a woman who sold the Lord for thirty pieces of silver. They were not women who forsook the Lord in the garden and fled. It was not a woman who denied Him three times in the high priest's house. But they were women who wailed and lamented when Jesus was led forth to be crucified. They were women who stood to the last by the cross. And they were women who were first to visit the grave "where the Lord lay." Great indeed is the power of the grace of God!

Let the recollection of these women encourage all the daughters of Adam who read of them, to take up the cross and to follow Christ. Let no sense of weakness, or fear of falling away, keep them back from a decided profession of religion. The mother of a large family, with limited means, may tell us that she has no time for religion. The wife of an ungodly husband may tell us that she dares not take up religion. The young daughter of worldly parents may tell us that it is impossible for her to have any religion. The maid-servant in the midst of unconverted companions, may tell us that in her place a person cannot follow religion.

But they are all wrong, quite wrong. With Christ nothing is impossible. Let them think again, and change their minds. Let them begin boldly in the strength of Christ, and trust Him for the consequences. The Lord Jesus never changes. He who enabled "many women" to serve Him faithfully while He was on earth, can enable women to serve Him, glorify Him, and be His disciples at the present day.

Let us mark lastly, in these verses, the peculiar privilege which our Lord grants to His faithful followers. We read that those who accompanied Him in His journeyings, "ministered to him of their substance." Of course He needed not their help. "All the beasts of the forest were his, and the cattle upon a thousand hills." (Psalm 50:10.) That mighty Savior who could multiply a few loaves and fish into food for thousands, could have called forth food from the earth for His own sustenance, if He had thought fit. But He did not do so, for two reasons.

One reason was, that He would show us that He was man like ourselves in all things, sin only excepted, and that He lived the life of faith in His Father's providence. The other reason was, that by allowing His followers to minister to Him, He might prove their love, and test their regard for Himself. True love will count it a pleasure to give anything to the object loved. False love will often talk and profess much, but do and give nothing at all.

This matter of "ministering to Christ" opens up a most important train of thought, and one which we shall do well to consider. The Lord Jesus Christ is continually providing His Church at the present day. No doubt it would be easy for Him to convert the Chinese or Hindoos in a moment, and to call grace into being with a word, as He created light on the first day of this world's existence. But He does not do so. He is pleased to work by means. He condescends to use the agency of missionaries, and the foolishness of man's preaching, in order to spread His Gospel. And by so doing, He is continually proving the faith and zeal of the churches. He lets Christians be fellow workers with Him, that He may prove who has a will to "minister" and who has none. He lets the spread of the Gospel be carried on by subscriptions, contributions, and religious Societies, that He may prove who are the covetous and unbelieving, and who are the truly "rich towards God." In short, the visible Church of Christ may be divided into two great parties, those who "minister" to Christ, and those who do not.

May we all remember this great truth and prove our own selves! While we live we are all upon our trial. Our lives are continually showing whose we are, and whom we serve, whether we love Christ or whether we love the world. Happy are they who know something of "ministering to Christ of their substance!" It is a thing which can still be done, though we do not see Him with our eyes. Those words which describe the proceedings of the Judgment day are very solemn, "I was an hungry and you gave me no food, I was thirsty and you gave me no drink." (Matt. 25:42.)

LUKE 8:4-15

THE PARABLE OF THE SOWER

And when a great multitude came together, and they of every city resorted unto him, he spake by a parable: The sower went forth to sow his seed: and as he sowed, some fell by the way side; and it was trodden under foot, and the birds of the heaven devoured it. And other fell on the rock; and as soon as it grew, it withered away, because it had no moisture. And other fell amidst the thorns; and the thorns grew with it, and choked it. And other fell into the good ground, and grew, and brought forth fruit a hundredfold. As he said these things, he cried, He that hath ears to hear, let him hear. And his disciples asked him what this parable might be. And he said, Unto you it is given to know the mysteries of the kingdom of God: but to the rest in parables; that seeing they may not see, and hearing they may not understand. Now the parable is this: The seed is the word of God. And those by the way side are they that have heard; then cometh the devil, and taketh away the word from their heart, that they may not believe and be saved. And those on the rock are they who, when they have heard, receive the word with joy; and these have no root, who for a while believe, and in time of temptation fall away. And that which fell among the thorns, these are they that have heard, and as they go on their way they are choked with cares and riches and pleasures of this life, and bring no fruit to perfection. And that in the good ground, these are such as in an honest and good heart, having heard the word, hold it fast, and bring forth fruit with patience.

The parable of the sower, contained in these verses, is reported more frequently than any parable in the Bible. It is a parable of universal application. The things it relates are continually going on in every congregation to which the Gospel is preached. The four kinds of hearts it describes are to be found in every assembly which hears the word. These circumstances should make us always read the parable with a deep sense of its importance. We should say to ourselves, as we read it—"This concerns me. My heart is to be seen in this parable. I, too, am here."

The passage itself requires little explanation. In fact, the meaning of the whole picture is so fully explained by our Lord Jesus Christ, that no exposition of man can throw much additional light on it. The parable is preeminently a parable of caution, and caution about a most important subject—the way of hearing the word of God. It was meant to be a warning to the apostles, not to expect too much from hearers. It was meant to be a warning to all ministers of the Gospel, not to look for too great results from sermons. It was meant, not least, to be a warning to hearers, to take heed how they hear. Preaching is an ordinance of which the value can never be overrated in the Church of Christ. But it should never be forgotten, that there must not only be good preaching, but good hearing.

The first caution that we learn from the parable of the sower, is to beware of the devil when we hear the Word. Our Lord tells us that the hearts of some hearers are like "the wayside." The seed of the Gospel is plucked away from them by the devil almost as soon as it is sown. It does not sink down into their consciences. It does not make the least impression on their minds.

The devil, no doubt, is everywhere. That malicious spirit is unwearied in his efforts to do us harm. He is ever watching for our halting, and seeking occasion to destroy our souls. But nowhere perhaps is the devil so active as in a congregation of Gospel-hearers. Nowhere does he labor so hard to stop the progress of that which is good, and to prevent men and women being saved. From him come wandering thoughts and roving imaginations—listless minds and dull memories—sleepy eyes and fidgety nerves, weary ears and distracted attention. In all these things Satan has a great hand. People wonder where they come from, and marvel how it is that they find sermons so dull, and remember them so badly! They forget the parable of the sower. They forget the devil.

Let us take heed that we are not way-side hearers. Let us beware of the devil. We shall always find him at Church. He never stays away from public ordinances. Let us remember this, and be upon our guard. Heat, and cold, and draughts, and damp, and wet, and rain, and snow, are often dreaded by Church goers, and alleged as reasons for not going to Church. But there is one enemy whom they ought to fear more than all these things together. That enemy is Satan.

The second caution that we learn from the parable of the sower, is to beware of resting on mere temporary impressions when we have heard the word. Our Lord tells us that the hearts of some hearers are like ROCKY ground. The seed of the word springs up immediately, as soon as they hear it, and bears a crop of joyful impressions, and pleasurable emotions. But these impressions, unhappily, are only on the surface. There is no deep and abiding work done in their souls. And hence, so soon as the scorching heat of temptation or persecution begins to be felt, the little bit of religion which they seemed to have attained, withers and vanishes away.

Feelings, no doubt, fill a most important office in our personal Christianity. Without them there can be no saving religion. Hope, and joy, and peace, and confidence, and resignation, and love, and fear, are things which must be felt, if they really exist. But it must never be forgotten that there are religious affections, which are spurious and false, and spring from nothing better than animal excitement. It is quite possible to feel great pleasure, or deep alarm, under the preaching of the Gospel, and yet to be utterly destitute of the grace of God. The tears of some hearers of sermons, and the extravagant delight of others, are no certain marks of conversion. We may be warm admirers of favorite preachers, and yet remain nothing better than stony-ground hearers. Nothing should content us but a deep, humbling, self-mortifying work of the Holy Spirit, and a heart-union with Christ.

The third caution contained in the parable of the sower is to beware of the cares of this world. Our Lord tells us that the hearts of many hearers of the word are like thorny ground. The seed of the word, when sown upon them, is choked by the multitude of other things, by which their affections are occupied. They have no objection to the doctrines and requirements of the Gospel. They even wish to believe and obey them. But they allow the things of earth to get such hold upon their minds, that they leave no room for the word of God to do its work. And hence it follows that however many sermons they hear, they seem nothing bettered by them. A weekly process of truth-stifling goes on within. They bring no fruit to perfection.

The things of this life form one of the greatest dangers which beset a Christian's path. The money, the pleasures, the daily business of the world, are so many traps to catch souls. Thousands of things, which in themselves are innocent, become, when followed to excess, little better than soul-poisons, and helps to hell. Open sin is not the only thing that ruins souls. In the midst of our families, and in the pursuit of our lawful callings, we have need to be on our guard. Unless we watch and pray, these temporal things may rob us of heaven, and smother every sermon we hear. We may live and die thorny ground hearers.

The last caution contained in the parable of the sower, is to beware of being content with any religion which does not bear FRUIT in our lives. Our Lord tells us that the hearts of those who hear the word aright, are like good ground. The seed of the Gospel sinks down deeply into their wills, and produces practical results in their faith and practice. They not only hear with pleasure, but act with decision. They repent. They believe. They obey.

Forever let us bear in mind that this is the only religion that saves souls. Outward profession of Christianity, and the formal use of Church ordinances and sacraments, never yet gave man a good hope in life, or peace in death, or rest in the world beyond the grave. There must be fruits of the Spirit in our hearts and lives, or else the Gospel is preached to us in vain. Those only who bear such fruits, shall be found at Christ's right hand in the day of His appearing.

Let us leave the parable with a deep sense of the danger and responsibility of all hearers of the Gospel. There are four ways in which we may hear, and of these four only one is right. There are three kinds of hearers whose souls are in imminent peril. How many of these three kinds are to be found in every congregation! There is only one class of hearers which is right in the sight of God. And what are we? Do we belong to that one?

Finally, let us leave the parable with a solemn recollection of the duty of every faithful preacher to divide his congregation, and give to each class his portion. The clergyman who ascends his pulpit every Sunday, and addresses his congregation as if he thought everyone was going to heaven, is surely not doing his duty to God or man. His preaching is flatly contradictory to the parable of the sower.

LUKE 8:16-21

A LAMP ON A STAND

And no man, when he hath lighted a lamp, covereth it with a vessel, or putteth it under a bed; but putteth it on a stand, that they that enter in may see the light. For nothing is hid, that shall not be made manifest; nor anything secret, that shall not be known and come to light. Take heed therefore how ye hear: for whosoever hath, to him shall be given; and whosoever hath not, from him shall be taken away even that which he thinketh he hath. And there came to him his mother and brethren, and they could not come at him for the crowd. And it was told him, Thy mother and thy brethren stand without, desiring to see thee. But he answered and said unto them, My mother and my brethren are these that hear the word of God, and do it.

These verses form a practical application of the famous parable of the sower. They are intended to nail and clench in our minds the mighty lesson which that parable contains. They deserve the especial attention of all true-hearted hearers of the Gospel of Christ.

We learn, firstly, from these verses, that spiritual knowledge ought to be diligently used. Our Lord tells us that it is like a lighted candle, utterly useless, when covered with a bushel, or put under a bed—only useful when set upon a candlestick, and placed where it can be made serviceable to the wants of men.

When we hear this lesson, let us first think of OURSELVES. The Gospel which we possess was not given us only to be admired, talked of, and professed—but to be practiced. It was not meant merely to reside in our intellect, and memories, and tongues—but to be seen is our lives. Christianity is a talent committed to our charge, and one which brings with it great responsibility. We are not in darkness like the heathen. A glorious light is put before us. Let us take heed that we use it. While we have the light let us walk in the light. (John 12:35.)

But let us not only think of ourselves. Let us also think of OTHERS. There are millions in the world who have no spiritual light at all. They are without God, without Christ, and without hope. (Ephes. 2:12.) Can we do nothing for them? There are thousands around us, in our own land, who are unconverted and dead in sins, seeing nothing and knowing nothing aright. Can we do nothing for them? These are questions to which every true Christian ought to find an answer. We should strive, in every way, to spread our religion. The highest form of selfishness is that of the man who is content to go to heaven alone. The truest charity is to endeavor to share with others every spark of religious light we possess ourselves, and so to hold up our own candle that it may give light to everyone around us. Happy is that soul, which, as soon as it receives light from heaven, begins to think of others as well as itself! No candle which God lights was ever meant to burn alone.

We learn, secondly, from these verses, the great importance of right hearing. The words of our Lord Jesus Christ ought to impress that lesson deeply on our hearts. He says, "Take heed how you hear."

The degree of benefit which men receive from all the means of grace depends entirely on the way in which they use them. Private PRAYER lies at the very foundation of religion; yet the mere formal repetition of a set of words, when "the heart is far away," does good to no man's soul. Reading the BIBLE is essential to the attainment of sound Christian knowledge; yet the mere formal reading of so many chapters as a task and duty, without a humble desire to be taught of God, is little better than a waste of time. Just as it is with praying and Bible reading, so it is with hearing. It is not enough that we go to Church and hear sermons. We may do so for fifty years, and "be nothing bettered, but rather worse." "Take heed," says our Lord, "how you hear."

Would anyone know how to hear aright? Then let him lay to heart three simple rules. For one thing, we must hear with FAITH, believing implicitly that every word of God is true, and shall stand. The word in old time did not profit the Jews, "not being mixed with faith in those who heard it." (Heb. 4:2.)—For another thing, we must hear with REVERENCE, remembering constantly that the Bible is the book of God. This was the habit of the Thessalonians. They received Paul's message, "not as the word of men, but the word of God." (1 Thess. 2:13.)—Above all, we must bear with PRAYER, praying for God's blessing before the sermon is preached, praying for God's blessing again when the sermon is over. Here lies the grand defect of the hearing of many. They ask no blessing, and so they have none. The sermon passes through their minds like water through a leaky vessel, and leaves nothing behind.

Let us bear these rules in mind every Sunday morning, before we go to hear the Word of God preached. Let as not rush into God's presence careless, reckless, and unprepared, as if it mattered not in what way such work was done. Let us carry with us faith, reverence, and prayer. If these three are our companions, we shall hear with profit, and return with praise.

We learn, finally, from these verses, the great privileges of those who hear the word of God and DO it. Our Lord Jesus Christ declares that He regards them as his "mother and his brethren."

The man who hears the word of God, and does it, is the true Christian. He hears the call of God to repent and be converted, and he obeys it. He ceases to do evil, and learns to do well. He puts off the old man, and puts on the new. He hears the call of God to believe on Jesus Christ for justification, and he obeys it. He forsakes his own righteousness, and confesses his need of a Savior. He receives Christ crucified as his only hope, and counts all things loss for the knowledge of Him. He hears the call of God to be holy, and he obeys it. He strives to mortify the deeds of his body, and to walk after the

Spirit. He labors to lay aside every weight, and the sin that so easily besets him. This is true vital Christianity. All men and women who are of this character are true Christians.

Now the TROUBLES of all who "hear the word of God and do it" are neither few nor small. The world, the flesh, and the devil continually vex them. They often groan, being burdened. (2 Cor. 5:4.) They often find the cross heavy, and the way to heaven rough and narrow. They often feel disposed to cry with Paul, "O wretched man that I am, who shall deliver me from the body of this death?" (Rom. 7:24.)

Let all such take comfort in the words of our Lord Jesus Christ which we are now considering. Let them remember that the Son of God himself regards them as his own near relations! Let them not heed the laughter, and mockery, and persecution of this world. The woman of whom Christ says, "She is my mother," and the man of whom Christ says, "He is my brother," have no cause to be ashamed.

LUKE 8:22-25

JESUS CALMS THE STORM

Now it came to pass on one of those days, that he entered into a boat, himself and his disciples; and he said unto them, Let us go over unto the other side of the lake: and they launched forth. But as they sailed he fell asleep: and there came down a storm of wind on the lake; and they were filling with water, and were in jeopardy. And they came to him, and awoke him, saying, Master, master, we perish. And he awoke, and rebuked the wind and the raging of the water: and they ceased, and there was a calm. And he said unto them, Where is your faith? And being afraid they marvelled, saying one to another, Who then is this, that he commandeth even the winds and the water, and they obey him?

The event in our Lord's life described in these verses is related three times in the Gospels. Matthew, Mark, and Luke were all inspired to record it. This circumstance should teach us the importance of the event, and should make us "give the more heed" to the lessons it contains.

We see, firstly, in these verses, that our Lord Jesus Christ was really man as well as God. We read that as he sailed over the Lake of Gennesaret in a ship with his disciples, "he fell asleep." Sleep, we must be all aware, is one of the conditions of our natural constitution as human beings. Angels and spirits require neither food nor refreshment. But flesh and blood, to keep up a healthy existence, must eat, and drink, and sleep. If the Lord Jesus could be weary, and need rest, He must have had two natures in one person—a human nature as well as a divine.

The truth now before us is full of deep consolation add encouragement for all true Christians. The one Mediator, in whom we are bid to trust, has been Himself "partaker of flesh and blood." The mighty High Priest, who is living for us at God's right hand, has had personal experience of all the sinless infirmities of the body. He has himself hungered, and thirsted, and suffered pain. He has himself endured weariness, and sought rest in sleep. Let us pour out our hearts before him with freedom, and tell Him our least troubles without reserve. He who made atonement for us on the cross is one who "can be touched with the feeling of our infirmities." (Heb. 4:15.) To be weary of working for God is sinful, but to be wearied and worn in doing God's work is no sin at all. Jesus himself was weary, and Jesus slept.

We see, secondly, in these verses, what fears and anxiety may assault the hearts of true disciples of Christ. We read, that "when a storm of wind came down on the lake," and the boat in which our Lord was sailing was filled with water, and in jeopardy, His companions were greatly alarmed. "They came to Him and awoke Him, saying, Master, Master, we perish." They forgot, for a moment, their Master's never-failing care for them in time past. They forgot that with Him they must be safe, whatever happened. They forgot everything but the sight and sense of present danger, and, under the impression of it, could not even wait until Christ awoke. It is only too true that sight, and sense, and feeling, make men very poor theologians.

Facts like these are sadly humbling to the pride of human nature. It ought to lower our self-conceit and high thoughts to see what a poor creature is man, even at his best estate—but facts like these are deeply instructive. They teach us what to watch and pray against in our own hearts. They teach of what we must make up our minds to find in other Christians. We must be moderate in our expectations. We must not suppose that men cannot be believers if they sometimes exhibit great weakness, or that men have no grace because they are sometimes overwhelmed with fears. Even Peter, James, and John, could cry, "Master, Master, we perish."

We see, thirdly, in these verses, how great is the power of our Lord Jesus Christ. We read that when His disciples awoke Him in the storm, "He arose, and rebuked the wind, and the raging of the waters, and they ceased, and there was a calm." This was, no doubt, a mighty miracle. It needed the power of Him who brought the flood on the earth in the days of Noah, and in due season took it away—who divided the Red Sea and the river Jordan into two parts, and made a path for His people through the waters—who brought the locusts on Egypt by an east wind, and by a west wind swept them away. (Exod. 10:13, 19.) No power short of this could in a moment turn a storm into a calm. "To speak to the winds and waves" is a common proverb for attempting that which is impossible. But here we see Jesus speaking, and at once the winds and waves obey! As man He had slept. As God He stilled the storm.

It is a blessed and comfortable thought, that all this almighty power of our Lord Jesus Christ is engaged on behalf of His believing people. He has undertaken to save every one of them to the uttermost, and He is "mighty to save." The trials of His people are often many and great. The devil never ceases to make war against them. The rulers of this world frequently persecute them. The very heads of the Church, who ought to be tender shepherds, are often bitterly opposed to the truth as it is in Jesus. Yet, notwithstanding all this, Christ's people shall never be entirely forsaken. Though severely harassed, they shall not be destroyed. Though cast down, they shall not be cast away. At the darkest time let true Christians rest in the thought, that "greater is He who is for them than all those who are against them." The winds and waves of political and ecclesiastical trouble may beat fiercely over them, and all hope may seem taken away. But still let them not despair. There is One living for them in heaven who can make these winds and waves to cease in a moment. The true Church, of which Christ is the Head, shall never perish. Its glorious Head is almighty, and lives for evermore, and His believing members shall all live, also, and reach home safe at last. (John 14:19.)

We see, lastly, in these verses, how needful it is for Christians to keep their faith ready for use. We read that our Lord said to His disciples when the storm had ceased, and their fears had subsided, "Where is your faith?" Well might He ask that question! Where was the profit of believing, if they could not believe in the time of need? Where was the real value of faith, unless they kept it in active exercise? Where was the benefit of trusting, if they were to trust their Master in sunshine only, but not in storms?

The lesson now before us is one of deep practical importance. To have true saving faith is one thing. To have that faith always ready for use is quite another. Many receive Christ as their Savior, and deliberately commit their souls to Him for time and eternity, who yet often find their faith sadly failing when something unexpected happens, and they are suddenly tried. These things ought not so to be. We ought to pray that we may have a stock of faith ready for use at a moment's notice, and may never be found unprepared. The highest style of Christian is the man who lives like Moses, "seeing Him who is invisible." (Heb. 11:27.) That man will never be greatly shaken by any storm. He will see Jesus near him in the darkest hour, and blue sky behind the blackest cloud.

LUKE 8:26-36

THE DEMON POSSESSED MAN

And they arrived at the country of the Gerasenes, which is over against Galilee. And when he was come forth upon the land, there met him a certain man out of the city, who had demons; and for a long time he had worn no clothes, and abode not in any house, but in the tombs. And when he saw Jesus, he cried out, and fell down before him, and with a loud voice said, What have I to do with thee, Jesus, thou Son of the Most High God? I beseech thee, torment me not. For he was commanding the unclean spirit to come out from the man. For oftentimes it had seized him: and he was kept under guard, and bound with chains and fetters; and breaking the bands asunder, he was driven of the demon into the deserts. And Jesus asked him, What is thy name? And he said, Legion; for many demons were entered into him. And they entreated him that he would not command them to depart into the abyss. Now there was there a herd of many swine feeding on the mountain: and they entreated him that he would give them leave to enter into them. And he gave them leave. And the demons came out from the man, and entered into the swine: and the herd rushed down the steep into the lake, and were drowned. And when they that fed them saw what had come to pass, they fled, and told it in the city and in the country. And they went out to see what had come to pass; and they came to Jesus, and found the man, from whom the demons were gone out, sitting, clothed and in his right mind, at the feet of Jesus: and they were afraid. And they that saw it told them how he that was possessed with demons was made whole.

The well-known narrative which we have now read, is carefully recorded by all of the first three Gospel-writers. It is a striking instance of our Lord's complete dominion over the prince of this world. We see the great enemy of our souls for once completely vanquished—the "strong man" foiled by One stronger than he, and the lion spoiled of his prey.

Let us mark, first, in this passage, the miserable condition of those over whom the devil reigns. The picture brought before us is a frightful one. We are told that when our Lord arrived in the country of the Gadarenes, there met Him "a certain man which had devils long time, and wore no clothes, neither abode in any house, but in the tombs." We are also told that although he had been "bound with chains and in fetters, he broke the bands, and was driven of the devil into the wilderness." In short, the case seems to have been one of the most aggravated forms of demoniacal possession. The unhappy sufferer was under the complete dominion of Satan, both in body and soul. So long as he continued in this state, he must have been a burden and a trouble to all around him. His mental faculties were under the direction of a "legion" of devils. His bodily strength was only employed for his own injury and shame. A more pitiable state for mortal man to be in, it is difficult to conceive.

Cases of bodily possession by Satan, like this, are, to say the least, very rarely met with in modern times. Yet we must not, on this account, forget that the devil is continually exercising a fearful power over many hearts and souls. He still urges many, in whose hearts he reigns, into self-dishonoring and self-destroying habits of life. He still rules many with a rod of iron—goads them on from vice to vice, and from profligacy to profligacy—drives them far from decent society, and the influence of respectable friends, plunges them into the lowest depths of wickedness—makes them little better than self-murderers-and renders them as useless to their families, the Church, and the world, as if they were dead, and not alive. Where is the faithful minister who could not put his finger on many such cases? What truer account can be given of many a young man, and many a young woman, than that they seem possessed of devils? It is vain to shut our eyes to facts. Demoniacal possession of men's bodies may be comparatively rare. But many, unhappily, are the cases in which the devil appears completely to possess men's souls.

These things are fearful to think upon. Fearful is it to see to what a wreck of body and mind Satan often brings young people! Fearful is it to observe how he often drives them out of the reach of all good influence, and buries them in a wilderness of bad companions and loathsome sins! Fearful, above all, is it to reflect that yet a little while Satan's slaves will be lost forever, and in hell! There often remains only one thing that can be done for them. They can be named before Christ in prayer. He that came to the country of the Gadarenes, and healed the miserable demoniac there, still lives in heaven, and pities sinners. The worst slave of Satan in England is not beyond a remedy. Jesus may yet take compassion on him, and set him free.

Let us mark, secondly, in these verses, the absolute power which the Lord Jesus Christ possesses over Satan. We are told that he "commanded the unclean spirit to come out of the man," whose miserable condition we have just heard described. At once the unhappy sufferer was healed. The "many devils" by whom he had been possessed were compelled to leave him. Nor is this all. Cast forth from their abode in the man's heart, we see these malignant spirits beseeching our Lord that He would "not torment" them, or "command them to go out into the deep," and so confessing His supremacy over them. Mighty as they were, they plainly felt themselves in the presence of One mightier than themselves. Full of malice as they were, they could not even hurt the "swine" of the Gadarenes until our Lord granted them permission.

Our Lord Jesus Christ's dominion over the devil should be a cheering thought to all true Christians. Without it, indeed, we might well despair of salvation. To feel that we have ever near us an invisible spiritual enemy, laboring night and day to compass our destruction, would be enough to crush our every hope, if we did not know a Friend and Protector. Blessed be God! The Gospel reveals such a One. The Lord Jesus is stronger than that "strong man armed," who is ever warring against our souls. The Lord Jesus is able to deliver us from the devil. He proved his power over him frequently when upon earth. He triumphed over him gloriously on the cross. He will never let him pluck any of His sheep out of His hand. He will one day bruise him under our feet, and bind him in the prison of hell. (Rom. 16:20; Rev. 20:1, 2.) Happy are they who hear Christ's voice and follow Him! Satan may vex them, but he cannot really hurt them! He may bruise their heel, but he cannot destroy their souls. They shall be "more than conquerors" through Him who loved them. (Rom 8:37.)

Let us mark, finally, the wonderful change which Christ can work in Satan's slaves. We are told that the Gadarenes "found the man out of whom the devil was departed, sitting at the feet of Jesus, clothed, and in his right mind." That sight must indeed have been strange and astonishing! The man's past history and condition, no doubt, were well known. He had probably been a nuisance and a terror to all the neighborhood. Yet here, in one moment, a complete change had come over him. Old things had passed away, and all things had become new. The power by which such a cure was wrought must indeed have been almighty. When Christ is the physician nothing is impossible.

One thing, however, must never be forgotten. Striking and miraculous as this cure was, it is not really more wonderful than every case of decided conversion to God. Marvelous as the change was which appeared in this demoniac's condition when healed, it is not one whit more marvelous than the change which passes over every one who is born again, and turned from the power of Satan to God. Never is a man in his right mind until he is converted, or in his right place until he sits by faith at the feet of Jesus, or rightly clothed until he has put on the Lord Jesus Christ. Have we ever considered what real conversion to God is? It is nothing else than the miraculous release of a captive, the miraculous restoration of a man to his right mind, the miraculous deliverance of a soul from the devil.

What are we ourselves? This, after all, is the grand question which concerns us. Are we bondsmen of Satan or servants of God? Has Christ made us free, or does the devil yet reign in our hearts? Do we sit at the feet of Jesus daily? Are we in our right minds? May the Lord help us to answer these questions aright!

LUKE 8:37-40

And all the people of the country of the Gerasenes round about asked him to depart from them, for they were holden with great fear: and he entered into a boat, and returned. But the man from whom the demons were gone out prayed him that he might be with him: but he sent him away, saying, Return to thy house, and declare how great things God hath done for thee. And he went his way, publishing throughout the whole city how great things Jesus had done for him.

And as Jesus returned, the multitude welcomed him; for they were all waiting for him.

We see in this passage two requests made to our Lord Jesus Christ. They were widely different one from the other, and were offered by people of widely different character. We see, moreover, how these requests were received by our Lord Jesus Christ. In either case the request received a most remarkable answer. The whole passage is singularly instructive.

Let us observe, in the first place, that the Gadarenes besought our Lord to depart from them, and their request was granted. We read these painfully solemn words—"Then all the people of the region of the Gerasenes asked Jesus to leave them, because they were overcome with fear. So he got into the boat and left." Now why did these unhappy men desire the Son of God to leave them? Why, after the amazing miracle of mercy which had just been wrought among them, did they feel no wish to know more of Him who wrought it? Why, in a word, did they become their own enemies, forsake their own mercies, and shut the door against the Gospel? There is but one answer to these questions. The Gadarenes loved the world, and the things of the world, and were determined not to give them up. They felt convinced, in their own consciences, that they could not receive Christ among them and keep their sins, and their sins they were resolved to keep. They saw, at a glance, that there was something about Jesus with which their habits of life would never agree, and having to choose between the new ways and their own old ones, they refused the new and chose the old.

And why did our Lord Jesus Christ grant the request of the Gadarenes, and leave them? He did it in judgment, to testify His sense of the greatness of their sin. He did it in mercy to His Church in every age, to show how great is the wickedness of those who wilfully reject the truth. It seems an eternal law of His government, that those who obstinately refuse to walk in the light shall have the light taken from them. Great is Christ's patience and long-suffering! His mercy endures forever. His offers and invitations are wide, and broad, and sweeping, and universal. He gives every church its day of grace and time of visitation. (Luke 19:44.) But if men persist in refusing His counsel, He has nowhere promised to persist in forcing it upon them. People who have the Gospel, and yet refuse to obey it, must not be surprised if the Gospel is removed from them. Hundreds of churches, and parishes, and families, are at this moment in the state of the Gadarenes. They said to Christ, "Depart from us," and He has taken them at their word. They were joined to idols, and are now "let alone." (Job 21:14; Hosea 4:17.)

Let us take heed that we do not sin the sin of the Gadarenes. Let us beware lest by coldness, and inattention, and worldliness, we drive Jesus from our doors, and compel Him to forsake us entirely. Of all sins which we can sin, this is the most sinful. Of all states of soul into which we can fall, none is so fearful as to be "let alone." Let it rather be our daily prayer that Christ may never leave us to ourselves. The old wreck, high and dry on the sand-bank, is not a more wretched sight than the man whose heart Christ has visited with mercies and judgments, but has at last ceased to visit, because He was not received. The barred door is a door at which Jesus will not always knock. The Gadarene mind must not be surprised to see Christ leaving it and going away.

Let us observe, in the second place, that the man out of whom the devils were departed, besought our Lord that he might be with Him, but his request was not granted. We read that Jesus sent him away, saying, "Return to your own house, and show how great things God has done unto you."

We can easily understand the request that this man made. He felt deeply grateful for the amazing mercy which he had just received in being cured. He felt full of love and warm affection toward Him, who had so wonderfully and graciously cured him. He felt that he could not see too much of Him, be too much in His company, cleave to Him too closely. He forgot everything else under the influence of these feelings. Family, relations, friends, home, house, country, all seemed as nothing in his eyes. He felt that he cared for nothing but to be with Christ. And we cannot blame him for his feelings. They may have been tinged with something of enthusiasm and inconsideration. There may have been about them a zeal not according to knowledge. In the first excitement of a newly felt cure, he may not have been fit to judge what his future line of life should be. But excited feelings in religion are far better than no feelings at all. In the petition he made, there was far more to praise than to blame.

But why did our Lord Jesus Christ REFUSE to grant this man's request? Why, at a time when he had few disciples, did He send this man away? Why, instead of allowing him to take place with Peter and James and John, did He bid him return to his own house? Our Lord did what He did in infinite wisdom. He did it for the benefit of the man's own soul. He saw it was more for his good to be a witness for the Gospel at home than a disciple abroad. He did it in mercy to the Gadarenes. He left among them one standing testimony of the truth of His own divine mission. He did it, above all, for the perpetual instruction of His whole church. He would have us know that there are various ways of glorifying Him, that He may be honored in private life as well as in the apostolic office, and that the first place in which we should witness for Christ is our own house.

There is a lesson of deep experimental wisdom in this little incident, which all true Christians would do well to lay to heart. That lesson is our own utter ignorance of what position is good for us in this world, and the necessity of submitting our own wills to the will of Christ. The place that we wish to fill is not always the place that is best for us. The line of life that we want to take up, is not always that which Christ sees to be most for the benefit of our souls. The place that we are obliged to fill is sometimes very distasteful, and yet it may be needful to our sanctification. The position we are compelled to occupy may be very disagreeable to flesh and blood, and yet it may be the very one that is necessary to keep us in our right mind. It is better to be sent away from Christ's bodily presence, by Christ Himself, than to remain in Christ's bodily presence without His consent.

Let us pray for the spirit of "contentment with such things as we have." Let us be fearful of choosing for ourselves in this life without Christ's consent, or moving in this world, when the pillar of cloud and fire is not moving before us. Let us ask the Lord to choose everything for us. Let our daily prayer be, "Give me what you will. Place me where you will. Only let me be Your disciple and abide in You."

LUKE 8:41-48

A SICK WOMAN HEALED

And behold, there came a man named Jairus, and he was a ruler of the synagogue: and he fell down at Jesus' feet, and besought him to come into his house; for he had an only daughter, about twelve years of age, and she was dying. But as he went the multitudes thronged him. And a woman having an issue of blood twelve years, who had spent all her living upon physicians, and could not be healed of any, came behind him, and touched the border of his garment: and immediately the issue of her blood stanched. And Jesus said, Who is it that touched me? And when all denied, Peter said, and they that were with him, Master, the multitudes press thee and crush thee. But Jesus said, Some one did touch me; for I perceived that power had gone forth from me. And when the woman saw that she was not hid, she came trembling, and falling down before him declared in the presence of all the people for what cause she touched him, and how she was healed immediately. And he said unto her, Daughter, thy faith hath made thee whole; go in peace.

How much misery and trouble sin has brought into the world! The passage we have just read affords a melancholy proof of this. First we see a distressed father in bitter anxiety about a dying daughter. Then we see a suffering woman, who has been afflicted twelve years with an incurable disease. And these are things which sin has sown broad-cast over the whole earth! These are but patterns of what is going on continually on every side. These are evils which God did not create at the beginning, but man has brought upon himself by the fall. There would have been no sorrow and no sickness among Adam's children, if there had been no sin.

Let us see in the case of the woman here described, a striking picture of the condition of many souls. We are told that she had been afflicted with a wearing disease for "twelve years," and that she "had spent all her living upon physicians," and that she could not be "healed of any." The state of many a sinner's heart is placed before us in this description as in a mirror. Perhaps it describes ourselves.

There are men and women in most congregations who have felt their sins deeply, and been sorely afflicted by the thought that they are not forgiven and not fit to die. They have desired relief and peace of conscience, but have not known where to find them. They have tried many false remedies, and found themselves "nothing bettered, but rather worse." They have gone the round of all the forms of religion, and wearied themselves with every imaginable man-made device for obtaining spiritual health. But all has been in vain. Peace of conscience seems as far off as ever. The wound within appears a fretting, intractable sore, which nothing can heal. They are still wretched, still unhappy, still thoroughly discontented with their own state. In short, like the woman of whom we read today, they are ready to say, "There is no hope for me. I shall never be saved."

Let all such take comfort in the miracle which we are now considering. Let them know that "there is balm in Gilead," which can cure them, if they will only seek it. There is one door at which they have never knocked, in all their efforts to obtain relief. There is one Physician to whom they have not applied, who never fails to heal. Let them consider the conduct of the woman before us in her necessity. When all other means had failed, she went to Jesus for help. Let them go and do likewise.

Let us see, secondly, in the conduct of the woman before us, a striking picture of the first beginnings of saving faith and its effect. We are told that she "came behind" our Lord, and "touched the hem of His garment, and immediately her bleeding stopped." The act appeared a most simple one, and utterly inadequate to produce any great result. But the effect of that act was most marvelous! In an instant the poor sufferer was healed. The relief that many physicians had failed to give in "twelve years," was obtained in one moment. It was but one touch, and she was well!

It is hard to conceive a more lively image of the experience of many souls than the history of this woman's cure. Hundreds could testify that, like her, they long sought spiritual help from physicians of no value, and wearied their souls by using remedies which brought no cure. At last, like her, they heard of One who healed laboring consciences, and forgave sinners, "without money and without price," if men would only come to Him by faith. The terms sounded too good to be credible. The tidings sounded too good to be true. But, like the woman before us, they resolved to try. They came to Christ by faith, with all their sins, and to their amazement at once found relief. And now they feel more comfort and hope than they ever felt before. The burden seems rolled off their backs. The weight seems taken off their minds. Light seems breaking in on their hearts. They begin to "rejoice in hope of the glory of God." (Rom. 5:2.) And all, they would tell us, is owing to one simple thing. They came to Jesus just as they were. They touched Him by faith, and were healed.

Forever let it be engraved on our hearts that faith in Christ is the grand secret of peace with God. Without it we shall never find inward rest, whatever we may do in religion. Without it we may go to services daily and receive the Lord's Supper every week—we may give our goods to the poor, and our bodies to be burned, we may fast and wear sackcloth, and live the lives of hermits—all this we may do, and be miserable after all. One true believing touch of Christ is worth all these things put together. The pride of human nature may not like it! But it is true! Thousands will rise up at the last day and testify that they never felt comfort of soul until they came to Christ by faith, and were content to cease from their own works, and be saved wholly and entirely by His grace.

Let us see, lastly, in this passage, how much our Lord desires that those who have received benefit from Him should confess Him before men. We are told that He did not allow this woman, whose case we have been reading, to retire from the crowd unnoticed. He enquired "who had touched Him." He enquired again, until the woman came forward and "declared" her case before all the people. And then came the gracious words, "Daughter, be of good comfort. Your faith has made you whole."

Confession of Christ is a matter of great importance. Let this never be forgotten by true Christians. The work that we can do for our blessed Master is little and poor. Our best endeavors to glorify Him are weak and full of imperfections. Our prayers and praises are sadly defective. Our knowledge and love are miserably small. But do we feel within that Christ has healed our souls? Then can we not confess Christ before men? Can we not plainly tell others that Christ has done everything for us—that we were dying of a deadly disease, and were cured—that we were lost, and are now found, that we were blind, and now see? Let us do this boldly, and not be afraid. Let us not be ashamed to let all men know what Jesus has done for our souls.

Our Master loves to see us doing so. He likes His people not to be ashamed of His name. It is a solemn saying of Paul, "If you shall confess with your mouth the Lord Jesus, and believe in your heart that God has raised Him from the dead, you shall be saved." (Rom. 10:9.) It is a still more solemn saying of Christ Himself, "Whoever shall be ashamed of me and my words, of him shall the Son of man be ashamed." (Luke 9:26.)

LUKE 8:49-56

JAIRUS' DAUGHTER RAISED FROM THE DEAD

While he yet spake, there cometh one from the ruler of the synagogue's house, saying, Thy daughter is dead; trouble not the Teacher. But Jesus hearing it, answered him, Fear not: only believe, and she shall be made whole. And when he came to the house, he suffered not any man to enter in with him, save Peter, and John, and James, and the father of the maiden and her mother. And all were weeping, and bewailing her: but he said, Weep not; for she is not dead, but sleepeth. And they laughed him to scorn, knowing that she was dead. But he, taking her by the hand, called, saying, Maiden, arise. And her spirit returned, and she rose up immediately: and he commanded that something be given her to eat. And her parents were amazed: but he charged them to tell no man what had been done.

The verses we have now read, contain one of the three great instances which the Holy Spirit has thought fit to record of our Lord restoring a dead person to life. The other two instances are those of Lazarus and the widow's son at Nain. There seems no reason to doubt that our Lord raised others beside these three. But these three cases are specially described as patterns of His almighty power. One was a young girl, who had just breathed her last. One was a young man, who was being carried to his burial. One was a man, who had already lain four days in the grave. In all three cases alike we see life at once restored at Christ's command.

Let us notice, in the verses before us, how universal is the dominion which death holds over the sons of men. We see him coming to a rich man's house, and tearing from him the desire of his eyes with a stroke. "There came one from the ruler of the synagogue's house, saying to him, Your daughter is dead." Such tidings as these are the bitterest cups which we have to drink in this world. Nothing cuts so deeply into man's heart as to part with beloved ones, and lay them in the grave. Few griefs are so crushing and heavy as the grief of a parent over an only child.

Death is indeed a cruel enemy! He makes no distinction in his attacks. He comes to the rich man's hall, as well as to the poor man's cottage. He does not spare the young, the strong, and the beautiful, any more than the old, the infirm, and the grey-haired. Not all the gold of Australia, nor all the skill of doctors, can keep the hand of death from our bodies, in the day of his power. When the appointed hour comes, and God permits him to smite, our worldly schemes must be broken off, and our darlings must be taken away and buried out of our sight.

These thoughts are melancholy, and few like to hear of them. The subject of death is one that men blink, and refuse to look at. "All men think all men mortal but themselves." But why should we treat this great reality in this way? Why should we not rather look the subject of death in the face, in order that when our turn comes we may be prepared to die? Death will come to our houses, whether we like it or not. Death will take each of us away, despite our dislike to hearing about it. Surely it is the part of a wise man to get ready for this great change. Why should we not be ready? There is one who can deliver us from the fear of death. (Heb. 2:15.) Christ has overcome death, and "brought life and immortality to light through the Gospel." (2 Tim. 1:10.) He that believes on Him has everlasting life, and though he were dead yet shall he live. (John 6:47; 11:25.) Let us believe in the Lord Jesus, and then death will lose his sting. We shall then be able to say with Paul, "To me to die is gain." (Phil. 1:21.)

Let us notice, secondly, in the verses before us, that faith in Christ's love and power is the best remedy in time of trouble. We are told that when Jesus heard the tidings, that the ruler's daughter was dead, He said to him, "Fear not, believe only, and she shall be made whole." These words, no doubt, were spoken with immediate reference to the miracle our Lord was going to perform. But we need not doubt that they were also meant for the perpetual benefit of the Church of Christ. They were meant to reveal to us the grand secret of comfort in the hour of need. That secret is to exercise faith, to fall back on the thought of Christ's loving heart and mighty hand—in one word, to believe.

Let a petition for more faith form a part of all our daily prayers. As ever we would have peace, and calmness, and quietness of spirit, let us often say, "Lord, increase our faith." A hundred painful things may happen to us every week in this evil world, of which our poor weak minds cannot see the reason. Without faith we shall be constantly disturbed and cast down. Nothing will make us cheerful and tranquil but an abiding sense of Christ's love, Christ's wisdom, Christ's care over us, and Christ's providential management of all our affairs. Faith will not sink under the weight of evil tidings. (Psalm. 112:7.) Faith can sit still and wait for better times. Faith can see light even in the darkest hour, and a needs-be for the heaviest trial. Faith can find room to build Ebenezers under any circumstances, and can sing songs in the night in any condition. "He that believes shall not make haste." "You will keep him in perfect peace whose mind is staid on you." (Isa. 28:16; 26:3.) Once more let the lesson be engraved on our minds. If we would travel comfortably through this world, we must "believe."

Let us notice, finally, in these verses, the almighty power which our Lord Jesus Christ possesses even over death. We are told that He came to the house of Jairus and turned the mourning into joy. He took by the hand the breathless body of the ruler's daughter, "and called saying, My child, arise." At once by that all-powerful voice life was restored. "Her spirit came again, and she arose immediately."

Let us take comfort in the thought that there is a limit to death's power. The king of terrors is very strong. How many generations he has mowed down and swept into the dust! How many of the wise and strong, and fair, he has swallowed down and snatched away in their prime! How many victories he has won, and how often he has written "vanity of vanities," on the pride of man! Patriarchs, and kings, and prophets, and apostles, have all in turn been obliged to yield to him. They have all died. But thanks be unto God, there is one stronger than death. There is one who has said, "O death! will be your plague—O grave! will be your destruction!" (Hosea 13:14.) That One is the Friend of sinners, Christ Jesus the Lord. He proved His power frequently when He came to the earth the first time, in the house of Jairus, by the tomb of Bethany, in the gate of Nain. He will prove to all the world when He comes again. "The last enemy that shall be destroyed is death." (1 Cor. 15:26.) "The earth shall cast out the dead." (Isa. 26:19.)

Let us leave the passage with the consoling thought, that the things which happened in Jairus' house are a type of good things to come. The hour comes and will soon be here, when the voice of Christ shall call all His people from their graves, and gather them together to part no more. Believing husbands shall once more see believing wives. Believing parents shall once more see believing children. Christ shall unite the whole family in the great home in heaven, and all tears shall be wiped from all eyes.

Chapter 9

JESUS SENDS OUT THE 12 APOSTLES

*A*nd he called the twelve together, and gave them power and authority over all demons, and to cure diseases. And he sent them forth to preach the kingdom of God, and to heal the sick. And he said unto them, Take nothing for your journey, neither staff, nor wallet, nor bread, nor money; neither have two coats. And into whatsoever house ye enter, there abide, and thence depart. And as many as receive you not, when ye depart from that city, shake off the dust from your feet for a testimony against them. And they departed, and went throughout the villages, preaching the gospel, and healing everywhere.

These verses contain our Lord's instructions to His twelve apostles, when He sent them forth the first time to preach the Gospel. The passage is one which throws much light on the work of Christian ministers in every age. No doubt the miraculous power which the apostles possessed, made their position very unlike that of any other body of men in the Church. No doubt, in many respects, they stood alone, and had no successors. Yet the words of our Lord in this place must not be confined entirely to the apostles. They contain deep wisdom for Christian teachers and preachers, for all time.

Let us observe, that the commission to the apostles contained special reference to the devil and bodily sickness. We read that Jesus gave them "authority over all devils, and to cure diseases."

We see here, as in a glass, two of the principal parts of the Christian minister's business. We must not expect him to cast out evil spirits, but we may fairly expect him to "resist the devil and all his works," and to keep up a constant warfare against the prince of this world. We must not expect him to work miraculous cures, but we may expect him to take a special interest in all sick people, to visit them, sympathize with them, and help them, if needful, as far as he can. The minister who neglects the sick members of his flock is no true pastor. He must not be surprised if people say that he cares for the fleece of his sheep more than for their health. The minister who allows drunkenness, blasphemy, uncleanness, fighting, reveling, and the like, to go on among his congregation unreproved, is omitting a plain duty of his office. He is not warring against the devil. He is no true successor of the apostles.

Let us observe, secondly, that one of the principal works which the apostles were commissioned to take up was preaching. We read that our Lord "sent them to preach the kingdom of God," and that "they went through the towns preaching the Gospel."

The importance of preaching, as a means of grace, might easily be gathered from this passage, even if it stood alone. But it is but one instance, among many, of the high value which the Bible everywhere sets upon preaching. It is, in fact, God's chosen instrument for doing good to souls. By it sinners are converted, inquirers led on, and saints built up. A preaching ministry is absolutely essential to the health and prosperity of a visible church. The pulpit is the place where the chief victories of the Gospel have always been won, and no Church has ever done much for the advancement of true religion in which the pulpit has been neglected. Would we know whether a minister is a truly apostolical man? If he is, he will give the best of his attention to his sermons. He will labor and pray to make his preaching effective, and he will tell his congregation that he looks to preaching for the chief results on souls. The minister who exalts the sacraments, or forms of the Church, above preaching, may be a zealous, earnest, conscientious, and respectable minister; but his zeal is not according to knowledge. He is not a follower of the apostles.

Let us observe, thirdly, that our Lord charges His apostles, when He sends them forth, to study simplicity of habits, and contentment with such things as they have. He bids them "take nothing for their journey, neither staffs, nor bag, neither bread nor money; neither have two coats apiece. And whatever house you enter into, there abide, and thence, depart." In part, these instructions apply only to a peculiar period. There came a day when our Lord Himself bade everyone who had "no sword, to sell his garment and buy one." (Luke 22:36.) But, in part, these instructions contain a lesson for all time. The spirit of these verses is meant to be remembered by all ministers of the Gospel.

The leading idea which the words convey is, a warning against worldliness and luxurious habits. Well would it be for the world and the Church if the warning had been more carefully heeded! From no quarter has Christianity received such damage as it has from the hands of its own teachers. On no point have its teachers erred so much, and so often, as in the matter of personal worldliness and luxury of life. They have often destroyed, by their daily lives, the whole work of their lips. They have given occasion to the enemies of religion to say, that they love ease, and money, and good things, far more than souls. From such ministers may we pray daily that the Church may be delivered! They are a living stumbling-block in the way to heaven. They are helpers to the cause of the devil, and not of God. The preacher whose affections are set on money, and dress and feasting, and pleasure-seeking, has clearly mistaken his vocation. He has forgotten his Master's instructions. He is not an apostolic man.

Let us observe, lastly, that our Lord prepares His disciples to meet with unbelief and impenitence in those to whom they preached. He speaks of those "who will not receive them" as a class which they must expect to see. He tells them how to behave, when not received, as if it was a state of things to which they must make up their mind.

All ministers of the Gospel would do well to read carefully this portion of our Lord's instructions. All missionaries, and district visitors, and Sunday-school teachers, would do well to lay it to heart. Let them not be cast down if their work seems in vain, and their labor without profit. Let them remember that the very first preachers and teachers whom Jesus employed were sent forth with a distinct warning that not all would believe. Let them work on patiently, and sow the good seed without fainting. Duties are theirs. Results are God's. Apostles may plant and water. The Holy Spirit alone can give spiritual life. The Lord Jesus knows what is in the heart of man. He does not despise his laborers because little of the seed they sow bears fruit. The harvest may be small. But every laborer shall be rewarded according to his work.

LUKE 9:7-11

THE APOSTLES RETURN

Now Herod the tetrarch heard of all that was done: and he was much perplexed, because that it was said by some, that John was risen from the dead; and by some, that Elijah had appeared; and by others, that one of the old prophets was risen again. And Herod said, John I beheaded: but who is this, about whom I hear such things? And he sought to see him.

And the apostles, when they were returned, declared unto him what things they had done. And he took them, and withdrew apart to a city called Bethsaida. But the multitudes perceiving it followed him: and he welcomed them, and spake to them of the kingdom of God, and them that had need of healing he cured.

Let us mark, in this passage, the power of a bad conscience. We are told that "when Herod the tetrarch heard of all that was done by our Lord, he was perplexed." He said, "John have I beheaded, but who is this?" Great and powerful as Herod was, the tidings of our Lord's ministry called his sins to remembrance, and disturbed him even in his royal palace. Surrounded as he was by everything which is considered to make life enjoyable, the report of another preacher of righteousness filled him with alarm. The recollection of his own wickedness in killing John the Baptist flashed on his mind. He knew he had done wrong. He felt guilty, self-condemned, and self-dissatisfied. Faithful and true is that saying of Solomon's, "The way of transgressors is hard." (Prov. 13:15.) Herod's sin had found him out. The prison and the sword had silenced John the Baptist's tongue, but they could not silence the voice of Herod's inward man. God's truth can neither be silenced, nor bound, nor killed.

Conscience is a most powerful part of our natural constitution. It cannot save our souls. It never leads a man to Christ. It is often blind, and ignorant, and misdirected. Yet conscience often raises a mighty testimony against sin in the sinner's heart, and makes him feel that "it is an evil and a bitter thing" to depart from God. Young people ought especially to remember this, and, remembering it, to take heed to their ways. Let them not flatter themselves that all is right, when their sins are past, and done, and forgotten by the world. Let them know that conscience can bring up each sin before the eyes of their minds, and make it bite like a serpent. Millions will testify at the last day that Herod's experience was their own. Conscience called old sins from their graves, and made them walk up and down in their hearts. In the midst of seeming happiness and prosperity they were inwardly miserable and distressed. Happy are they who have found the only cure for a bad conscience! Nothing will ever heal it but the blood of Christ.

Let us mark, secondly, the importance to Christians of occasional privacy and retirement. We are told, that when the apostles returned from their first ministerial work, our Lord "took them and went aside privately into a desert place." We cannot doubt that this was done with a deep meaning. It was meant to teach the great lesson that those who do public work for the souls of others, must be careful to make time for being alone with God.

The lesson is one which many Christians would do well to remember. Occasional retirement, self-inquiry, meditation, and secret communion with God, are absolutely essential to spiritual health. The man who neglects them is in great danger of a fall. To be always preaching, teaching, speaking, writing, and working public works, is, unquestionably, a sign of zeal. But it is not always a sign of zeal according to knowledge. It often leads to untoward consequences. We must make time occasionally for sitting down and calmly looking within, and examining how matters stand between our own selves and Christ. The omission of the practice is the true account of many a backsliding which shocks the Church, and gives occasion to the world to blaspheme. Many could say with sorrow, in the words of Canticles, "They made me keeper of the vineyards, but my own vineyard have I not kept." (Cant. 1:6.)

Let us mark, lastly, in this passage, our Lord Jesus Christ's readiness to receive all who come to Him. We are told, that when the multitude followed Him into the desert, where He had retired, "he received them, and spoke unto them of the kingdom of God, and healed those who had need of healing." Unmannerly and uninvited as this intrusion on his privacy seems to have been, it met with no rebuff from our Lord. He was always more ready to give instruction than people were to ask it, and more willing to teach than people were to be taught.

But the incident, trifling as it may seem, exactly tallies with all that we read in the Gospels of the gentleness and compassion of Christ. We never see Him dealing with people according to their deserts. We never find Him scrutinizing the motives of His hearers, or refusing to allow them to learn of Him, because their hearts were not right in the sight of God. His ear was always ready to hear, and His hand to work, and His tongue to preach. None that came to Him were ever cast out. Whatever they might think of His doctrine, they could never say that Jesus of Nazareth was "an austere man."

Let us remember this in all our dealings with Christ about our own souls. We may draw near to Him with boldness, and open our hearts to Him with confidence. He is a Savior of infinite compassion and loving-kindness. He will not break the bruised reed, nor quench the smoking flax. The secrets of our spiritual life may be such as we would not have our dearest friends know. The wounds of our consciences may be deep and sore, and require most delicate handling. But we need not fear anything, if we commit all to Jesus, the Son of God. We shall find that His kindness is unbounded. His own words shall be found abundantly true—"I am meek and lowly of heart, and you shall find rest to your souls." (Matt. 11:29.)

Let us remember this, finally, in our dealing with other people, if we are called upon to give them help about their souls. Let us strive to walk in the steps of Christ's example, and, like Him, to be kind, and patient, and always willing to aid. The ignorance of young beginners in religion is sometimes very provoking. We are apt to be wearied of their instability, and fickleness, and halting between two opinions. But let us remember Jesus, and not be weary. He "received all," spoke to all, and did good to all. Let us go and do likewise. As Christ deals with us, so let us deal one with another.

LUKE 9:12-17

JESUS FEEDS THE FIVE THOUSAND

And the day began to wear away; and the twelve came, and said unto him, Send the multitude away, that they may go into the villages and country round about, and lodge, and get provisions: for we are here in a desert place. But he said unto them, Give ye them to eat. And they said, We have no more than five loaves and two fishes; except we should go and buy food for all this people. For they were about five thousand men. And he said unto his disciples, Make them sit down in companies, about fifty each. And they did so, and made them all sit down. And he took the five loaves and the two fishes, and looking up to heaven, he blessed them, and brake; and gave to the disciples to set before the multitude. And they ate, and were all filled: and there was taken up that which remained over to them of broken pieces, twelve baskets.

The miracle described in these verses is more frequently related in the Gospels than any that our Lord wrought. There is no doubt a meaning in this repetition. It is intended to draw our special attention to the things which it contains.

We see, for one thing, in these verses, a striking example of our Lord Jesus Christ's DIVINE POWER. He feeds an assembly of five thousand men with five loaves and two fish. He makes a scanty supply of food, which was barely sufficient for the daily needs of Himself and His disciples, satisfy the hunger of a company as large as a Roman legion. There could be no mistake about the reality and greatness of this miracle. It was done publicly, and before many witnesses. The same power which at the beginning made the world out of nothing, caused food to exist, which before had not existed. The circumstances of the whole event made deception impossible. Five thousand hungry men would not have agreed that they were "all filled," if they had not received real food. "Twelve baskets full of fragments" would never have been taken up, if real material loaves and fish had not been miraculously multiplied. Nothing, in short, can explain the whole transaction, but the finger of God. The same hand which sent manna from heaven in the wilderness to feed Israel, was the hand which made five loaves and two fish supply the needs of five thousand men.

The miracle before us is one among many proofs that with Christ nothing is impossible. The Savior of sinners is Almighty. He "calls those things which be not as though they were." (Rom. 4:17.) When He wills a thing, it shall be done. When He commands a thing, it shall come to pass. He can create light out of darkness, order out of disorder, strength out of weakness, joy out of sorrow, and food out of nothing at all. Forever let us bless God that it is so! We might well despair, when we see the corruption of human nature, and the desperate hardness and unbelief of man's heart, if we did not know the power of Christ. "Can these dry bones live? Can any man or woman be saved? Can any child, or friend of ours ever become a true Christian? Can we ourselves ever win our way through to heaven?"—Questions like these could never be answered, if Jesus was not Almighty. But thanks be to God, Jesus has all power in heaven and earth. He lives in heaven for us, able to save to the uttermost, and therefore we may hope.

We see, for another thing, in these verses, a striking emblem of Christ's ability to supply the spiritual needs of mankind. The whole miracle is a picture. We see in it, as in a mirror, some of the most important truths of Christianity. It is, in fact, a great acted parable of the glorious Gospel.

What is that multitude which surrounded our Lord in the wilderness; poor and helpless, and destitute of food? It is a figure of mankind. We are a company of poor sinners, in the midst of a wicked world, without strength, or power to save ourselves, and severely in danger of perishing from spiritual famine.

Who is that gracious Teacher who had compassion on this starving multitude in the wilderness, and said to His disciples, "Give them something to eat?" It is Jesus Himself, ever full of pity, ever kind, ever ready to show mercy, even to the unthankful and the evil. And He is not altered. He is just the same today as He was eighteen hundred years ago. High in heaven at the right hand of God, He looks down on the vast multitude of starving sinners, who cover the face of the earth. He still pities them, still cares for them, still feels for their helplessness and need. And He still says to His believing followers, "Behold this multitude, give them something to eat."

What is that wonderful provision which Christ miraculously made for the famishing multitude before Him? It is a figure of the Gospel. Weak and contemptible as that Gospel appears to many, it contains "enough and to spare" for the souls of all mankind. Poor and despicable as the story of a crucified Savior seems to the wise and prudent, it is the power of God unto salvation to everyone that believes. (Rom. 1:16.)

What are those disciples who received the loaves and fish from Christ's hand, and carried them to the multitude, until all were filled? They are a figure of all faithful preachers and teachers of the Gospel. Their word is simple, and yet deeply important. They are appointed to set before men the provision that Christ has made for their souls. Of their own invention they are not commissioned to give anything. All that they convey to men, must be from Christ's hands. So long as they faithfully discharge this office, they may confidently expect their Master's blessing. Many, no doubt, will always refuse to eat of the food that Christ has provided. But if ministers offer the bread of life to men faithfully, the blood of those who are lost will not be required at their hands.

What are we doing ourselves? Have we discovered that this world is a wilderness, and that our souls must be fed with bread from heaven, or die eternally? Happy are they who have learned this lesson, and have tasted by experience, that Christ crucified is the true bread of life! The heart of man can never be satisfied with the things of this world. It is always empty, and hungry, and thirsty, and dissatisfied, until it comes to Christ. It is only they who hear Christ's voice, and follow Him, and feed on Him by faith, who are "filled."

LUKE 9:18-22

PETER'S CONFESSION OF CHRIST

And it came to pass, as he was praying apart, the disciples were with him: and he asked them, saying, Who do the multitudes say that I am? And they answering said, John the Baptist; but others say, Elijah; and others, that one of the old prophets is risen again. And he said unto them, But who say ye that I am? And Peter answering said, The Christ of God. But he charged them, and commanded them to tell this to no man; saying, The Son of man must suffer many things, and be rejected of the elders and chief priests and scribes, and be killed, and the third day be raised up.

Let us notice in this passage, the variety of opinions about our Lord Jesus Christ, which prevailed during His earthly ministry. We are told that some said that He was John the Baptist—some that He was Elijah—and some that one of the old prophets was risen again. One common remark applies to all these opinions. All were agreed that our Lord's doctrine was not like that of the Scribes and Pharisees. All saw in Him a bold witness against the evil that was in the world.

Let it never surprise us, to find the same variety of opinions about Christ and His Gospel in our own times. God's truth disturbs the spiritual laziness of men. It obliges them to think. It makes them begin to talk, and reason, and speculate, and invent theories to account for its spread in some quarters, and its rejection in others. Thousands in every age of the Church spend their lives in this way, and never come to the point of drawing near to God. They satisfy themselves with a miserable round of gossip about this preacher's sermons, or that writer's opinions. They think "this man goes too far," and "that man does not go far enough." Some doctrines they approve, and others they disapprove. Some teachers they call "sound," and others they call "unsound." They cannot quite make up their own minds what is true, or what is right. Year rolls on after year, and finds them in the same state—talking, criticizing, faultfinding, speculating, but never getting any further—hovering like the moth round religion, but never settling down like the bee, to feed on its treasures. They never boldly lay hold of Christ. They never set themselves heartily to the great business of serving God. They never take up the cross and become thorough Christians. And at last, after all their talking, they die in their sins, unprepared to meet God.

Let us not be content with a religion of this kind. It will not save us to talk and speculate, and exchange opinions about the Gospel. The Christianity that saves, is a thing personally grasped, personally experienced, personally felt, and personally possessed. There is not the slightest excuse for stopping short in talk, opinion, and speculation. The Jews of our Lord's time might have found out, if they had been honest inquirers, that Jesus of Nazareth was neither John the Baptist, nor Elijah, nor an old prophet, but the Christ of God. The speculative Christian of our own day, might easily satisfy himself on every point which is needful to salvation, if he would really, candidly, and humbly seek the teaching of the Spirit. The words of our Lord are weighty and solemn, "If any man will do God's will, he shall know of the doctrine, whether it be of God." (John 7:17.) Honest, practical obedience, is one of the keys of the gate of knowledge.

Let us notice, secondly, in this passage, the singular knowledge and faith displayed by the Apostle Peter. We read, that when our Lord said to His disciples, "Whom do you say that I am? Peter answering, said, the Christ of God."

This was a noble confession, and one of which, in these days, we can hardly realize the full value. To estimate it aright we should place ourselves in the position of our Lord's disciples. We should call to mind that the great, and wise, and learned of their own nation, saw no beauty in their Master, and would not receive Him as the Messiah. We should recollect that they saw no royal dignity about our Lord—no crown—no army—no earthly dominion. They saw nothing but a poor man, who often had no place in which to lay his head. And yet it was at this time, and under these circumstances, that Peter boldly declares his belief that Jesus is the Christ of God Truly, this was a great faith! It was mingled, no doubt, with much of ignorance and imperfection. But such as it was, it was a faith that stood alone. He that had it was a remarkable man, and far in advance of the age in which he lived.

We should pray frequently that God would raise up more Christians of the stamp of the apostle Peter. Erring, and unstable, and ignorant of his own heart as he sometimes proved, that blessed apostle was in some respects one in ten thousand. He had faith, and zeal, and love to Christ's cause, when almost all Israel was unbelieving and cold. We need more men of this sort. We need men who are not afraid to stand alone, and to cleave to Christ when the many are against Him. Such men, like Peter, may err sadly at times, but in the long run of life will do more good than any. Knowledge, no doubt, is an excellent thing; but knowledge without zeal and warmth will never do much for the world.

Let us notice, thirdly, in this passage, our Lord's prediction of His own coming death. We read that He said, "The Son of Man must suffer many things, and be rejected of the elders, and chief priests, and scribes, and be slain, and be raised the third day." These words, as we read them now, sound simple and plain; but there lie beneath the surface of them two truths which ought to be carefully remembered.

For one thing, our Lord's prediction shows us that His death upon the cross was the voluntary act of His own free will. He was not delivered up to Pilate and crucified because He could not help it, and had no power to crush His enemies. His death was the result of the eternal counsels of the blessed Trinity. He had undertaken to suffer for man's sin, the just for the unjust, that He might bring us to God. He had engaged to bear our sins, as our Substitute and Surety, and He bore them willingly in His own person on the tree. He saw Calvary and the cross before Him all the days of His ministry. He went up to them willingly, knowingly, and with full consent, that He might pay our debts in His own blood. His death was not the death of a mere weak son of man, who could not escape; but the death of One who was very God of very God, and had undertaken to be punished in our stead.

For another thing, our Lord's prediction shows us the blinding effect of PREJUDICE on men's minds. Clear and plain as His words now seem to us, His disciples did not understand them. They heard as though they heard not. They could not understand that Messiah was to be "cut off." They could not receive the doctrine that their own Master must die. And hence, when His death really took place, they were amazed and confounded. Often as He had told them of it, they had never realized it as a fact.

Let us watch and pray against prejudice. Many a zealous man has been grievously misled by it, and has pierced himself through with many sorrows. Let us beware of allowing traditions, old preconceived notions, unsound interpretations, baseless theories in religion, to find root in our hearts. There is but one test of truth "What says the Scripture?" Before this let every prejudice go down.

LUKE 9:23-27

THE TEST OF DISCIPLESHIP

And he said unto all, If any man would come after me, let him deny himself, and take up his cross daily, and follow me. For whosoever would save his life shall lose it; but whosoever shall lose his life for my sake, the same shall save it. For what is a man profited, if he gain the whole world, and lose or forfeit his own self? For whosoever shall be ashamed of me and of my words, of him shall the Son of man be ashamed, when he cometh in his own glory, and the glory of the Father, and of the holy angels. But I tell you of a truth, There are some of them that stand here, who shall in no wise taste of death, till they see the kingdom of God.

These words of our Lord Jesus Christ contain three great lessons for all Christians. They apply to all ranks and classes without exception. They are intended for every age and time, and for every branch of the visible church.

We learn, for one thing, the absolute necessity of daily self-denial. We ought every day to crucify the flesh, to overcome the world, and to resist the devil. We ought to keep under our bodies, and bring them into subjection. We ought to be on our guard, like soldiers in an enemy's country. We ought to fight a daily battle, and war a daily warfare. The command of our Master is clear and plain—"If any man will come after Me, let him deny himself, and take up his cross daily, and follow Me."

Now what do we know of all this? Surely this is a question which ought to be asked. A little formal church-going, and a decent attendance at a place of worship, can never be the Christianity of which Christ speaks in this place. Where is our self-denial? Where is our daily carrying of the cross? Where is our following of Christ? Without a religion of this kind we shall never be saved. A crucified Savior will never be content to have a self-pleasing, self-indulging, worldly-minded people. No self-denial—no real grace! No cross—no crown! "Those who are Christ's," says Paul, "have crucified the flesh with its affections and lusts." (Gal. 5:24.) "Whoever will save his life," says the Lord Jesus, "shall lose it; but whoever will lose his life for My sake shall save it."

We learn, for another thing, from our Lord's words in this passage, the unspeakable value of the soul. A question is asked, which admits of only one answer—"And how do you benefit if you gain the whole world but lose or forfeit your own soul in the process?" The possession of the whole world, and all that it contains, would never make a man happy. Its pleasures are false and deceptive. Its riches, rank, and honors, have no power to satisfy the heart. So long as we have not got them they glitter, and sparkle, and seem desirable. The moment we have them we find that they are empty bubbles, and cannot make us feel content. And, worst of all, when we possess this world's good things, to the utmost bound of our desire, we cannot keep them. Death comes in and separates us from all our property forever. Naked we came upon earth, and naked we go forth, and of all our possessions we can carry nothing with us. Such is the world, which occupies the whole attention of thousands! Such is the world, for the sake of which millions are every year destroying their souls!

The loss of the soul is the heaviest loss that can befall a man. The worst and most painful of diseases—the most distressing bankruptcy of fortune—the most disastrous shipwrecks—are a mere scratch of a pin compared to the loss of a soul. All other losses are bearable, or but for a short time, but the loss of the soul is for evermore. It is to lose God, and Christ, and heaven, and glory, and happiness, to all eternity. It is to be cast away forever, helpless and hopeless in hell!

What are we doing ourselves? Are we losing our souls? Are we, by willful neglect or by open sin—by sheer carelessness and idleness, or deliberate breach of Gods law—compassing our own destruction? These questions demand an answer. The plain account of many professing Christians is this, that they are daily sinning against the sixth commandment. They are murdering their own souls!

We learn, in the last place, from our Lord's words, the guilt and danger of being ashamed of Christ and His words. We read that He says—"Whoever shall be ashamed of Me and My words, of Him shall the Son of Man be ashamed when He shall come in His own glory, and in His Father's, and of the holy angels."

There are many ways of being ashamed of Christ. We are guilty of it whenever we are afraid of letting men know that we love His doctrines, His precepts, His people, and His ordinances. We are guilty of it when ever we allow the fear of man to prevail over us, and to keep us back from letting others see that we are decided Christians. Whenever we act in this way, we are denying our Master, and committing a great sin.

The wickedness of being ashamed of Christ is very great. It is a proof of unbelief. It shows that we care more for the praise of men whom we can see, than that of God whom we cannot see. It is a proof of ingratitude. It shows that we fear confessing Him before man who was not ashamed to die for us upon the cross. Wretched indeed are they who give way to this sin. Here, in this world, they are always miserable. A bad conscience robs them of peace. In the world to come they can look for no comfort. In the day of judgment they must expect to be disowned by Christ to all eternity, if they will not confess Christ for a few years upon earth.

Let us resolve never to be ashamed of Christ. Of sin and worldliness we may well be ashamed. Of Christ and His cause we have no right to be ashamed at all. Boldness in Christ's service always brings its own reward. The boldest Christian is always the happiest man.

LUKE 9:28-36
THE TRANSFIGURATION

And it came to pass about eight days after these sayings, that he took with him Peter and John and James, and went up into the mountain to pray. And as he was praying, the fashion of his countenance was altered, and his raiment became white and dazzling. And behold, there talked with him two men, who were Moses and Elijah; who appeared in glory, and spake of his decease which he was about to accomplish at Jerusalem. Now Peter and they that were with him were heavy with sleep: but when they were fully awake, they saw his glory, and the two men that stood with him. And it came to pass, as they were parting from him, Peter said unto Jesus, Master, it is good for us to be here: and let us make three tabernacles; one for thee, and one for Moses, and one for Elijah: not knowing what he said. And while he said these things, there came a cloud, and overshadowed them: and they feared as they entered into the cloud. And a voice came out of the cloud, saying, This is my Son, my chosen: hear ye him. And when the voice came, Jesus was found alone. And they held their peace, and told no man in those days any of the things which they had seen.

The event described in these verses, commonly called "the transfiguration," is one of the most remarkable in the history of our Lord's earthly ministry. It is one of those passages which we should always read with peculiar thankfulness. It lifts a corner of the veil which hangs over the world to come, and throws light on some of the deepest truths of our religion.

In the first place, this passage shows us something of the glory which Christ will have at His second coming. We read that "the fashion of His countenance was altered, and His clothing was white and glistering," and that the disciples who were with Him "saw His glory."

We need not doubt that this marvelous vision was meant to encourage and strengthen our Lord's disciples. They had just been hearing of the cross and passion, and the self-denial and sufferings to which they must submit themselves, if they would be saved. They were now cheered by a glimpse of the "glory that should follow," and the reward which all faithful servants of their Master would one day receive. They had seen their Master's day of weakness. They now saw, for a few minutes, a pattern and specimen of His future power.

Let us take comfort in the thought, that there are good things laid up in store for all true Christians, which shall make ample amends for the afflictions of this present time. Now is the season for carrying the cross, and sharing in our Savior's humiliation. The crown, the kingdom, the glory, are all yet to come. Christ and His people are now, like David in the cave of Adullam, despised, and lightly esteemed by the world. There seems no form or loveliness in Him, or in His service. But the hour comes, and will soon be here, when Christ shall take to Himself His great power and reign, and put down every enemy under His feet. And then the glory which was first seen for a few minutes, by three witnesses on the Mount of Transfiguration, shall be seen by all the world, and never hidden to all eternity.

In the second place, this passage shows us the safety of all true believers who have been removed from this world. We are told that when our Lord appeared in glory, Moses and Elijah were seen with Him, standing and speaking with Him. Moses had been dead nearly fifteen hundred years. Elijah had been taken up by a whirlwind from the earth more than nine hundred years before this time. Yet here these holy men were seen once more alive, and not only alive, but in glory!

Let us take comfort in the blessed thought that there is a resurrection and a life to come. All is not over, when the last breath is drawn. There is another world beyond the grave. But, above all, let us take comfort in the thought, that until the day dawns, and the resurrection begins, the people of God are safe with Christ. There is much about their present condition, no doubt, which is deeply mysterious. Where is their local habitation? What knowledge have they of things on earth? These are questions we cannot answer. But let it suffice us to know that Jesus is taking care of them, and will bring them with Him at the last day. He showed Moses and Elijah to His disciples on the Mount of Transfiguration, and He will show us all who have fallen asleep in Him, at His second advent. Our brethren and sisters in Christ are in good keeping. They are not lost, but gone before us.

In the third place, this passage shows us that the Old Testament saints in glory take a deep interest in Christ's atoning death. We are told that when Moses and Elijah appeared in glory with our Lord on the Mount of

Transfiguration, they "talked with Him." And what was the subject of their conversation? We are not obliged to make conjectures and guesses about this. Luke tells us, "they spoke of His decease, which He should accomplish at Jerusalem." They knew the meaning of that death. They knew how much depended on it. Therefore they "talked" about it.

It is a grave mistake to suppose that holy men and women under the Old Testament knew nothing about the sacrifice which Christ was to offer up for the sin of the word. Their light, no doubt, was far less clear than ours. They saw things afar off and indistinctly, which we see, as it were, close at hand. But there is not the slightest proof that any Old Testament saint ever looked to any other satisfaction for sin, but that which God promised to make by sending Messiah. From Abel downwards the whole company of old believers appear to have been ever resting on a promised sacrifice, and a blood of almighty efficacy yet to be revealed. From the beginning of the world there has never been but one foundation of hope and peace for sinners—the death of an Almighty Mediator between God and man. That foundation is the center truth of all revealed religion. It was the subject of which Moses and Elijah were seen speaking when they appeared in glory. They spoke of the atoning death of Christ.

Let us take heed that this death of Christ is the ground of all our confidence. Nothing else will give us comfort in the hour of death and the day of judgment. Our own works are all defective and imperfect. Our sins are more in number than the hairs of our heads. (Psalm 40:12.) Christ dying for our sins, and rising again for our justification, must be our only plea, if we wish to be saved. Happy is that man who has learned to cease from his own works, and to glory in nothing but the cross of Christ! If saints in glory see in Christ's death so much beauty, that they must needs talk of it, how much more ought sinners on earth!

In the last place, the passage shows us the immense distance between Christ and all other teachers whom God has given to man. We are told that when Peter, "not knowing what he said," proposed to make three tabernacles on the mount, one for Jesus, one for Moses, and one for Elijah, as if all three deserved equal honor, this proposal was at once rebuked in a remarkable way—"There came a voice out of the cloud, saying, This is my beloved Son, hear Him." That voice was the voice of God the Father, conveying both reproof and instruction. That voice proclaimed to Peter's ear that however great Moses and Elijah might be, there stood One before him far greater than they. They were but servants; He was the King's Son. They were but stars; He was the Sun. They were but witnesses; He was the Truth.

Forever let that solemn word of the Father ring in our ears, and give the keynote to our religion. Let us honor ministers for their Master's sake. Let us follow them so long as they follow Christ. But let it be our principal aim to hear Christ's voice, and follow Him wherever He goes. Let some talk, if they will, of the voice of the Church. Let others be content to say, "I hear this preacher, or that clergyman." Let us never be satisfied unless the Spirit witnesses within us that we hear Christ Himself, and are His disciples.

LUKE 9:37-45
THE HEALING OF A BOY WITH AN EVIL SPIRIT

And it came to pass, on the next day, when they were come down from the mountain, a great multitude met him. And behold, a man from the multitude cried, saying, Teacher, I beseech thee to look upon my son; for he is mine only child: and behold, a spirit taketh him, and he suddenly crieth out; and it teareth him that he foameth, and it hardly departeth from him, bruising him sorely. And I besought thy disciples to cast it out; and they could not. And Jesus answered and said, O faithless and perverse generation, how long shall I be with you, and bear with you? bring hither thy son. And as he was yet a coming, the demon dashed him down, and tare him grievously. But Jesus rebuked the unclean spirit, and healed the boy, and gave him back to his father.

And they were all astonished at the majesty of God. But while all were marvel-ling at all the things which he did, he said unto his disciples, Let these words sink into your ears: for the Son of man shall be delivered up into the hands of men. But they understood not this saying, and it was concealed from them, that they should not perceive it; and they were afraid to ask him about this saying.

The event described in these verses took place immediately after the transfiguration. The Lord Jesus, we should remark, did not tarry long on the Mount of Olives. His communion with Moses and Elijah was very short. He soon returned to His accustomed work of doing good to a sin-stricken world. In His life on earth, to receive honor and have visions of glory was the exception. To minister to others, to heal all who were oppressed by the devil, to do acts of mercy to sinners, was the rule. Happy are those Christians who have learned of Jesus to live for others more than for themselves, and who understand that it is "more blessed to give than to receive." (Acts 20:35.)

We have first, in these verses, an example of what a parent should do when he is troubled about his children. We are told of a man in severe distress about his only son. This son was possessed by an evil spirit, and grievously tormented by him, both in body and soul. In his distress the father makes application to our Lord Jesus Christ for relief. "Master," he says, "I beseech You, look upon my son—for he is my only child."

There are many Christian fathers and mothers at this day who are just as miserable about their children as the man of whom we are reading. The son who was once the "desire of their eyes," and in whom their lives were bound up, turns out a spendthrift, a profligate, and a companion of sinners. The daughter who was once the flower of the family, and of whom they said, "This girl shall be the comfort of our old age," becomes self-willed, worldly minded, and a lover of pleasure more than a lover of God. Their hearts are well near broken. The iron seems to enter into their souls. The devil appears to triumph over them, and rob them of their choicest jewels. They are ready to cry, "I shall go to the grave sorrowing. What good shall my life do to me?"

Now what should a father or mother do in a case like this? They should do as the man before us did. They should go to Jesus in prayer, and cry to Him about their child. They should spread before that merciful Savior the tale of their sorrows, and entreat Him to help them. Great is the power of prayer and intercession! The child of many prayers shall seldom be cast away. God's time of conversion may not be ours. He may think fit to prove our faith by keeping us long waiting. But so long as a child lives, and a parent prays, we have no right to despair about that child's soul.

We have, secondly, in these verses, an example of Christ's readiness to show mercy to young people. We are told in the case before us, that the prayer of the afflicted parent was graciously granted. He said to him, "Bring your son here." And then "He rebuked the unclean spirit, and healed the child, and delivered him again to his father." We have many similar cases in the Gospels. The daughter of Jairus, the nobleman's son at Capernaum, the daughter of the Canaanitish woman, the widow's son at Nain, are all instances of our Lord's interest in those who are young. The young are exactly those whom the devil labors to lead captive and make His own. The young seem to have been exactly the people whom our Lord took a special delight in helping. Three He plucked out of the very jaws of death. Two, as in the case before us, He rescued from the complete dominion of the devil.

There is a meaning in facts like these. They are not recorded without a special purpose. They are meant to encourage all who try to do good to the souls of the young. They are meant to remind us that young men and young women are special objects of interest to Christ. They supply us with an antidote to the common idea that it is useless to press religion on the attention of young people. Such an idea, let us remember, comes from the devil and not from Christ. He who cast out the evil spirit from the child before us, still lives, and is still mighty to save. Let us then work on, and try to do good to the young. Whatever the world may think, Jesus is well pleased.

We have, lastly, in these verses, an example of the spiritual ignorance which may be found even in the hearts of good men. We are told that our Lord said to His disciples, "The Son of man shall be delivered into the hands of men." They had heard the same thing from His lips little more than a week before. But now, as then, the words seemed lost upon them. They heard as though they heard not. They could not realize the fact that their Master was to die. They could not realize the great truth that Christ was to be "cut off" before He was to reign, and that this cutting off was a literal death upon the cross. It is written, "They understood not this saying"—"it was hidden from them," they perceived it not."

Such slowness of understanding may surprise us much at this period of the world. We are apt to forget the power of early habits of thought, and national prejudices, in the midst of which the disciples had been trained. "The throne of David," says a great divine, "did so fill their eyes that they could not see the cross." Above all, we forget the enormous difference between the position we occupy who know the history of the crucifixion and the Scriptures which it fulfilled, and the position of a believing Jew who lived before Christ died and the veil was rent in twain. Whatever we may think of it, the ignorance of the disciples should teach us two useful lessons, which we shall all do well to learn.

For one thing, let us learn that men may understand spiritual things very feebly, and yet be true children of God. The head may be very dull when the heart is right. Grace is far better than gifts, and faith than knowledge. If a man has faith and grace enough to give up all for Christ's sake, and to take up the cross and follow Him, he shall be saved in spite of much ignorance. Christ shall own him at the last day.

Finally, let us learn to bear with ignorance in others, and to deal patiently with beginners in religion. Let us not make men offenders for a word. Let us not set our brother down as having no grace, because he does not exhibit clear knowledge. Has he faith in Christ? Does he love Christ? These are the principal things. If Jesus could endure so much weakness in His disciples, we may surely do likewise.

LUKE 9:46-50

WHO WILL BE THE GREATEST

And there arose a reasoning among them, which of them was the greatest. But when Jesus saw the reasoning of their heart, he took a little child, and set him by his side, and said unto them, Whosoever shall receive this little child in my name receiveth me: and whosoever shall receive me receiveth him that sent me: for he that is least among you all, the same is great. And John answered and said, Master, we saw one casting out demons in thy name; and we forbade him, because he followeth not with us. But Jesus said unto him, Forbid him not: for he that is not against you is for you.

The verses we have now read contain two most important warnings. They are directed against two of the commonest evils which are to be found in the Church of Christ. He who gave them knew well what was in the heart of man. Well would it have been for the Church of Christ, if His words in this passage had received more attention!

In the first place, the Lord Jesus gives us a warning against pride and self-conceit. We are told that "there arose a reasoning among the disciples which of them should be the greatest." Astonishing as it may seem, this little company of fishermen and publicans was not beyond the plague of a self-seeking and ambitious spirit. Filled with the vain notion that our Lord's kingdom was to appear immediately, they were ready to wrangle about their place and precedency in it. Each thought his own claim the strongest. Each thought his own deserts and right to honor most unquestionable. Each thought that whatever place was assigned to his brethren, a principal place ought to be assigned to himself. And all this happened in the company of Christ Himself, and under the noon-tide blaze of His teaching. Such is the heart of man.

There is something very instructive in this fact. It ought to sink down deeply into the heart of every Christian reader. Of all sins there is none against which we have such need to watch and pray, as pride. It is a pestilence that walks in darkness, and a sickness that destroys at noon-day. No sin is so deeply rooted in our nature. It cleaves to us like our skin. Its roots never entirely die. They are ready, at any moment, to spring up, and exhibit a most pernicious vitality. No sin is so senseless and deceitful. It can wear the garb of humility itself. It can lurk in the hearts of the ignorant, the ungifted, and the poor, as well as in the minds of the great, the learned, and the rich. It is a quaint and homely saying, but only too true, that no pope has ever received such honor as pope "self."

Let a prayer for humility and the spirit of a little child, form part of our daily supplications. Of all creatures none has so little right to be proud as man, and of all men none ought to be so humble as the Christian. Is it really true that we confess ourselves to be "miserable sinners," and daily debtors to mercy and grace? Are we the followers of Jesus, who was "meek and lowly of heart," and "made himself of no reputation" for our sakes? Then let that same mind be in us which was in Christ Jesus. Let us lay aside all high thoughts and self-conceit. In lowliness of mind, let us esteem others better than ourselves. Let us be ready, on all occasions, to take the lowest place. And let the words of our Savior ring in our ears continually, "He that is least among you all the same shall be great."

In the second place, our Lord Jesus Christ gives us a warning against a bigoted and illiberal spirit. As in the preceding verses, so here, the occasion of the warning is supplied by the conduct of His own disciples. We read that John said to Him, "Master, we saw one casting out devils in your name—and we forbade him, because he follows not with us." Who this man was, and why he did not associate with the disciples, we do not know. But we do know that he was doing a good work in casting out devils, and that he was doing what he did in the name of Christ. And yet John says, "we forbade him." Very striking is the reply which the Lord at once gave him—"Forbid him not—for he that is not against us is for us."

The conduct of John and the disciples on this occasion is a curious illustration of the sameness of human nature, in every age. Thousands, in every period of Church history, have spent their lives in copying John's mistake. They have labored to stop every man who will not work for Christ in their way, from working for Christ at all. They have imagined, in their petty self-conceit, that no man can be a soldier of Christ, unless he wears their uniform, and fights in their regiment. They have been ready to say of every Christian who does not see everything with their eyes, "Forbid him! Forbid him! for he follows not with us."

The solemn remark of our Lord Jesus Christ, on this occasion, demands our special notice. He pronounces no opinion upon the conduct of the man of whom John speaks. He neither praises nor blames him for following an independent course, and not working with His disciples. He simply declares that he must not be forbidden, and that those who work the same kind of work that we do, should be regarded not as enemies, but allies. "He that is not against us is for us."

The principle laid down in this passage is of great importance. A right understanding of it will prove most useful to us in these latter days. The divisions and varieties of opinion which exist among Christians are undeniably very great. The schisms and separations which are continually arising about Church-government, and modes of worship, are very perplexing to tender consciences. Shall we approve those divisions? We cannot do so. Union is strength. The disunion of Christians is one cause of the slow progress of vital Christianity. Shall we denounce, and hold up to public reprobation, all who will not agree to work with us, and to oppose Satan in our way? It is useless to do so. Hard words never yet made men of one mind. Unity was never yet brought about by force. What then ought we to do? We must leave alone those who do not agree with us, and wait quietly until God shall think fit to bring us together. Whatever we may think of our divisions, the words of our Lord must never be forgotten—"Forbid them not."

The plain truth is, that we are all too ready to say, "We are the men, and wisdom shall die with us." (Job 12:2.) We forget that no individual Church on earth has an absolute monopoly of all wisdom, and that people may be right in the main, without agreeing with us. We must learn to be thankful if sin is opposed, and the Gospel preached, and the devil's kingdom pulled down, though the work may not be done exactly in the way we like. We must try to believe that men may be true-hearted followers of Jesus Christ, and yet for some wise reason may be kept back from seeing all things in religion just as we do. Above all, we must praise God if souls are converted, and Christ is magnified—no matter who the preacher may be, and to what Church he may belong. Happy are those who can say with Paul, "If Christ be preached, I rejoice, yes and will rejoice," (Phil. 1:18.) and with Moses, "Are you jealous for my sake? I wish that all the Lord's people were prophets, and that the Lord would put his Spirit upon them all!" (Num. 11:29.)

LUKE 9:51-56

SAMARITAN OPPOSITION

And it came to pass, when the days were well-nigh come that he should be received up, he stedfastly set his face to go to Jerusalem, and sent messengers before his face: and they went, and entered into a village of the Samaritans, to make ready for him. And they did not receive him, because his face was as though he were going to Jerusalem. And when his disciples James and John saw this, they said, Lord, wilt thou that we bid fire to come down from heaven, and consume them? But he turned, and rebuked them. And they went to another village.

Let us notice in these verses, the steady determination with which our Lord Jesus Christ regarded His own crucifixion and death. We read that "when the time was come that He should be received up, He steadfastly set His face to go to Jerusalem." He knew full well what was before Him. The betrayal, the unjust trial, the mockery, the scourging, the crown of thorns, the spitting, the nails, the spear, the agony on the cross—all, all were doubtless spread before His mind's eye, like a picture. But He never flinched for a moment from the work that He had undertaken. His heart was set on paying the price of our redemption, and going even to the prison of the grave, as our surety. He was full of tender love towards sinners. It was the desire of His whole soul to procure for them salvation. And so, "for the joy set before Him, He endured the cross, despising the shame." (Heb. 12:2.)

Forever let us bless God that we have such a ready and willing Savior. Forever let us remember that as He was ready to suffer, so He is always ready to save. The man that comes to Christ by faith should never doubt Christ's willingness to receive Him. The mere fact that the Son of God willingly came into the world to die, and willingly suffered, should silence such doubts entirely. All the unwillingness is on the part of man, not of Christ. It consists in the ignorance, and pride, and unbelief, and half-heartedness of the sinner himself. But there is nothing lacking in Christ.

Let us strive and pray that the same mind may be in us which was in our blessed Master. Like Him, let us be willing to go anywhere, do anything, suffer anything when the path of duty is clear, and the voice of God calls. Let us set our faces steadfastly to our work, when our work is plainly marked out, and drink our bitter cups patiently, when they come from a Father's hand.

Let us notice, secondly, in these verses, the unusual conduct of two of the apostles, James and John. We are told that a certain Samaritan village refused to show hospitality to our Lord. "They did not receive him, because his face was as though he would go to Jerusalem." And then we read of a strange proposal which James and John made. "They said, Lord, do you want us to command fire to come down from heaven and consume them, even as Elijah did?"

Here was zeal indeed, and zeal of a most plausible kind—zeal for the honor of Christ! Here was zeal, justified and supported by a scriptural example, and that the example of no less a prophet than Elijah! But it was not a zeal according to knowledge. The two disciples, in their heat, forgot that circumstances alter cases, and that the same action which may be right and justifiable at one time, may be wrong and unjustifiable at another. They forgot that punishments should always be proportioned to offences, and that to destroy a whole village of ignorant people for a single act of discourtesy, would have been both unjust and cruel. In short, the proposal of James and John was a wrong and inconsiderate one. They meant well, but they greatly erred.

Facts like this in the Gospels are carefully recorded for our learning. Let us see to it that we mark them well, and treasure them up in our minds. It is possible to have much zeal for Christ, and yet to exhibit it in most unholy and unchristian ways. It is possible to mean well and have good intentions, and yet to make most grievous mistakes in our actions. It is possible to imagine that we have Scripture on our side, and to support our conduct by scriptural quotations, and yet to commit serious errors. It is as clear as daylight, from this and other cases related in the Bible, that it is not enough to be zealous and well-meaning. Very grave faults are frequently committed with good intentions. From no quarter perhaps has the Church received so much injury as from ignorant but well-meaning men.

We must seek to have knowledge as well as zeal. Zeal without knowledge is an army without a general, and a ship without a rudder. We must pray that we may understand how to make a right application of Scripture. The word is no doubt "a light to our feet, and a lantern to our path." But it must be the word rightly handled, and properly applied.

Let us notice, lastly, in these verses, what a solemn rebuke our Lord gives to persecution carried on under color of religion. We are told that when James and John made the strange proposal on which we have just been dwelling, "He turned and rebuked them, and said, You know not what manner of spirit you are of. For the Son of man is not come to destroy men's lives, but to save them." Uncourteous as the Samaritan villagers had been, their conduct was not to be resented by violence. The mission of the Son of man was to do good, when men would receive Him, but never to do harm. His kingdom was to be extended by patient continuance in well doing, and by meekness and gentleness in suffering, but never by violence and severity.

No saying of our Lord's, perhaps, has been so totally overlooked by the Church of Christ as that which is now before us. Nothing can be imagined more contrary to the will of Christ than the religious wars and persecutions which disgrace the annals of Church history. Thousands and tens of thousands have been put to death for their religion's sake all over the world. Thousands have been burned, or shot, or hanged, or drowned, or beheaded, in the name of the Gospel, and those who have slain them have actually believed that they were doing God service! Unhappily, they have only shown their own ignorance of the spirit of the Gospel, and the mind of Christ.

Let it be a settled principle in our minds, that whatever men's errors may be in religion, we must never persecute them. Let us, if needful, argue with them, reason with them, and try to show them a more excellent way. But let us never take up the "carnal" weapon to promote the spread of truth. Let us never be tempted, directly or indirectly, to persecute any man, under pretense of the glory of Christ and the good of the Church. Let us rather remember, that the religion which men profess from fear of death, or dread of penalties, is worth nothing at all, and that if we swell our ranks by fear and threatening, in reality we gain no strength. "The weapons of our warfare," says Paul, "are not carnal." (2 Cor. 10:4.) The appeals that we make must be to men's consciences and wills. The arguments that we use must not be sword, or fire, or prison, but doctrines, and precepts, and texts. It is a quaint and homely saying, but as true in the Church as it is in the army, that "one volunteer is worth ten men who have been pressed into service."

LUKE 9:57-62

THE COST OF FOLLOWING JESUS

And as they went on the way, a certain man said unto him, I will follow thee whithersoever thou goest. And Jesus said unto him, The foxes have holes, and the birds of the heaven have nests; but the Son of man hath not where to lay his head. And he said unto another, Follow me. But he said, Lord, suffer me first to go and bury my father. But he said unto him, Leave the dead to bury their own dead; but go thou and publish abroad the kingdom of God. And another also said, I will follow thee, Lord; but first suffer me to bid farewell to them that are at my house.

But Jesus said unto him, No man, having put his hand to the plow, and looking back, is fit for the kingdom of God.

The passage of Scripture we have just read is a very remarkable one. It contains three short sayings of peculiar solemnity, addressed by our Lord Jesus Christ to three different people. We know nothing of the names of those people. We know nothing of the effect which our Lord's words produced upon them. But we need not doubt that each was addressed in the way which his character required, and we may be sure that the passage is specially intended to promote self-inquiry.

The first of these sayings was addressed to one who offered to be a disciple unconditionally, and of his own accord. "Lord," said this man, "I will follow you wherever you go"—That offer sounded well. It was a step in advance of many. Thousands of people heard our Lord's sermons who never thought of saying what this man said. Yet he who made this offer was evidently speaking without thought. He had never considered what belonged to discipleship. He had never counted the cost. And hence he needed the grave reply which his offer called forth—"Foxes have holes, and birds of the air have nests, but the Son of man has not where to lay his head." He must weigh well what he was taking in hand. He must not suppose that Christ's service was all pleasure and smooth sailing. Was he prepared for this? Was he ready to "endure hardness?" (2 Tim. 2:3.) If not, he had better withdraw his application to be a disciple.

Let us learn from our Lord's words on this occasion, that He would have all who profess and call themselves Christians reminded that they must carry the cross. They must lay their account to be despised, and afflicted, and tried, like their Master. He would have no man enlisted on false pretenses. He would have it distinctly understood that there is a battle to be fought, and a race to be run—a work to be done, and many hard things to be endured—if we propose to follow Him. Salvation He is ready to bestow, without money and without price. Grace by the way, and glory in the end, shall be given to every sinner who comes to Him. But He would not have us ignorant that we shall have deadly enemies—the world, the flesh, and the devil, and that many will hate us, slander us, and persecute us, if we become His disciples. He does not wish to discourage us, but He does wish us to know the truth.

Well would it have been for the Church if our Lord's warning had been more frequently pondered! Many a man begins a religious life, full of warmth and zeal, and by and bye loses all his first love, and turns back again to the world. He liked the new uniform, and the bounty money, and the name of a Christian soldier. He never considered the watching, and warring, and wounds, and conflicts, which Christian soldiers must endure. Let us never forget this lesson. It need not make us afraid to begin serving Christ, but it ought to make us begin carefully, humbly, and with much prayer for grace. If we are not ready to take part in the afflictions of Christ, we must never expect to share His glory.

The second of our Lord's sayings is addressed to one whom Jesus invited to follow Him. The answer He received was a very remarkable one. "Lord," said the man, "allow me first to go and bury my father." The thing he requested was in itself harmless. But the time at which the request was made was unseasonable. Affairs of far greater importance than even a father's funeral demanded the man's immediate attention. There would always be plenty of people ready and fit to take charge of a funeral. But there was at that moment a pressing need of laborers to do Christ's work in the world. And hence the man's request drew from our Lord the solemn reply—"Let the dead bury their dead, but you go and preach the kingdom of God."

Let us learn, from this saying, to beware of allowing family and social duties to interfere with our duty to Christ. Funerals, and marriages, and visits of courtesy, and the like, unquestionably are not in themselves sinful. But when they are allowed to absorb a believer's time, and keep him back from any plain religious duty, they become a snare to his soul. That the children of the world, and the unconverted, should allow these kind of things to occupy all their time and thoughts is not astonishing. They know nothing higher, and better, and more important. "Let the dead bury their dead." But the heirs of glory, and children of the King of kings, should be men of a different stamp. They should declare plainly, by their conduct, that the world to come is the great reality which fills their thoughts. They should not be ashamed to let men see that they have no time either to rejoice or to sorrow like others who have no hope. (1 Thess. 4:13.) Their Master's work waits for them, and their Master's work must have the chief place in their hearts. They are God's priests in the world, and, like the priests of old, their mourning must be kept carefully within bounds, (Lev. 21:1.) "Weeping," says an old divine, "must not hinder working," and mourning must not be allowed to run into excess.

The third of our Lord's sayings in this passage was addressed to one who volunteered to follow Him, but marred the grace of His offer by interposing a request. "Lord," he said, "I will follow you; but let me first go bid them farewell which are at home at my house." The answer he received shows plainly that the man's heart was not yet thoroughly engaged in Christ's service, and that he was therefore unfit to be a disciple. "Jesus said unto him, No man having put his hand to the plough, and looking back, is fit for the kingdom of God."

We learn from this saying that it is impossible to serve Christ with a divided heart. If we are looking back to anything in this world we are not fit to be disciples. Those who look back, like Lot's wife, want to go back. Jesus will not share His throne with anyone—no, not with our dearest relatives. He must have all our heart, or none. No doubt we are to honor father and mother, and love all around us. But when love to Christ and love to relatives come in collision, Christ must have the preference. We must be ready, like Abraham, if needs be, to come out from kindred and father's house for Christ's sake. We must be prepared in case of necessity, like Moses, to turn our backs even on those who have brought us up, if God calls us, and the path is plain.

Such decided conduct may entail sore trials on our affections. It may crush our hearts to go contrary to the opinions of those we love. But such conduct may sometimes be positively necessary to our salvation, and without it, when it becomes necessary, we are unfit for the kingdom of God. The good soldier will not allow his heart to be entangled too much with his home. If he daily gives way to unmanly repinings about those he has left behind him, he will never be fit for a campaign. His present duties—the watching, the marching, the fighting—must have the principal place in his thoughts. So must it be with all who would serve Christ. They must beware of softness spoiling their characters as Christians. They must endure hardness, as good soldiers of Jesus Christ. (2 Tim. 2:3.)

Let us leave the whole passage with many searchings of heart. The times are undoubtedly much changed since our Lord spoke these words. Not many are called to make such real sacrifices for Christ's sake as when Christ was upon earth. But the heart of man never changes. The difficulties of salvation are still very great. The atmosphere of the world is still very unfavorable to spiritual religion. There is still need for thorough, unflinching, whole-hearted decision, if we would reach heaven. Let us aim at nothing less than this decision, Let us be willing to do anything, and suffer anything, and give up everything for Christ's sake. It may cost us something for a few years, but great will be the reward in eternity.

Chapter 10

*N*ow after these things the Lord appointed seventy others, and sent them two and two before his face into every city and place, whither he himself was about to come. And he said unto them, The harvest indeed is plenteous, but the laborers are few: pray ye therefore the Lord of the harvest, that he send forth laborers into his harvest. Go your ways; behold, I send you forth as lambs in the midst of wolves. Carry no purse, no wallet, no shoes; and salute no man on the way. And into whatsoever house ye shall enter, first say, Peace be to this house. And if a son of peace be there, your peace shall rest upon him: but if not, it shall turn to you again. And in that same house remain, eating and drinking such things as they give: for the laborer is worthy of his hire. Go not from house to house.*

The verses before us relate a circumstance which is not recorded by any Gospel writer except Luke. That circumstance is our Lord's appointment of seventy disciples to go before Him, in addition to the twelve apostles. We do not know the names of any of these disciples. Their subsequent history has not been revealed to us. But the instructions with which they are sent forth are deeply interesting, and deserve the close attention of all ministers and teachers of the Gospel.

The first point in our Lord's charge to the seventy disciples is the importance of prayer and intercession. This is the leading thought with which our Lord opens His address. Before He tells His ambassadors what to do,

He first bids them to pray. "Ask the Lord of the harvest that He would send forth laborers into his harvest."

Prayer is one of the best and most powerful means of helping forward the cause of Christ in the world. It is a means within the reach of all who have the Spirit of adoption. Not all believers have money to give to missions. Very few have great intellectual gifts, or extensive influence among men. But all believers can pray for the success of the Gospel—and they ought to pray for it daily. Many and marvelous are the answers to prayer which are recorded for our learning in the Bible. "The effectual fervent prayer of a righteous man avails much." (James 5:16.) Prayer is one of the principal weapons which the minister of the Gospel ought to use. To be a true successor of the apostles, he must give himself to prayer as well as to the ministry of the word. (Acts 6:4.) He must not only use the sword of the Spirit, but pray always, with all prayer and supplication. (Eph. 6:17,18.) This is the way to win a blessing on his own ministry. This, above all, is the way to procure helpers to carry on Christ's work. Colleges may educate men. Bishops may ordain them. Patrons may give them livings. But God alone can raise up and send forth "laborers" who will do work among souls. For a constant supply of such laborers let us daily pray.

The second point in our Lord's charge to the seventy disciples, is the perilous nature of the work in which they were about to be engaged. He does not keep back from them the dangers and trials which are before them. He does not enlist them under false pretenses, or prophesy smooth things, or promise them unvarying success. He tells them plainly what they must expect. "Behold," He says, "I send you forth as lambs among wolves."

These words, no doubt, had a special reference to the life-time of those to whom they were spoken. We see their fulfillment in the many persecutions described in the Acts of the Apostles. But we must not conceal from ourselves that the words describe a state of things which may be seen at this very day. So long as the Church stands believers must expect to be like "lambs among wolves." They must make up their minds to be hated, and persecuted, and ill-treated, by those who have no real religion. They must look for no favor from unconverted people, for they will find none. It was a strong but a true saying of Martin Luther, that "Cain will murder Abel, if he can, to the very end of the world." "Marvel not," says John, "if the world hates you." "All that will live godly in Jesus Christ," says Paul, "shall suffer persecution." (1 John 3:13; 2 Tim. 3:12.)

The third point in our Lord's charge to the seventy disciples is, the thorough devotion to their work which He enjoined upon them. They were to abstain even from the appearance of covetousness, or love of money, or luxury—"Carry neither purse, nor bag, nor shoes." They were to behave like men who had no time to waste on the empty compliments and conventional courtesies of the world—"Salute no man by the way."

These remarkable words must, doubtless be interpreted with some qualification. The time came when our Lord Himself, at the end of His ministry, said to the disciples, "He that has a purse let him take it, and likewise his bag." (Luke 22:36.) The apostle Paul was not ashamed to use salutations. The apostle Peter expressly commands us to "be courteous." (1 Pet. 3:8.) But still, after every deduction and qualification, there remains a deep lesson beneath these words of our Lord, which ought not to be overlooked. They teach us that ministers and teachers of the Gospel should beware of allowing the world to eat up their time and thoughts, and to hinder them in their spiritual work. They teach us that care about money, and excessive attention to what are called "the courtesies of life," are mighty snares in the way of Christ's laborers, and snares into which they must take heed lest they fall.

Let us consider these things. They concern ministers especially, but they concern all Christians more or less. Let us strive to show the men of the world that we have no time for their mode of living. Let us show them that we find life too precious to be spent in perpetual feasting, and visiting, and calling, and the like, as if there were no death, or judgment, or life to come. By all means let us be courteous. But let us not make the courtesies of life an idol, before which everything else must bow down. Let us declare plainly that we seek a country beyond the grave, and that we have no time for that incessant round of eating, and drinking, and dressing, and civility, and exchange of compliments, in which so many try to find their happiness, but evidently try in vain. Let our principle be that of Nehemiah, "I am doing a great work, so that I cannot come down." (Neh. 6:3.)

The fourth point in our Lord's charge to the seventy disciples is the simpleminded and contented spirit which He bade them to exhibit. Wherever they tarried, in traveling about upon their Master's business, they were to avoid the appearance of being fickle, changeable, delicate livers, or hard to please about food and lodging. They were to "eat and drink such things" as were given them. They were not to "go from house to house."

Instructions like these no doubt have a primary and special reference to the ministers of the Gospel. They are the men above all who, in their style of living, ought to be careful to avoid the spirit of the world. Simplicity in food and household arrangements, and readiness to put up with any accommodation, so long as health can be preserved uninjured, should always be the mark of the "man of God." Once let a preacher get the reputation of being fond of eating and drinking and worldly comforts, and his ministerial usefulness is at an end. The sermon about "things unseen" will produce little effect when the life preaches the importance of the "things that are seen."

But we ought not to confine our Lord's instructions to ministers alone. They ought to speak loudly to the consciences of all believers, of all who are called by the Holy Spirit and made priests to God. They ought to remind us of the necessity of simplicity and unworldliness in our daily life. We must beware of thinking too much about our meals, and our furniture, and our houses, and all those many things which concern the life of the body. We must strive to live like men whose first thoughts are about the immortal soul. We must endeavor to pass through the world like men who are not yet at home, and are not overmuch troubled about the fare they meet with on the road and at the inn. Blessed are they who feel like pilgrims and strangers in this life, and whose best things are all to come!

LUKE 10:8-16

And into whatsoever city ye enter, and they receive you, eat such things as are set before you: and heal the sick that are therein, and say unto them, The kingdom of God is come nigh unto you. But into whatsoever city ye shall enter, and they receive you not, go out into the streets thereof and say, Even the dust from your city, that cleaveth to our feet, we wipe off against you: nevertheless know this, that the kingdom of God is come nigh. I say unto you, it shall be more tolerable in that day for Sodom, than for that city. Woe unto thee, Chorazin! woe unto thee, Bethsaida! for if the mighty works had been done in Tyre and Sidon, which were done in you, they would have repented long ago, sitting in sackcloth and ashes. But it shall be more tolerable for Tyre and Sidon in the judgment, than for you. And thou, Capernaum, shalt thou be exalted unto heaven? thou shalt be brought down unto Hades. He that heareth you heareth me; and he that rejecteth you rejecteth me; and he that rejecteth me rejecteth him that sent me.

These verses comprise the second part of our Lord Jesus Christ's charge to the seventy disciples. Its lessons, like those of the first part, have a special reference to ministers and teachers of the Gospel. But they contain truths which deserve the serious attention of all members of the Church of Christ.

The first point we should notice in these verses is the simplicity of the tidings which our Lord commanded some of His first messengers to proclaim. We read that they were commissioned to say, "The kingdom of God is come near unto you."

These words we should probably regard as the key-note to all that the seventy disciples said. We can hardly suppose that they said nothing else but this single sentence. The words no doubt implied far more to a Jewish hearer at the time when they were spoken, than they convey to our minds at the present day. To a well instructed Israelite, they would sound like an announcement that the times of Messiah had come—that the long promised Savior was about to be revealed—that the "desire of all nations" was about to appear. (Hag. 2:7.) All this is unquestionably true. Such an announcement suddenly made by seventy men, evidently convinced of the truth of what they said, traveling over a thickly peopled country, could hardly fail to draw attention and excite inquiry. But still the message is peculiarly and strikingly simple.

It may be doubted whether the modern way of teaching Christianity, as a general rule, is sufficiently simple. It is a certain fact that deep reasoning and elaborate arguments are not the weapons by which God is generally pleased to convert souls. Simple plain statements, boldly and solemnly made, and made in such a manner that they are evidently felt and believed by him who makes them, seem to have the most effect on hearts and consciences. Parents and teachers of the young, ministers and missionaries, Scripture readers and district visitors, would all do well to remember this. We need not be so anxious as we often are about fencing, and proving, and demonstrating, and reasoning, out the doctrines of the Gospel. Not one soul in a hundred was ever brought to Christ in this fashion. We need more simple, plain, solemn, earnest, affectionate statements of simple Gospel truths. We may safely leave such statements to work and take care of themselves. They are arrows from God's own quiver, and will often pierce hearts which have not been touched by the most eloquent sermon.

The second point we should notice in these verses is the great sinfulness of those who reject the offers of Christ's Gospel. Our Lord declares that it shall be "more tolerable at the last day for Sodom," than for those who receive not the message of His disciples. And He proceeds to say that the guilt of Chorazin and Bethsaida, cities in Galilee, where He had often preached and worked miracles, but where the people had nevertheless not repented, was greater than the guilt of Tyre and Sidon.

Declarations like these are peculiarly dreadful. They throw light on some truths which men are very apt to forget. They teach us that all will be judged according to their spiritual light, and that from those who have enjoyed most religious privileges, most will be required. They teach us the exceeding hardness and unbelief of the human heart. It was possible to hear Christ preach, and to see Christ's miracles, and yet to remain unconverted. They teach us, not least, that man is responsible for the state of his own soul. Those who reject the Gospel, and remain impenitent and unbelieving, are not merely objects of pity and compassion, but deeply guilty and blameworthy in God's sight. God called, but they refused. God spoke to them, but they would not regard. The condemnation of the unbelieving will be strictly just. Their blood will be upon their own heads. The Judge of all the earth will do right.

Let us lay these things to heart, and beware of unbelief. It is not open sin and flagrant profligacy alone which ruin souls. We have only to sit still and do nothing, when the Gospel is pressed on our acceptance, and we shall find ourselves one day in the pit. We need not run into any excess of riot. We need openly oppose true religion. We have only to remain cold, careless, indifferent, unmoved, and unaffected, and our end will be in hell. This was the ruin of Chorazin and Bethsaida. And this, it may be feared, will be the ruin of thousands, as long as the world stands. No sin makes less noise, but none so surely damns the soul, as unbelief.

The last point that we should notice in these verses is the honor which the Lord Jesus is pleased to put upon His faithful ministers. We see this brought out in the words with which He concludes His charge to the seventy disciples. He says to them, "He that hears you hears me, and he that despises you despises me, and he that despises me despises Him that sent me."

The language here used by our Lord is very remarkable, and the more so when we remember that it was addressed to the seventy disciples, and not to the twelve apostles. The lesson it is intended to convey is clear and unmistakable. It teaches us that ministers are to be regarded as Christ's messengers and ambassadors to a sinful world. So long as they do their work faithfully, they are worthy of honor and respect for their Master's sake. Those who despise them, are not despising them so much as their Master. Those who reject the terms of salvation which they are commissioned to proclaim, are doing an injury not so much to them as to their King. When Hanun, king of Ammon, ill-used the ambassadors of David, the insult was resented as if it had been done to David himself. (2 Sam. 10:1-19.)

Let us remember these things, in order that we may form a right estimate of the position of a minister of the Gospel. The subject is one on which error abounds. On the one side the minister's office is regarded with idolatrous and superstitious reverence. On the other side it is often regarded with ignorant contempt. Both extremes are wrong. Both errors arise from forgetfulness of the plain teaching of Scripture. The minister who does not do Christ's work faithfully, or deliver Christ's message correctly, has no right to look for the respect of the people.

But the minister who declares all the counsel of God, and keeps back nothing that is profitable, is one whose words cannot be disregarded without great sin. He is on the King's business. He is a herald. He is an ambassador. He is the bearer of a flag of truce. He brings the glad tidings of terms off peace. To such a man the words of our Lord will prove strictly applicable. The rich may trample on him. The wicked may hate him. The pleasure-lover may be annoyed at him. The covetous may be vexed by him. But he may take comfort daily in His Master's words, "He that despises you despises me." The last day will prove that these words were not spoken in vain.

LUKE 10:17-20

And the seventy returned with joy, saying, Lord, even the demons are subject unto us in thy name. And he said unto them, I beheld Satan fallen as lightning from heaven. Behold, I have given you authority to tread upon serpents and scorpions, and over all the power of the enemy: and nothing shall in any wise hurt you. Nevertheless in this rejoice not, that the spirits are subject unto you; but rejoice that your names are written in heaven.

We learn, from this passage, how ready Christians are to be puffed up with success. It is written, that the seventy returned from their first mission with joy, "saying, Lord, even the devils are subject unto us through your name." There was much false fire in that joy. There was evidently self-satisfaction in that report of achievements. The whole tenor of the passage leads us to this conclusion. The remarkable expression which our Lord uses about Satan's fall from heaven, was most probably meant to be a caution. He read the hearts of the young and inexperienced soldiers before Him. He saw how much they were lifted up by their first victory. He wisely checks them in their undue exultation. He warns there against pride.

The lesson is one which all who work for Christ should mark and remember. Success is what all faithful laborers in the Gospel field desire. The minister at home and the missionary abroad, the district visitor and the city missionary, the tract distributor and the Sunday-school teacher, all alike long for success. All long to see Satan's kingdom pulled down, and souls converted to God. We cannot wonder. The desire is right and good.

Let it, however, never be forgotten, that the time of success is a time of danger to the Christian's soul. The very hearts that are depressed when all things seem against them are often unduly exalted in the day of prosperity. Few men are like Samson, and can kill a lion without telling others of it. (Judges 14:6.) No wonder that Paul says of a bishop, that he ought not to be "a novice, lest being lifted up with pride, he fall into the condemnation of the devil." (1 Tim. 3:6.) Most of Christ's laborers probably have as much success as their souls can bear.

Let us pray much for humility, and especially for humility in our days of peace and success. When everything around us seems to prosper, and all our plans work well—when family trials and sicknesses are kept from us, and the course of our worldly affairs runs smooth—when our daily crosses are light, and all within and without like a morning without clouds—then, then is the time when our souls are in danger! Then is the time when we have need to be doubly watchful over our own hearts. Then is the time when seeds of evil are sown within us by the devil, which may one day astound as by their growth and strength.

There are few Christians who can carry a full cup with a steady hand. There are few whose souls prosper in their days of uninterrupted success. We are all inclined to sacrifice to our net, and burn incense to our own drag. (Hab. 1:16.) We are ready to think that our own might and our own wisdom have procured us the victory. The caution of the passage before us ought never to be forgotten. In the midst of our triumphs, let us cry earnestly, "Lord, clothe us with humility."

We learn, for another thing, from these verses, that gifts, and power of working miracles, are very inferior to grace. It is written that our Lord said to the seventy disciples, "In this rejoice not, that the spirits are subject unto you, but rather rejoice because your names are written in heaven." It was doubtless an honor and a privilege to be allowed to cast out devils. The disciples were right to be thankful. But it was a far higher privilege to be converted and pardoned men, and to have their names written in the register of saved souls.

The distinction here drawn between grace and gifts is one of deep importance, and often and sadly overlooked in the present day. GIFTS, such as mental vigor, vast memory, striking eloquence, ability in argument, power in reasoning, are often unduly valued by those who possess them, and unduly admired by those who possess them not. These things ought not so to be. Men forget that gifts without grace save no one's soul, and are the characteristic of Satan himself.

GRACE, on the contrary, is an everlasting inheritance, and, lowly and despised as its possessor may be, will land him safe in glory. He that has gifts without grace is dead in sins, however splendid his gifts may be. But he that has grace without gifts is alive to God, however unlearned and ignorant he may appear to man. And "a living dog is better than a dead lion." (Eccles. 9:4.)

Let the religion which we aim to possess be a religion in which grace is the main thing. Let it not content us to be able to speak eloquently, or preach powerfully, or reasonably, or argue cleverly, or profess loudly, or talk fluently. Let it not satisfy us to know the whole system of Christian doctrines, and to have texts and words at our command. These things are all well in their way. They are not to be undervalued. They have their use. But these things are not the grace of God, and they will not deliver us from hell. Let us never rest until we have the witness of the Spirit within us that we are "washed, and sanctified, and justified, in the name of the Lord Jesus and by the Spirit of God." (1 Cor. 6:11.) Let us seek to know that "our names are written in heaven," and that we are really one with Christ and Christ in us.

Let us strive to be "epistles of Christ known and read of all men," and to show by our humility, and charity, and faith, and spiritual-mindedness, that we are the children of God. This is true religion. These are the real marks of saving Christianity. Without such marks, a man may have abundance of gifts and turn out nothing better than a follower of Judas Iscariot, the false apostle, and go at last to hell. With such marks, a man may be like Lazarus, poor and despised upon earth, and have no gifts at all. But his name is written in heaven, and Christ shall own him as one of His people at the last day.

LUKE 10:21-24

In that same hour he rejoiced in the Holy Spirit, and said, I thank thee, O Father, Lord of heaven and earth, that thou didst hide these things from the wise and understanding, and didst reveal them unto babes: yea, Father; for so it was well-pleasing in thy sight. All things have been delivered unto me of my Father: and no one knoweth who the Son is, save the Father; and who the Father is, save the Son, and he to whomsoever the Son willeth to reveal him. And turning to the disciples, he said privately, Blessed are the eyes which see the things that ye see: for I say unto you, that many prophets and kings desired to see the things which ye see, and saw them not; and to hear the things which ye hear, and heard them not.

There are five remarkable points in these verses which deserve the attention of all who wish to be well-instructed Christians. Let us take each of the five in order.

We should observe, in the first place, the one instance on record of our Lord Jesus Christ rejoicing. We read, that in "that hour Jesus rejoiced in spirit." Three times we are told in the Gospels that our Lord Jesus Christ wept. Once only we are told that He rejoiced.

And what was the cause of our Lord's joy? It was the conversion of souls. It was the reception of the Gospel by the weak and lowly among the Jews, when the "wise and prudent" on every side were rejecting it. Our blessed Lord no doubt saw much in this world to grieve Him. He saw the obstinate blindness and unbelief of the vast majority of those among whom He ministered. But when He saw a few poor men and women receiving the glad tiding of salvation, even His heart was refreshed. He saw it and was glad.

Let all Christians mark our Lord's conduct in this matter, and follow His example. They find little in the world to cheer them. They see around them a vast multitude walking in the broad way that leads to destruction, careless, hardened, and unbelieving. They see a few here and there, and only a few, who believe to the saving of their souls. But let this sight make them thankful. Let them bless God that any at all are converted, and that any at all believe. We do not realize the sinfulness of man sufficiently. We do not reflect that the conversion of any soul is a miracle—a miracle as great as the raising of Lazarus from the dead. Let us learn from our blessed Lord to be more thankful. There is always some blue sky as well as black clouds, if we will only look for it. Though only a few are saved, we should find reason for rejoicing. It is only through free grace and undeserved mercy that any are saved at all.

We should observe, secondly, the sovereignty of God in saving sinners. We read that our Lord says to His Father, "You have hidden these things from the wise and prudent, and revealed them unto babes." The meaning of these words is clear and plain. There are some from whom salvation is "hidden." There are others to whom salvation is "revealed."

The truth here laid down is deep and mysterious. "It is as high as heaven—what can we do? It is as deep as hell—what do we know?" Why some around us are converted and others remain dead in sins, we cannot possibly explain. Why England is a Christian country and China buried in idolatry, is a problem we cannot solve. We only know that it is so. We can only acknowledge that the words of our Lord Jesus Christ supply the only answer that mortal man ought to give—"Even so, Father, for so it seemed good in your sight."

Let us, however, never forget that God's sovereignty does not destroy man's responsibility. That same God who does all things according to the counsel of His own will, always addresses us as accountable creatures, as beings whose blood will be on their own heads if they are lost. We cannot understand all His dealings. We see in part and know in part. Let us rest in the conviction that the judgment day will clear up all, and that the Judge of all will not fail to do right. In the meantime, let us remember that God's offers of salvation are free, wide, broad, and unlimited, and that "in our doings that will of God is to be followed which we have expressly declared unto us in the Word of God." (17th Article of Church of England.) If truth is hidden from some and revealed to others, we may be sure that there is a cause.

We should observe, thirdly, the character of those from whom truth is hidden, and of those to whom truth is revealed. We read that our Lord says, "You have hidden these things from the wise and prudent and have revealed them unto babes."

We must not gather from these words a wrong lesson. We must not infer that any people on earth are naturally more deserving of God's grace and salvation than others. All are alike sinners, and merit nothing but wrath and condemnation. We must simply regard the words as stating a fact. The wisdom of this world often makes people proud, and increases their natural enmity to Christ's Gospel. The man who has no pride of knowledge, or fancied morality, to fall back on, has often fewest difficulties to get over in coming to the knowledge of the truth. The publicans and sinners are often the first to enter the kingdom of God, while the Scribes and Pharisees stand outside.

Let us learn from these words to beware of self-righteousness. Nothing so blinds the eyes of our souls to the beauty of the Gospel as the vain, delusive idea, that we are not so ignorant and wicked as some, and that we have got a character which will bear inspection. Happy is that man who has learned to feel that he is "wretched, and miserable, and poor, and blind, and naked." (Rev. 3:17.) To see that we are bad, is the first step towards being really good. To feel that we are ignorant is the first beginning of all saving knowledge.

We should observe, in the fourth place, the majesty and dignity of our Lord Jesus Christ. We read that He said, "My Father has given me authority over everything. No one really knows the Son except the Father, and no one really knows the Father except the Son and those to whom the Son chooses to reveal him." These are the words of one who was very God of very God, and no mere man. We read of no patriarch, or prophet, or apostle, or saint, of any age, who ever used words like these. They reveal to our wondering eyes a little of the mighty majesty of our Lord's nature and person. They show Him to us, as the Head over all things, and King of kings—"all things are delivered to me of my Father." They show Him as one distinct from the Father, and yet entirely one with Him, and knowing Him in an unspeakable manner. "No man knows who the Son is but the Father—and who the Father is but the Son." They show Him, not least, as the Mighty Revealer of the Father to the sons of men, as the God who pardons iniquity, and loves sinners for His Son's sake-"no one really knows the Father except the Son and those to whom the Son chooses to reveal him."

Let us repose our souls confidently on our Lord Jesus Christ. He is one who is "mighty to save." Many and weighty as our sins are, Christ can bear them all. Difficult as is the work of our salvation, Christ is able to accomplish it. If Christ was not God as well as man we might indeed despair. But with such a Savior as this we may begin boldly, and press on hopefully, and await death and judgment without fear. Our help is laid on one that is mighty. (Psalm 89:19.) Christ over all, God blessed forever, will not fail any one that trusts in Him.

Let us observe, finally, the peculiar privileges of those who hear the Gospel of Christ. We read that our Lord said to His disciples, "Blessed are the eyes which see the things that you see. For I tell you that many prophets and kings have desired to see those things which you see, and have not seen them, and to hear those things which you hear, and have not heard them."

The full significance of these words will probably never be understood by Christians until the last day. We have probably a most faint idea of the enormous advantages enjoyed by believers who have lived since Christ came into the world, compared to those of believers who died before Christ was born. The difference between the knowledge of an Old Testament saint and a saint in the apostles' days is far greater than we conceive. It is the difference of twilight and noon-day, of winter and summer, of the mind of a child and the mind of a full-grown man. No doubt the Old Testament saints looked to a coming Savior by faith, and believed in a resurrection and a life to come. But the coming and death of Christ unlocked a hundred Scriptures which before were closed, and cleared up scores of doubtful points which before had never been solved. In short, "the way into the holiest was not made manifest, while the first tabernacle was standing." (Heb. 9:8.) The humblest Christian believer understands things which David and Isaiah could never explain.

Let us leave the passage with a deep sense of our own debt to God and of our great responsibility for the full light of the Gospel. Let us see that we make a good use of our many privileges. Having a full Gospel, let us beware that we do not neglect it. It is a weighty saying, "To whomsoever much is given, of them will much be required." (Luke 12:48.)

LUKE 10:25-28

THE PARABLE OF THE GOOD SAMARITAN

And behold, a certain lawyer stood up and made trial of him, saying, Teacher, what shall I do to inherit eternal life? And he said unto him, What is written in the law? how readest thou? And he answering said, Thou shalt love the Lord thy God with all thy heart, and with all thy soul, and with all thy strength, and with all thy mind; and thy neighbor as thyself. And he said unto him, Thou hast answered right: this do, and thou shalt live.

We should notice in this passage, the solemn question which was addressed to our Lord Jesus Christ. We are told that a certain lawyer asked Him, "What shall I do to inherit eternal life?" The motive of this man was evidently not right. He only asked this question to "tempt" our Lord, and to provoke Him to say something on which His enemies might lay hold. Yet the question he propounded was undoubtedly one of the deepest importance.

It is a question which deserves the principal attention of every man, woman, and child on earth. We are all sinners—dying sinners, and sinners going to be judged after death. "How shall our sins be pardoned? With which shall we come before God? How shall we escape the damnation of hell? Where shall we flee from the wrath to come? What must we do to be saved?"—These are inquiries which people of every rank ought to put to themselves, and never rest until they find an answer.

It is a question which unhappily few care to consider. Thousands are constantly inquiring, "What shall we eat? What shall we drink? With what shall we be clothed? How can we get money? How can we enjoy ourselves? How can we prosper in the world?" Few, very few, will ever give a moment's thought to the salvation of their souls. They hate the subject. It makes them uncomfortable. They turn from it and put it away. Faithful and true is that saying of our Lord's, "Wide is the gate and broad is the way that leads unto destruction, and many there be that go in thereat." (Matt. 7:13.)

Let us not be ashamed of putting the lawyer's question to our own souls. Let us rather ponder it, think about it, and never be content until it fills the first place in our minds. Let us seek to have the witness of the Spirit within us, that we repent us truly of sin, that we have a lively faith in God's mercy through Christ, and that we are really walking with God. This is the character of the heirs of eternal life. These are they who shall one day receive the kingdom prepared for the children of God.

We should notice, secondly, in this passage, the high honor which our Lord Jesus Christ places on the Bible. He refers the lawyer at once to the Scriptures, as the only rule of faith and practice. He does not say in reply to his question—"What does the Jewish Church say about eternal life? What do the Scribes, and Pharisees, and priests think? What is taught on the subject in the traditions of the elders?"—He takes a far simpler and more direct course. He sends his questioner at once to the writings of the Old Testament—"What is written in the law? How read you it?"

Let the principle contained in these words, be one of the foundation principles of our Christianity. Let the Bible, the whole Bible, and nothing but the Bible, be the rule of our faith and practice. Holding this principle we travel upon the king's highway. The road may sometimes seem narrow, and our faith may be severely tried, but we shall not be allowed greatly to err. Departing from this principle we enter on a pathless wilderness. There is no telling what we may be led to believe or do. Forever let us bear this in mind. Here let us cast anchor. Here let us abide.

It matters nothing who says a thing in religion, whether an ancient father, or a modern Bishop, or a learned divine. Is it in the Bible? Can it be proved by the Bible? If not, it is not to be believed. It matters nothing how beautiful and clever sermons or religious books may appear. Are they in the smallest degree contrary to Scripture? If they are, they are rubbish and poison, and guides of no value. What says the Scripture? This is the only rule, and measure, and gauge of religious truth. "To the law and to the testimony," says Isaiah, "if they speak not according to this word, it is because there is no light in them." (Isaiah 8:20.)

We should notice, lastly, in this passage, the clear knowledge of duty to God and man, which the Jews in our Lord's time possessed. We read that the lawyer said, in reply to our Lord's question, "You shall love the Lord your God with all your heart, and with all your soul, and with all your strength, and with all your mind; and your neighbor as yourself." That was well spoken. A clearer description of daily practical duty could not be given by the most thoroughly instructed Christian in the present day. Let not this be forgotten.

The words of the lawyer are very instructive in two points of view. They throw a strong light on two subjects, about which many mistakes abound. For one thing, they show us how great were the privileges of religious knowledge which the Jews enjoyed under the Old Testament, compared to the heathen world. A nation which possessed such principles of duty as those now before us, was immeasurably in advance of Greece and Rome. For another thing, the lawyer's words show us how much clear head-knowledge a person may possess, while his heart is full of wickedness. Here is a man who talks of loving God with all his soul, and loving his neighbor as himself, while he is actually "tempting" Christ, and trying to do Him harm, and, anxious to justify himself and make himself out a charitable man! Let us ever beware of this kind of religion. Clear knowledge of the head, when accompanied by determined impenitence of heart, is a most dangerous state of soul. "If you know these things," says Jesus, "happy are you if you do them." (John 13:17.)

Let us not forget, in leaving this passage, to apply the high standard of duty which it contains, to our own hearts, and to prove our own selves. Do we love God with all our heart, and soul, and strength, and mind? Do we love our neighbor as ourselves? Where is the person that could say with perfect truth, "I do?" Where is the man that ought not to lay his hand on his mouth, when he hears these questions? Verily we are all guilty in this matter! The best of us, however holy we may be, come far short of perfection. Passages like this, should teach us our need of Christ's blood and righteousness. To Him we must go, if we would ever stand with boldness at the bar of God. From Him we must seek grace, that the love of God and man may become ruling principles of our lives. In Him we must abide, that we may not forget our principles, and that we may show the world that by them we desire to live.

LUKE 10:29-37

But he, desiring to justify himself, said unto Jesus, And who is my neighbor? Jesus made answer and said, A certain man was going down from Jerusalem to Jericho; and he fell among robbers, who both stripped him and beat him, and departed, leaving him half dead. And by chance a certain priest was going down that way: and when he saw him, he passed by on the other side. And in like manner a Levite also, when he came to the place, and saw him, passed by on the other side. But a certain Samaritan, as he journeyed, came where he was: and when he saw him, he was moved with compassion, and came to him, and bound up his wounds, pouring on them oil and wine; and he set him on his own beast, and brought him to an inn, and took care of him. And on the morrow he took out two shillings, and gave them to the host, and said, Take care of him; and whatsoever thou spendest more, I, when I come back again, will repay thee. Which of these three, thinkest thou, proved neighbor unto him that fell among the robbers? And he said, He that showed mercy on him. And Jesus said unto him, Go, and do thou likewise.

These words contain the well-known parable of the good Samaritan. In order to understand the drift of this parable, we must carefully remember the occasion on which it was spoken. It was spoken in reply to the question of a certain lawyer, who asked, "who is my neighbor?" Our Lord Jesus Christ answers that question by telling the story we have just read, and winds up the narrative by an appeal to the lawyer's conscience. Let these things not be forgotten. The object of the parable is to show the nature of true charity and brotherly love. To lose sight of this object, and discover deep allegories in the parable, is to trifle with Scripture, and deprive our souls of most valuable lessons.

We are taught, first, in this parable, how rare and uncommon is true brotherly love. This is a lesson which stands out prominently on the face of the narrative before our eyes. Our Lord tells us of a traveler who fell among thieves, and was left naked, wounded, and half dead on the road. He then tells us of a priest and a Levite, who, one after the other, came traveling that way, and saw the poor wounded man, but gave him no help. Both were men, who from their religious office and profession, ought to have been ready and willing to do good to one in distress. But both, in succession, were too selfish, or too unfeeling to offer the slightest assistance. They doubtless reasoned with themselves, that they knew nothing of the wounded traveler—that he had perhaps got into trouble by his own misconduct—that they had no time to stop to help him—and that they had enough to do to mind their own business, without troubling themselves with strangers. And the result was, that one after the other, they both "passed by on the other side."

We have in this striking description, an exact picture of what is continually going on in the world. Selfishness is the leading characteristic of the great majority of mankind. That cheap charity which costs nothing more than a trifling subscription or contribution, is common enough. But that self-sacrificing kindness of heart, which cares not what trouble is entailed, so long as good can be done, is a grace which is rarely met with. There are still thousands in trouble who can find no friend or helper. And there are still hundreds of "priests and Levites" who see them, but "pass by on the other side."

Let us beware of expecting much from the kindness of man. If we do, we shall certainly be disappointed. The longer we live the more clearly we shall see that few people care for others except from interested motives, and that unselfish, unselfish, pure brotherly love, is as scarce as diamonds and rubies. How thankful we ought to be that the Lord Jesus Christ is not like man! His kindness and love are unfailing. He never disappoints any of His friends. Happy are they who have learned to say, "My soul, wait only upon God; my expectation is from Him." (Psalm 62:5.)

We are taught, secondly, in this parable, who they are to whom we should show kindness, and whom we are to love as neighbors. We are told that the only person who helped the wounded traveler, of whom we are reading, was a certain Samaritan. This man was one of a nation who had "no dealings" with the Jews. (John 4:9.), He might have excused himself by saying that the road from Jerusalem to Jericho was through the Jewish territory, and that cases of distress ought to be cared for by the Jews. But he does nothing of the sort. He sees a man stripped of his clothing, and lying half dead. He asks no questions, but at once has compassion on him. He makes no difficulties, but at once gives aid. And our Lord says to us, "Go and do you likewise."

Now, if these words mean anything, a Christian ought to be ready to show kindness and brotherly love to everyone that is in need. Our kindness must not merely extend to our families, and friends, and relations. We must love all men, and be kind to all, whenever occasion requires. We must beware of an excessive strictness in scrutinizing the past lives of those who need our aid. Are they in real trouble? Are they in real distress? Do they really need help? Then, according to the teaching of this parable, we ought to be ready to assist them.

We should regard the whole world as our parish, and the whole race of mankind as our neighbors. We should seek to be the friend of every one who is oppressed, or neglected, or afflicted, or sick, or in prison, or poor, or an orphan, or a heathen, or a slave, or an idiot, or starving, or dying. We should exhibit such world-wide friendship, no doubt, wisely, discreetly, and with good sense, but of such friendship we never need be ashamed. The ungodly may sneer at it as extravagance and fanaticism. But we need not mind that. To be friendly to all men in this way, is to show something of the mind that was in Christ.

We are taught, lastly, in this parable, after what manner, and to what extent we are to show kindness and love to others. We are told that the Samaritan's compassion towards the wounded traveler was not confined to feelings and passive impressions. He took much trouble to give him help. He acted as well as felt. He spared no pains or expense in befriending him. Stranger as the man was, he went to him, bound up his wounds, set him on his own beast, brought him to an inn, and took care of him. Nor was this all. On the morrow he gave the host of the inn money, saying, "Take care of him, and whatever you spend more, when I come again I will repay you." And our Lord says to each of us, "Go and do likewise."

The lesson of this part of the parable is plain and unmistakable. The kindness of a Christian towards others should not be in word and in tongue only, but in deed and in truth. His love should be a practical love, a love which entails on him self-sacrifice and self-denial, both in money, and time, and trouble. His charity should be seen not merely in his talking, but his acting—not merely in his profession, but in his practice. He should think it no misspent time to work as hard in doing good to those who need help, as others work in trying to get money. He should not be ashamed to toil as much to make the misery of this world rather smaller, as those toil who hunt or shoot all day long. He should have a ready ear for every tale of sorrow, and a ready hand to help every one in affliction, so long as he has the power. Such brotherly love the world may not understand. The returns of gratitude which such love meets with may be few and small. But to show such brotherly love, is to walk in the steps of Christ, and to reduce to practice the parable of the good Samaritan.

And now let us leave the parable with grave thoughts and deep searchings of heart. How few Christians seem to remember that such a parable was ever written! What an enormous amount of stinginess, and baseness, and ill-nature, and suspicion there is to be seen in the Church, and that even among people who repeat the creed and go to the Lord's table! How seldom we see a man who is really kind, and feeling, and generous, and liberal and good-natured, except to himself and his children! Yet the Lord Jesus Christ spoke the parable of the good Samaritan, and meant it to be remembered.

What are we ourselves? Let us not forget to put that question to our hearts. What are we doing, each in our own station, to prove that this mighty parable is one of the rules of our daily life? What are we doing for the heathen, at home and abroad? What are we doing to help those who are troubled in mind, body, or estate? There are many such in this world. There are always some near our own door. What are we doing for them? Anything, or nothing at all? May God help us to answer these questions! The world would be a happier world if there was more practical Christianity.

LUKE 10:38-42

MARTHA AND MARY

Now as they went on their way, he entered into a certain village: and a certain woman named Martha received him into her house. And she had a sister called Mary, who also sat at the Lord's feet, and heard his word. But Martha was cumbered about much serving; and she came up to him, and said, Lord, dost thou not care that my sister did leave me to serve alone? bid her therefore that she help me. But the Lord answered and said unto her, Martha, Martha, thou art anxious and troubled about many things: but one thing is needful: for Mary hath chosen the good part, which shall not be taken away from her.

The little history which these verses contain, is only recorded in the Gospel of Luke. So long as the world stands, the story of Mary and Martha will furnish the Church with lessons of wisdom which ought never to be forgotten. Taken together with the eleventh chapter of John's Gospel, it throws a most instructive light on the inner life of the family which Jesus loved.

Let us observe, for one thing, how different the characters and personalities of true Christians may be. The two sisters of whom we read in this passage were faithful disciples. Both had believed. Both had been converted. Both had honored Christ when few gave Him honor. Both loved Jesus, and Jesus loved both of them. Yet they were evidently women of very different turn of mind. Martha was active, stirring, and impulsive, feeling strongly, and speaking out all she felt. Mary was quiet, still, and contemplative, feeling deeply, but saying less than she felt. Martha, when Jesus came to her house, rejoiced to see Him, and busied herself with preparing a suitable refreshment. Mary, also, rejoiced to see Him, but her first thought was to sit at His feet and hear His word. Grace reigned in both hearts, but each showed the effects of grace at different times, and in different ways.

We shall find it very useful to ourselves to remember this lesson. We must not expect all believers in Christ to be exactly like one another. We must not set down others as having no grace, because their experience does not entirely tally with our own. The sheep in the Lord's flock have each their own peculiarities. The trees in the Lord's garden are not all precisely alike. All true servants of God agree in the principal things of religion. All are led by one Spirit. All feel their sins, and all trust in Christ. All repent, all believe, and all are holy. But in minor matters they often differ widely. Let not one despise another on this account. There will be Marthas and there will be Marys in the Church until the Lord comes again.

Let us observe, for another thing, what a snare to our souls the cares of this world may be, if allowed to take up too much attention. It is plain from the tone of the passage before us, that Martha allowed her anxiety to provide a suitable entertainment for the Lord, to carry her away. Her excessive zeal for temporal provisions, made her forget, for a time, the things of her soul. "She was cumbered about much serving." By and bye her conscience pierced her when she found herself alone serving tables, and saw her sister sitting at Jesus' feet and hearing His word. Under the pressure of a conscience ill at ease, her temper became ruffled, and the 'old Adam' within broke out into open complaint. "Lord," she said, "do not you care that my sister has left me to serve alone? Bid her therefore that she help me."

In so saying, this holy woman sadly forgot what she was, and to whom she was speaking. She brought down on herself a solemn rebuke, and had to learn a lesson which probably made a lasting impression. Alas! "how great a matter a little fire kindles." The beginning of all this was a little over-anxiety about the innocent household affairs of this world!

The fault of Martha should be a perpetual warning to all Christians. If we desire to grow in grace, and to enjoy soul-prosperity, we must beware of the cares of this world. Except we watch and pray, they will insensibly eat up our spirituality, and bring leanness on our souls. It is not open sin, or flagrant breaches of God's commandments alone, which lead men to eternal ruin. It is far more frequently an excessive attention to things in themselves lawful, and the being "cumbered about much serving." It seems so right to provide for our own! It seems so proper to attend to the duties of our station! It is just here that our danger lies. Our families, our business, our daily callings, our household affairs, our interaction with society, all, all may become snares to our hearts, and may draw us away from God. We may go down to the pit of hell from the very midst of lawful things.

Let us take heed to ourselves in this matter. Let us watch our habits of mind jealously, lest we fall into sin unawares. If we love life, we must hold the things of this world with a very loose hand, and beware of allowing anything to have the first place in our hearts, excepting God. Let us mentally write "poison" on all temporal good things. Used in moderation they are blessings, for which we ought to be thankful. Permitted to fill our minds, and trample upon holy things, they become an inevitable curse. Profits and pleasures are dearly purchased, if in order to obtain them we thrust aside eternity from our thoughts, abridge our Bible-reading, become careless hearers of the Gospel, and shorten our prayers. A little earth upon the fire within us will soon make that fire burn low.

Let us observe, for another thing, what a solemn rebuke our Lord Jesus Christ gave to His servant Martha. Like a wise physician He saw the disease which was preying upon her, and at once applied the remedy. Like a tender parent, He exposed the fault into which His erring child had fallen, and did not spare the chastening which was required. "Martha, Martha," He said, "you are anxious and troubled about many things—but one thing is needful." Faithful are the wounds of a friend! That little sentence was a precious balm indeed! It contained a volume of practical divinity in a few words.

"One thing is needful." How true that saying! The longer we live in the world, the more true it will appear. The nearer we come to the grave, the more thoroughly we shall assent to it. Health, and money, and lands, and rank, and honors, and prosperity, are all well in their way. But they cannot be called needful. Without them thousands are happy in this world, and reach glory in the world to come. The "many things" which men and women are continually struggling for, are not really necessaries. The grace of God which brings salvation is the one thing needful.

Let this little sentence be continually before the eyes of our minds. Let it check us when we are ready to murmur at earthly trials. Let it strengthen us when we are tempted to deny our Master on account of persecution. Let it caution us when we begin to think too much of the things of this world. Let it quicken us when we are disposed to look back, like Lot's wife. In all such seasons, let the words of our Lord ring in our ears like a trumpet, and bring us to a right mind. "One thing is needful." If Christ is ours, we have all and abound.

We should observe, lastly, what high commendation our Lord Jesus Christ pronounced on Mary's choice. We read that He said, "Mary has chosen that good part, which shall not be taken from her." There was a deep meaning in these words. They were spoken not only for Mary's sake, but for the sake of all Christ's believing people in every part of the world. They were meant to encourage all true Christians to be single-eyed and whole-hearted—to follow the Lord fully, and to walk closely with God, to make soul-business immeasurably their first business, and to think comparatively little of the things of this world.

The true Christian's portion is the grace of God. This is the "good part" which he has chosen, and it is the only portion which really deserves the name of "good." It is the only good thing which is substantial, satisfying, real, and lasting. It is good in sickness and good in health—good in youth and good in age, good in adversity and good in prosperity—good in life and good in death, good in time and good in eternity. No circumstance and no position can be imagined in which it is not good for man to have the grace of God.

The true Christian's possession shall never be taken from him. He alone, of all mankind, shall never be stripped of his inheritance. Kings must one day leave their palaces. Rich men must one day leave their money and lands. They only hold them until they die. But the poorest saint on earth has a treasure of which he will never be deprived. The grace of God, and the favor of Christ, are riches which no man can take from him. They will go with him to the grave when he dies. They will rise with him in the resurrection morning, and be his to all eternity.

What do we know of this "good part" which Mary chose? Have we chosen it for ourselves? Can we say with truth that it is ours? Let us never rest until we can. Let us "choose life," while Christ offers it to us without money and without price. Let us seek treasure in heaven, lest we awake to find that we are paupers for evermore.

Chapter 11

LUKE 11:1-4

JESUS' TEACHING ON PRAYER

And it came to pass, as he was praying in a certain place, that when he ceased, one of his disciples said unto him, Lord, teach us to pray, even as John also taught his disciples. And he said unto them, When ye pray, say, Father, Hallowed be thy name. Thy kingdom come. Give us day by day our daily bread. And forgive us our sins; for we ourselves also forgive every one that is indebted to us. And bring us not into temptation.

These verses contain the prayer commonly called the Lord's Prayer. Few passages of Scripture perhaps are so well known as this. The most benighted Roman Catholic can tell us that there is a prayer called "Pater Noster." The most ignorant English child has heard something about "Our Father."

The importance of the Lord's Prayer appears in the simple fact, that our Lord Jesus Christ delivered it twice with very slight variations. He who never spoke a word without good reason, has thought fit to teach us this prayer upon two distinct occasions. Twice the Lord God wrote the ten commandments on tables of stone. (Deut. 9:10; 10:4.) Twice the Lord Jesus delivered the Lord's Prayer.

The occasion of the Lord's Prayer being delivered a second time, in the verses before us, is full of interest. It appears that "one of the disciples" said, "Lord, teach us to pray." The answer to that request was the well-known prayer which we are now considering. Who this "disciple" was we do not know. What he did will be remembered as long as the world stands. Happy are those who partake of his feelings, and often cry, "Lord, teach me to pray."

The substance of the Lord's Prayer is a mine of spiritual treasure. To expound it fully in a work like this, is manifestly impossible. The prayer, on which volumes have been written, does not admit of being handled properly in a few pages. For the present it must suffice us to notice its leading divisions, and to mark the leading trains of thought which it should suggest to us for private meditation.

The first division of the Lord's Prayer respects the God whom we worship. We are taught to approach Him as our Father in heaven—our Father no doubt as our Creator, but specially as our Father reconciled to us in Christ Jesus—our Father whose dwelling is "in heaven," and whom no temple on earth can contain. We then make mention of three great things—our Father's name, our Father's kingdom, and our Father's will.

We are taught to pray that the name of God may be sanctified—"Hallowed be your name." In using these words, we do not mean that God's NAME admits of degrees of holiness, or that any prayers of ours can make it more holy than it is. But we declare our hearty desire that God's character, and attributes, and perfection, may be more known, and honored, and glorified by all His intelligent creatures. In fact, it is the very petition which the Lord Jesus Himself puts up on another occasion, "Father, glorify your name." (John 12:28.)

We are next taught to pray that God's KINGDOM may come—"Your kingdom come." In so saying, we declare our desire that the usurped power of Satan may speedily be cast down—that all mankind may acknowledge God as their lawful King, and that the kingdoms of this world may become in fact, as they are in promise, the kingdoms of our God and of His Christ. The final setting up of this kingdom has been long predicted, even from the day of Adam's fall. The whole creation groans in expectation of it. The last prayer in the Bible points to it. The canon of Scripture almost closes with the words, "Come Lord Jesus." (Rev. 11:15; Gen. 3:15; Rom. 8:22; Rev. 22:20.)

We are taught, thirdly, to pray that God's WILL may be done—"Your will be done on earth as it is in heaven." In so saying, we express our longing desire that the number of God's converted and obedient people on earth may greatly increase, that His enemies, who hate His laws, may be diminished and brought low, and that the time may speedily arrive when all men shall do their willing service to God on earth, even as all the angels do in heaven. (Hab. 2:14; Heb. 8:11.)

Such is the first division of the Lord's Prayer. Its marvelous fullness and deep importance cannot be overrated. Blessed indeed are those Christians who have learned that God's name is far more honorable than that of any earthly potentate; God's kingdom the only kingdom that shall stand forever—and God's law the rule to which all laws ought to be conformed! The more these things are understood and believed in a land, the happier that land will be. The days when all acknowledge these things will be the "days of heaven upon earth."

The second division of the Lord's Prayer respects our own daily needs. We are taught to make mention of two things which we need every day. These two things are, one of them temporal, and the other spiritual. One of them is "bread." The other is "forgiveness of sins."

We are taught to ask for BREAD—"Give us this day our daily bread." Under this word "bread," no doubt, is included everything which our bodies can require. We acknowledge our entire dependence upon God for life, and breath, and all things. We ask Him to take charge of us, and provide for us in all that concerns this world. It is the prayer of Solomon under another form, "Feed me with food convenient for me." (Prov. 30:8.)

We are taught to ask, in the next place, for FORGIVENESS—"Forgive us our sins, for we also forgive everyone that is indebted to us." In so saying, we confess that we are fallen, guilty, and corrupt creatures, and in many things offend daily. We make no excuse for ourselves. We plead nothing in our own behalf. We simply ask for the free, full, gracious mercy of our Father in Christ Jesus. And we accompany the petition by the only profession which the whole Lord's Prayer contains. We profess that we "forgive every one that is indebted to us."

The combined simplicity and richness of the second division of the Lord's Prayer can never be sufficiently admired. How soon the words are spoken! And yet how much the words take in! Daily bread and daily mercy are by far the first and principal things that mortal man needs. He is the rich man who possesses them. He is the wise man who is not ashamed to pray for them every day. The child of God, no doubt, is fully justified before God, and all things are working for his good. But it is the life of true faith to apply daily for fresh supplies for all our needs. Though the promises are all ours, our Father likes His children to remind Him of them. Though washed, we need daily to wash our feet. (John 13:10.)

The third division of the Lord's Prayer respects our daily dangers. We are taught to make mention of two things which we ought to fear every day, and which we must expect to meet with as long as we are in this world. One of these things is "temptation." The other is "evil."

We are taught to pray against TEMPTATION—"Lead us not into temptation." We do not mean by this expression that God is the author of evil, or that He tempts man to sin. (James 1:13.) But we entreat Him who orders all things in heaven and earth, and without whom nothing can happen, so to order the course of our lives that we may not be tempted above what we can bear. We confess our weakness and readiness to fall. We entreat our Father to preserve us from trials, or else to make a way for us to escape. We ask that our feet may be kept, and that we may not bring discredit on our profession and misery on our souls.

We are taught, lastly, to pray against EVIL—"Deliver us from evil." We include under the word evil, everything that can hurt us, either in body or soul, and especially every weapon of that great author of evil, the devil. We confess that ever since the fall, the world "lies in the wicked one." (1 John 5:19.) We confess that evil is in us, and about us, and near us, and on every side, and that we have no power to deliver ourselves from it. We apply to the strong for strength. We cast ourselves on Him for protection. In short, we ask what our Savior Himself asked for us, when He said, "I pray not that you should take them out of the world, but that you should keep them from the evil one." (John 17:15.)

Such is the last division of the Lord's Prayer. In real importance it is not a whit inferior to the two other divisions, which we have already considered. It leaves man precisely in the position which he ought to occupy. It puts in his mouth the language of humility. The most dangerous state in which we can be, is not to know and feel our spiritual danger.

And now let us use the Lord's Prayer for the trial of our own state before God. Its words have probably passed over our lips thousands of times. But have we really felt it? Do we really desire its petitions to be granted? Is God really our Father? Are we born again, and made His children by faith in Christ? Do we care much for His name and will? Do we really wish the kingdom of God to come? Do we feel our need of daily temporal mercies, and of daily pardon of sin? Do we fear falling into temptation? Do we dread evil above all things? These are serious questions. They deserve serious consideration.

Let us strive to make the Lord's Prayer our model and pattern in all our approaches to God. Let it suggest to us the sort of things which we should pray for and pray against. Let it teach us the relative place and proportion which we should give to each subject in our prayers. The more we ponder and examine the Lord's Prayer, the more instructive and suggestive shall we find it to be.

LUKE 11:5-13

PARABLE OF THE IMPORTUNATE FRIEND

And he said unto them, Which of you shall have a friend, and shall go unto him at midnight, and say to him, Friend, lend me three loaves; for a friend of mine is come to me from a journey, and I have nothing to set before him; and he from within shall answer and say, Trouble me not: the door is now shut, and my children are with me in bed; I cannot rise and give thee? I say unto you, Though he will not rise and give him because he is his friend, yet because of his importunity he will arise and give him as many as he needeth. And I say unto you, Ask, and it shall be given you; seek, and ye shall find; knock, and it shall be opened unto you. For every one that asketh receiveth; and he that seeketh findeth; and to him that knocketh it shall be opened. And of which of you that is a father shall his son ask a loaf, and he give him a stone? or a fish, and he for a fish give him a serpent? Or if he shall ask an egg, will he give him a scorpion? If ye then, being evil, know how to give good gifts unto your children, how much more shall your heavenly Father give the Holy Spirit to them that ask him?

In these verses our Lord Jesus Christ instructs us about prayer. The subject is one which can never be too strongly pressed on our attention. Prayer lies at the very root of our practical Christianity. It is part of the daily business of our religious life. We have reason to thank God, that upon no point has our Lord Jesus Christ spoken so fully and frequently as upon prayer.

We learn for one thing, from these verses, the importance of perseverance in prayer. This lesson is conveyed to us in the simple parable, commonly called the "Friend at Midnight." We are there reminded what man can obtain from man by dint of importunity. Selfish and indolent as we naturally are, we are capable of being roused to exertion by continual asking. The man who would not give three loaves at midnight for friendship's sake, at length gave them to save himself the trouble of being further entreated. The application of the parable is clear and plain. If importunity succeeds so well, between man and man, how much more may we expect it to obtain mercies when used in prayer to God.

The lesson is one which we shall do well to remember. It is far more easy to begin a habit of prayer than to keep it up. Myriads of professing Christians are regularly taught to pray when they are young, and then gradually leave off the practice as they grow up. Thousands take up a habit of praying for a little season, after some special mercy or special affliction, and then little by little become cold about it, and at last lay it aside. The secret thought comes stealing over men's minds, that "it is no use to pray." They see no visible benefit from it. They persuade themselves that they get on just as well without prayer. Laziness and unbelief prevail over their hearts, and at last they altogether "restrain prayer before God." (Job 15:4.)

Let us resist this feeling, whenever we feel it rising within us. Let us resolve by God's grace, that however poor and feeble our prayers may seem to be, we will pray on. It is not for nothing that the Bible tells us so frequently, to "watch unto prayer," to "pray without ceasing," to "continue in prayer," to "pray always and not to faint," to be "instant in prayer." These expressions all look one way. They are all meant to remind us of a danger and to quicken us to a duty.

The time and way in which our prayers shall be answered are matters which we must leave entirely to God. But that every petition which we offer in faith shall certainly be answered, we need not doubt. Let us lay our matters before God again and again, day after day, week after week, month after month, year after year. The answer may be long in coming, as it was in the cases of Hannah and Zachariah. (1 Sam. 1:27; Luke 1:13.) But though it tarry, let us pray on and wait for it. At the right time it will surely come and not tarry.

We learn, for another thing, from these verses, how wide and encouraging are the promises which the Lord Jesus holds out to prayer. The striking words in which they are clothed are familiar to us if any are in the Bible—"Ask, and you shall receive; seek, and you shall find; knock, and it shall be opened unto you." The solemn declaration which follows, appears intended to make assurance doubly sure—"Everyone that asks receives, and he that seeks finds, and to him that knocks it shall be opened." The heart-searching argument which concludes the passage, leaves faithlessness and unbelief without excuse—"If you being evil, know how to give good gifts unto your children—how much more shall your heavenly Father give the Holy Spirit to those who ask him."

There are few promises in the Bible so broad and unqualified as those contained in this wonderful passage. The last in particular deserves especial notice. The Holy Spirit is beyond doubt the greatest gift which God can bestow upon man. Having this gift, we have all things—life, light, hope and heaven. Having this gift we have God the Father's boundless love, God the Son's atoning blood, and full communion with all three Persons of the blessed Trinity. Having this gift, we have grace and peace in the world that now is, glory and honor in the world to come. And yet this mighty gift is held out by our Lord Jesus Christ as a gift to be obtained by prayer! "Your heavenly Father shall give the Holy Spirit to those who ask him."

There are few passages in the Bible which so completely strip the unconverted man of his common excuses as this passage. He says he is "weak and helpless." But does he ask to be made strong? He says he is "wicked and corrupt." But does he seek to be made better? He says he "can do nothing of himself." But does he knock at the door of mercy, and pray for the grace of the Holy Spirit? These are questions to which many, it may be feared, can make no answer. They are what they are, because they have no real desire to be changed. They have not, because they ask not. They will not come to Christ, that they may have life; and therefore they remain dead in trespasses and sins.

And now, as we leave the passage, let us ask ourselves whether we know anything of real prayer? Do we pray at all? Do we pray in the name of Jesus, and as needy sinners? Do we know what it is to "ask," and "seek," and "knock," and wrestle in prayer, like men who feel that it is a matter of life or death, and that they must have an answer? Or are we content with saying over some old form of words, while our thoughts are wandering, and our hearts far away? Truly we have learned a great lesson when we have learned that "saying prayers" is not praying!

If we do pray, let it be a settled rule with us, never to leave off the habit of praying, and never to shorten our prayers. A man's state before God may always be measured by his prayers. Whenever we begin to feel careless about our private prayers, we may depend upon it, there is something very wrong in the condition of our souls. There are breakers ahead. We are in imminent danger of a shipwreck.

LUKE 11:14-20

JESUS AND BEELZEBUB

And he was casting out a demon that was dumb. And it came to pass, when the demon was gone out, the dumb man spake; and the multitudes marvelled. But some of them said, By Beelzebub the prince of the demons casteth he out demons.

And others, trying him, sought of him a sign from heaven. But he, knowing their thoughts, said unto them, Every kingdom divided against itself is brought to desolation; and a house divided against a house falleth. And if Satan also is divided against himself, how shall his kingdom stand? because ye say that I cast out demons by Beelzebub. And if I by Beelzebub cast out demons, by whom do your sons cast them out? therefore shall they be your judges. But if I by the finger of God cast out demons, then is the kingdom of God come upon you.

The connection between these verses and those which immediately precede them, is striking and instructive. In the preceding verses, our Lord Jesus Christ had been showing the power and importance of prayer. In the verses before us, he delivers a man from a 'mute' devil. The miracle is evidently intended to throw fresh light on the lesson. The same Savior who encourages us to pray, is the Savior who destroys Satan's power over our members, and restores our tongues to their proper use.

Let us notice, firstly, in these verses, the variety of ways in which Satan exhibits his desire to injure man. We read of a 'mute' devil. Sometimes in the Gospel we are told of an "unclean" devil. Sometimes we are told of a raging and violent devil. Here we are told of one under whose influence the unhappy person possessed by him became "mute." Many are the devices of Satan. It is foolish to suppose that he always works in the same manner. One thing only is the common mark of all his operations—he delights to inflict injury and do harm.

There is something very instructive in the case before us. Do we suppose, because bodily possession by Satan is not so glaringly manifest as it once was, that the great enemy is less active in doing mischief than he used to be? If we think so we have much to learn. Do we suppose that there is no such thing as the influence of a "mute" devil in the present day? If we do, we had better think again. What shall we say of those who never speak to God, who never use their tongues in prayer and praise, who never employ that organ which is a man's "glory," in the service of Him who made it? What shall we say, in a word, of those who can speak to everyone but God? What can we say but that Satan has despoiled them of the truest use of a tongue? What ought we to say but that they are possessed with a "mute devil?" The prayerless man is dead while he lives. His members are rebels against the God who made them. The "mute devil" is not yet extinct.

Let us watch and pray that we may never be given over to the influence of a mute spirit. Thanks be to God, that same Jesus still lives, who can make the deaf to hear and the mute to speak! To Him let us flee for help. In Him let us abide. It is not enough to avoid open profligacy, and to keep clear of glaring sins. It is not enough to be moral, and proper, and respectable in our lives. All this is negative goodness, and nothing more. Is there anything positive about our religion? Do we yield our members as instruments of righteousness to God? (Rom. 6:13.) Having eyes, do we see God's kingdom? Having ears, do we hear Christ's voice? Having a tongue, do we use it for God's praise? These are very serious inquiries. The number of people who are deaf and mute before God is far greater than many suppose.

Let us notice, secondly, in these verses, the amazing power of prejudice over the hearts of unconverted men. We read, that when our Lord cast out the mute spirit, there were some who said, "He casts out devils through Beelzebub, the chief of the devils." They could not deny the miracle. They then refused to allow that it was wrought by divine power. The work before their eyes was plain and indisputable. They then attempted to discredit the character of Him who did it, and to blacken His reputation by saying that he was in league with the devil.

The state of mind here described is a most formidable disease, and one unhappily not uncommon. There are never lacking men who are determined to see no good in the servants of Christ, and to believe all manner of evil about them. Such men appear to throw aside their common sense. They refuse to listen to evidence, or to attend to plain arguments. They seem resolved to believe that whatever a Christian does must be wrong, and whatever he says must be false! If he does right at any time, it must be from corrupt motives! If he speaks truth, it must be with sinister views! If he does good works, it is from selfish reasons! If he casts out devils, it is through Beelzebub! Such prejudiced men are to be found in many a congregation. They are the severest trials of the ministers of Christ. No wonder that Paul said, "Pray that we may be delivered from unreasonable as well as wicked men." (2 Thess. 3:2.)

Let us strive to be of a fair, and honest, and candid spirit in our judgment of men and things in religion. Let us be ready to give up old and cherished opinions the moment that anyone can show us a "more excellent way." The honest and good heart is a great treasure. (Luke 8:15.) A prejudiced spirit is the very jaundice of the soul. It affects a man's mental eyesight, and makes him see everything in an unnatural color. From such a spirit may we pray to be delivered!

Let us notice, lastly, in these verses, the great evil of religious divisions. This is a truth which our Lord impresses on us in the answer He gives to His prejudiced enemies. He shows the folly of their charge that He cast out devils by Beelzebub. He quotes the proverbial saying that "a house divided against itself falls." He infers the absurdity of the idea that Satan would cast out Satan, or the devil cast out his own agents. And in so doing, He teaches Christians a lesson which they have been mournfully slow to learn in every age of the church. That lesson is the sin and folly of needless divisions.

Religious divisions of some kind there must always be, so long as false doctrine prevails, and men will cleave to it. What communion can there be between light and darkness? How can two walk together except they be agreed? What unity can there be where there is not the unity of the Spirit? Division and separation from those who adhere to false and unscriptural doctrine is a duty and not a sin.

But there are divisions of a very different kind, which are deeply to be deplored. Such, for example, are divisions between men who agree on main points—divisions about matters not needful to salvation—divisions about forms and ceremonies, and ecclesiastical arrangements upon which Scripture is silent. Divisions of this kind are to be avoided and discouraged by all faithful Christians. The existence of them is a melancholy proof of the fallen state of man, and the corruption of his understanding as well as his will. They bring scandal on religion, and weakness on the church. "Every kingdom divided against itself is brought to desolation."

What are the best remedies against needless divisions? A humble spirit, a readiness to make concessions, and an enlightened acquaintance with holy Scripture. We must learn to distinguish between things in religion which are essential, and things which are not essential—things which are needful to salvation, and things which are not needful, things which are of first rate importance, and things which are of second rate importance. On the one class of things we must be stiff and unbending as the oak tree—"If any man preach any other Gospel than that which we have preached, let him be accursed." (Gal. 1:8.)—On the other we may be yielding and compliant as the willow, "I am made all things to all men, that I might by all means save some." (1 Cor. 9:22.)

To draw such clear distinctions requires no small practical wisdom. But such wisdom is to be had for the asking. "If any man lack wisdom, let him ask of God." (James 1:5.) When Christians keep up needless divisions they show themselves more foolish than Satan himself.

LUKE 11:21-26

When the strong man fully armed guardeth his own court, his goods are in peace: but when a stronger than he shall come upon him, and overcome him, he taketh from him his whole armor wherein he trusted, and divideth his spoils. He that is not with me is against me; and he that gathereth not with me scattereth. The unclean spirit when he is gone out of the man, passeth through waterless places, seeking rest, and finding none, he saith, I will turn back unto my house whence I came out. And when he is come, he findeth it swept and garnished. Then goeth he, and taketh to him seven other spirits more evil than himself; and they enter in and dwell there: and the last state of that man becometh worse than the first.

The subject of these words of Christ is mysterious, but deeply important. They were spoken concerning Satan and his agency. They throw light on the power of Satan, and the nature of his operations. They deserve the close attention of all who would fight the Christian warfare with success. Next to his friends and allies, a soldier ought to be well acquainted with his enemies. We ought not to be ignorant of Satan's devices.

Let us observe in these verses what a fearful picture our Lord draws of Satan's power. There are four points in His description, which are peculiarly instructive.

Christ speaks of Satan as a "STRONG man." The strength of Satan has been only too well proved by his victories over the souls of men. He who tempted Adam and Eve to rebel against God, and brought sin into the world— he who has led captive the vast majority of mankind, and robbed them of heaven; that evil one is indeed a mighty foe. He who is called the "Prince of this world," is not an enemy to be despised. The devil is very strong.

Christ speaks of Satan as a "strong man, fully ARMED." Satan is well supplied with defensive armor. He is not to be overcome by slight assaults, and feeble exertions. He that would overcome him must put forth all his strength. "This kind goes not out but by prayer and fasting." And Satan is also well supplied with offensive weapons. He is never at a loss for means to injure the soul of man. He has snares of every kind, and devices of every description. He knows exactly how every rank, and class, and age, and nation, and people can be assailed with most advantage. The devil is well armed.

Christ speaks of man's heart as being Satan's "palace." The natural heart is the favorite abode of the evil one, and all its faculties and powers are his servants, and do his will. He sits upon the throne which God ought to occupy, and governs the inward man. The devil is the "spirit that works in the children of disobedience." (Ephes. 2:2.)

Christ speaks of Satan's "goods being at PEACE." So long as a man is dead in trespasses and sin, so long his heart is at ease about spiritual things. He has no fear about the future. He has no anxiety about his soul. He has no dread of falling into hell. All this is a FALSE PEACE no doubt. It is a sleep which cannot last, and from which there must be one day a dreadful waking. But there is such a peace beyond question. Thoughtless, stolid, reckless insensibility about eternal things is one of the worst symptoms of the devil reigning over a man's soul.

Let us never think lightly of the devil. That common practice of idle jesting about Satan which we may often mark in the world, is a great evil. A prisoner must be a very hardened man who jests about the executioner and the gallows. The heart must be in a very bad state, when a man can talk with levity about hell and the devil.

Let us thank God that there is One who is stronger even than Satan. That One is the Friend of sinners, Jesus the Son of God. Mighty as the devil is, he was overcome by Jesus on the cross, when He triumphed over him openly. Strong as the devil is, Christ can pluck his captives out of his hands, and break the chains which bind them. May we never rest until we know that deliverance by experience, and have been set free by the Son of God!

Let us observe, for another thing, in these verses, how strongly our Lord teaches the impossibility of neutrality. He says, "he that is not with me, is against me; and he that gathers not with me, scatters."

The principle laid down in these words should be constantly remembered by all who make any profession of decided religion. We all naturally love an easy Christianity. We dislike collisions and separation. We like, if possible, to keep in with both sides. We fear extremes. We dread being righteous overmuch. We are anxious not to go too far. Such thoughts as these are full of peril to the soul. Once allowed to get the upper hand, they may do us immense harm. Nothing is so offensive to Christ as lukewarmness in religion. To be utterly dead and ignorant, is to be an object of pity as well as blame. But to know the truth and yet "halt between two opinions," is one of the chief of sins.

Let it be the settled determination of our minds that we will serve Christ with all our hearts, if we serve Him at all. Let there be no reserve, no compromise, no half-heartedness, no attempt to reconcile God and mammon in our Christianity. Let us resolve, by God's help, to be "with Christ," and "gather" by Christ's side, and allow the world to say and do what it will. It may cost us something at first. It will certainly repay us in the long run. Without decision there is no happiness in religion. He that follows Jesus most fully, will always follow Him most comfortably. Without decision in religion, there is no usefulness to others. The half-hearted Christian attracts none by the beauty of his life, and wins no respect from the world.

Let us observe, finally, in these verses, how dangerous it is to be content with any change in religion short of thorough conversion to God. This is a truth which our Lord teaches by an dreadful picture of one from whom a devil has been cast forth, but into whose heart the Holy Spirit has not entered. He describes the evil spirit, after his expulsion, as seeking rest and finding none. He describes him planning a return to the heart which he once inhabited, and carrying his plan into execution—He describes him finding that heart empty of any good, and, like a house "swept and garnished" for his reception. He describes him as entering in once more, with seven spirits worse than himself, and once more making it his abode. And He winds up all by the solemn saying, "the last state of that man is worse than the first."

We must feel in reading these fearful words, that Jesus is speaking of things which we faintly comprehend. He is lifting a corner of the veil which hangs over the unseen world. His words, no doubt, illustrate the state of things which existed in the Jewish nation during the time of His own ministry. But the main lesson of his words, which concerns us, is the danger of our own individual souls. They are a solemn warning to us, never to be satisfied with religious reformation without heart conversion.

There is no safety except in 'thorough Christianity'. To lay aside open sin is nothing, unless grace reigns in our hearts. To cease to do evil is a small matter, if we do not also learn to do well. The house must not only be swept and whitewashed. A new tenant must be introduced, or else the leprosy may yet appear again in the walls. The outward life must not only be garnished with the formal trappings of religion. The power of vital religion must be experienced in the inward man. The devil must not only be cast out. The Holy Spirit must take his place. Christ must dwell in our hearts by faith. We must not only be moralized, but spiritualized. We must not only be reformed, but born again.

Let us lay these things to heart. Many professing Christians, it may be feared, are deceiving themselves. They are not what they once were, and so they flatter themselves, they are what they ought to be. They are no longer sabbath-breaking, daring sinners, and so they dream that they are Christians.

They see not that they have only changed one kind of devil for another. They are governed by a decent, Pharisaic devil, instead of an audacious, riotous, unclean devil. But the tenant within is the devil still. And their last end will be worse than their first. From such an end may we pray to be delivered!

Whatever we are in religion, let us be thorough. Let us not be houses swept and garnished, but uninhabited by the Spirit. Let us not be potsherds covered with silver, fair on the outside, but worthless on the inside. Let our daily prayer be, "Search me, O God—and see whether there be any wicked way in me, and lead me in the way everlasting." (Psalm 139:24.)

LUKE 11:27-32
THE SIGN OF JONAH

And it came to pass, as he said these things, a certain woman out of the multitude lifted up her voice, and said unto him, Blessed is the womb that bare thee, and the breasts which thou didst suck. But he said, Yea rather, blessed are they that hear the word of God, and keep it.

And when the multitudes were gathering together unto him, he began to say, This generation is an evil generation: it seeketh after a sign; and there shall no sign be given to it but the sign of Jonah. For even as Jonah became a sign unto the Ninevites, so shall also the Son of man be to this generation. The queen of the south shall rise up in the judgment with the men of this generation, and shall condemn them: for she came from the ends of the earth to hear the wisdom of Solomon; and behold, a greater than Solomon is here. The men of Nineveh shall stand up in the judgment with this generation, and shall condemn it: for they repented at the preaching of Jonah; and behold, a greater than Jonah is here.

A woman is brought before us in this passage of Scripture of whose name and history we know nothing. We read that, as our Lord spoke, "A certain woman of the company lifted up her voice and said unto him, Blessed is the mother that gave you birth." At once our Lord founds on her remark a great lesson. His perfect wisdom turned every incident within His reach to profit.

We should observe in these verses how great are the privileges of those who hear and keep God's word. They are regarded by Christ with as much honor as if they were His nearest relatives. It is more blessed to be a believer in the Lord Jesus than it would have been to have been one of the family in which He was born after the flesh. It was a greater honor to the Virgin Mary herself to have Christ dwelling in her heart by faith, than to have been the mother of Christ, and to have nursed Him on her bosom.

Truths like these we are generally very slow to receive. We are apt to fancy that to have seen Christ, and heard Christ, and lived near Christ, and been a relative of Christ according to the flesh, would have had some mighty effect upon our souls. We are all naturally inclined to attach great importance to a religion of sight, and sense, and touch, and eye, and ear. We love a physical, tangible , material Christianity, far better than one of faith. And we need reminding that seeing is not always believing. Thousands saw Christ continually, while He was on earth, and yet clung to their sins. Even His brethren at one time "did not believe in him." (John 7:5.) A mere fleshly knowledge of Christ saves no one. The words of Paul are very instructive- "Though we have known Christ after the flesh, yet now henceforth know we him no more." (2 Cor. 5:16.)

Let us learn from our Lord's words before us that the highest privileges our souls can desire are close at hand, and within our reach, if we only believe. We need not idly wish that we had lived near Capernaum, or nearby Joseph's house at Nazareth. We need not dream of a deeper love and a more thorough devotion if we had really pressed Christ's hand, or heard Christ's voice, or been numbered among Christ's relatives. All this could have done nothing more for us than simple faith can do now. Do we hear Christ's voice and follow Him? Do we take Him for our only Savior and our only Friend, and forsaking all other hopes, cleave only unto Him? If this be so, all things are ours. We need no higher privilege. We can have no higher, until Christ comes again. No man can be nearer and dearer to Jesus than the man who simply believes.

We should observe, secondly, in these verses, the desperate unbelief of the Jews in our Lord's time. We are told that though they "gathered thick together" to hear Christ preach, they still professed to be waiting for a sign. They pretended to need more evidence before they believed. Our Lord declares that the Queen of Sheba and the men of Nineveh would put the Jews to shame at the last day. The Queen of Sheba had such faith that she traveled a vast distance in order to hear the wisdom of Solomon. Yet Solomon, with all his wisdom, was an erring and imperfect king. The Ninevites had such faith that they believed the message which Jonah brought from God, and repented. Yet even Jonah was a weak and unstable prophet. The Jews of our Lord's time had far higher light and infinitely clearer teachings than either

Solomon or Jonah could supply. They had among them the King of kings, the Prophet greater than Moses. Yet the Jews neither repented nor believed!

Let it never surprise us to see unbelief abounding, both in the church and in the world. So far from wondering that there have been men like Hobbes, and Paine, and Rousseau, and Voltaire, we ought rather to wonder that such men have been so few. So far from marveling that the vast majority of professing Christians remain unaffected and unmoved by the preaching of the Gospel, we ought to marvel that any around us believe at all. Why should we wonder to see that old disease which began with Adam and Eve infecting all their children? Why should we expect to see more faith among men and women now than was seen in our Lord's time? The enormous amount of unbelief and hardness on every side may well grieve and pain us. But it ought not to cause surprise.

Let us thank God if we have received the gift of faith. It is a great thing to believe all the Bible. We do not sufficiently realize the corruption of human nature. We do not see the full virulence of the disease by which all Adam's children are infected, and the small number of those who are saved. Have we faith, however weak and small? Let us praise God for the privilege. Who are we that God should have made us to differ?

Let us watch against UNBELIEF. The root of it often lies within us even after the tree is cut down. Let us guard our faith with a godly jealousy. It is the shield of the soul. It is the grace above all others which Satan labors to overthrow. Let us hold it fast. Blessed are those who believe!

We should observe, lastly, in these verses, how our Lord Jesus Christ testifies to the truth of a resurrection, and a life to come. He speaks of the queen of the south, whose name and dwelling-place are now alike unknown to us. He says "she shall rise up in the judgment." He speaks of the men of Nineveh, a people who have passed away from the face of the earth. He says of them also, "they shall rise up."

There is something very solemn and instructive in the language which our Lord here uses. It reminds us that this world is not all, and that the life which man lives in the body on earth is not the only life of which we ought to think. The kings and queens of olden time are all to live again one day, and to stand before the bar if God. The vast multitudes who once swarmed round the palaces of Nineveh are all to come forth from their graves, and to give an account of their works. To our eyes they seem to have passed away forever. We read with wonder of their empty halls, and talk of them as a people who have completely perished. Their dwelling-places are a desolation. Their very bones are dust. But to the eye of God they all live still. The queen of the south and the men of Nineveh will all rise again. We shall yet see them face to face.

Let the truth of the resurrection be often before our minds. Let the life to come be frequently before our thoughts. All is not over when the grave receives its tenant, and man goes to his 'long home'. Other people may dwell in our houses, and spend our money. Our very names may soon be forgotten. But still all is not over! Yet a little time and we shall all live again. "The earth shall cast out the dead." (Isaiah 26:19.) Many, like Felix, may well tremble when they think of such things. But men who live by faith in the Son of God, like Paul, should lift up their heads and rejoice.

LUKE 11:33-36
THE LAMP OF THE BODY

No man, when he hath lighted a lamp, putteth it in a cellar, neither under the bushel, but on the stand, that they which enter in may see the light. The lamp of thy body is thine eye: when thine eye is single, thy whole body also is full of light; but when it is evil, thy body also is full of darkness. Look therefore whether the light that is in thee be not darkness. If therefore thy whole body be full of light, having no part dark, it shall be wholly full of light, as when the lamp with its bright shining doth give thee light.

We learn from these words of the Lord Jesus, the importance of making a good use of religious light and privileges. We are reminded of what men do when they light a candle. They do not "put it in a hidden place," under a bushel measure. They place it on a candlestick, that it may be serviceable and useful by giving light.

When the Gospel of Christ is placed before a man's soul, it is as if God offered to him a lighted candle. It is not sufficient to hear it, and assent to it, and admire it, and acknowledge its truth. It must be received into the heart, and obeyed in the life. Until this takes place the Gospel does him no more good than if he were an African heathen, who has never heard the Gospel at all. A lighted candle is before him, but he is not turning it to account. The guilt of such conduct is very great. God's light neglected will be a heavy charge against many at the last day.

But even when a man professes to value the light of the Gospel he must take care that he is not selfish in the use of it. He must endeavor to reflect the light on all around him. He must strive to make others acquainted with the truths which he finds good for himself. He must let his light so shine before men, that they may see whose he is and whom he serves, and may be induced to follow his example, and join the Lord's side. He must regard the light which he enjoys as a loan, for the use of which he is accountable. He must strive to hold his candle in such a way, that many may see it, and as they see it, admire and believe.

Let us take heed to ourselves that we do not neglect our light. The sin of many in this matter is far greater than they suppose. Thousands flatter themselves that their souls are not in a very bad state, because they abstain from gross and glaring acts of wickedness, and are decent and respectable in their outward lives. But are they neglecting the Gospel when it is offered to them? Are they coolly sitting still year after year, and taking no decided steps in the service of Christ? If this be so, let them know that their guilt is very great in the sight of God. To have the light and yet not walk in the light, is of itself a great sin. It is to treat with contempt and indifference the King of kings.

Let us beware of selfishness in our religion, even after we have learned to value the light. We should labor to make all men see that we have found "the pearl of great price," and that we want them to find it as well as ourselves. A man's religion may well be suspected, when he is content to go to heaven alone. The true Christian will have a large heart. If a parent, he will long for the salvation of his children. If a master, he will desire to see his servants converted. If a landlord, he will want his tenants to come with him into God's kingdom. This is healthy religion! The Christian who is satisfied to burn his candle alone, is in a very weak and sickly state of soul.

We learn, secondly, from these verses, the value of a single and undivided heart in religion. This is a lesson which our Lord illustrates from the office of the eye in the human body. He reminds us that when the eye is "single," or 'thoroughly healthy', the action of the whole body is influenced by it. But when, on the contrary, the eye is evil or diseased, it affects the physical comfort and activity of the whole man. In an eastern country, where eye diseases are painfully common, the illustration is one which would be particularly striking.

But when can it be truly said that a man's heart is single in religion? What are the MARKS of a single heart? The question is one of deep importance. Well would it be for the church and the world if single hearts were more common.

The single heart is a heart which is not only changed, converted, and renewed; but thoroughly, powerfully, and habitually under the influence of the Holy Spirit. It is a heart which abhors all compromises, all luke-warmness, all halting between two opinions in religion. It sees one mighty object—the love of Christ dying for sinners. It has one mighty aim—to glorify God and do His will. It has one mighty desire, to please God and be commended by Him. Compared with such objects, aims, and desires, the single heart knows nothing worthy to be named. The praise and favor of man are nothing. The blame and disapprobation of man are trifles light as air. "One thing I desire-one thing I do—one thing I live for," this is the language of the single heart. (Psalm. 27:4.; Luke 10:42; Philip. 3:13.) Such were the hearts of Abraham, and Moses, and David, and Paul, and Luther, and Latimer. They all had their weaknesses and infirmities. They erred no doubt in some things. But they all had this grand peculiarity. They were men of one thing. They had single hearts. They were unmistakably "men of God."

The BLESSINGS of a single heart in religion are almost incalculable. He who has it, does good by wholesale. He is like a light-house in the midst of a dark world. He reflects light on hundreds whom he knows nothing of. "His whole body is full of light." His Master is seen through every window of his conversation and conduct. His grace shines forth in every department of his behavior. His family, his servants, his relations, his neighbors, his friends, his enemies, all see the bias of his character, and all are obliged to confess, whether they like it or not, that his religion is a real and influential thing.

And not least, the man of a single heart finds a rich reward in the inward experience of his own soul. He has food to eat the world knows not of. He has a joy and peace in believing to which many indolent Christians never attain. His face is toward the sun, and so his heart is seldom cold.

Let us pray and labor that we may have a single eye and a whole heart in our Christianity. If we have a religion, let us have a thorough one. If we are Christians, let us be decided. Inward peace and outward usefulness are at stake in this matter. Our eye must be single, if our whole body is to be full of light.

LUKE 11:37-44

JESUS PRONOUNCES 3 WOES ON THE PHARISEES

Now as he spake, a Pharisee asketh him to dine with him: and he went in, and sat down to meat. And when the Pharisee saw it, he marvelled that he had not first bathed himself before dinner. And the Lord said unto him, Now ye the Pharisees cleanse the outside of the cup and of the platter; but your inward part is full of extortion and wickedness. Ye foolish ones, did not he that made the outside make the inside also? But give for alms those things which are within; and behold, all things are clean unto you. But woe unto you Pharisees! for ye tithe mint and rue and every herb, and pass over justice and the love of God: but these ought ye to have done, and not to leave the other undone. Woe unto you Pharisees! for ye love the chief seats in the synagogues, and the salutations in the marketplaces. Woe unto you! for ye are as the tombs which appear not, and the men that walk over them know it not.

Let us notice in this passage, our Lord Jesus Christ's readiness, when needful, to go into the company of the unconverted. We read that a certain Pharisee invited Jesus to eat with him. The man was evidently not one of our Lord's disciples. Yet we are told that "Jesus went in and reclined at the table."

The conduct of our Lord on this occasion, as on others, is meant to be an example to all Christians. Christ is our pattern as well as our propitiation. There are evidently times and occasions when the servant of Christ must mix with the ungodly and the children of this world. There may be seasons when it may be a duty to hold social dealings with them, to accept their invitations, and sit down at their tables. Nothing, of course, must induce the Christian to be a partaker in the sins or frivolous amusements of the world. But he must not be uncourteous. He must not entirely withdraw himself from the society of the unconverted, and become a hermit or an ascetic. He must remember that good may be done in the private room as well as in the pulpit.

One qualification, however, should never be forgotten, when we act upon our Lord's example in this matter. Let us take heed that we go down into the company of the unconverted in the same spirit in which Christ went. Let us remember His boldness in speaking of the things of God. He was always "about His Father's business." Let us remember His faithfulness in rebuking sin. He spared not even the sins of those that entertained Him, when His attention was publicly called to them. Let us go into company in the same frame of mind, and our souls will take no harm. If we feel that we dare not imitate Christ in the company which we, are invited to join, we may be sure that we had better stay at home.

Let us notice, secondly, in this passage, the foolishness which accompanies hypocrisy in religion. We are told that the Pharisee with whom our Lord dined marveled that our Lord "had not first washed before dinner." He thought, like most of his order, that there was something unholy in not doing it, and that the neglect of it was a sign of moral impurity. Our Lord points out the absurdity of attaching such importance to the mere cleansing of the body, while the cleansing of the heart is overlooked. He reminds His host that God looks at the inward part of as, the hidden man of the heart, far more than at our skins. And He asks the searching question, "Did not He that made that which is outside, make that which is inside also?" The same God who formed our poor dying bodies, is the God who gave us a heart and soul.

Forever let us bear in mind that the state of our hearts is the principal thing that demands our attention, if we would know what we are in religion. Bodily washings, and fastings, and gestures, and postures, and self-imposed mortifications of the flesh, are all utterly useless if the heart is wrong. External devoutness of conduct, a grave face, and a bowed head, and a solemn countenance, and a loud amen, are all abominable in God's sight, so long as our hearts are not washed from their wickedness, and renewed by the Holy Spirit. Let this caution never be forgotten.

The idea that men can be devout before they are converted, is a grand delusion of the devil, and one against which we all need to be on our guard. There are two Scriptures which are very weighty on this subject. In one it is written, "Out of the heart are the issues of life." (Prov. 4:23.) In the other it is written, "Man looks on the outward appearance, but the Lord looks at the heart." (1 Sam. 16:7.) There is a question which we should always ask ourselves in drawing near to God, whether in public or private. We should say to ourselves, "Where is my heart?"

Let us notice, thirdly, in this passage, the gross inconsistency which is often exhibited by hypocrites in religion. We read that our Lord says to the Pharisees, "Woe to you Pharisees, because you give God a tenth of your mint, rue and all other kinds of garden herbs, but you neglect justice and the love of God." They carried to an extreme their zeal to pay tithes for the service of the temple—and yet they neglected the plainest duties towards God and their neighbors. They were scrupulous to an extreme about small matters in the ceremonial law; and yet they were utterly regardless of the simplest first principles of justice to man and love toward God. In the one direction they were rigidly careful to do even more than was needful. In the other direction they would do nothing at all. In the secondary things of their religion they were downright zealots and enthusiasts. But in the great primary things they were no better than the heathen.

The conduct of the Pharisees in this matter, unhappily, does not stand alone. There have never been lacking religious professors who have exalted the second things of Christianity far above the first, and in their zeal for the second things have finally neglected the first things entirely. There are thousands at the present day who make a great ado about daily services, and keeping Lent, and frequent communion, and turning to the east in churches, and a gorgeous ceremonial, and intoning public prayers—but never get any further. They know little or nothing of the great practical duties of humility, charity, meekness, spiritual-mindedness, Bible reading, private devotion, and separation from the world. They plunge into every gaiety with greediness. They are to be seen at every worldly assembly and revel, at the race, the opera, the theater, and the ball. They exhibit nothing of the mind of Christ in their daily life. What is all this but walking in the steps of the Pharisees? Well says the wise man, "There is no new thing under the sun." (Eccles. 1:9.) The generation which tithed mint but passed over "judgment and the love of God," is not yet extinct.

Let us watch and pray that we may observe a scriptural proportion in our religion. Let us beware of putting the second things out of their place, and so by degrees losing sight of the first entirely. Whatever importance we attach to the ceremonial part of Christianity, let us never forget its great practical duties. The religious teaching which inclines us to pass them over, has something about it which is radically defective.

Let us notice, lastly, the falseness and hollowness which characterize the 'religious hypocrite'. We read that our Lord compared the Pharisees to "unmarked graves, which men walk over without knowing it." Even so these boasting teachers of the Jews were inwardly full of corruption and uncleanness, to an extent of which their deluded hearers had no conception.

The picture here drawn is painful and disgusting. Yet the accuracy and truthfulness of it have often been proved by the conduct of hypocrites in every age of the church. What shall we say of, the lives of monks and nuns, which were exposed at the time of the Reformation? Thousands of so called "holy" men and women were found to be sunk in every kind of wickedness.

What shall we say of the lives of some of the leaders of sects and heresies who have professed a peculiarly pure standard of doctrine? Not infrequently the very men who have promised to others liberty have turned out to be themselves "servants of corruption." The morbid anatomy of human nature is a loathsome study. Hypocrisy and unclean living have often been found side by side.

Let us leave the whole passage with a settled determination to watch and pray against hypocrisy in religion. Whatever we are as Christians, let us be real, thorough, genuine and sincere. Let us abhor all disguise and pretense, and masquerading in the things of God, as that which is utterly loathsome in Christ's eyes. We may be weak, and erring, and frail, and come far short of our aims and desires. But at any rate, if we profess to believe in Christ, let us be true.

LUKE 11:45-54

JESUS PRONOUNCES 3 WOES ON THE SCRIBES

And one of the lawyers answering saith unto him, Teacher, in saying this thou reproachest us also. And he said, Woe unto you lawyers also! for ye load men with burdens grievous to be borne, and ye yourselves touch not the burdens with one of your fingers. Woe unto you! for ye build the tombs of the prophets, and your fathers killed them. So ye are witnesses and consent unto the works of your fathers: for they killed them, and ye build their tombs. Therefore also said the wisdom of God, I will send unto them prophets and apostles; and some of them they shall kill and persecute; that the blood of all the prophets, which was shed from the foundation of the world, may be required of this generation; from the blood of Abel unto the blood of Zachariah, who perished between the altar and the sanctuary: yea, I say unto you, it shall be required of this generation. Woe unto you lawyers! for ye took away the key of knowledge: ye entered not in yourselves, and them that were entering in ye hindered. And when he was come out from thence, the scribes and the Pharisees began to press upon him vehemently, and to provoke him to speak of many things; laying wait for him, to catch something out of his mouth.

The passage before us is an example of our Lord Jesus Christ's faithful dealing with the souls of men. We see Him without fear or favor rebuking the sins of the Jewish expounders of God's law. That false charity which calls it "unkind" to say that any one is in error, finds no encouragement in the language used by our Lord. He calls things by their right names. He knew that acute diseases need severe remedies. He would have us know that the truest friend to our souls, is not the man who is always "speaking smooth things," and agreeing with everything we say, but the man who tells us the most truth.

We learn, firstly, from our Lord's words, how great is the sin of professing to teach others what we do not practice ourselves. He says to the lawyers, "You laden men with burdens grievous to be borne, while you yourselves touch not the burdens with one of your fingers." They required others to observe wearisome ceremonies in religion which they themselves neglected. They had the impudence to lay yokes upon the consciences of other men, and yet to grant exemptions from these yokes for themselves. In a word, they had one set of measures and weights for their hearers, and another set for their own souls.

The stern reproof which our Lord here administers, should come home with special power to certain classes in the church. It is a word in season to all teachers of young people. It is a word to all masters of families and heads of households. It is a word to all fathers and mothers. Above all, it is a word to all clergymen and ministers of religion. Let all such mark well our Lord's language in this passage. Let them beware of telling others to aim at a standard which they do not aim at themselves. Such conduct, to say the least, is gross inconsistency.

Perfection, no doubt, is unattainable in this world. If nobody is to lay down rules, or teach, or preach, until he is faultless himself, the whole fabric of society would be thrown into confusion. But we have a right to expect 'some agreement' between a man's words and a man's work—between his teaching and his doing—between his preaching and his practice. One thing at all events is very certain. No lessons produce such effects on men as those which the teacher illustrates by his own daily life. Happy is he who can say with Paul, "Those things which you have heard and seen in me, do." (Philip.4:9.)

We learn, secondly, from our Lord's words, how much more easy it is to admire dead saints than living ones. He says to the lawyers, "You build the sepulchers of the prophets, and your fathers killed them." They professed to honor the memory of the prophets, while they lived in the very same ways which the prophets had condemned! They openly neglected their advice and teaching, and yet they pretended to respect their graves!

The practice which is here exposed has never been without followers in spirit, if not in the letter. Thousands of wicked men in every age of the church have tried to deceive themselves and others by loud professions of admiration for the saints of God after their decease. By so doing they have endeavored to ease their own consciences, and blind the eyes of the world. They have sought to raise in the minds of others the thought, "If these men love the memories of the good so dearly they must surely be of one heart with them." They have forgotten that even a child can see that "dead men tell no tales," and that to admire men when they can neither reprove us by their lips, nor put us to shame by their lives, is a very cheap admiration indeed.

Would we know what a man's religious character really is? Let us inquire what he thinks of true Christians while they are yet alive. Does he love them, and cleave to them, and delight in them, as the excellent of the earth? Or does he avoid them, and dislike them, and regard them as fanatics, and enthusiasts, and extreme, and righteous overmuch? The answers to these questions are a pretty safe test of a man's true character. When a man can see no beauty in living saints, but much in dead ones, his soul is in a very rotten state. The Lord Jesus has pronounced his condemnation. He is a hypocrite in the sight of God.

We learn, thirdly, from our Lord's words, how surely a reckoning day for persecution will come upon the persecutors. He says that the "blood of all the prophets shall be required."

There is something peculiarly solemn in this statement. The number of those who have been put to death for the faith of Christ in every age of the world, is exceedingly great. Thousands of men and women have laid down their lives rather than deny their Savior, and have shed their blood for the truth. At the time they died they seemed to have no helper. Like Zachariah, and James, and Stephen, and John the Baptist, and Ignatius, and Huss, and Hooper, and Latimer, they died without resistance. They were soon buried and forgotten on earth, and their enemies seemed to triumph utterly.

But their deaths were not forgotten in heaven. Their blood was had in remembrance before God. The persecutions by Herod, and Nero, and Diocletian, and bloody Mary, and Charles IX, are not forgotten. There shall be a great judgement one day, and then all the world shall see that "precious in the sight of the Lord is the death of his saints." (Psalm 116:15.)

Let us often look forward to the judgment day. There are many things going on in the world which are trying to our faith. The frequent triumphing of the wicked is perplexing. The frequent depression of the godly is a problem that appears hard to solve. But it shall all be made clear one day. The great white throne and the books of God shall put all things in their right places. The tangled maze of God's providence shall be unraveled. All shall be proved to a wondering world to have been "well done." Every tear that the wicked have caused the godly to shed shall be reckoned for. Every drop of righteous blood that has been spilled shall at length be required.

We learn, lastly, from our Lord's words, how great is the wickedness of keeping back others from religious knowledge. He says to the lawyers, "You have taken away the key of knowledge—you entered not in yourselves, and those that were entering in you hindered."

The sin here denounced is awfully common. The guilt of it lies at far more doors than at first sight many are aware. It is the sin of the Romish priest who forbids the poor man to read his Bible. It is the sin of the unconverted Protestant minister who warns his people against "extreme views," and sneers at the idea of conversion. It is the sin of the ungodly, thoughtless husband who dislikes his wife becoming "serious." It is the sin of the worldly-minded mother who cannot bear the idea of her daughter thinking of spiritual things, and giving up theaters and balls. All these, wittingly or unwittingly, are bringing down on themselves our Lord's emphatic "woe." They are hindering others from entering heaven!

Let us pray that this dreadful sin may never be ours. Whatever we are ourselves in religion, let us dread discouraging others, if they have the least serious concern about their souls. Let us never check any of those around us in their religion, and specially in the matter of reading the Bible, hearing the Gospel, and private prayer. Let us rather cheer them, encourage them, help them, and thank God if they are better than ourselves. "Deliver me from blood-guiltiness," was a prayer of David's. (Psalm 51:14.) It may be feared that the blood of relatives will be heavy on the heads of some at the last day. They saw them about to "enter" the kingdom of God, and they "hindered" them.

Chapter 12

In the meantime, when the many thousands of the multitude were gathered together, insomuch that they trod one upon another, he began to say unto his disciples first of all, Beware ye of the leaven of the Pharisees, which is hypocrisy. But there is nothing covered up, that shall not be revealed; and hid, that shall not be known. Wherefore whatsoever ye have said in the darkness shall be heard in the light; and what ye have spoken in the ear in the inner chambers shall be proclaimed upon the housetops. And I say unto you my friends, Be not afraid of them that kill the body, and after that have no more that they can do. But I will warn you whom ye shall fear: Fear him, who after he hath killed hath power to cast into hell; yea, I say unto you, Fear him. Are not five sparrows sold for two pence? and not one of them is forgotten in the sight of God. But the very hairs of your head are all numbered. Fear not: ye are of more value than many sparrows.

The words which begin this chapter are very striking when we consider its contents. We are told that "a crowd of many thousands had gathered, so that they were trampling on one another." And what does our Lord do? In the hearing of this multitude He delivers warnings against false teachers, and denounces the sins of the times in which he lived unsparingly, unflinchingly, and without partiality. This was true charity. This was doing the work of a physician. This was the pattern which all His ministers were intended to follow. Well would it have been for the church and the world if the ministers of Christ had always spoken out as plainly and faithfully as their Master used to do! Their own lives might have been made more uncomfortable by such a course of action. But they would have saved far more souls.

The first thing that demands our attention in these verses is Christ's warning against hypocrisy. He says to His disciples, "Beware you of the leaven of the Pharisees, which is hypocrisy."

This is a warning of which the importance can never be overrated. It was delivered by our Lord more than once, during His earthly ministry. It was intended to be a standing caution to His whole church in every age, and in every part of the world. It was meant to remind us that the principles of the Pharisees are deeply ingrained in human nature, and that Christians should be always on their guard against them. Pharisaism is a subtle leaven which the natural heart is always ready to receive. It is a leaven which once received into the heart infects the whole character of a man's Christianity. Of this leaven, says our Lord, in words that should often ring in our ears—of this leaven, beware!

Let us ever nail this caution in our memories, and bind it on our hearts. The plague is about us on every side. The danger is at all times. What is the essence of Romanism, and semi-Romanism, and formalism, and sacrament worship and church-adorning, and ceremonialism? What is it all but the leaven of the Pharisees under one shape or another? The Pharisees are not extinct. Pharisaism lives still.

If we would not become Pharisees, let us cultivate a 'heart religion'. Let us realize daily that the God with whom we have to do, looks far below the outward surface of our profession, and that He measures us by the state of our hearts. Let us be real and true in our Christianity. Let us abhor all partacting, and affectation, and semblance of devotion, put on for public occasions, but not really felt within. It may deceive man, and get us the reputation of being very religious, but it cannot deceive God. "There is nothing covered that shall not be revealed." Whatever we are in religion, let us never wear a cloak or a mask.

The second thing that demands our attention in these verses is Christ's warning against the fear of man. "Be not afraid," He says, "of those who kill the body, and after that have no more that they can do." But this is not all. He not only tells us whom we ought not to fear, but of whom we ought to be afraid. "Fear him," He says, "who after he has killed, has power to cast into hell; yes, I say unto you, fear him." The manner in which the lesson is conveyed is very striking and impressive. Twice over the exhortation is enforced. "Fear him," says our Lord—"yes, I say unto you, fear him."

The fear of man is one of the greatest obstacles which stand between the soul and heaven. "What will men say of me? What will they think of me? What will they do to me?"—How often these little questions have turned the balance against the soul, and kept men bound hand and foot by sin and the devil! Thousands would never hesitate a moment to storm a breach or face a lion, who dare not face the laughter of relatives, neighbors, and friends. Now if the fear of man has such influence in these times, how much greater must its influence have been in the days when our Lord was upon earth! If it be hard to follow Christ through ridicule and ill-natured words, how much harder must it have been to follow Him through prisons, beatings, scourgings, and violent deaths! All these things our Lord Jesus knew well. No wonder that He cries, "Be not afraid."

But what is the best remedy against the fear of man? How are we to overcome this powerful feeling, and break the chains which it throws around us? There is no remedy like that which our Lord recommends. We must supplant the fear of man by a higher and more powerful principle—the fear of God. We must look away from those who can only hurt the body to Him who has all dominion over the soul. We must turn our eyes from those who can only injure us in the life that now is, to Him who can condemn us to eternal misery in the life to come. Armed with this mighty principle, we shall not play the coward. Seeing Him that is invisible, we shall find the lesser fear melting away before the greater, and the weaker before the stronger.

"I fear God," said Colonel Gardiner, "and therefore there is no one else that I need fear." It was a noble saying of martyred Bishop Hooper, when a Roman Catholic urged him to save his life by recanting at the stake—"Life is sweet and death is bitter. But eternal life is more sweet, and eternal death is more bitter."

The last thing that demands our attention in these verses, is Christ's encouragement to persecuted believers. He reminds them of God's providential care over the least of His creatures—"Not one sparrow is forgotten before God." He goes on to assure those who the same Fatherly care is engaged on behalf of each one of themselves—"The very hairs of your head are all numbered." Nothing whatever, whether great or small, can happen to a believer, without God's ordering and permission.

The providential government of God over everything in this world is a truth of which the Greek and Roman philosophers had no conception. It is a truth which is specially revealed to us in the word of God. Just as the telescope and microscope show us that there is order and design in all the works of God's hand, from the greatest planet down to the least insect, so does the Bible teach us that there is wisdom, order, and design in all the events of our daily life. There is no such thing as "chance," "luck," or "accident" in the Christian's journey through this world. All is arranged and appointed by God. And all things are "working together" for the believer's good. (Rom. 8:28.)

Let us seek to have an abiding sense of God's hand in all that befalls us, if we profess to be believers in Jesus Christ. Let us strive to realize that a Father's hand is measuring out our daily portion, and that our steps are ordered by Him. A daily practical faith of this kind, is one grand secret of happiness, and a mighty antidote against murmuring and discontent. We should try to feel in the day of trial and disappointment, that all is right and all is well done. We should try to feel on the bed of sickness that there must be a "needs be." We should say to ourselves, "God could keep away from me these things if He thought fit. But He does not do so, and therefore they must be for my advantage. I will lie still, and bear them patiently. I have 'an everlasting covenant ordered in all things and sure.' (2 Sam. 23:5.) What pleases God shall please me."

LUKE 12:8-12

And I say unto you, Everyone who shall confess me before men, him shall the Son of man also confess before the angels of God: but he that denieth me in the presence of men shall be denied in the presence of the angels of God. And every one who shall speak a word against the Son of man, it shall be forgiven him: but unto him that blasphemeth against the Holy Spirit it shall not be forgiven. And when they bring you before the synagogues, and the rulers, and the authorities, be not anxious how or what ye shall answer, or what ye shall say: for the Holy Spirit shall teach you in that very hour what ye ought to say.

We are taught, firstly, in these verses, that we must confess Christ upon earth, if we expect Him to own us as His saved people at the last day. We must not be ashamed to let all men see that we believe in Christ, and serve Christ, and love Christ, and care more for the praise of Christ than for the praise of man.

The duty of confessing Christ is incumbent on all Christians in every age of the Church. Let us never forget that. It is not for martyrs only, but for all believers, in every rank of life. It is not for great occasions only, but for our daily walk through an evil world. The rich man among the rich, the laborer among laborers, the young among the young, the servant among servants-each and all must be prepared, if they are true Christians, to confess their Master. It needs no blowing a trumpet. It requires no noisy boasting. It needs nothing more than using the daily opportunity. But one thing is certain—if a man loves Jesus, he ought not to be ashamed to let people know it.

The difficulty of confessing Christ is undoubtedly very great. It never was easy at any period. It never will be easy as long as the world stands. It is sure to entail on us laughter, ridicule, contempt, mockery, enmity, and persecution. The wicked dislike to see any one better than themselves. The world which hated Christ will always hate true Christians. But whether we like it or not, whether it be hard or easy, our course is perfectly clear. In one way or another Christ must be confessed.

The grand motive to stir us up to bold confession is forcibly brought before us in the words which we are now considering. Our Lord declares, that if we do not confess Him before men, He will "not confess us before the angels of God" at the last day. He will refuse to acknowledge us as His people. He will disown us as cowards, faithless, and deserters. He will not plead for us. He will not be our Advocate. He will not deliver us from the wrath to come. He will leave us to reap the consequences of our cowardice, and to stand before the bar of God helpless, defenseless, and unforgiven.

What a dreadful prospect is this! How much turns on this one hinge of "confessing Christ before men!" Surely we ought not to hesitate for a moment. To doubt between two such alternatives is the height of folly. For us to deny Christ or be ashamed of His Gospel, may get us a little of man's good opinion for a few years, though it will bring us no real peace. But for Christ to deny us at the last day will be ruin in hell to all eternity! Let us cast away our cowardly fears. Come what will, let us confess Christ.

We are taught, secondly, in these verses, that there is such a thing as an unpardonable sin. Our Lord Jesus Christ declares that "unto him that blasphemes against the Holy Spirit, it shall not be forgiven."

These dreadful words must doubtless be interpreted with scriptural qualification. We must never so expound one part of Scripture as to make it contradict another. Nothing is impossible with God. The blood of Christ can cleanse away all sin. The very chief of sinners have been pardoned in many instances. These things must never be forgotten. Yet notwithstanding all this, there remains behind a great truth which must not be evaded. There is such a thing as a sin "which shall not be forgiven."

The sin to which our Lord refers in this passage appears to be the sin of deliberately rejecting God's truth with the heart, while the truth is clearly known with the head. It is a combination of light in the understanding and determined wickedness in the will. It is the very sin into which many of the Scribes and Pharisees appear to have fallen, when they rejected the ministry of the Spirit after the day of Pentecost, and refused to believe the preaching of the apostles. It is a sin into which, it may be feared, many constant hearers of the Gospel nowadays fall, by determined clinging to the world. And worst of all, it is a sin which is commonly accompanied by utter deadness, hardness, and insensibility of heart. The man whose sins will not be forgiven, is precisely the man who will never seek to have them forgiven. This is exactly the root of his dreadful disease. He might be pardoned, but he will not seek to be pardoned. He is Gospel-hardened and "twice dead." His conscience is "seared with a hot iron." (1 Tim. 4:2.)

Let us pray that we may be delivered from a cold, speculative, unsanctified head-knowledge of Christianity. It is a rock on which thousands make shipwreck to all eternity. No heart becomes so hard as that on which the light shines, but finds no admission. The same fire which melts the wax hardens the clay. Whatever light we have let us use it. Whatever knowledge we possess, let us live fully up to it. To be an ignorant heathen, and bow down to idols and stones, is bad enough. But to be called a Christian, and know the theory of the Gospel, and yet cleave to sin and the world with the heart, is to be a candidate for the worst and lowest place in hell. It is to be as like as possible to the devil.

We are taught, lastly, in this passage, that Christians need not be over anxious as to what they shall say, when suddenly required to speak for Christ's cause.

The promise which our Lord gives on this subject has a primary reference, no doubt, to public trials like those of Paul before Felix and Festus. It is a promise which hundreds in similar circumstances have found fulfilled to their singular comfort. The lives of many of the Reformers, and others of God's witnesses, are full of striking proofs that the Holy Spirit can teach Christians what to say in time of need.

But there is a secondary sense, in which the promise belongs to all believers, which ought not be overlooked. Occasions are constantly arising in the lives of Christians, when they are suddenly and unexpectedly called upon to speak on behalf of their Master, and to render a reason of their hope. The home circle, the family fireside, the society of friends, the communion with relatives, the very business of the world, will often furnish such sudden occasions. On such occasions the believer should fall back on the promise now before us. It may be disagreeable, and especially to a young Christian, to be suddenly required to speak before others of religion, and above all if religion is attacked. But let us not be alarmed, and flurried, or cast down, or excited. If we remember the promise of Christ, we have no cause to be afraid.

Let us pray for a good memory about Bible promises. We shall find it an inestimable comfort. There are far more, and far wider promises laid down in Scripture for the comfort of Christ's people, than most of Christ's people are aware of. There are promises for almost every position in which we can be placed, and every event that can befall us. Among other promises, let us not forget that one which is now before us. We are sometimes called upon to go into company which is not congenial to us, and we go with a troubled and anxious heart. We fear saying what we ought not to say, and not saying what we ought. At such seasons, let us remember this blessed promise, and put our Master in remembrance of it also. So doing He will not fail us or forsake us. A mouth shall be given to us and wisdom to speak rightly—"The Holy Spirit shall teach us" what to say.

LUKE 12:13-21

PARABLE OF THE RICH FOOL

And one out of the multitude said unto him, Teacher, bid my brother divide the inheritance with me. But he said unto him, Man, who made me a judge or a divider over you? And he said unto them, Take heed, and keep yourselves from all covetousness: for a man's life consisteth not in the abundance of the things which he possesseth. And he spake a parable unto them, saying, The ground of a certain rich man brought forth plentifully: and he reasoned within himself, saying, What shall I do, because I have not where to bestow my fruits? And he said, This will I do: I will pull down my barns, and build greater; and there will I bestow all my grain and my goods. And I will say to my soul, Soul, thou hast much goods laid up for many years; take thine ease, eat, drink, be merry. But God said unto him, Thou foolish one, this night is thy soul required of thee; and the things which thou hast prepared, whose shall they be? So is he that layeth up treasure for himself, and is not rich toward God.

The passage we have read now affords a singular instance of man's readiness to bring the things of this world into the midst of his religion. We are told that a certain hearer of our Lord asked Him to assist him about his temporal affairs. "Master," he said, "speak to my brother, that he divide the inheritance with me." He probably had some vague idea that Jesus was going to set up a kingdom in this world, and to reign upon earth. He resolves to make an early application about his own pecuniary matters. He entreats our Lord's arbitration about his earthly inheritance. Other hearers of Christ might be thinking of a portion in the world to come. This man was one whose chief thoughts evidently ran upon this present life.

How many hearers of the Gospel are just like this man! How many are incessantly planning and scheming about the things of time, even under the very sound of the things of eternity! The natural heart of man is always the same. Even the preaching of Christ did not arrest the attention of all His hearers. The minister of Christ in the present day must never be surprised to see worldliness and inattention in the midst of his congregation. The servant must not expect his sermons to be more valued than his Master's.

Let us mark in these verses what a solemn warning our Lord pronounces against covetousness. "He said unto them, take heed and beware of covetousness."

It would be vain to decide positively which is the most common sin in the world. It would be safe to say that there is none, at any rate, to which the heart is more prone, than covetousness. It was this sin which helped to cast down the angels who fell. They were not content with their first estate. They coveted something better. It was this sin which helped to drive Adam and Eve out of paradise, and bring death into the world. Our first parents were not satisfied with the things which God gave them in Eden. They coveted, and so they fell. It is a sin which, ever since the fall, has been the productive cause of misery and unhappiness upon earth. Wars, quarrels, strifes, divisions, envyings, disputes, jealousies, hatreds of all sorts, both public and private, may nearly all be traced up to this fountain-head.

Let the warning which our Lord pronounces, sink down into our hearts, and bear fruit in our lives. Let us strive to learn the lesson which Paul had mastered, when he says, "I have learned in whatever state I am therewith to be content." (Phil. 4:11.) Let us pray for a thorough confidence in God's superintending providence over all our worldly affairs, and God's perfect wisdom in all His arrangements concerning us. If we have little, let us be sure that it would be not good for us to have much. If the things that we have are taken away, let us be satisfied that there is a needs be. Happy is he who is persuaded that whatever is, is best, and has ceased from vain wishing, and become "content with such things as he has." (Hebrews 13:5.)

Let us mark, secondly, in these verses, what a withering exposure our Lord makes of the folly of worldly-mindedness. He draws the picture of a rich man of the world, whose mind is wholly set on earthly things. He paints him scheming and planning about his property, as if he was master of his own life, and had but to say, "I will do a thing," and it would be done. And then he turns the picture, and shows us God requiring the worldling's soul, and asking the heart-searching question, "Whose shall these things be which you have provided?" "Folly," he bids us learn, nothing less than "folly," is the right word by which to describe the conduct of the man who thinks of nothing but his money. The man who "lays up treasure for himself, and is not rich towards God," is the man whom God declares to be a "fool."

It is a dreadful thought that the character which Jesus brings before us in this parable, is far from being uncommon. Thousands in every age of the world have lived continually doing the very things which are here condemned. Thousands are doing them at this very day. They are laying up treasure upon earth, and thinking of nothing but how to increase it. They are continually adding to their hoards, as if they were to enjoy them forever, and as if there was no death, no judgment, and no world to come. And yet these are the men who are called clever, and prudent, and wise! These are the men who are commended, and flattered, and held up to admiration! Truly the Lord sees not as man sees! The Lord declares that rich men who live only for this world are "fools."

Let us pray for rich men. Their souls are in great danger. "Heaven," said a great man on his death-bed, "is a place to which few kings and rich men come." Even when converted, the rich carry a great weight, and run the race to heaven under great disadvantages. The possession of money has a most hardening effect upon the conscience. We never know what we may do when we become rich. "The love of money is the root of all evil. While some have coveted after it, they have erred from the faith and pierced themselves through with many sorrows." (1 Tim. 6:10.) Poverty has many disadvantages. But riches destroy far more souls than poverty!

Let us mark, lastly, in these verses, how important it is to be rich towards God. This is true wisdom. This is true providing for time to come. This is genuine prudence. The wise man is he who does not think only of earthly treasure, but of treasure in heaven.

When can it be said of a man, that he is rich towards God? Never until he is rich in grace, and rich in faith, and rich in good works! Never until he has applied to Jesus Christ, and bought of him gold tried in the fire! (Rev. 3:18.) Never until he has a house not made with hands, eternal in the heavens! Never until he has a name inscribed in the book of life, and is an heir of God and a joint heir with Christ! Such a man is truly rich. His treasure is incorruptible. His bank never breaks. His inheritance fades not away. Man cannot deprive him of it. Death cannot snatch it out of his hands. All things are his already—life, death, things present, and things to come. (1 Cor. 3:22.) And best of all, what he has now is nothing to what he will have hereafter.

Riches like these are within reach of every sinner who will come to Christ and receive them. May we never rest until they are ours! To obtain them may cost us something in this world. It may bring on us persecution, ridicule, and scorn. But let the thought console us, that the Judge of all says, "You are rich." (Rev. 2:9.) The true Christian is the only man who is really wealthy and wise.

LUKE 12:22-31

WARNINGS ABOUT WORRY

And he said unto his disciples, Therefore I say unto you, Be not anxious for your life, what ye shall eat; nor yet for your body, what ye shall put on. For the life is more than the food, and the body than the raiment. Consider the ravens, that they sow not, neither reap; which have no store-chamber nor barn; and God feedeth them: of how much more value are ye than the birds! And which of you by being anxious can add a cubit unto the measure of his life? If then ye are not able to do even that which is least, why are ye anxious concerning the rest? Consider the lilies, how they grow: they toil not, neither do they spin; yet I say unto you, Even Solomon in all his glory was not arrayed like one of these. But if God doth so clothe the grass in the field, which to-day is, and to-morrow is cast into the oven; how much more shall he clothe you, O ye of little faith? And seek not ye what ye shall eat, and what ye shall drink, neither be ye of doubtful mind. For all these things do the nations of the world seek after: but your Father knoweth that ye have need of these things. Yet seek ye his kingdom, and these things shall be added unto you.

We have in these verses a collection of striking arguments against over-anxiety about the things of this world.

At first sight they may seem to some minds simple and common place. But the more they are pondered, the more weighty will they appear. An abiding recollection of them would save many Christians an immense amount of trouble.

Christ bids us consider the RAVENS. "They neither sow nor reap. They have neither storehouse nor barn. But God feeds them." Now if the Maker of all things provides for the needs of birds, and orders things so that they have a daily supply of food, we ought surely not to fear that He will let His spiritual children starve.

Christ bids us look at the LILIES. "They toil not, they spin not; Yet Solomon in all his glory was not arrayed like one of these." Now if God every year provides these flowers with a fresh supply of living leaves and blossoms, we surely ought not to doubt His power and willingness to furnish His believing servants with all needful clothing.

Christ bids us remember that a Christian man should be ashamed of being as anxious as a heathen. The "pagan world" may well be anxious about food, and clothing, and the like. They are sunk in deep ignorance, and know nothing of the real nature of God. But the man who can say of God, "He is my Father," and of Christ, "He is my Savior, ought surely to be above such anxieties and cares. A clear faith should produce a light heart.

Finally, Christ bids us think of the perfect knowledge of God. "Our Father knows that we have need" of food and clothing. That thought alone ought to make us content. All our needs are perfectly known to the Lord of heaven and earth. He can relieve those needs, whenever He sees fit. He will relieve them, whenever it is good for our souls.

Let the four arguments now adduced sink deep into our hearts, and bear fruit in our lives. Nothing is more common than an anxious and troubled spirit, and nothing so mars a believer's usefulness, and diminishes his inward peace. Nothing, on the contrary, glorifies God so much as a cheerful spirit in the midst of temporal troubles. It carries a reality with it which even the worldly can understand. It commends our Christianity, and makes it beautiful in the eyes of men. Faith, and faith only, will produce this cheerful spirit. The man who can say boldly, "The Lord is my shepherd," is the man who will be able to add, "I shall not lack." (Psalm. 23:1.)

We have, secondly, in these verses, a high standard of living commended to all Christians. It is contained in a short and simple injunction, "Seek the kingdom of God." We are not to give our principal thoughts to the things of this world. We are not so to live as if we had nothing but a body. We are to live like beings who have immortal souls to be lost or saved—a death to die—a God to meet—a judgment to expect—and an eternity in heaven or in hell awaiting us.

When can we be said to "seek the kingdom of God?" We do so when we make it the chief business of our lives to secure a place in the number of saved people—to have our sins pardoned, our hearts renewed, and ourselves made fit for the inheritance of the saints in light. We do so when we give a primary place in our minds to the interests of God's kingdom—when we labor to increase the number of God's subjects—when we strive to maintain God's cause, and advance God's glory in the world.

The kingdom of God is the only kingdom worth laboring for. All other kingdoms shall, sooner or later, decay and pass away. The statesmen who raise them are like men who build houses of cards, or children, who make palaces of sand on the sea shore. The wealth which constitutes their great-ness is as liable to melt away as the snow in spring. The kingdom of God is the only kingdom which shall endure forever. Happy are they who belong to it, love it, live for it, pray for it, and labor for its increase and prosperity. Their labor shall not be in vain. May we give all diligence to make our calling into this kingdom sure! May it be our constant advice to children, relatives, friends, servants, neighbors, "Seek the kingdom!" Whatever else you seek, "Seek first the kingdom of God!"

We have, lastly, in these verse, a marvelous promise held out to those who seek the kingdom of God. Our Lord Jesus declares, "All these things shall be added unto you."

We must take heed that we do not misunderstand the meaning of this passage. We have no right to expect that the Christian tradesman, who neglects his business under pretense of zeal for God's kingdom, will find his trade prosper, and his affairs do well. To place such a sense upon the promise would be nothing less than fanaticism and enthusiasm. It would encourage slothfulness in business, and give occasion to the enemies of God to blaspheme.

The man to whom the promise before us belongs, is the Christian who gives to the things of God their right order and their right place. He does not neglect the worldly duties of his station, but he regards them as of infinitely less importance than the requirements of God. He does not omit due atten-tion to his temporal affairs, but he looks on them as of far less moment than the affairs of his soul. In short, he aims in all his daily life to put God first and the world second—to give the second place to the things of his body, and the first place to the things of his soul. This is the man to whom Jesus says, "All these things shall be added unto you."

But how is the promise fulfilled? The answer is short and simple. The man who seeks first God's kingdom shall never lack anything that is for his good. He may not have so much health as some. He may not have so much wealth as others. He may not have a richly spread table, or royal dainties. But he shall always have enough. "Bread shall be given him. His water shall be sure." (Isaiah 33:16.) "All things shall work together for good to those who love God." (Rom. 8:28.) "No good thing will the Lord withhold from those who walk uprightly." (Psalm 84:11.) "I have been young," said David, "and now am old, yet never have I seen the righteous forsaken, nor his seed begging their bread." (Psalm 37:25.)

LUKE 12:32-40

WATCHFULNESS

Fear not, little flock; for it is your Father's good pleasure to give you the kingdom. Sell that which ye have, and give alms; make for yourselves purses which wax not old, a treasure in the heavens that faileth not, where no thief draweth near, neither moth destroyeth. For where your treasure is, there will your heart be also. Let your loins be girded about, and your lamps burning; and be ye yourselves like unto men looking for their lord, when he shall return from the marriage feast; that, when he cometh and knocketh, they may straightway open unto him. Blessed are those servants, whom the lord when he cometh shall find watching: verily I say unto you, that he shall gird himself, and make them sit down to meat, and shall come and serve them. And if he shall come in the second watch, and if in the third, and find them so blessed are those servants. But know this, that if the master of the house had known in what hour the thief was coming, he would have watched, and not have left his house to be broken through. Be ye also ready: for in an hour that ye think not the Son of man cometh.

Let us mark what a gracious word of consolation this passage contains for all true believers. The Lord Jesus knew well the hearts of His disciples. He knew how ready they were to be filled with fears of every description—fears because of the fewness of their number—fears because of the multitude of their enemies, fears because of the many difficulties in their way—fears because of their sense of weakness and unworthiness. He answers these many fears with a single golden sentence—"Fear not, little flock, it is your Father's good pleasure to give you the kingdom."

Believers are a "little flock." They always have been, ever since the world began. Professing servants of God have sometimes been very many. Baptized people at the present day are a great company. But true Christians are very few. It is foolish to be surprised at this. It is vain to expect it will be otherwise until the Lord comes again. "Strait is the gate, and narrow is the way, that leads unto life, and few there be that find it." (Matt. 7:14.)

Believers have a glorious "kingdom" awaiting them. Here upon earth they are often mocked and ridiculed, and persecuted, and, like their Master, despised and rejected of men. But "the sufferings of this present time are not worthy to be compared with the glory which shall be revealed." "When Christ, who is our life, shall appear, then shall you also appear with him in glory." (Rom. 8:18. Coloss. 3:4.)

Believers are tenderly loved by God the Father. It is "the Father's good pleasure" to give them a kingdom. He does not receive them grudgingly, unwillingly, and coldly. He rejoices over them as members of His beloved Son in whom He is well pleased. He regards them as His dear children in Christ. He sees no spot in them. Even now, when He looks down on them from heaven, in the midst of their infirmities, He is well pleased, and hereafter, when presented before His glory, He will welcome them with exceeding joy. (Jude 24.)

Are we members of Christ's little flock? Then surely we ought not to be afraid. There are given to us exceeding great and precious promises. (2 Pet. 1:4.) God is ours, and Christ is ours. Greater are those that are for us than all that are against us. The world, the flesh, and the devil, are mighty enemies. But with Christ on our side we have no cause to fear.

Let us mark, secondly, what a striking exhortation these verses contain to seek treasure in heaven. "Sell your possessions and give to the poor. Provide purses for yourselves that will not wear out, a treasure in heaven that will not be exhausted, where no thief comes near and no moth destroys." But this is not all. A mighty, heart-searching principle is laid down to enforce the exhortation. "Where your treasure is, there will your heart be also."

The language of this charge is doubtless somewhat figurative. Yet the meaning of it is clear and unmistakable. We are to sell—to give up anything, and deny ourselves anything which stands in the way of our soul's salvation. We are to give—to show charity and kindness to everyone, and to be more ready to spend our money in relieving others, than to hoard it for our own selfish purposes. We are to provide ourselves treasures in heaven, to make sure that our names are in the book of life—to lay hold of eternal life—to lay up for ourselves evidences which will bear the inspection of the day of judgment.

This is true wisdom. This is real prudence. The man who does well for himself is the man who gives up everything for Christ's sake. He makes the best of bargains. He carries the cross for a few years in this world, and in the world to come has everlasting life. He obtains the best of possessions. He carries his riches with him beyond the grave. He is rich in grace here, and he is rich in glory hereafter. And, best of all, what he obtains by faith in Christ he never loses. It is "that good part which is never taken away."

Would we know what we are ourselves? Let us see whether we have treasure in heaven, or whether all our good things are here upon earth. Would we know what our treasure is? Let us ask ourselves what we love most? This is the true test of character. This is the pulse of our religion. It matters little what we say, or what we profess, or what preaching we admire, or what place of worship we attend. What do we love? On what are our affections set? This is the great question. "Where our treasure is there will our hearts be also."

Let us mark, lastly, what an instructive picture these verses contain of the frame of mind which the true Christian should endeavor to keep up. Our Lord tells us that we ought to be "like men that wait for their Lord." We ought to live like servants who expect their Master's return, fulfilling our duties in our several stations, and doing nothing which we would not like to be found doing when Christ comes again.

The standard of life which our Lord has set up here is an exceedingly high one—so high, indeed, that many Christians are apt to flinch from it, and feel cast down. And yet there is nothing here which ought to make a believer afraid. Readiness for the return of Christ to this world implies nothing which is impossible and unattainable. It requires no angelic perfection. It requires no man to forsake his family, and retire into solitude. It requires nothing more than the life of repentance, faith, and holiness.

The man who is living the life of faith in the Son of God is the man whose "loins are girded," and whose "light is burning." Such a man may have the care of kingdoms on him, like Daniel—or be a servant in a Nero's household, like some in Paul's time. All this matters nothing. If he lives looking unto Jesus, he is a servant who can "open to Him immediately." Surely it is not too much to ask Christians to be men of this kind. Surely it was not for nothing that our Lord said, "The Son of Man comes at an hour when you do not think."

Are we ourselves living as if we were ready for the second coming of Christ? Well would it be if this question were put to our consciences more frequently. It might keep us back from many a false step in our daily life. It might prevent many a backsliding. The true Christian should not only believe in Christ, and love Christ. He should also look and long for Christ's appearing. If he cannot say from his heart, "Come, Lord Jesus," there must be something wrong about his soul.

LUKE 12:41-48

And Peter said, Lord, speakest thou this parable unto us, or even unto all? And the Lord said, Who then is the faithful and wise steward, whom his lord shall set over his household, to give them their portion of food in due season? Blessed is that servant, whom his lord when he cometh shall find so doing. Of a truth I say unto you, that he will set him over all that he hath. But if that servant shall say in his heart, My lord delayeth his coming; and shall begin to beat the menservants and the maidservants, and to eat and drink, and to be drunken; the lord of that servant shall come in a day when he expecteth not, and in an hour when he knoweth not, and shall cut him asunder, and appoint his portion with the unfaithful. And that servant, who knew his lord's will, and made not ready, nor did according to his will, shall be beaten with many stripes; but he that knew not, and did things worthy of stripes, shall be beaten with few stripes. And to whomsoever much is given, of him shall much be required: and to whom they commit much, of him will they ask the more.

We learn from these verses, the importance of doing, in our Christianity. Our Lord is speaking of His own second coming. He is comparing His disciples to servants waiting for their master's return, who have each their own work to do during His absence. "Blessed," He says, "is that servant, whom his master, when he comes, shall find so doing."

The warning has doubtless a primary reference to ministers of the Gospel. They are the stewards of God's mysteries, who are specially bound to be found "doing," when Christ comes again. But the words contain a further lesson, which all Christians would do well to consider. That lesson is, the immense importance of a working, practical, diligent, useful religion.

The lesson is one which is greatly needed in the churches of Christ. We hear a great deal about people's intentions, and hopes, and wishes, and feelings, and professions. It would be well if we could hear more about people's practice. It is not the servant who is found wishing and professing, but the servant who is found "doing" whom Jesus calls "blessed."

The lesson is one which many, unhappily, shrink from giving, and many more shrink from receiving. We are gravely told that to talk of "working," and "doing," is 'legalistic', and brings Christians into bondage! Remarks of this kind should never move us. They savor of ignorance or perverseness. The lesson before us is not about justification, but about sanctification—not about faith, but about holiness. The point is not what a man should do to be saved—but what ought a saved man to do! The teaching of Scripture is clear and express upon this subject, A saved man ought to be "careful to maintain good works." (Tit. 3:8.) The desire of a true Christian ought to be, to be found "doing."

If we love life, let us resolve by God's help, to be "doing" Christians. This is to be like Christ. He "went about doing good." (Acts 10:38.) This is to be like the apostles, they were men of deeds even more than of words. This is to glorify God—"Herein is my Father glorified, that you bear much fruit." (John 15:8.) This is to be useful to the world—"Let your light so shine before men, that they may see your good works, and glorify your Father in heaven." (Matt. 5:16.)

We learn, secondly, from these verses, the dreadful danger of those who neglect the duties of their calling. Of such our Lord declares, that they shall be "cut in pieces, and their portion appointed with the unbelievers." These words no doubt apply especially to the ministers and teachers of the Gospel. Yet we must not flatter ourselves that they are confined to them. They are probably meant to convey a lesson to all who fill offices of high responsibility. It is a striking fact that when Peter says at the beginning of the passage, "are you telling this parable to us, or to all?" our Lord gives him no answer. Whoever occupies a position of trust, and neglects his duties, would do well to ponder this passage, and learn wisdom.

The language which our Lord Jesus uses about slothful and unfaithful servants, is peculiarly severe. Few places in the Gospels contain such strong expressions as this. It is a vain delusion to suppose that the Gospel speaks nothing but "smooth things." The same loving Savior who holds out mercy to the uttermost to the penitent and believing, never shrinks from holding up the judgments of God against those who despise His counsel. Let no man deceive us on this subject. There is a hell for such an one as goes on still in his wickedness, no less than a heaven for the believer in Jesus. There is such a thing as "the wrath of the Lamb." (Rev. 6:16.)

Let us strive so to live, that whenever the heavenly Master comes, we may be found ready to receive Him. Let us watch our hearts with a godly jealousy, and beware of the least symptom of unreadiness for the Lord's appearing. Specially let us beware of any rising disposition to lower our standard of Christian holiness—to dislike people who are more spiritually-minded than ourselves, and to conform to the world. The moment we detect such a disposition in our hearts, we may be sure that our souls are in great peril. The Christian professor who begins to persecute God's people, and to take pleasure in worldly society, is on the high road to ruin.

We learn, lastly, from these verses, that the greater a man's religious light is, the greater is his guilt if he is not converted. The servant which "knew his master's will, but did it not, shall be beaten with many stripes." "Unto whomsoever much is given, of him shall be much required."

The lesson of these words is one of wide application. It demands the attention of many classes. It should come home to the conscience of every British Christian. His judgment shall be far more strict than that of the heathen who never saw the Bible. It should come home to every Protestant who has the liberty to read the Scriptures. His responsibility is far greater than that of the priest-ridden Romanist, who is debarred from the use of God's word. It should come home to every hearer of the Gospel. If he remains unconverted he is far more guilty than the inhabitant of some dark parish, who never hears any teaching but a sort of semi-heathen morality. It should come home to every child and servant in religious families. All such are far more blameworthy, in God's sight, than those who live in houses where there is no honor paid to the word of God and prayer. Let these things never be forgotten. Our judgment at the last day will be according to our light and opportunities.

What are we doing ourselves with our religious knowledge? Are we using it wisely, and turning it to good account? Or are we content with the barren saying, "We know it—we know it," and secretly flattering ourselves that the knowledge of our Lord's will makes us better than others, while that will is not done? Let us beware of mistakes. The day will come, when knowledge unimproved will be found the most perilous of possessions. Thousands will awake to find that they are in a lower place than the most ignorant and idolatrous heathen. Their knowledge not used, and their light not followed, will only add to their condemnation.

LUKE 12:49-53
NOT PEACE BUT DIVISION

I came to cast fire upon the earth; and what do I desire, if it is already kindled? But I have a baptism to be baptized with; and how am I straitened till it be accomplished! Think ye that I am come to give peace in the earth? I tell you, Nay; but rather division: for there shall be from henceforth five in one house divided, three against two, and two against three. They shall be divided, father against son, and son against father; mother against daughter, and daughter against her mother; mother in law against her daughter in law, and daughter in law against her mother in law.

The sayings of the Lord Jesus in these five verses are particularly weighty and suggestive. They unfold truths which every true Christian would do well to mark and digest. They explain things in the Church, and in the world, which at first sight are hard to be understood.

We learn for one thing from these verses how thoroughly the heart of Christ was set on finishing the work which He came into the world to do. He says, "I have a baptism to undergo"—a baptism of suffering, of wounds, of agony, of blood, and of death. Yet none of these things moved Him. He adds, "How am I straitened until this baptism is accomplished!" The prospect of coming trouble did not deter Him for a moment. He was ready and willing to endure all things in order to provide eternal redemption for His people. Zeal for the cause He had taken in hand was like a burning fire within Him. To advance His Father's glory, to open the door of life to a lost world, to provide a fountain for all sin and uncleanness by the sacrifice of Himself, were continually the uppermost thoughts of His mind. He was pressed in spirit until this mighty work was finished.

Forever let us bear in mind that all Christ's sufferings on our behalf were endured willingly, voluntarily, and of His own free choice. They were not submitted to patiently merely because He could not avoid them. They were not borne without a murmur merely because He could not escape them. He lived a humble life for thirty-three years merely because He loved to do so. He died a death of agony with a willing and a ready mind. Both in life and death He was carrying out the eternal counsel whereby God was to be glorified and sinners were to be saved. He carried it out with all His heart, mighty as the struggle was which it entailed upon His flesh and blood. He delighted to do God's will. He was straitened until it was accomplished.

Let us not doubt that the heart of Christ in heaven is the same that it was when He was upon earth. He feels as deep an interest now about the salvation of sinners as He did formerly about dying in their stead. Jesus never changes. He is the same yesterday, and today, and forever. There is in Him an infinite willingness to receive, pardon, justify, and deliver the souls of men from hell. Let us strive to realize that willingness, and learn to believe it without doubting, and repose on it without fear. It is a certain fact, if men would only believe it, that Christ is far more willing to save us than we are to be saved.

Let the zeal of our Lord and Master be an example to all His people. Let the recollection of His burning readiness to die for us be like a glowing coal in our memories, and constrain us to live to Him, and not to ourselves. Surely the thought of it should waken our sleeping hearts, and warm our cold affections, and make us anxious to redeem the time, and do something for His Praise. A zealous Savior ought to have zealous disciples.

We learn, for another thing, from these verses, how useless it is to expect universal peace and harmony from the preaching of the Gospel. The disciples, like most Jews of their day, were probably expecting Messiah's kingdom immediately to appear. They thought the time was at hand when the wolf would lie down with the lamb, and men would not hurt or destroy any more. (Isaiah 11:9.) Our Lord saw what was in their hearts, and checked their untimely expectations with a striking saying—"do you think that I have come to send peace on earth? I tell you, No, but rather division."

There is something at first sight very startling in this saying. It seems hard to reconcile it with the song of angels, which spoke of "peace on earth" as the companion of Christ's Gospel. (Luke 2:14.) Yet startling as the saying sounds, it is one which facts have proved to be literally true. Peace is undoubtedly the result of the Gospel wherever it is believed and received. But wherever there are hearers of the Gospel who are hardened, impenitent, and determined to have their sins, the very message of peace becomes the cause of division. Those who live after the flesh will hate those that live after the Spirit. Those who are resolved to live for the world will always be wickedly affected towards those that are resolved to serve Christ. We may lament this state of things, but we cannot prevent it. Grace and nature can no more amalgamate than oil and water. So long as men are disagreed upon first principles in religion, there can be no real cordiality between them. So long as some men are converted and some are unconverted, there can be no true peace.

Let us beware of unscriptural expectations. If we expect to see people of one heart and one mind, before they are converted, we shall continually be disappointed. Thousands of well-meaning people now-a-days are continually crying out for more "unity" among Christians. To attain this they are ready to sacrifice almost anything, and to throw overboard even sound doctrine, if, by so doing, they can secure peace. Such people would do well to remember that even gold may be bought too dear, and that peace is useless if purchased at the expense of truth. Surely they have forgotten the words of Christ, "I came not to send peace but division."

Let us never be moved by those who charge the Gospel with being the cause of strife and divisions upon earth. Such men only show their ignorance when they talk in this way. It is not the Gospel which is to blame, but the corrupt heart of man. It is not God's glorious remedy which is in fault, but the diseased nature of Adam's race, which, like a self-willed child, refuses the medicine provided for its cure. So long as some men and women will not repent and believe, and some will, there must needs be division. To be surprised at it is the height of folly. The very existence of division is one proof of Christ's foresight, and of the truth of Christianity.

Let us thank God that a time is coming when there shall be no more divisions on earth, but all shall be of one mind. That time shall be when Jesus, the Prince of Peace, comes again in person, and puts down every enemy under His feet. When Satan is bound, when the wicked are separated from the righteous, and cast down to their own place, then, and not until then, will be perfect peace. For that blessed time let us wait, and watch, and pray. The night is far spent. The day is at hand. Our divisions are but for a little season. Our peace shall endure to eternity.

LUKE 12:54-59

And he said to the multitudes also, When ye see a cloud rising in the west, straightway ye say, There cometh a shower; and so it cometh to pass. And when ye see a south wind blowing, ye say, There will be a scorching heat; and it cometh to pass. Ye hypocrites, ye know how to interpret the face of the earth and the heaven; but how is it that ye know not how to interpret this time? And why even of yourselves judge ye not what is right? For as thou art going with thine adversary before the magistrate, on the way give diligence to be quit of him; lest haply he drag thee unto the judge, and the judge shall deliver thee to the officer, and the officer shall cast thee into prison. I say unto thee, Thou shalt by no means come out thence, till thou have paid the very last mite.

The first thing which this passage teaches us is the duty of noticing the signs of the times. The Jews in our Lord's days neglected this duty. They shut their eyes against events occurring in their own day of the most significant character. They refused to see that prophecies were being fulfilled around those who were bound up with the coming of Messiah, and that Messiah Himself must be in the midst of them. The scepter had departed from Judah, and the lawgiver from between his feet. The seventy weeks of Daniel were fulfilled. (Gen. 49:10. Dan. 9:24.) The ministry of John the Baptist had excited attention from one end of the land to the other. The miracles of Christ were great, undeniable, and notorious. But still the eyes of the Jews were blinded. They still obstinately refused to believe that Jesus was the Christ. And hence they drew from our Lord the question—"How is it that you do not discern this time?"

It becomes the servants of God, in every age, to observe the public events of their own day, and to compare them with the predictions of unfulfilled prophecy. There is nothing commendable in an ignorant indifference to contemporary history. The true Christian should rather watch the career of governments and nations with a jealous watchfulness, and hail with gladness the slightest indication of the day of the Lord being at hand. The Christian who cannot see the hand of God in history, and does not believe in the gradual movement of all kingdoms towards the final subjection of all things to Christ, is as blind as the Jew.

Have we no signs of the times to observe? The question is soon answered. The history of the last seventy years is full of events which demand the prayerful attention of every servant of Christ. The things that have happened within these seventy years ought to send us to our watch towers, and raise in us great searchings of heart. The rise and progress of a missionary spirit among all Protestant Churches—the wide-spread interest felt about the Jews-the evident decay of the Mohammedan power—the shaking of all the kingdoms of Europe by the French Revolution—the extraordinary spread of knowledge and education—the astonishing revival of Romanism—the steady growth of the most subtle forms of infidelity—all these are facts which cannot be denied, and facts which ought to speak loudly to every well-informed Christian. Surely they deserve to be called signs of our times.

Let us remember the words of our Lord in the passage before us, and not err after the manner of the Jews. Let us not be blind, and deaf, and insensible to all that God is doing, both in the Church and in the world. The things of which we have just been reminded are surely not without meaning. They have not come on the earth by chance or by accident, but by the appointment of God. We ought not to doubt that they are a call to watchfulness, and to preparation for the day of God. May we all have an ear to hear, and a heart to understand! May we not sleep as do many, but watch and discern our time! It is a solemn saying in the book of Revelation—"If therefore you shall not watch, I will come on you as a thief, and you shall not know what hour I will come upon you." (Rev. 3:3.)

The second thing which this passage teaches us, is the immense importance of seeking reconciliation with God before it is too late. This is a lesson which our Lord illustrates by a parable or comparison. He compares us to a man on his way to a magistrate with an adversary, in consequence of a difference or dispute, and describes the course which such a man ought to take. Like him, we are upon our way to the presence of a Judge. We shall all stand at the bar of God. Like him, we have an adversary. The holy law of God is against us, and contrary to us, and its demands must be satisfied. Like him, we ought to give diligence to get our case settled, before it comes before the Judge. We ought to seek pardon and forgiveness before we die. Like him, if we let our opportunity slip, the judgment will go against us, and we shall be cast into the prison of hell. Such appears to be the meaning of the parable in the passage before us. It in a vivid picture of the care which men ought to take in the great matter of reconciliation with God.

Peace with God is by far the first thing in religion. We are born in sin, and children of wrath. We have no natural love towards God. The carnal mind is enmity against God. It is impossible that God can take pleasure in us. "The wicked his soul hates." (Psalm. 11:5.) The chief and foremost desire of everyone who professes to have any religion, should be to obtain reconciliation. Until this is done, nothing is done. We have got nothing worth having in Christianity, until we have peace with God. The law brings us in guilty. The judgment is sure to go against us. Without reconciliation, the end of our Life's journey will be hell.

Peace with God is the principal thing which the Gospel of Christ offers to the soul. Peace and pardon stand in the forefront of its list of privileges, and are tendered freely to everyone that believes on Jesus. There is One who can deliver us from the adversary. Christ is the end of the law for righteousness to everyone that believes. Christ has redeemed us from the curse of the law, being made a curse for us. Christ has blotted out the handwriting that was against us, and has taken it out of the way, nailing it to His cross. Being justified by faith, we have peace with God, through our Lord Jesus Christ. There is no condemnation to those who are in Christ Jesus. The claims of our adversary are all satisfied by Christ's blood. God can now be just, and yet the justifier of every one that believes on Jesus. A full atonement has been made. The debt has been completely paid. The Judge can say, "Deliver them, I have found a ransom." (Job 33:24.)

Let us never rest until we know and feel that we are reconciled to God. Let it not content us to go to Church, use means of grace, and be reckoned Christians, without knowing whether our sins are pardoned, and our souls justified. Let us seek to know that we are one with Christ, and Christ in us-that our iniquities are forgiven, and our sins covered. Then, and then only, may we lie down in peace, and look forward to judgment without fear. The time is short. We are traveling on to a day when our lot for eternity must be decided. Let us give diligence that we may be found safe in that day. The souls that are found without Christ shall be cast into a hopeless prison.

Chapter 13

*N*ow there were some present at that very season who told him of the Galilaeans, whose blood Pilate had mingled with their sacrifices. 2And he answered
and said unto them, Think ye that these Galilaeans were sinners above all the
Galilaeans, because they have suffered these things? 3I tell you, Nay: but, except
ye repent, ye shall all in like manner perish. 4Or those eighteen, upon whom the
tower in Siloam fell, and killed them, think ye that they were offenders above all
the men that dwell in Jerusalem? 5I tell you, Nay: but, except ye repent, ye shall
all likewise perish.

The murder of the Galileans, mentioned in the first verse of this passage,
is an event of which we know nothing certain. The motives of those who
told our Lord of the event, we are left to conjecture. At any rate, they gave
Him an opportunity of speaking to them about their own souls, which He
did not fail to employ. He seized the event, as His manner was, and made a
practical use of it. He bade His informants look within, and think of their
own state before God. He seems to say, "What though these Galileans did
die a sudden death? What is that to you? Consider your own ways. Except
you repent, you shall all likewise perish."

Let us observe, for one thing, in these verses, how much more ready
people are to talk of the deaths of others than their own. The death of the
Galileans, mentioned here, was probably a common subject of conversation
in Jerusalem and all Judea. We can well believe that all the circumstances

and particulars belonging to it were continually discussed by thousands who never thought of their own latter end. It is just the same in the present day. A murder—a sudden death—a shipwreck, or a railway accident, will completely occupy the minds of a neighborhood, and be in the mouth of every one you meet. And yet these very people dislike talking of their own deaths, and their own prospects in the world beyond the grave. Such is human nature in every age. In religion, men are ready to talk of anybody's business rather than their own.

The state of our own souls should always be our first concern. It is eminently true that real Christianity will always begin at home. The converted man will always think first of his own heart, his own life, his own deserts, and his own sins. Does he hear of a sudden death? He will say to himself, "Should I have been found ready, if this had happened to me?" Does he hear of some dreadful crime, or deed of wickedness? He will say to himself, "Are my sins forgiven? and have I really repented of my own transgressions?" Does he hear of worldly men running into every excess of sin? He will say to himself, "Who has made me to differ? What has kept me from walking in the same road, except the free grace of God?"

May we ever seek to be men of this frame of mind! Let us take a kind interest in all around us. Let us feel tender pity and compassion for all who suffer violence, or are removed by sudden death. But let us never forget to look at home, and to learn wisdom for ourselves from all that happens to others.

Let us observe, for another thing, in these verses, how strongly our Lord lays down the universal necessity of repentance. Twice He declares emphatically, "Except you repent, you shall all likewise perish."

The truth here asserted, is one of the foundations of Christianity. "All have sinned and come short of the glory of God." All of us are born in sin. We are fond of sin, and are naturally unfit for friendship with God. Two things are absolutely necessary to the salvation of every one of us. We must repent, and we must believe the Gospel. Without repentance towards God, and faith towards our Lord Jesus Christ, no man can be saved.

The nature of true repentance is clearly and unmistakably laid down in holy Scripture. It begins with knowledge of sin. It goes on to work sorrow for sin. It leads to confession of sin before God. It shows itself before man by a thorough breaking off from sin. It results in producing a habit of deep hatred for all sin. Above all, it is inseparably connected with lively faith in the Lord Jesus Christ. Repentance like this is the characteristic of all true Christians.

The necessity of repentance to salvation will be evident to all who search the Scriptures, and consider the nature of the subject. Without it there is no forgiveness of sins. There never was a pardoned man who was not also a penitent. There never was one washed in the blood of Christ who did not feel, and mourn, and confess, and hate his own sins. Without it there can be no fitness for heaven. We could not be happy if we reached the kingdom of glory with a heart loving sin. The company of saints and angels would give us no pleasure. Our minds would not be in tune for an eternity of holiness. Let these things sink down into our hearts. We must repent as well as believe, if we hope to be saved.

Let us leave the subject with the solemn inquiry—Have we ourselves repented? We live in a Christian land. We belong to a Christian Church. We have Christian ordinances and means of grace. We have heard of repentance with the hearing of the ear, and that hundreds of times. But have we ever repented? Do we really know our own sinfulness? Do our sins cause us any sorrow? Have we cried to God about our sins, and sought forgiveness at the throne of grace? Have we ceased to do evil, and broken off from our bad habits? Do we cordially and heartily hate everything that is evil? These are serious questions. They deserve serious consideration. The subject before us is no light matter. Nothing less than life—eternal life—is at stake! If we die impenitent, and without a new heart, we had better never have been born.

If we never yet repented, let us begin without delay. For this we are accountable. "Repent you, and be converted," were the words of Peter to the Jews who had crucified our Lord. (Acts 3:19.) "Repent and pray," was the charge addressed to Simon Magus when he was in the "gall of bitterness and bond of iniquity." (Acts 8:22.) There is everything to encourage us to begin. Christ invites us. Promises of Scripture are held out to us. Glorious declarations of God's willingness to receive us abound throughout the word. "There is joy in heaven over one sinner that repents." Then let us arise and call upon God. Let us repent without delay.

If we have already repented in time past, let us go on repenting to the end of our lives. There will always be sins to confess and infirmities to deplore, so long as we are in the body. Let us repent more deeply, and humble ourselves more thoroughly, every year. Let every returning birthday find us hating sin more, and loving Christ more. He was a wise old saint who said, "I hope to carry my repentance to the very gate of heaven."

LUKE 13:6-9

THE BARREN FIG TREE

And he spake this parable; A certain man had a fig tree planted in his vine-
yard; and he came seeking fruit thereon, and found none. And he said unto the
vinedresser, Behold, these three years I come seeking fruit on this fig tree, and find
none: cut it down; why doth it also cumber the ground? And he answering saith
unto him, Lord, let it alone this year also, till I shall dig about it, and dung it: and
if it bear fruit thenceforth, well; but if not, thou shalt cut it down.

The parable we have now read is peculiarly humbling and heart-searching.
The Christian who can hear it and not feel sorrow and shame as he looks at
the state of Christendom, must be in a very unhealthy state of soul.

We learn first from this passage that where God gives spiritual privileges
He expects proportionate returns.

Our Lord teaches this lesson by comparing the Jewish Church of His day
to a "fig tree planted in a vineyard." This was exactly the position of Israel in
the world. They were separated from other nations by the Mosaic laws and
ordinances, no less than by the situation of their land. They were favored
with revelations of God, which were granted to no other people. Things were
done for them that were never done for Egypt, or Nineveh, or Babylon, or
Greece, or Rome. It was only just and right that they should bear fruit to
God's praise. It might reasonably be expected that there would be more faith,
and penitence, and holiness, and godliness in Israel than among the heathen.
This is what God looked for. The owner of the fig tree "came seeking fruit."

But we must look beyond the Jewish Church if we mean to get the full
benefit of the parable before us. We must look to the Christian churches.
They have light, and truth, and doctrines, and precepts, of which the heathen
never hear. How great is their responsibility! Is it not just and right that God
should expect from them "fruit?"

We must look to our own hearts. We live in a land of Bibles, and liberty,
and Gospel preaching. How vast are the advantages we enjoy compared to
the Chinese and Hindoo! Never let us forget that God expects from us "fruit."

These are solemn truths. Few things are so much forgotten by men as
the close connection between privilege and responsibility. We are all ready
enough to eat the fat and drink the sweet, and bask in the sunshine of our
position both as Christians and Englishmen—and even to spare a few pitying
thoughts for the half naked savage who bows down to stocks and stones.

But we are very slow to remember that we are accountable to God for all we enjoy; and that to whomsoever much is given, of them much will be required. Let us awake to a sense of these things. We are the most favored nation upon earth. We are in the truest sense "a fig tree planted in a vineyard." Let us not forget that the great Master looks for "fruit."

We learn, secondly, from this passage, that it is a most dangerous thing to be unfruitful under great religious privileges.

The manner in which our Lord conveys this lesson to us is deeply impressive. He shows us the owner of the barren fig tree complaining that it bore no fruit-"These three years I come seeking fruit and find none." He describes him as even ordering the destruction of the tree as a useless cumberer of the ground-"Cut it down; why cumbers it the ground?" He brings in the dresser of the vineyard pleading for the fig tree, that it may be spared a little longer—"Lord, let it alone this year also." And He concludes the parable by putting these dreadful words into the vinedresser's mouth—"If it bears fruit, well—and if not, then after that you shall cut it down."

There is a plain warning here to all professing churches of Christ. If their ministers do not teach sound doctrine, and their members do not live holy lives, they are in imminent peril of destruction. God is every year observing them, and taking account of all their ways. They may abound in ceremonial religion. They may be covered with the leaves of forms, and services, and ordinances. But if they are destitute of the fruits of the Spirit, they are reckoned useless cumberers of the ground. Except they repent, they will be cut down. It was so with the Jewish Church forty years after our Lord's ascension. It has been so since with the African Churches. It will be so yet with many others, it may be feared, before the end comes. The axe is lying near the root of many an unfruitful Church. The sentence will yet go forth, "Cut it down."

There is a plainer warning still in the passage for all 'unconverted professing Christians'. There are many in every congregation who hear the Gospel, who are literally hanging over the brink of the pit. They have lived for years in the best part of God's vineyard, and yet borne no fruit. They have heard the Gospel preached faithfully for hundreds of Sundays, and yet have never embraced it, and taken up the cross, and followed Christ. They do not perhaps run into open sin. But they do nothing for God's glory. There is nothing positive about their religion. Of each of these the Lord of the vineyard might say with truth, "I come these many years seeking fruit on this tree and find none. Cut it down. It cumbers the ground."

There are myriads of respectable professing Christians in this plight. They have not the least idea how near they are to destruction. Never let us forget that to be content with sitting in the congregation and hearing sermons, while we bear no fruit in our lives, is conduct which is most offensive to God. It provokes Him to cut us off suddenly, and that without remedy.

We learn, lastly, from this parable, what an infinite debt we all owe to God's mercy and Christ's intercession. It seems impossible to draw any other lesson from the earnest pleading of the dresser of the vineyard—"Lord, let it alone this year also." Surely we see here, as in a glass, the loving kindness of God, and the mediation of Christ.

Mercy has been truly called the darling attribute of God. Power, justice, purity, holiness, wisdom, unchangeableness, are all parts of God's character, and have all been manifested to the world in a thousand ways, both in His works and in His word. But if there is one part of His perfections which He is pleased to exhibit to man more clearly than another, beyond doubt that part is mercy. He is a God that "delights in mercy." (Micah 7:18.)

Mercy founded on the mediation of a coming Savior, was the cause why Adam and Eve were not cast down to hell, in the day that they fell. Mercy has been the cause why God has borne so long with this sin-laden world, and not come down to judgment. Mercy is even now the cause why unconverted sinners are so long spared, and not cut off in their sins. We have probably not the least conception how much we all owe to God's long-suffering. The last day will prove that all mankind were debtors to God's mercy, and Christ's mediation. Even those who are finally lost will discover to their shame, that it was "of the Lord's mercies they were not consumed" long before they died. As for those who are saved, covenant-mercy will be all their plea.

And now are we fruitful or unfruitful? This, after all, is the question that concerns us most. What does God see in us year after year? Let us take heed so to live that He may see in us fruit.

LUKE 13:10-17

A CRIPPLED WOMAN HEALED

And he was teaching in one of the synagogues on the sabbath day. And behold, a woman that had a spirit of infirmity eighteen years; and she was bowed together, and could in no wise lift herself up. And when Jesus saw her, he called her, and said to her, Woman, thou art loosed from thine infirmity. And he laid his hands upon her: and immediately she was made straight, and glorified God. And the ruler of the synagogue, being moved with indignation because Jesus had healed on the sabbath, answered and said to the multitude, There are six days in which men ought to work: in them therefore come and be healed, and not on the day of the sabbath. But the Lord answered him, and said, Ye hypocrites, doth not each one of you on the sabbath loose his ox or his ass from the stall, and lead him away to watering? And ought not this woman, being a daughter of Abraham, whom Satan had bound, lo, these eighteen years, to have been loosed from this bond on the day of the sabbath? And as he said these things, all his adversaries were put to shame: and all the multitude rejoiced for all the glorious things that were done by him.

We see in these verses a striking example of diligence in the use of means of grace. We are told of a "woman which had a spirit of infirmity eighteen years, and was bowed together, and could not straighten up." We know not who this woman was. Our Lord's saying that she was "a daughter of Abraham," would lead us to infer that she was a true believer. But her name and history are hidden from us. This only we know, that when Jesus was "teaching in one of the synagogues on the Sabbath," this woman was there. Sickness was no excuse with her for tarrying from God's house. In spite of suffering and infirmity, she found her way to the place where the day and the word of God were honored, and where the people of God met together. And truly she was blessed in her deed! She found a rich reward for all her pains. She came sorrowing, and went home rejoicing.

The conduct of this suffering Jewess may well put to shame many a strong and healthy professing Christian. How many in the full enjoyment of bodily vigor, allow the most frivolous excuses to keep them away from the house of God! How many are constantly spending the whole Sunday in idleness, pleasure-seeking, or business, and scoffing and sneering at those who "keep the Sabbath holy!" How many think it a great matter if they attend the public worship of God once on Sunday, and regard a second attendance as a needless excess of zeal akin to fanaticism! How many find religious services a weariness while they attend them, and feel relieved when they are over! How few know anything of David's spirit, when he said, "I was glad when they said to me, Let us go into the house of the Lord." "How lovely are your tabernacles, O Lord of Hosts!" (Psalm 122:1; Psalm 84:1.)

Now what is the explanation of all this? What is the reason why so few are like the woman of whom we read this day? The answer to these questions is short and simple. The most have no heart for God's service. They have no delight in God's presence or God's day. "The carnal mind is enmity against

God." The moment a man's heart is converted, these pretended difficulties about attending public worship vanish away. The new heart finds no trouble in keeping the Sabbath holy. Where there is a will there is always a way.

Let us never forget that our feelings about Sundays are sure tests of the state of our souls. The man who can find no pleasure in giving God one day in the week, is manifestly unfit for heaven. Heaven itself is nothing but an eternal Sabbath. If we cannot enjoy a few hours in God's service once a week in this world, it is plain that we could not enjoy an eternity in His service in the world to come. Happy are those who walk in the steps of her of whom we read today! They shall find Christ and a blessing while they live, and Christ and glory when they die.

We see, secondly, in these verses, the almighty power of our Lord Jesus Christ. We are told that when He saw the suffering woman of whom we are reading, "He called her to Him, and said unto her, Woman, you are loosed from your infirmity. And He laid His hands on her." That touch was accompanied by miraculous healing virtue. At once a disease of eighteen years' standing gave way before the Lord of Life. "Immediately she was made straight and glorified God."

We need not doubt that this mighty miracle was intended to supply hope and comfort to sin-diseased souls. With Christ nothing is impossible. He can soften hearts which seem hard as the nether mill-stone. He can bend stubborn wills which "for eighteen years" have been set on self-pleasing, on sin, and the world. He can enable sinners who have been long poring over earthly things, to look upward to heaven, and see the kingdom of God. Nothing is too hard for the Lord. He can create, and transform, and renew, and break down, and build, and quicken, with irresistible power. He lives, who formed the world out of nothing, and He never changes.

Let us hold fast this blessed truth, and never let it go. Let us never despair about our own salvation. Our sins may be countless. Our lives may have been long spent in worldliness and folly. Our youth may have been wasted in soul defiling excesses, of which we are lamentably ashamed. But are we willing to come to Christ, and commit our souls to Him? If so, there is hope. He can heal us thoroughly, and say, "you are loosed from your infirmity."

Let us never despair about the salvation of others so long as they are alive. Let us name them before the Lord night and day, and cry to Him on their behalf. We may perhaps have relatives whose case seems desperate because of their wickedness. But it is not really so. There are no incurable cases with Christ. If He were to lay His healing hand on them, they would be "made straight, and glorify God." Let us pray on, and faint not. That saying of Job is worthy of all acceptation—"I know that you can do everything." (Job 42:2.) Jesus is "able to save to the uttermost."

We see, lastly, in these verses, the right observance of the Sabbath day asserted and defended by our Lord Jesus Christ. The ruler of the synagogue in which the infirm woman was healed, found fault with her as a breaker of the Sabbath. He drew down upon himself a stern but just rebuke—"You hypocrite, does not each one of you on the Sabbath loose his ox or his donkey from the stall, and lead him away to watering?" If it was allowable to attend to the needs of beasts on the Sabbath, how much more to human creatures! If it was no breach of the fourth commandment to show kindness to oxen and donkeys, much less to show kindness to a daughter of Abraham.

The principle here laid down by our Lord is the same that we find elsewhere in the Gospels. He teaches us that the command to "do no work" on the Sabbath, was not intended to prohibit works of necessity and mercy. The Sabbath was made for man's benefit, and not for his hurt. It was appointed to promote man's best and highest interests, and not to debar him of anything that is really for his good. It requires nothing but what is reasonable and wise. It forbids nothing that is really necessary to man's comfort.

Let us pray for a right understanding of the law of the Sabbath. Of all the commandments that God has given, none is more essential to the happiness of man, and none is so frequently misrepresented, abused, and trampled underfoot. Let us lay down for ourselves two special rules for the observance of the Sabbath. For one thing let us do no work which is not absolutely needful. For another, let us keep the day "holy," and give it to God. From these two rules let us never swerve. Experience shows that there is the closest connection between Sabbath sanctification and healthy Christianity.

LUKE 13:18-21

PARABLES OF THE MUSTARD SEED, AND THE YEAST

He said therefore, Unto what is the kingdom of God like? and whereunto shall I liken it? It is like unto a grain of mustard seed, which a man took, and cast into his own garden; and it grew, and became a tree; and the birds of the heaven lodged in the branches thereof. And again he said, Whereunto shall I liken the kingdom of God? It is like unto leaven, which a woman took and hid in three measures of meal, till it was all leavened.

There is a peculiar interest belonging to the two parables contained in these verses. We find them twice delivered by our Lord, and at two distinct periods in His ministry. This fact alone should make us give the more earnest heed to the lessons which the parables convey. They will be found rich both in prophetical and experimental truths.

The parable of the mustard seed is intended to show the progress of the Gospel in the WORLD.

The BEGINNINGS of the Gospel were exceedingly small. It was like "a mustard seed cast into the garden." It was a religion which seemed at first so feeble, and helpless, and powerless, that it could not live. Its first founder was One who was poor in this world, and ended His life by dying the death of a malefactor on the cross. Its first adherents were a little company, whose number probably did not exceed a thousand when the Lord Jesus left the world. Its first preachers were a few fishermen and publicans, who were, most of them, unlearned and ignorant men. Its first starting point was a despised corner of the earth, called Judea, a petty tributary province of the vast empire of Rome. Its first doctrine was eminently calculated to call forth the enmity of the natural heart. Christ crucified was to the Jews a stumbling-block, and to the Greeks foolishness. Its first movements brought down on its friends persecution from all quarters. Pharisees and Sadducees, Jews and Gentiles, ignorant idolaters and self-conceited philosophers, all agreed in hating and opposing Christianity. It was a sect everywhere spoken against. These are no empty assertions. They are simple historical facts, which no one can deny. If ever there was a religion which was a little grain of seed at its beginning, that religion was the Gospel.

But the PROGRESS of the Gospel, after the seed was once cast into the earth, was great, steady and continuous. The grain of mustard seed "grew and became a great tree." In spite of persecution, opposition, and violence, Christianity gradually spread and increased. Year after year its adherents became more numerous. Year after year idolatry withered away before it. City after city, and country after country, received the new faith. Church after church was formed in almost every quarter of the earth then known. Preacher after preacher rose up, and missionary after missionary came forward to fill the place of those who died.

Roman emperors and heathen philosophers, sometimes by force and sometimes by argument, tried in vain to check the progress of Christianity. They might as well have tried to stop the tide from flowing, or the sun from rising. In a few hundred years, the religion of the despised Nazarene—the religion which began in the upper chamber at Jerusalem—had overrun the civilized world. It was professed by nearly all Europe, by a great part of Asia, and by the whole northern part of Africa. The prophetic words of the parable before us were literally fulfilled. The grain of mustard seed "became a great tree; and the birds of the air lodged in the branches of it." The Lord Jesus said it would be so. And so it came to pass.

Let us learn from this parable never to despair of any work for Christ, because its first beginnings are feeble and small. A single minister in some large neglected town-district—a single missionary amid myriads of savage heathen-a single reformer in the midst of a fallen and corrupt church—each and all of these may seem at first sight utterly unlikely to do any good. To the eye of man, the work may appear too great, and the instrument employed quite unequal to it. Let us never give way to such thoughts. Let us remember the parable before us and take courage. When the line of duty is plain, we should not begin to count numbers, and confer with flesh and blood. We should believe that one man with the living seed of God's truth on his side, like Luther or Knox, may turn a nation upside down. If God is with him, none shall stand against him. In spite of men and devils, the seed that he sows shall become a great tree.

The parable of the leaven is intended to show the progress of the Gospel in the heart of a BELIEVER.

The first beginnings of the work of grace in a sinner are generally exceedingly small. It is like the mixture of leaven with a lump of dough. A single sentence of a sermon, or a single verse of Holy Scripture—a word of rebuke from a friend, or a casual religious remark overheard—a tract given by a stranger, or a trifling act of kindness received from a Christian, some one of these things is often the starting-point in the life of a soul. The first actings of the spiritual life are often small in the extreme—so small, that for a long time they are not known except by him who is the subject of them, and even by him not fully understood. A few serious thoughts and prickings of conscience—a desire to pray really and not formally—a determination to begin reading the Bible in private—a gradual drawing towards means of grace—an increasing interest in the subject of religion—a growing distaste for evil habits and bad companions, these, or some of them, are often the first symptoms of grace beginning to move the heart of man. They are symptoms which worldly men may not perceive, and ignorant believers may despise, and even old Christians may mistake. Yet they are often the first steps in the mighty business of conversion. They are often the "leaven" of grace working in a heart.

The work of grace once begun in the soul will never stand still. It will gradually "leaven the whole lump." Like leaven once introduced, it can never be separated from that with which it is mingled. Little by little it will influence the conscience, the affections, the mind, and the will, until the whole man is affected by its power, and a thorough conversion to God takes place. In some cases no doubt the progress is far quicker than in others. In some cases the result is far more clearly marked and decided than in others. But wherever a real work of the Holy Spirit begins in the heart, the whole character is sooner or later leavened and changed. The tastes of the man are altered. The whole bias of his mind becomes different. "Old things pass away, and all things become new." (2 Cor. 5:17.) The Lord Jesus said that it would be so, and all experience shows that so it is.

Let us learn from this parable never to "despise the day of small things" in religion. (Zec. 4:10.) The soul must creep before it can walk, and walk before it can run. If we see any sign of grace beginning in a brother, however feeble, let us thank God and be hopeful. The leaven of grace once planted in his heart, shall yet leaven the whole lump. "He that begins the work, will perform it unto the day of Jesus Christ." (Phil. 1:6.)

Let us ask ourselves whether there is any work of grace in our own hearts. Are we resting satisfied with a few vague wishes and convictions? Or do we know anything of a gradual, growing, spreading, increasing, leavening process going on in our inward man? Let nothing short of this content us. The true work of the Holy Spirit will never stand still. It will leaven the whole lump.

LUKE 13:22-30

THE NARROW DOOR

And he went on his way through cities and villages, teaching, and journeying on unto Jerusalem.

And one said unto him, Lord, are they few that are saved? And he said unto them, Strive to enter in by the narrow door: for many, I say unto you, shall seek to enter in, and shall not be able. When once the master of the house is risen up, and hath shut to the door, and ye begin to stand without, and to knock at the door, saying, Lord, open to us; and he shall answer and say to you, I know you not whence ye are; then shall ye begin to say, We did eat and drink in thy presence, and thou didst teach in our streets; and he shall say, I tell you, I know not whence ye are; depart from me, all ye workers of iniquity. There shall be the weeping and the gnashing of teeth, when ye shall see Abraham, and Isaac, and Jacob, and all the prophets, in the kingdom of God, and yourselves cast forth without. And they shall come from the east and west, and from the north and south, and shall sit down in the kingdom of God. And behold, there are last who shall be first, and there are first who shall be last.

We see in these verses a remarkable question asked. We are told that a certain man said to our Lord, "Are there few that be saved?"

We do not know who this enquirer was. He may have been a self-righteous Jew, trained to believe that there was no hope for the uncircumcised, and no salvation for any but the children of Abraham. He may have been an idle trifler with religion, who was ever wasting his time on curious and speculative questions. In any case, we must all feel that he asked a question of deep and momentous importance.

He that desires to know the number of the saved, in the present dispensation, need only turn to the Bible, and his curiosity will be satisfied. He will read in the sermon on the mount these solemn words, "Strait is the gate and narrow is the way that leads unto life, and few there be that find it." (Matt. 7:14.)—He has only to look around him, and compare the ways of the many with the word of God, and he will soon come to the conclusion, if he is an honest man, that the saved are few. It is a dreadful conclusion. Our souls naturally turn away from it. But Scripture and facts alike combine to shut us up to it. Salvation to the uttermost is offered to men. All things are ready on God's part. Christ is willing to receive sinners. But sinners are not willing to come to Christ. And hence few are saved.

We see, secondly, in these verses, a striking exhortation given. We are told that when our Lord Jesus Christ was asked whether few would be saved, He said, "Strive to enter in at the strait gate." He addressed these words to the whole company of His hearers. He thought it not good to gratify the curiosity of his questioner by a direct reply. He chose rather to press home on him, and all around him, their own immediate duty. In minding their own souls, they would soon find the question answered. In striving to enter in at the strait gate they would soon see whether the saved were many or few.

Whatever others may do in religion the Lord Jesus would have us know that our duty is clear. The gate is strait. The work is great. The enemies of our souls are many. We must be up and doing. We are to wait for nobody. We are not to inquire what other people are doing, and whether many of our neighbors, and relatives, and friends are serving Christ. The unbelief and indecision of others will be no excuse at the last day. We must never follow a multitude to do evil. If we go to heaven alone, we must resolve that by God's grace we will go. Whether we have many with us or a few, the command before us is plain—"Strive to enter in."

Whatever others may think in religion, the Lord Jesus would have us know, that we are responsible for exertion. We are not to sit still in sin and worldliness, waiting for the grace of God. We are not to go on still in our wickedness, sheltering ourselves under the vain plea that we can do nothing until God draws us. We are to draw near to Him in the use of the means of grace. How we can do it is a question with which we have nothing to do. It is in obedience that the knot will be untied. The command is express and unmistakable—"Strive to enter in."

We see, thirdly, in these verses, a day of dreadful solemnity described. We are told of a time when "the master of the house shall rise and shut the door," when some shall "sit down in the kingdom of God," and others be "shut out" for evermore. About the meaning of these words there can be no doubt. They describe the second coming of Christ and the day of judgment.

A day is coming on the earth when the patience of God towards SIN-NERS shall have an end. The door of mercy, which has been so long open, shall at last be shut. The fountain opened for all sin and uncleanness shall at length be closed. The throne of grace shall be removed, and the throne of judgment shall be set up in its place. The great assize of the world shall begin. All that are found impenitent and unbelieving shall be thrust out forever from God's presence. Men shall find that there is such a thing as "the wrath of the Lamb." (Rev. 6:16.)

A day is coming when BELIEVERS in Christ shall receive a full reward. The Master of the great house in heaven shall call His servants together, and give to each a crown of glory that fades not away. They shall sit down with Abraham, and Isaac, and Jacob, and rest forever from warfare and work. They shall be shut in with Christ, and saints, and angels, in the kingdom of heaven, and sin, and death, and sorrow, and the world, and the devil, shall be eternally shut out. Men shall see at last that "To him that sows righteousness there is a sure reward." (Prov. 11:18.)

We see, lastly, in these verses, a heart-searching prophecy delivered. Our Lord tells us that in the day of His second coming, ' Many will seek to enter in at the strait gate, and shall not be able." They will "knock at the door, saying, Lord, Lord, open to us," but will find no admission. They will even plead earnestly, that "they have eaten and drunk in Christ's presence, and that he has taught in their streets." But their plea will be unavailing. They will receive the solemn answer, "I don't know you. Go away, all you who do evil." Religious profession, and formal knowledge of Christ will save none who have served sin and the world.

There is something peculiarly striking in our Lord's language in this prophecy. It reveals to us the dreadful fact, that men may see what is right when it is too late for them to be saved. There is a time coming when many will repent too late, and believe too late—sorrow for sin too late, and begin to pray too late-be anxious about salvation too late, and long for heaven too late. Myriads shall wake up in another world, and be convinced of truths which on earth they refused to believe. Earth is the only place in God's creation where there is any infidelity. Hell itself is nothing but truth known too late.

The recollection of this passage should help us to set a right estimate on things around us. Money, and pleasure, and rank, and greatness, occupy the first place now in the world. Praying, and believing, and holy living, and acquaintance with Christ, are despised, and ridiculed, and held very cheap. But there is a change coming one day! The last shall be first, and the first last. For that change let us be prepared.

And now let us ask ourselves whether we are among the many or among the few? Do we know anything of striving and warring against sin, the world, and the devil? Are we ready for the Master's coming to shut the door? The man who can answer these questions satisfactorily is a true Christian.

LUKE 13:31-35

JESUS' SORROW OVER JERUSALEM

In that very hour there came certain Pharisees, saying to him, Get thee out, and go hence: for Herod would fain kill thee. And he said unto them, Go and say to that fox, Behold, I cast out demons and perform cures to-day and to-morrow, and the third day I am perfected. Nevertheless I must go on my way to-day and to-morrow and the day following: for it cannot be that a prophet perish out of Jerusalem. O Jerusalem, Jerusalem, that killeth the prophets, and stoneth them that are sent unto her! how often would I have gathered thy children together, even as a hen gathereth her own brood under her wings, and ye would not! Behold, your house is left unto you desolate: and I say unto you, Ye shall not see me, until ye shall say, Blessed is he that cometh in the name of the Lord.

Let us learn from these verses, how entirely our times are in God's hands. Our Lord Jesus Christ teaches us this lesson by His reply to those who bade Him depart, because Herod would kill Him. He said, "I cast out devils, and I do cures today and tomorrow." His time was not yet come for leaving the world. His work was not yet finished. Until that time came it was not in the power of Herod to hurt Him. Until that work was finished no weapon forged against Him could prosper.

There is something in our Lord's words which demands the attention of all true Christians. There is a frame of mind exhibited to us which we should do well to copy. Our Lord, no doubt, spoke with a prophetic foresight of coming things. He knew the time of His own death, and He knew that this time was not yet come. Foreknowledge like this, of course, is not granted to believers in the present day. But still there is a lesson here which we ought not to overlook. We ought, in a certain measure, to aim at having the mind that was in Christ Jesus. We ought to seek to possess a spirit of calm, unshaken confidence about things to come. We should study to have a heart "not afraid of evil tidings," but quiet, steady, and trusting in the Lord. (Psalm 112:7.)

The subject is a delicate one, but one which concerns our happiness so much that it deserves consideration. We are not intended to be idle fatalists, like the Muhammadans, or cold, unfeeling statues, like the Stoics. We are not to neglect the use of means, or to omit all prudent provision for the unseen future. To neglect means is fanaticism, and not faith. But still, when we have done all, we should remember, that though DUTIES are ours, EVENTS are God's. We should therefore endeavor to leave things to come in God's hands, and not to be over-anxious about health, or family, or money, or plans.

To cultivate this frame of mind would add immensely to our peace. How many of our cares and fears are about things which never come to pass! Happy is that man who can walk in our Lord's steps, and say, "I shall have what is good for me. I shall live on earth until my work is done, and not a moment longer. I shall be taken when I am ripe for heaven, and not a minute before. All the powers of the world cannot take away my life, until God permits. All the physicians of earth cannot preserve it, when God calls me away."

Is there anything beyond the reach of man in this spirit? Surely not. Believers have a covenant ordered in all things and sure. The very hairs of their heads are numbered. Their steps are ordered by the Lord. All things are working together for their good. When they are afflicted, it is for their profit. When they are sick, it is for some wise purpose. All things are said to be theirs, life, death, things present, and things to come. (2 Sam. 23:5; Matt. 10:30; Psalm 37:23; Rom. 8:28; Heb. 12:10; John 11:4; 1 Cor. 3:22.)

There is no such thing as chance, luck, or accident, in the life of a believer. There is but one thing needful, in order to make a believer calm, quiet, unruffled, undisturbed in every position, and under every circumstance. That one thing is faith in active exercise. For such faith let us daily pray. Few indeed know anything of it. The faith of most believers is very fitful and spasmodic. It is for lack of steady, constant faith, that so few can say with Christ, "I must proceed on my way today and tomorrow, and not die until my work is done."

Let us learn, for another thing, from these verses, how great is the compassion of our Lord Jesus Christ towards sinners. We see this brought out in a most forcible manner by our Lord's language about Jerusalem. He knew well the wickedness of that city. He knew what crimes had been committed there in times past. He knew what was coming on Himself, at the time of His crucifixion. Yet even to Jerusalem He says, "How often would I have gathered your children together as a hen gathers her chicks under her wings, but you were not willing."

It grieves the Lord Jesus Christ to see sinners going on still in their wickedness. "As I live," are His words, "I have no pleasure in the death of the wicked." (Ezek. 33:11.) Let all unconverted people remember this. It is not enough that they grieve parents, and ministers, and neighbors, and friends. There is one higher than all these, whom they deeply grieve by their conduct. They are daily grieving Christ.

The Lord Jesus is willing to save sinners. "He is not willing that any should perish, but that all should come to repentance." He would have all men saved and come to the knowledge of the truth." (2 Pet 3:9; 1 Tim. 2:4.) This is a mighty principle of the Gospel, and one which severely perplexes narrow-minded and shallow theologians. But what says the Scripture? The words before us, no less than the texts just quoted, are distinct and express. "I would have gathered your children," says Christ, "but you were not willing." The will of poor hardened unbelieving man, and not the will of Christ, is the cause why sinners are lost for evermore. Christ "would" save them, but they were not willing.

Let the truth before us sink down into our hearts, and bear fruit in our lives. Let us thoroughly understand that if we die in our sins and go to hell, our blood will be upon our own heads. We cannot lay the blame on God the Father, nor on Jesus Christ the Redeemer, nor on the Holy Spirit the

Comforter. The promises of the Gospel are wide, broad, and general. The readiness of Christ to save sinners is unmistakably declared. If we are lost, we shall have none to find fault with but ourselves. The words of Christ will be our condemnation—"You will not come unto me, that you might have life." (John 5:40.)

Let us take heed, with such a passage as this before us, that we are not more systematic than Scripture. It is a serious thing to be "wise above that which is written." Our SALVATION is wholly of God. Let that never be forgotten. None but the elect shall be finally saved. "No man can come unto Christ except the Father draws him." (John 6:44.) But our RUIN, if we are lost, will be wholly of ourselves. We shall reap the fruit of our own choice. We shall find that we have lost our own souls. Linked between these two principles lies truth which we must maintain firmly, and never let go. There is doubtless deep mystery about it. Our minds are too feeble to understand it now. But we shall understand it all hereafter. God's sovereignty and man's responsibility shall appear perfectly harmonious one day. In the meantime, whatever we doubt, let us never doubt Christ's infinite willingness to save.

Chapter 14

*A*nd it came to pass, when he went into the house of one of the rulers of the *Pharisees on a sabbath to eat bread, that they were watching him. 2And behold, there was before him a certain man that had the dropsy. 3And Jesus answering spake unto the lawyers and Pharisees, saying, Is it lawful to heal on the sabbath, or not? 4But they held their peace. And he took him, and healed him, and let him go. 5And he said unto them, Which of you shall have an ass or an ox fallen into a well, and will not straightway draw him up on a sabbath day? 6And they could not answer again unto these things.*

Let us mark in this passage, how our Lord Jesus Christ accepted the hospitality of those who were not His disciples. We read that "He went into the house of one of the chief Pharisees to eat bread." We cannot reasonably suppose that this Pharisee was a friend of Christ. It is more probable that he only did what was customary for a man in his position. He saw a stranger teaching religion, whom some regarded as a prophet, and he invited Him to eat at his table. The point that most concerns us, is this, that when the invitation was given it was accepted.

If we want to know how our Lord carried Himself at a Pharisee's table, we have only to read attentively the first twenty-four verses of this chapter. We shall find Him the same there that He was elsewhere, always about His Father's business. We shall see Him first defending the true observance of the Sabbath-day—then expounding the nature of true humility—then urging on

His host the character of true hospitality—and finally delivering that most relevant and striking parable—the parable of the great supper. And all this is done in the most wise, and calm, and dignified manner. The words are all words in season. The speech is "always with grace, seasoned with salt." (Coloss. 4:6.) The perfection of our Lord's conduct appears on this, as on all other occasions. He always said the right thing, at the right time, and in the right way. He never forgot, for a moment, who He was and where He was.

The example of Christ in this passage deserves the close attention of all Christians, and specially of ministers of the Gospel. It throws strong light on some most difficult points—our communion with unconverted people—the extent to which we should carry it—the manner in which we should behave when we are with them. Our Lord has left us a pattern for our conduct in this chapter. It will be our wisdom to endeavor to walk in His steps.

We ought not to withdraw entirely from all communion with unconverted people. It would be cowardice and indolence to do so, even if it were possible. It would shut us out from many opportunities of doing good. But we ought to go into their society moderately, watchfully, and prayerfully, and with a firm resolution to carry our Master and our Master's business with us.

The house from which Christ is deliberately excluded is not the house at which Christians ought to receive hospitalities, and keep up intimacy. The extent to which we should carry our communion with the unconverted, is a point which each believer must settle for himself. Some can go much further than others in this direction, with advantage to their company, and without injury to themselves. "Every man has his proper gift." (1 Cor. 7:7.) There are two questions which we should often put to ourselves, in reference to this subject. "Do I, in company, spend all my time in light and worldly conversation? Or do I endeavor to follow, however feebly, the example of Christ?" The society in which we cannot answer these questions satisfactorily, is society from which we had better withdraw. So long as we go into company as Christ went to the Pharisee's house, we shall take no harm.

Let us mark, secondly, in this passage, how our Lord was watched by His enemies. We read that when He went to eat bread on the Sabbath day, in the house of a Pharisee, "they watched Him."

The circumstance here recorded, is only a type of what our Lord was constantly subjected to, all through His earthly ministry. The eyes of His enemies were continually observing Him. They watched for His halting, and waited eagerly for some word or deed on which they could lay hold and build an accusation. Yet they found none. Our blessed Lord was ever holy, harmless, undefiled, and separate from evil. Perfect indeed must that life have been, in which the bitterest enemy could find no flaw, or blemish, or spot, or wrinkle, or any such thing!

He that desires to serve Christ must make up his mind to be "watched" and observed, no less than His Master. He must never forget that the eyes of the world are upon him, and that the wicked are looking narrowly at all his ways. Specially ought he to remember this when he goes into the society of the unconverted. If he makes a slip there, in word or deed, and acts inconsistently, be may rest assured it will not be forgotten.

Let us endeavor to live daily as in the sight of a holy God. So living, it will matter little how much we are "watched" by an ill-natured and malicious world. Let us exercise ourselves to have a conscience void of offence toward God and man, and to do nothing which can give occasion to the Lord's enemies to blaspheme. The thing is possible. By the grace of God it can be done. The haters of Daniel were obliged to confess, "we shall not find any occasion against this Daniel, except we find it against him concerning the law of his God." (Dan. 6:5.)

Let us mark, lastly, in this passage, how our Lord asserts the lawfulness of doing works of mercy on the Sabbath day. We read that he healed a man who had the dropsy on the Sabbath day, and then said to the lawyers and Pharisees, "Which of you shall have an donkey or an ox fallen into a pit, and will not immediately pull him out on the Sabbath day?" This was a home thrust, which could not be fended off. It is written, "They could not answer Him."

The qualification which our Lord here puts on the requirements of the fourth commandment, is evidently founded on Scripture, reason, and common sense. The Sabbath was made for man, for his benefit, not for his injury, for his advantage, not for his hurt. The interpretation of God's law respecting the Sabbath was never intended to be strained so far as to interfere with charity, kindness, and the real needs of human nature. All such interpretations only defeat their own end. They require that which fallen man cannot perform, and thus bring the whole commandment into disrepute. Our Lord saw this clearly, and labored throughout His ministry to restore this precious part of God's law to its just position.

The principle which our Lord lays down about Sabbath observance needs carefully fencing with cautions. The right to do works of necessity and mercy is fearfully abused in these latter days. Thousands of Christians appear to have trampled down the hedge, and burst the bounds entirely with respect to this holy day. They seem to forget that though our Lord repeatedly explains the requirements of the fourth commandment, He never struck it out of the law of God, or said that it was not binding on Christians at all.

Can any one say that Sunday traveling, except on very rare emergencies, is a work of mercy? Will anyone tell us that Sunday trading, Sunday dinner parties, Sunday excursion-trains on railways, Sunday deliveries of letters and newspapers, are works of mercy? Have servants, and shop-men, and engine drivers, and coachmen, and clerks, and porters, no souls? Do they not need rest for their bodies and time for their souls, like other men? These are serious questions, and ought to make many people think.

Whatever others do, let us resolve to "keep the Sabbath holy." God has a controversy with the churches about Sabbath desecration. It is a sin of which the cry goes up to heaven, and will be reckoned for one day. Let us wash our hands of this sin, and have nothing to do with it. If others are determined to rob God, and take possession of the Lord's day for their own selfish ends, let us not be partakers in their sins.

LUKE 14:7-14
PLACES OF HONOR

And he spake a parable unto those that were bidden, when he marked how they chose out the chief seats; saying unto them, When thou art bidden of any man to a marriage feast, sit not down in the chief seat; lest haply a more honorable man than thou be bidden of him, and he that bade thee and him shall come and say to thee, Give this man place; and then thou shalt begin with shame to take the lowest place. But when thou art bidden, go and sit down in the lowest place; that when he that hath bidden thee cometh, he may say to thee, Friend, go up higher: then shalt thou have glory in the presence of all that sit at meat with thee. For everyone that exalteth himself shall be humbled; and he that humbleth himself shall be exalted. And he said to him also that had bidden him, When thou makest a dinner or a supper, call not thy friends, nor thy brethren, nor thy kinsmen, nor rich neighbors; lest haply they also bid thee again, and a recompense be made thee. But when thou makest a feast, bid the poor, the maimed, the lame, the blind: and thou shalt be blessed; because they have not wherewith to recompense thee: for thou shalt be recompensed in the resurrection of the just.

Let us learn from these verses the value of humility. This is a lesson which our Lord teaches in two ways. Firstly, He advises those who are bidden to a wedding to "sit down in the lowest place." Secondly, He backs up His advice by declaring a great principle, which frequently fell from His lips—"Whoever exalts himself shall be abased, and he that humbles himself shall be exalted."

Humility may well be called the queen of the Christian graces. To know our own sinfulness and weakness, and to feel our need of Christ, is the very beginning of saving religion. It is a grace which has always been the distinguishing feature in the character of the holiest saints in every age. Abraham, and Moses, and Job, and David, and Daniel, and Paul, were all eminently humble men. Above all, it is a grace within the reach of every true Christian. All have not money to give away. All have not time and opportunities for working directly for Christ. All have not gifts of speech, and tact, and knowledge, in order to do good in the world. But all converted men should labor to adorn the doctrine they profess by humility. If they can do nothing else, they can strive to be humble.

Would we know the root and spring of humility? One word describes it. The root of humility is right knowledge. The man who really knows himself and his own heart—who knows God and His infinite majesty and holiness—who knows Christ, and the price at which he was redeemed—that man will never be a proud man. He will count himself, like Jacob, unworthy of the least of all God's mercies. He will say of himself, like Job, "I am vile." He will cry, like Paul, "I am chief of sinners." (Genes. 32:10; Job 40:4; 1 Tim. 1:15.) He will think anything good enough for him. In lowliness of mind be will esteem everyone else to be better than himself. (Philip. 2:3.) Ignorance— nothing but sheer ignorance—ignorance of self, of God, and of Christ, is the real secret of pride. From that miserable self-ignorance may we daily pray to be delivered! He is the wise man who knows himself—and he who knows himself, will find nothing within to make him proud.

Let us learn, secondly, from these verses, the duty of caring for the poor. Our Lord teaches this lesson in a peculiar manner. He tells the Pharisee who invited Him to his feast, that, when he made "a dinner or a supper," he ought not to "call his friends," or relatives, or rich neighbors. On the contrary, He says, "When you make a feast, call the poor, the maimed, the lame, the blind."

The precept contained in these words must evidently be interpreted with considerable limitation. It is certain that our Lord did not intend to forbid men showing any hospitality to their relatives and friends. It is certain that He did not mean to encourage a useless and profuse expenditure of money in giving to the poor. To interpret the passage in this manner would make it contradict other plain Scriptures. Such interpretations cannot possibly be correct.

284 | J.C. RYLE

But when we have said this, we must not forget that the passage contains a deep and important lesson. We must be careful that we do not limit and qualify that lesson until we have pared it down and refined it into nothing at all. The lesson of the passage is plain and distinct. The Lord Jesus would have us care for our poorer brethren, and help them according to our power. He would have us know that it is a solemn duty never to neglect the poor, but to aid them and relieve them in their time of need.

Let the lesson of this passage sink down deeply into our hearts. "The poor shall never cease out of the land." (Deut. 15:11.) A little help conferred upon the poor judiciously and in season, will often add immensely to their happiness, and take away immensely from their cares, and promote good feeling between class and class in society. This help it is the will of Christ that all His people who have the means should he willing and ready to bestow. That stingy, calculating spirit, which leads some people to talk of "the workhouse," and condemn all charity to the poor, is exceedingly opposed to the mind of Christ. It is not for nothing that our Lord declares that He will say to the wicked in the day of judgment, "I was an hungry and you gave me no food—I was thirsty and you gave me no drink." It is not for nothing that Paul writes to the Galatians, "All they asked was that we should continue to remember the poor, the very thing I was eager to do." (Matt. 25:42. Gal. 2:10.)

Let us learn, lastly, from these verses, the great importance of looking forward to the resurrection of the dead. This lesson stands out in a striking manner in the language used by our Lord on the subject of showing charity to the poor. He says to the Pharisee who entertained Him, "The poor cannot repay you-you shall be repaid at the resurrection of the just."

There is a resurrection after death. Let this never be forgotten. The life that we live here in the flesh is not all. The visible world around us is not the only world with which we have to do. All is not over when the last breath is drawn, and men and women are carried to their long home in the grave. The trumpet shall one day sound, and the dead shall be raised incorruptible. All that are in the graves shall hear Christ's voice and come forth—those who have done good to the resurrection of life, and those who have done evil to the resurrection of damnation. This is one of the great foundation truths of the Christian religion. Let us cling to it firmly, and never let it go.

Let us strive to live like men who believe in a resurrection and a life to come, and desire to be always ready for another world. So living, we shall look forward to death with calmness. We shall feel that there remains some better portion for us beyond the grave. So living, we shall take patiently all that we have to bear in this world. Trial, losses, disappointments, ingratitude, will affect us little. We shall not look for our reward here. We shall feel that all will be rectified one day, and that the Judge of all the earth will do right. (Gen. 18:25.)

But how can we bear the thought of a resurrection? What shall enable us to look forward to a world to come without alarm? Nothing can do it, but faith in Christ. Believing on Him, we have nothing to fear. Our sins will not appear against us. The demands of God's law will be found completely satisfied. We shall stand firm in the great day, and none shall lay anything to our charge. (Rom. 8:33.) Worldly men like Felix, may well tremble when they think of a resurrection. But believers, like Paul, may rejoice.

LUKE 14:15-24
PARABLE OF THE GREAT BANQUET

And when one of them that sat at meat with him heard these things, he said unto him, Blessed is he that shall eat bread in the kingdom of God. But he said unto him, A certain man made a great supper; and he bade many: and he sent forth his servant at supper time to say to them that were bidden, Come; for all things are now ready. And they all with one consent began to make excuse. The first said unto him, I have bought a field, and I must needs go out and see it; I pray thee have me excused. And another said, I have bought five yoke of oxen, and I go to prove them; I pray thee have me excused. And another said, I have married a wife, and therefore I cannot come. And the servant came, and told his lord these things. Then the master of the house being angry said to his servant, Go out quickly into the streets and lanes of the city, and bring in hither the poor and maimed and blind and lame. And the servant said, Lord, what thou didst command is done, and yet there is room. And the lord said unto the servant, Go out into the highways and hedges, and constrain them to come in, that my house may be filled. For I say unto you, that none of those men that were bidden shall taste of my supper.

The verses before us contain one of our Lord's most instructive parables. It was spoken in consequence of a remark made by one who was sitting at table with Him in a Pharisee's house. "Blessed," said this man, "is he that shall eat the feast in the kingdom of God." The object of this remark we are left to conjecture. It is likely that he who made it was one of that class of people who wish to go to heaven, and like to hear good things talked of, but never get any further. Our Lord takes occasion to remind him and all the company, by means of the parable of the great supper, that men may have the kingdom of God offered to them, and yet may willingly neglect it, and be lost forever.

We are taught, firstly, in this parable, that God has made a great provision for the salvation of men's souls. This is the meaning of the words, "a certain man made a great banquet, and invited many." This is the Gospel.

The Gospel contains a full supply of everything that sinners need in order to be saved. We are all naturally starving, empty, helpless, and ready to perish. Forgiveness of all sin, and peace with God, justification of the person, and sanctification of the heart—grace by the way, and glory in the end—are the gracious provision which God has prepared for the wants of our souls. There is nothing that sin-laden hearts can wish, or weary consciences require, which is not spread before men in rich abundance in Christ. Christ, in one word, is the sum and substance of the "great supper." "I am the bread of life." "Him that comes unto me shall never hunger, and he that believes on me shall never thirst." "My flesh is food indeed, and my blood is drink indeed." "He that eats my flesh and drinks my blood, has eternal life." (John 6:35-55, 56.)

We are taught, secondly, in this parable, that the offers and invitations of the Gospel are most broad and liberal. We read that he who made the supper "sent his servant at the time of the banquet to say to those who were invited, Come for all things are now ready."

There is nothing lacking on God's part for the salvation of man. If man is not saved, the fault is not on God's side. The Father is ready to receive all who come to Him by Christ. The Son is ready to cleanse all from their sins who apply to Him by faith. The Spirit is ready to come to all who ask for Him. There is an infinite willingness in God to save man, if man is only willing to be saved.

There is the fullest warrant for sinners to draw near to God by Christ. The word "Come," is addressed to all without exception. Are men laboring and heavy-laden? "Come unto me," says Jesus, "and I will give you rest." Are men thirsting? "If any man thirst," says Jesus, "let him come unto me and drink." Are men poor and hungry? "Come," says Jesus, "buy wine and milk without money and without price." No man shall ever be able to say that he had no encouragement to seek salvation. That word of the Lord shall silence every objector—"Him that comes to me, I will in no wise cast out."

We are taught, thirdly, in this parable, that many who receive Gospel invitations refuse to accept them. We read that when the servant announced that all things were ready, those who were invited "all with one consent began to make excuse." One had one trivial excuse, and another had another. In one point only all were agreed—they would not come.

We have in this part of the parable a vivid picture of the reception which the Gospel is continually meeting with wherever it is proclaimed. Thousands are continually doing what the parable describes. They are invited to come to Christ, and they will not come. It is not ignorance of religion that ruins most men's souls. It is lack of will to use knowledge; or love of this present world. It is not open profligacy that fills hell. It is excessive attention to things which in themselves are lawful. It is not avowed dislike to the Gospel which is so much to be feared. It is that procrastinating, excuse-making spirit, which is always ready with a reason why Christ cannot be served today. Let the words of our Lord on this subject sink down into our hearts. Infidelity and immorality, no doubt, slay their thousands. But decent, plausible, smooth-spoken excuses slay their tens of thousands. No excuse can justify a man in refusing God's invitation, and not coming to Christ.

We are taught, lastly, in this parable, that God earnestly desires the salvation of souls, and would have all means used to procure acceptance for His Gospel. We read that when those who were first invited to the supper refused the invitation, "the master of the house said to his servant, Go out quickly into the streets, and bring in here the poor, and the maimed, and the halt, and the blind." We read that when this was done, and there was yet room, "the master said unto his servant, Go out into the high ways and hedges, and compel them to come in, that my house may be filled."

The meaning of these words can admit of little dispute. They surely justify us in asserting the exceeding love and compassion of God towards sinners. His patience is inexhaustible. If some will not receive the truth, He will have others invited in their stead. His pity for the lost is no pretended and imaginary thing. He is infinitely willing to save souls. Above all, the words justify every preacher and teacher of the Gospel in employing all possible means to awaken sinners, and turn them from their sins. If they will not come to us in public, we must visit them in private. If they will not attend our preaching in the congregation, we must be ready to preach from house to house.

We must even not be ashamed to use a gentle violence. We must be instant in season, out of season. (2 Tim. 4:2.) We must deal with many an unconverted man, as one who is half-asleep, half out of his mind, and not fully conscious of the state he is in. We must press the Gospel on his notice again and again. We must cry aloud and spare not. We must deal with him as we would with a man about to commit suicide. We must try to snatch him as a brand from the burning. We must say, "I cannot—I will not—I dare not let you go on ruining your own soul." The men of the world may not understand such earnest dealing. They may sneer at all zeal and fervor in religion as fanaticism. But the "man of God," who desires to do the work of an evangelist, will heed little what the world says. He will remember the words of our parable. He will "compel men to come in."

Let us leave this parable with serious self-inquiry. It ought to speak to us in the present day. To us this invitation of the Gospel is addressed as well as to the Jews. To us the Lord is saying constantly, "Come unto the supper— Come unto me." Have we accepted His invitation? Or are we practically saying, "I cannot come." If we die without having come to Christ, we had better never have been born.

LUKE 14:25-35
THE COST OF BEING A DISCIPLE

Now there went with him great multitudes: and he turned, and said unto them, If any man cometh unto me, and hateth not his own father, and mother, and wife, and children, and brethren, and sisters, yea, and his own life also, he cannot be my disciple. Whosoever doth not bear his own cross, and come after me, cannot be my disciple. For which of you, desiring to build a tower, doth not first sit down and count the cost, whether he have wherewith to complete it? Lest haply, when he hath laid a foundation, and is not able to finish, all that behold begin to mock him, saying, This man began to build, and was not able to finish. Or what king, as he goeth to encounter another king in war, will not sit down first and take counsel whether he is able with ten thousand to meet him that cometh against him with twenty thousand? Or else, while the other is yet a great way off, he sendeth an ambassage, and asketh conditions of peace. So therefore whosoever he be of you that renounceth not all that he hath, he cannot be my disciple. Salt therefore is good: but if even the salt have lost its savor, wherewith shall it be seasoned? It is fit neither for the land nor for the dunghill: men cast it out. He that hath ears to hear, let him hear.

We learn, firstly, from this passage, that true Christians must be ready, if need be, to give up everything for Christ's sake. This is a lesson which is taught in very remarkable language. Our Lord says, "If any man come to me, and hate not his father and mother, and wife and children, and brethren and sisters, yes, and his own life also, he cannot be my disciple."

This expression must doubtless be interpreted with some qualification. We must never explain any text of Scripture in such a manner as to make it contradict another. Our Lord did not mean us to understand that it is the duty of Christians to hate their relatives. This would have been to contradict the fifth commandment. He only meant that those who follow Him must love Him with a deeper love even than their nearest and dearest relatives, or their own lives. He did not mean that it is an essential part of Christianity to quarrel with our relatives and friends. But He did mean that if the claims of our relatives and the claims of Christ come into collision, the claims of relatives must give way. We must choose rather to displease those we love most upon earth, than to displease Him who died for us on the cross.

The demand which our Lord makes upon us here is peculiarly stringent and heart-searching. Yet it is a wise and a necessary one. Experience shows, both in the church at home, and in the mission-field abroad, that the greatest foes to a man's soul are sometimes those of his own house. It sometimes happens that the greatest hindrance in the way of an awakened conscience, is the opposition of relatives and friends. Ungodly fathers cannot bear to see their sons "taking up new views" of religion. Worldly mothers are vexed to see their daughters unwilling to enter into the gaieties of the world. A collision of opinion takes place frequently, as soon as grace enters into a family. And then comes the time when the true Christian must remember the spirit of our Lord's words in this passage. He must be willing to offend his family, rather than offend Christ.

The line of duty in such cases is doubtless very painful. It is a heavy cross to disagree with those we love, and especially about spiritual things. But if this cross be laid upon us, we must remember that firmness and decision are true kindness. It can never be true love to relatives to do wrong, in order to please them. And, best of all, firmness accompanied by gentleness and consistency, in the long run of life, often brings its own reward. Thousands of Christians will bless God at the last day, that they had relatives and friends who chose to displease them rather than Christ. That very decision was the first thing that made them think seriously, and led finally to the conversion of their souls.

We learn secondly, from this passage, that those who are thinking of following Christ should be warned to "count the cost." This is a lesson which was intended for the multitudes who followed our Lord without thought

290 | J.C. RYLE

and consideration, and was enforced by examples drawn from building and from war. It is a lesson which will be found useful in every age of the church.

It costs something to be a true Christian. Let that never be forgotten. To be a mere nominal Christian, and go to church, is cheap and easy work. But to hear Christ's voice, and follow Christ, and believe in Christ, and confess Christ, requires much self-denial. It will cost us our sins, and our self-righteousness, and our ease, and our worldliness. All—all must be given up. We must fight an enemy who comes against us with twenty thousand followers. We must build a tower in troublous times. Our Lord Jesus Christ would have us thoroughly understand this. He bids us "count the cost."

Now, why did our Lord use this language? Did He wish to discourage men from becoming His disciples? Did He mean to make the gate of life appear more narrow than it is? It is not difficult to find an answer to these questions. Our Lord spoke as He did to prevent men following Him lightly and inconsiderately, from mere carnal feeling or temporary excitement, who in time of temptation would fall away. He knew that nothing does so much harm to the cause of true religion as backsliding, and that nothing causes so much backsliding as enlisting disciples without letting them know what they take in hand. He had no desire to swell the number of His followers by admitting soldiers who would fail in the hour of need. For this reason He raises a warning voice. He bids all who think of taking service with Him count the cost before they begin.

Well would it be for the Church and the world if the ministers of Christ would always remember their Master's conduct in this passage. Often—far too often-people are built up in self-deception, and encouraged to think they are converted when in reality they are not converted at all. Feelings are supposed to be faith. Convictions are supposed to be grace. These things ought not so to be. By all means let us encourage the first beginnings of religion in a soul. But never let us urge people forward without telling them what true Christianity entails. Never let us hide from them the battle and the toil. Let us say to them "come with us"—but let us also say, "count the cost."

We learn, lastly, from this passage, how miserable is the condition of backsliders and apostates. This is a lesson which is intimately connected with the preceding one. The necessity of "counting the cost" is enforced by a picture of the consequences of neglecting to do so. The man who has once made a profession of religion, but has afterwards gone back from it, is like salt which has "lost its savor." Such salt is comparatively useless. "It is neither fit for the land, nor fit for the ash-heap—but men cast it out." Yet the state of that salt is a lively emblem of the state of a backslider. No wonder that our Lord said, "He that has ears to hear let him hear."

The truth which our Lord brings out in this place is very painful, but very useful and needful to be known. No man, be it remembered, is in so dangerous a state as he who has once known the truth and professed to love it, and has afterwards fallen away from his profession, and gone back to the world. You can tell such a man nothing that he does not know. You can show him no doctrine that he has not heard. He has not sinned in ignorance like many. He has gone away from Christ with his eyes open. He has sinned against a known, and not an unknown God. His case is well near desperate. All things are possible with God. Yet it is written, "It is impossible for those who were once enlightened—if they shall fall away, to renew them again unto repentance." (Heb. 6:4-6.)

Let us ponder these things well. The subject is one which is not sufficiently considered. Let us never be afraid of beginning to serve Christ. But let us begin seriously, thoughtfully, and with a due consideration of the step we take. And having once begun, let us pray for grace that we may persevere, and never fall away.

Chapter 15

LUKE 15:1-10

THE PARABLES OF THE LOST SHEEP,

AND THE LOST COIN

Now all the publicans and sinners were drawing near unto him to hear him. And both the Pharisees and the scribes murmured, saying, This man receiveth sinners, and eateth with them. And he spake unto them this parable, saying, What man of you, having a hundred sheep, and having lost one of them, doth not leave the ninety and nine in the wilderness, and go after that which is lost, until he find it? And when he hath found it, he layeth it on his shoulders, rejoicing. And when he cometh home, he calleth together his friends and his neighbors, saying unto them, Rejoice with me, for I have found my sheep which was lost. I say unto you, that even so there shall be joy in heaven over one sinner that repenteth, more than over ninety and nine righteous persons, who need no repentance. Or what woman having ten pieces of silver, if she lose one piece, doth not light a lamp, and sweep the house, and seek diligently until she find it? And when she hath found it, she calleth together her friends and neighbors, saying, Rejoice with me, for I have found the piece which I had lost. Even so, I say unto you, there is joy in the presence of the angels of God over one sinner that repenteth.

The chapter which begins with these verses is well known to Bible readers if any is in the Scriptures. Few chapters perhaps have done more good to the souls of men. Let us take heed that it does good to us.

We should first observe in these verses, the striking testimony which was borne to our Lord by His enemies. We read that when "all the publicans and sinners drew near to hear Him, the Scribes and Pharisees murmured, saying, This man receives sinners, and eats with them."

These words were evidently spoken with surprise and scorn, and not with pleasure and admiration. These ignorant guides of the Jews could not understand a preacher of religion having anything to do with wicked people! Yet their words worked for good. The very saying which was meant for a reproach was adopted by the Lord Jesus as a true description of His office. It led to His speaking three of the most instructive parables which ever fell from His lips.

The testimony of the Scribes and Pharisees was strictly and literally true. The Lord Jesus is indeed one that "receives sinners." He receives them to pardon them, to sanctify them, and to make them fit for heaven. It is His special office to do so. For this end He came into the world. He came not to call the righteous, but sinners to repentance. He came into the world to save sinners. What He was upon earth He is now at the right hand of God, and will be to all eternity. He is emphatically the sinner's Friend.

Have we any sense of sin? Do we feel bad, and wicked, and guilty, and deserving of God's anger? Is the remembrance of our past lives bitter to us? Does the recollection of our past conduct make us ashamed? Then we are the very people who ought to apply to Christ, just as we are, pleading nothing of our own, making no useless delay. Christ will receive us graciously, pardon us freely, and give us eternal life. He is One that "receives sinners." Let us not be lost for lack of applying to Him that we may be saved.

We should observe, secondly, in these verses, the remarkable figures under which our Lord describes His own love towards sinners. We read that in reply to the taunting remark of His enemies He spoke three parables—the parables of the lost sheep, the lost piece of silver, and the prodigal son. The first two of these parables are now before us. All three are meant to illustrate one and the same truth. They all throw strong light on Christ's willingness to save sinners.

Christ's love is an active, working love. Just as the shepherd did not sit still bewailing his lost sheep, and the woman did not sit still bewailing her lost money, so our blessed Lord did not sit still in heaven pitying sinners. He left the glory which He had with the Father, and humbled Himself to be made in the likeness of man. He came down into the world to seek and save that which was lost. He never rested until He had made atonement for our transgressions, brought in everlasting righteousness, provided eternal redemption, and opened a door of life to all who are willing to be saved.

Christ's love is a self-denying love. The shepherd brought his lost sheep home on his own shoulders rather than leave it in the wilderness. The woman lighted a candle, and swept the house, and searched diligently, and spared no pains, until she found her lost money. And just so did Christ not spare Himself, when he undertook to save sinners. "He endured the cross, despising the shame." He "laid down His life for His friends." Greater love than this cannot be shown. (John 15:13. Heb. 12:2.)

Christ's love is a deep and mighty love. Just as the shepherd rejoiced to find his sheep, and the woman to find her money, so does the Lord Jesus rejoice to save sinners. It is a real pleasure to Him to pluck them as brands from the burning. It was His "food and drink," when upon earth, to finish the work which He came to do. He felt straitened in spirit until it was accomplished. It is still His delight to show mercy. He is far more willing to save sinners than sinners are to be saved.

Let us strive to know something of this love of Christ. It is a love that truly passes knowledge. It is unspeakable and unsearchable. It is that on which we must wholly rest our souls, if we would have peace in time, and glory in eternity. If we take comfort in our own love to Christ, we are building on a sandy foundation. But if we lean on Christ's love to us, we are on a rock.

We should observe, lastly, in these verses, the wide encouragement which our Lord holds out to repentance. We read these striking words, "Joy shall be in heaven over one sinner that repents." We read the same thought again after a few verses—"There is joy in the presence of the angels of God over one sinner that repents." The thing is doubled, to make doubt impossible. The idea is repeated, in order to meet man's unbelief.

There are deep things in these sayings, beyond doubt. Our poor weak minds are little able to understand how the perfect joy of heaven can admit of increase. But one thing, at any rate, stands out clearly on the face of these expressions. There is an infinite willingness on God's part to receive sinners. However wicked a man may have been, in the day that he really turns from his wickedness and comes to God by Christ, God is well-pleased. God has no pleasure in the death of him that dies, and God has pleasure in true repentance.

Let the man who is afraid to repent, consider well the verses we are now looking at, and be afraid no more. There is nothing on God's part to justify his fears. An open door is set before him. A free pardon awaits him. "If we confess our sins, God is faithful and just to forgive our sins, and cleanse us from all unrighteousness." (1 John 1:9.)

Let the man who is ashamed to repent, consider these verses, and cast shame aside. What though the world mocks and jests at his repentance? While man is mocking, angels are rejoicing. The very change which sinners call foolishness, is a change which fills heaven with joy.

Have we repented ourselves? This, after all, is the principal question which concerns us. What shall it profit us to know Christ's love, if we do not use it? "If you know these things, happy are you if you do them." (John 13:17.)

LUKE 15:11-24

PARABLE OF THE LOST SON

And he said, A certain man had two sons: and the younger of them said to his father, Father, give me the portion of thy substance that falleth to me. And he divided unto them his living. And not many days after, the younger son gathered all together and took his journey into a far country; and there he wasted his substance with riotous living. And when he had spent all, there arose a mighty famine in that country; and he began to be in want. And he went and joined himself to one of the citizens of that country; and he sent him into his fields to feed swine. And he would fain have filled his belly with the husks that the swine did eat: and no man gave unto him. But when he came to himself he said, How many hired servants of my father's have bread enough and to spare, and I perish here with hunger! I will arise and go to my father, and will say unto him, Father, I have sinned against heaven, and in thy sight: I am no more worthy to be called your son: make me as one of thy hired servants. And he arose, and came to his father. But while he was yet afar off, his father saw him, and was moved with compassion, and ran, and fell on his neck, and kissed him. And the son said unto him, Father, I have sinned against heaven, and in thy sight: I am no more worthy to be called thy son. But the father said to his servants, Bring forth quickly the best robe, and put it on him; and put a ring on his hand, and shoes on his feet: and bring the fatted calf, and kill it, and let us eat, and make merry: for this my son was dead, and is alive again; he was lost, and is found. And they began to be merry.

The parable before us is commonly known as the parable of "the prodigal son." It may be truly called a mighty spiritual picture. Unlike some of our Lord's parables, it does not convey to us one great lesson only, but many. Every part of it is peculiarly rich in instruction.

We see, firstly, in this parable, a man following the natural bent of his own heart. Our Lord shows us a "younger son" making haste to set up for himself, going far away from a kind father's house, and "wasting his substance in riotous living."

We have in these words a faithful portrait of the mind with which we are all born. This is our likeness. We are all naturally proud and self-willed. We have no pleasure in fellowship with God. We depart from Him, and go afar off. We spend our time, and strength, and faculties, and affections, on things that cannot profit. The covetous man does it in one fashion; the slave of lusts and passions in another; the lover of pleasure in another. In one point only are all agreed. Like sheep, we all naturally "go astray, and turn everyone to his own way." (Isaiah. 53:6.) In the younger son's first conduct we see the natural heart.

He that knows nothing of these things has yet much to learn. He is spiritually blind. The eyes of his understanding need to be opened. The worst ignorance in the world is not to know ourselves. Happy is he who bas been delivered from the kingdom of darkness, and been made acquainted with himself! Of too many it may be said, "They know not, neither will they understand. They walk on in darkness." (Psalm 82:5.)

We see, secondly, in this parable, man finding out that the ways of sin are hard, by bitter experience. Our Lord shows us the younger son spending all his property and reduced to poverty—obliged to take service and "feed swine"-so hungry that he is ready to eat swine's food—and cared for by none.

These words describe a common case. Sin is a hard master, and the servants of sin always find it out, sooner or later, to their cost. Unconverted people are never really happy. Under a profession of high spirits and cheerfulness, they are often ill at ease within. Thousands of them are sick at heart, dissatisfied with themselves, weary of their own ways, and thoroughly uncomfortable. "There be many that say, who will show us any good." "There is no peace, says my God, to the wicked." (Psalm. 4:6. Isaiah 57:21.)

Let this truth sink down into our hearts. It is a truth, however loudly unconverted people may deny it. "The way of transgressors is hard." (Prov. 13:15.) The secret wretchedness of natural man is exceedingly great. There is a famine within, however much they may try to conceal it. They are "in need." He that "sows to the flesh shall of the flesh reap corruption." No wonder that Paul said, "What profit had you in those things whereof you are now ashamed?" (Gal. 6:8. Rom. 6:21.)

EXPOSITORY THOUGHTS ON THE GOSPELS: LUKE | 297

We see, thirdly, in this parable, man awaking to a sense of his natural state, and resolving to repent. Our Lord tells us that the younger son "came to himself and said, how many servants of my father have bread enough and to spare, and I perish with hunger? I will arise and go to my father, and say unto him, Father, I have sinned."

The thoughts of thousands are vividly painted in these words. Thousands have reasoned in this way, and are saying such things to themselves every day. And we must be thankful when we see such thoughts arise. Thinking is not change of heart, but it may be the beginning of it. Conviction is not conversion, but it is one step, at any rate, in a right direction. The ruin of many people's souls is simply this, that they never think at all.

One caution, however, must always be given. Men must beware that they do not stop short in "thinking." Good thoughts are all very well, but they are not saving Christianity. If the younger son had never got beyond thinking, he might have kept from home to the day of his death.

We see, fourthly, in this parable, man turning to God with true repentance and faith. Our Lord shows us the younger son leaving the far country where he was, and going back to his father's house, carrying into practice the good intentions he had formed, and unreservedly confessing his sin. "He arose and went."

These words are a life-like outline of true repentance and conversion. The man in whose heart a true work of the Holy Spirit has begun, will never be content with thinking and resolving. He will break off from sin. He will come out from its fellowship. He will cease to do evil. He will learn to do well. He will turn to God in humble prayer. He will confess his iniquities. He will not attempt to excuse his sins. He will say with David, "I acknowledge my transgression." He will say with the tax-collector, "God be merciful to me a sinner." (Psalm 51:3. Luke 18:13.)

Let us beware of any repentance, falsely so called, which is not of this character. Action is the very life of "repentance unto salvation." Feelings, and tears, and remorse, and wishes, and resolutions, are all useless, until they are accompanied by action and a change of life. In fact they are worse than useless. Insensibly they sear the conscience and harden the heart.

We see, fifthly, in this parable, the penitent man received readily, pardoned freely, and completely accepted with God. Our Lord shows us this, in this part of the younger son's history, in the most touching manner. We read that "he got up and went to his father. But while he was still a long way off, his father saw him and was filled with compassion for him; he ran to his son, threw his arms around him and kissed him. The son said to him, 'Father, I have sinned against heaven and against you. I am no longer worthy to be called your son.' But the father said to his servants, 'Quick! Bring the best robe and put it on him. Put a ring on his finger and sandals on his feet. Bring the fattened calf and kill it. Let's have a feast and celebrate.'"

More deeply affecting words than these, perhaps, were never written. To comment on them seems almost needless. It is like gilding refined gold, and painting the lily. They show us in great broad letters the infinite love of the Lord Jesus Christ towards sinners. They teach how infinitely willing He is to receive all who come to Him, and how complete, and full, and immediate is the pardon which He is ready to bestow. "By Him all who believe are justified from all things." "He is plenteous in mercy." (Acts 13:39. Psalm 86:5.)

Let this boundless mercy of our Lord Jesus Christ be engraved deeply in our memories, and sink into our minds. Let us never forget that He is One "that receives sinners." With Him and His mercy sinners ought to begin, when they first begin to desire salvation. On Him and His mercy saints must live, when they have been taught to repent and believe. "The life which I live in the flesh," says Paul, "I live by the faith of the Son of God, who loved me and gave Himself for me." (Gal. 2:20.)

LUKE 15:25-32

Now his elder son was in the field: and as he came and drew nigh to the house, he heard music and dancing. And he called to him one of the servants, and inquired what these things might be. And he said unto him, Thy brother is come; and thy father hath killed the fatted calf, because he hath received him safe and sound. But he was angry, and would not go in: and his father came out, and entreated him. But he answered and said to his father, Lo, these many years do I serve thee, and I never transgressed a commandment of thine; and yet thou never gavest me a kid, that I might make merry with my friends: but when this thy son came, who hath devoured thy living with harlots, thou killedst for him the fatted calf. And he said unto him, Son, thou art ever with me, and all that is mine is thine. But it was meet to make merry and be glad: for this thy brother was dead, and is alive again; and was lost, and is found.

These verses form the conclusion of the parable of the prodigal son. They are far less well known than the verses which go before them. But they were spoken by the same lips which described the younger son's return to his father's house. Like everything which those lips spoke, they will be found deeply profitable.

We are taught, firstly, in this passage, how unkind and ill-natured are the feelings of self-righteous men towards sinners.

This is a lesson which our Lord conveys to us by describing the conduct of the "elder brother" of the prodigal son. He shows him to us "angry" and finding fault because of the rejoicings over his brother's return. He shows him complaining that his father treated the returning prodigal too well, and that he himself had not been treated as well as his merits deserved. He shows him utterly unable to share in the joy which prevailed when his younger brother came home, and giving away to ill-natured and envious thoughts. It is a painful picture, but a very instructive one.

For one thing, this elder brother is an exact picture of the Jews of our Lord's times. They could not bear the idea of their 'Gentile' younger brother being made partaker of their privileges. They would gladly have excluded him from God's favor. They steadily refused to see that the Gentiles were to be fellow heirs and partakers of Christ with themselves. In all this they were precisely acting the part of the "elder brother."

For another thing, the elder brother is an exact type of the Scribes and Pharisees of our Lord's times. They objected that our Lord received sinners and ate with them. They murmured because He opened the door of salvation to publicans and harlots. They would have been better pleased if our Lord had confined His ministry to them and their party, and had left the ignorant and sinful entirely alone. Our Lord saw this state of things clearly; and never did He paint it with such graphic power as in the picture of the "elder brother."

Last, but not least, the elder brother is an exact type of a large class in the Church of Christ in the present day. There are thousands on every side who dislike a free, full, unfettered Gospel to be preached. They are always complaining that ministers throw the door too wide open, and that the doctrine of grace tends to promote licentiousness. Whenever we come across such people, let us remember the passage we are now considering. Their voice is the voice of the "elder brother."

Let us beware of this spirit infecting our own heart. It arises partly from ignorance. Men begin by not seeing their own sinfulness and unworthiness, and then they fancy that they are much better than others, and that nobody is worthy to be put by their side. It arises partly from lack of charity. Men are lacking in kind feeling towards others, and then they are unable to take pleasure when others are saved. Above all, it arises from a thorough misunderstanding of the true nature of gospel forgiveness. The man who really feels that we all stand by grace and are all debtors, and that the best of us has nothing to boast of, and has nothing which he has not received—such a man will not be found talking like the "elder brother."

We are taught, secondly, in this passage, that the conversion of any soul ought to be an occasion of joy to all who see it. Our Lord shows us this by putting the following words into the mouth of the prodigal's father—"We had to celebrate this happy day. For your brother was dead and has come back to life! He was lost, but now he is found!"

The lesson of these words was primarily meant for the Scribes and Pharisees. If their hearts had been in a right state, they would never have murmured at our Lord for receiving sinners. They would have remembered that the worst of publicans and sinners were their own brethren, and that if they themselves were different, it was grace alone that had made the difference. They would have been glad to see such helpless wanderers returning to the fold. They would have been thankful to see them plucked as brands from the burning, and not cast away forever. Of all these feelings, unhappily, they knew nothing. Wrapped in their own self-righteousness they murmured and found fault, when in reality they ought to have thanked God and rejoiced.

The lesson is one which we shall all do well to lay to heart. Nothing ought to give us such true pleasure as the conversion of souls. It makes angels rejoice in heaven. It ought to make Christians rejoice on earth. What if those who are converted were lately the vilest of the vile? What if they have served sin and Satan for many long years, and wasted their substance in riotous living? It matters nothing. "Has grace come into their hearts? Are they truly penitent? Have they come back to their father's house? Are they new creatures in Christ Jesus? Are the dead made alive and the lost found?"

These are the only questions we have any right to ask. If they can be answered satisfactorily we ought to rejoice and be glad. Let the worldly, if they please, mock and sneer at such conversions. Let the self-righteous, if they will, murmur and find fault, and deny the reality of all great and sudden changes. But let the Christian who reads the words of Christ in this chapter, remember them and act upon them. Let him thank God and be merry. Let him praise God that one more soul is saved. Let him say, "this my brother was dead and is alive again; and was lost, and is found."

What are our own feelings on the subject? This after all is the question that concerns us most. The man who can take deep interest in politics, or field sports, or money-making, or farming, but none in the conversion of souls, is no true Christian. He is himself "dead" and must be made "alive again." He is himself "lost" and must be "found."

Chapter 16

THE PARABLE OF THE SHREWD MANAGER

*A*nd he said also unto the disciples, There was a certain rich man, who had a steward; and the same was accused unto him that he was wasting his goods. And he called him, and said unto him, What is this that I hear of thee? render the account of thy stewardship; for thou canst be no longer steward. And the steward said within himself, What shall I do, seeing that my lord taketh away the steward-ship from me? I have not strength to dig; to beg I am ashamed. I am resolved what to do, that, when I am put out of the stewardship, they may receive me into their houses. And calling to him each one of his lord's debtors, he said to the first, How much owest thou unto my lord? And he said, A hundred measures of oil. And he said unto him, Take thy bond, and sit down quickly and write fifty. Then said he to another, And how much owest thou? And he said, A hundred measures of wheat. He saith unto him, Take thy bond, and write fourscore. And his lord commended the unrighteous steward because he had done wisely: for the sons of this world are for their own generation wiser than the sons of the light. And I say unto you, Make to yourselves friends by means of the mammon of unrighteousness; that, when it shall fail, they may receive you into the eternal tabernacles. He that is faithful in a very little is faithful also in much: and he that is unrighteous in a very little is unrighteous also in much. If therefore ye have not been faithful in the unrighteous mammon, who will commit to your trust the true riches? And if ye have not been faithful in that which is another's, who will give you that which is your own?

The passage we have now read is a difficult one. There are knots in it which perhaps will never be untied, until the Lord comes again. We might reasonably expect that a book written by inspiration, as the Bible is, would contain things hard to be understood. The fault lies not in the book, but in our own feeble understandings. If we learn nothing else from the passage before us, let us learn humility.

Let us beware, in the first place, that we do not draw from these verses lessons which they were never meant to teach.

The steward, whom our Lord describes, is not set before us as a pattern of morality. He is distinctly called the "unjust steward." The Lord Jesus never meant to sanction dishonesty, and unfair dealing between man and man. This steward cheated his master, and broke the eighth commandment. His master was struck with his cunning and forethought, when he heard of it, and "commended" him, as a shrewd and far-seeing man. But there is no proof that his master was pleased with his conduct. Above all, there is not a word to show that the man was praised by Christ. In short, in his treatment of his master, the steward is a beacon to be avoided, and not a pattern to be followed.

The caution, now laid down, is very necessary. Commercial dishonesty is unhappily very common in these latter days. Fair dealing between man and man is increasingly rare. Men do things in the way of business, which will not stand the test of the Bible. In "making haste to be rich," thousands are continually committing actions which are not strictly innocent. (Prov. 28:20.)

Sharpness and smartness, in bargaining, and buying, and selling, and pushing trade, are often covering over things that ought not to be. The generation of "the unjust steward" is still a very large one. Let us not forget this. Whenever we do to others what we would not like others to do to us, we may be sure, whatever the world may say, that we are wrong in the sight of Christ.

Let us observe, in the second place, that one principal lesson of the parable before us, is the wisdom of providing against coming evil.

The conduct of the unjust steward, when he received notice to give up his place, was undeniably skillful. Dishonest as he was in striking off from the bills of debtors anything that was due to his master, he certainly by so doing made for himself friends. Wicked as he was, he had an eye to the future. Disgraceful as his measures were, he provided well for himself. He did not sit still in idleness, and see himself reduced to poverty without a struggle.

He schemed, and planned, and contrived, and boldly carried his plans into execution. And the result was that when he lost one home he secured another.

What a striking contrast between the steward's conduct about his earthly prospects, and the conduct of most men about their souls! In this general point of view, and in this only, the steward sets us all an example which we should do well to follow. Like him, we should look far forward to things to come. Like him, we should provide against the day when we shall have to leave our present habitation. Like him, we should secure "a house in heaven," which may be our home, when we put off our earthly tabernacle of the body. (2 Cor. 5:1.) Like him we should use all means to provide for ourselves everlasting habitations.

The parable, in this point of view, is deeply instructive. It may well raise within us great searchings of heart. The diligence of worldly men about the things of time, should put to shame the coldness of professing Christians about the things of eternity. The zeal and pertinacity of men of business in compassing sea and land to get earthly treasures, may well reprove the slackness and indolence of believers about treasures in heaven. The words of our Lord are indeed weighty and solemn, "The children of this world are in their generation wiser than the children of light." May these words sink into our hearts and bear fruit in our lives!

Let us notice, lastly, in this passage, the remarkable expressions which our Lord uses about little things, in close connection with the parable of the unjust steward. We read that He said, "He that is faithful in that which is least, is faithful also in much—and he that is unjust in the least, is unjust also in much."

Our Lord here teaches us the great importance of strict faithfulness about "little things." He guards us against supposing that such conduct about money as that of the unjust steward, ought ever to be considered a light and trifling thing among Christians. He would have us know that "little things" are the best test of character—and that unfaithfulness about "little things" is the symptom of a bad state of heart. He did not mean, of course, that honesty about money can justify our souls, or put away sin. But He did mean that dishonesty about money is a sure sign of a heart not being "right in the sight of God." The man who is not dealing honestly with the gold and silver of this world, can never be one who has true riches in heaven. "If you have not been faithful in that which is another man's, who shall give you that which is your own?"

The doctrine laid down by our Lord in this place, deserves most serious consideration in the present day. An idea appears to prevail in some men's minds, that true religion may be separated from common honesty, and that soundness about matters of doctrine may cover over swindling and cheating in matters of practice! Against this wretched idea our Lord's words were a plain protest. Against this idea let us watch and be on our guard. Let us contend earnestly for the glorious doctrines of salvation by grace, and justification by faith. But let us never allow ourselves to suppose that true religion sanctions any trifling with the second table of the law. Let us never forget for a moment, that true faith will always be known by its fruits. We may be very sure that where there is no honesty, there is no grace.

LUKE 16:13-18

SERVING TWO MASTERS

No servant can serve two masters: for either he will hate the one, and love the other; or else he will hold to one, and despise the other. Ye cannot serve God and mammon. And the Pharisees, who were lovers of money, heard all these things; and they scoffed at him. And he said unto them, Ye are they that justify yourselves in the sight of men; but God knoweth your hearts: for that which is exalted among men is an abomination in the sight of God. The law and the prophets were until John: from that time the gospel of the kingdom of God is preached, and every man entereth violently into it. But it is easier for heaven and earth to pass away, than for one tittle of the law to fall. Every one that putteth away his wife, and marrieth another, committeth adultery: and he that marrieth one that is put away from a husband committeth adultery.

These verses teach us, firstly, the uselessness of attempting to serve God with a divided heart. Our Lord Jesus Christ says, "No servant can serve two masters—for either he will hate the one and love the other—or else he will hold to the one and despise the other. You cannot serve God and mammon."

The truth here propounded by our Lord appears, at first sight, too obvious to admit of being disputed. And yet the very attempt which is here declared to be useless is constantly being made by many in the matter of their souls. Thousands on every side are continually trying to do the thing which Christ pronounces impossible. They are endeavoring to be friends of the world and friends of God at the same time. Their consciences are so far enlightened, that they feel they must have some religion. But their affections are so chained down to earthly things, that they never come up to the mark of being true Christians. And hence they live in a state of constant discomfort. They have too much religion to be happy in the world, and they have too much of the world in their hearts to be happy in their religion. In short, they waste their time in laboring to do that which cannot be done. They are striving to "serve God and mammon."

He that desires to be a happy Christian, will do well to ponder our Lord's sayings in this verse. There is perhaps no point on which the experience of all God's saints is more uniform than this, that decision is the secret of comfort in Christ's service. It is the half-hearted Christian who brings up an evil report of the good land. The more thoroughly we give ourselves to Christ, the more sensibly shall we feel within "the peace of God which passes all understanding." (Phil. 4:7.) The more entirely we live, not to ourselves, but to Him who died for us, the more powerfully shall we realize what it is to have "joy and peace in believing." (Rom. 15:13.) If it is worthwhile to serve Christ at all, let us serve Him with all our heart, and soul, and mind and strength. Life, eternal life, after all, is the matter at stake, no less than happiness. If we cannot make up our minds to give up everything for Christ's sake, we must not expect Christ to own us at the last day. He will have all our hearts or none. "Whoever will be a friend of the world is the enemy of God." (James 4:4) The end of undecided and half-hearted Christians will be to be cast out forever.

These verses teach us, secondly, how widely different is the estimate set on things by man from that which is set on things by God. Our Lord Jesus Christ declares this in a severe rebuke which he addresses to the covetous Pharisees who derided Him. He says, "You are they which justify yourselves before men; but God knows your hearts—for that which is highly esteemed among men is abomination in the sight of God."

The truth of this solemn saying appears on every side of us. We have only to look round the world and mark the things on which most men set their affections, in order to see it proved in a hundred ways. Riches, and honors, and rank, and pleasure, are the chief objects for which the greater part of mankind are living. Yet these are the very things which God declares to be "vanity," and of the love of which He warns us to beware! Praying, and Bible reading, and holy living, and repentance, and faith, and grace, and communion with God, are things for which few care at all. Yet these are the very things which God in His Bible is ever urging on our attention! The disagreement is glaring, painful, and appalling. What God calls good, that man calls evil! What God calls evil, that man calls good!

Whose words, after all, are true? Whose estimate is correct? Whose judgment will stand at the last day? By whose standard will all be tried, before they receive their eternal sentence? Before whose bar will the current opinions of the world be tested and weighed at last? These are the only questions which ought to influence our conduct; and to these questions the Bible returns a plain answer. The counsel of the Lord, it alone shall stand forever. The word of Christ, it alone shall judge man at the last day. By that word let us live. By that word let us measure everything, and every person in this evil world. It matters nothing what man thinks. "What says the Lord?"—It matters nothing what it is fashionable or customary to think. "Let God be true, and every man a liar." (Rom. 3:4.) The more entirely we are of one mind with God, the better we are prepared for the judgment day. To love what God loves, to hate what God hates, and to approve what God approves, is the highest style of Christianity. The moment we find ourselves honoring anything which in the sight of God is lightly esteemed, we may be sure there is something wrong in our souls.

These verses teach us, lastly, the dignity and sanctity of the law of God. Our Lord Jesus Christ declares that "it is easier for heaven and earth to pass, than for one tittle of the law to fail."

The honor of God's holy law was frequently defended by Christ during the time of His ministry on earth. Sometimes we find Him defending it against man-made additions, as in the case of the fourth commandment. Sometimes we find Him defending it against those who would lower the standard of its requirements, and allow it to be transgressed, as in the case of the law of marriage. But never do we find Him speaking of the law in any terms but those of respect. He always "magnified the law and made it honorable." (Isaiah 43:21.) Its 'ceremonial' part was a type of His own gospel, and was to be fulfilled to the last letter. Its 'moral' part was a revelation of God's eternal mind, and was to be perpetually binding on Christians.

The honor of God's holy law needs continually defending in the present day. On few subjects does ignorance prevail so widely among professing Christians. Some appear to think that Christians have nothing to do with the law—that its moral and ceremonial parts were both of only temporary obligation—and that the daily sacrifice and the ten commandments were both alike put aside by the gospel. Some on the other hand think that the law is still binding on us, and that we are to be saved by obedience to it, but that its requirements are lowered by the gospel, and can be met by our imperfect obedience. Both these views are erroneous and unscriptural. Against both let us be on our guard.

Let us settle it in our minds that "the law is good if man uses it lawfully." (1 Tim. 1:8.) It is intended to show us God's holiness and our sinfulness—to convince us of sin and to lead us to Christ—to show us how to live after we have come to Christ, and to teach us what to follow and what to avoid. He that so uses the law will find it a true friend to his soul. The establishes Christian will always say, "I delight in the law of God after the inward man." (Rom. 7:22.)

LUKE 16:19-31
THE RICH MAN AND LAZARUS

Now there was a certain rich man, and he was clothed in purple and fine linen, faring sumptuously every day: and a certain beggar named Lazarus was laid at his gate, full of sores, and desiring to be fed with the crumbs that fell from the rich man's table; yea, even the dogs came and licked his sores. And it came to pass, that the beggar died, and that he was carried away by the angels into Abraham's bosom: and the rich man also died, and was buried. And in Hades he lifted up his eyes, being in torments, and seeth Abraham afar off, and Lazarus in his bosom. And he cried and said, Father Abraham, have mercy on me, and send Lazarus, that he may dip the tip of his finger in water, and cool my tongue; for I am in anguish in this flame. But Abraham said, Son, remember that thou in thy lifetime receivedst thy good things, and Lazarus in like manner evil things: but now here he is comforted and thou art in anguish. And besides all this, between us and you there is a great gulf fixed, that they that would pass from hence to you may not be able, and that none may cross over from thence to us. And he said, I pray thee therefore, father, that thou wouldest send him to my father's house; for I have five brethren; that he may testify unto them, lest they also come into this place of torment. But Abraham saith, They have Moses and the prophets; let them hear them. And he said, Nay, father Abraham: but if one go to them from the dead, they will repent. And he said unto him, If they hear not Moses and the prophets, neither will they be persuaded, if one rise from the dead.

The parable we have now read, in one respect stands alone in the Bible. It is the only passage of Scripture which describes the feelings of the unconverted after death. For this reason, as well as for many others, the parable deserves especial attention.

We learn, firstly, from this parable, that a man's worldly condition is no test of his state in the sight of God. The Lord Jesus describes to us two men, of whom one was very rich, and the other very poor. The one "fared sumptuously every day." The other was a mere "beggar," who had nothing that he could call his own. And yet of these two the poor man had grace, and the rich had none. The poor man lived by faith, and walked in the steps of Abraham. The rich man was a thoughtless, selfish worldling, dead in trespasses and sins.

Let us never give way to the common idea that men are to be valued according to their income, and that the man who has most money is the one who ought to be the most highly esteemed. There is no authority for this notion in the Bible. The general teaching of Scripture is flatly opposed to it. "Not many wise, not many mighty, not many noble are called." (1 Cor. 1:26.) "Let not the rich man glory in his riches. But let him that glories glory in this, that he knows and understands me." (Jer. 9:24.) Wealth is no mark of God's favor. Poverty is no mark of God's displeasure. Those whom God justifies and glorifies are seldom the rich of this world. It we would measure men as God measures them, we must value them according to their grace.

We learn, secondly, from this parable, that death is the common end to which all classes of mankind must come. The trials of the "beggar," and the sumptuous faring of the "rich man," alike ceased at last. There came a time when both of them died. "All go to one place." (Eccles. 3:20.)

Death is a great fact that all acknowledge, but very few seem to realize. Most men eat, and drink, and talk, and plan, as if they were going to live upon earth forever. The true Christian must be on his guard against this spirit. "He that would live well," said a great divine, "should often think of his last day, and make it his company-keeper." Against murmuring, and discontent, and envy, in the state of poverty—against pride, and self-sufficiency, and arrogance, in the possession of wealth, there are few better antidotes than the remembrance of death. "The beggar died," and his bodily wants were at an end. "The rich man died," and his feasting was stopped for evermore.

We learn, thirdly, from this parable, that the souls of believers are specially cared for by God in the hour of death. The Lord Jesus tells us that when the beggar died he "was carried by angels to Abraham's bosom."

There is something very comforting in this expression. We know little or nothing of the state and feelings of the dead. When our own last hour comes, and we lie down to die, we shall be like those who journey into an unknown country. But it may satisfy us to know that all who fall asleep in Jesus are in good keeping. They are not houseless, homeless wanderers between the hour of death and the day of resurrection. They are at rest in the midst of friends, with all who have had like faith with Abraham. They have no lack of anything. And, best of all, Paul tells us they are "with Christ." (Phil. 1:23.)

We learn, fourthly, from this parable, the reality and eternity of hell. The Lord Jesus tells us plainly, that after death the rich man was "in hell—tormented with fire." He gives us a fearful picture of his longing for a drop of "water to cool his tongue," and of "the gulf" between him and Abraham, which could not be passed. There are few more dreadful passages perhaps in the whole Bible than this. And He from whose lips it came, be it remembered, was one who delighted in mercy!

The certainty and endlessness of the future punishment of the wicked, are truths which we must hold fast and never let go. From the day when Satan said to Eve, "You shall not surely die," there never have been lacking men who have denied them. Let us not be deceived. There is a hell for the impenitent, as well as a heaven for believers. There is a wrath to come for all who "obey not the Gospel of Christ." (2 Thess. 1:8.) From that wrath let us flee betimes to the great hiding-place, Jesus Christ the Lord. If men find themselves "in torment" at last, it will not be because there was no way to escape.

We learn, fifthly, from this parable, that unconverted men find out the value of a soul, after death, when it is too late. We read that the rich man desired Lazarus might be sent to his five brethren who were yet alive, "lest they also should come to the place of torment." While he lived he had never done anything for their spiritual good. They had probably been his companions in worldliness, and, like him, had neglected their souls entirely. When he is dead he finds out too late the folly of which they had all been guilty, and desires that, if possible, they might be called to repentance.

The change that will come over the minds of unconverted men after death is one of the most fearful points in their future condition. They will see, and know, and understand a hundred things to which they were obstinately blind while they were alive. They will discover that, like Esau, they have bartered away eternal happiness for a mere mess of pottage. There is no infidelity, or skepticism, or unbelief after death. It is a wise saying of an old divine, that "hell is nothing more than truth known too late."

We learn, lastly, from this parable, that the greatest miracles would have no effect on men's hearts, if they will not believe God's Word. The rich man thought that "if one went to his brethren from the dead they would repent." He argued that the sight of one who came from another world must surely make them feel, though the old familiar words of Moses and the prophets had been heard in vain. The reply of Abraham is solemn and instructive— "If they hear not Moses and the prophets, neither will they be persuaded though one rose from the dead."

The principle laid down in these words is of deep importance. The Scriptures contain all that we need to know in order to be saved, and a messenger from the world beyond the grave could add nothing to them. It is not 'more evidence' that is needed in order to make men repent, but more heart and will to make use of what they already know.

The 'dead' could tell us nothing more than the Bible contains, if they rose from their graves to instruct us. After the first novelty of their testimony was worn away, we would care no more for their words than the words of any other.

This wretched waiting for something which we have not, and neglect of what we already have, is the ruin of thousands of souls. Faith, simple faith in the Scriptures which we already possess, is the first thing needful to salvation. The man who has the Bible, and can read it, and yet waits for more evidence before he becomes a decided Christian, is deceiving himself. Except he awakens from his delusion he will die in his sins.

Chapter 17

LUKE 17:1-4

STUMBLING BLOCKS

*A*nd he said unto his disciples, It is impossible but that occasions of stumbling *should come; but woe unto him, through whom they come! It were well for him if a millstone were hanged about his neck, and he were thrown into the sea, rather than that he should cause one of these little ones to stumble. Take heed to yourselves: if thy brother sin, rebuke him; and if he repent, forgive him. And if he sin against thee seven times in the day, and seven times turn again to thee, saying, I repent; thou shalt forgive him.*

We are taught for one thing in these verses, the great sinfulness of putting stumbling-blocks in the way of other men's souls. The Lord Jesus says, "Woe unto him through whom offences come! It were better for him that a mill-stone were hung about his neck, and he cast into the sea, than that he should offend one of these little ones."

When do men make others stumble? When do they cause "offences" to come? They do it, beyond doubt, whenever they persecute believers, or endeavor to deter them from serving Christ. But this, unhappily, is not all. Professing Christians do it whenever they bring discredit on their religion by inconsistencies of temper, of word, or of deed. We do it whenever we make our Christianity unlovely in the eyes of the world, by conduct not in keeping with our profession. The world may not understand the doctrines and principles of believers. But the world is very keen-sighted about their practice.

The sin against which our Lord warns us was the sin of David. When he had broken the seventh commandment, and taken the wife of Uriah to be his wife, the prophet Nathan said to him, "You have given great occasion to the enemies of the Lord to blaspheme." (2 Sam. 12:14.) It was the sin which Paul charges on the Jews, when he says, "the name of God is blasphemed among the Gentiles through you." (Rom. 2:24.) It is the sin of which he frequently entreats Christians to beware—"Give no offence, neither to the Jews nor to the Gentiles, nor to the Church of God." (1 Cor. 10:32.)

The subject is a deeply searching one. The sin which our Lord brings before us is unhappily very common. The inconsistencies of professing Christians too often supply the men of the world with an excuse for neglecting religion altogether. An inconsistent believer, whether he knows it or not, is daily doing harm to souls. His life is a positive injury to the Gospel of Christ.

Let us often ask ourselves whether we are doing good or harm in the world. We cannot live to ourselves, if we are Christians. The eyes of many will always be upon us. Men will judge by what they see, far more than by what they hear. If they see the Christian contradicting by his practice what he professes to believe, they are justly stumbled and offended. For the world's sake, as well as for our own, let us labor to be eminently holy. Let us endeavor to make our religion beautiful in the eyes of men, and to adorn the doctrine of Christ in all things. Let us strive daily to lay aside every weight, and the sin which most easily besets us, and so to live that men can find no fault in us, except concerning the law of our God. Let us watch jealously over our tempers and tongues, and the discharge of our social duties. Anything is better than doing harm to souls. The cross of Christ will always give offence. Let us not increase that offence by carelessness in our daily life. The natural man cannot be expected to love the Gospel. But let us not disgust him by inconsistency.

We are taught, for another thing, in these verses, the great importance of a forgiving spirit. The Lord Jesus says, "if your brother sins against you, rebuke him, and if he repents, forgive him—and if he sins against you seven times in a day, and seven times in a day turn again to you, saying, I repent, forgive him."

There are few Christian duties which are so frequently and strongly dwelt upon in the New Testament as this of 'forgiving injuries'. It fills a prominent place in the Lord's prayer. The only profession we make in all that prayer, is that of forgiving "those who trespass against us." It is a test of being forgiven ourselves. The man who cannot forgive his neighbor the few trifling offences he may have committed against him, can know nothing experimentally of that free and full pardon which is offered no by Christ. (Matt. 18:35; Ephes. 4:32.)

Not least, it is one leading mark of the indwelling of the Holy Spirit. The presence of the Spirit in the heart may always be known by the fruits He causes to be brought forth in the life. Those fruits are both active and passive. The man who has not learned to bear and forbear, to put up with much and look over much, is not born of the Spirit. (1 John 3:14; Matt. 5:44, 45.)

The doctrine laid down by our Lord in this place is deeply humbling. It shows most plainly the wide contrariety which exists between the ways of the world and the Gospel of Christ. Who does not know that pride, and arrogance, and high-mindedness, and readiness to take offence, and implacable determination never to forget and never to forgive, are common among baptized men and women? Thousands will go to the Lord's table, and even profess to love the Gospel, who fire up in a moment at the least appearance of what they call "offensive" conduct, and make a quarrel out of the merest trifles. Thousands are perpetually quarreling with all around them, always complaining how ill other people behave, and always forgetting that their own quarrelsome disposition is the spark which causes the flame.

One general remark applies to all such people. They are making their own lives miserable and showing their unfitness for the kingdom of God. An unforgiving and quarrelsome spirit is the surest mark of an unregenerate heart. What says the Scripture? "Whereas there is among you envying, and strife, and divisions, are you not carnal, and walk as men?" (1 Cor. 3:3; 1 John 3:18-20; 4:20.)

Let us leave the whole passage with jealous self-inquiry. Few passages ought to humble Christians so much, and to make them feel so deeply their need of the blood of atonement, and the mediation of Christ. How often we have given offence, and caused others to stumble! How often we have allowed unkind, and angry, and revengeful thoughts to nestle undisturbed in our hearts! These things ought not so to be. The more carefully we attend to such practical lessons as this passage contains, the more shall we recommend our religion to others, and the more inward peace shall we find in our own souls.

LUKE 17:5-10

UNWORTHY SERVANTS

And the apostles said unto the Lord, Increase our faith. And the Lord said, If ye had faith as a grain of mustard seed, ye would say unto this sycamine tree, Be thou rooted up, and be thou planted in the sea; and it would obey you. But who is there of you, having a servant plowing or keeping sheep, that will say unto him, when he is come in from the field, Come straightway and sit down to meat; and will not rather say unto him, Make ready wherewith I may sup, and gird thyself, and serve me, till I have eaten and drunken; and afterward thou shalt eat and drink? Doth he thank the servant because he did the things that were commanded? Even so ye also, when ye shall have done all the things that are commanded you, say, We are unprofitable servants; we have done that which it was our duty to do.

Let us notice, in these verses, the important request which the apostles made. They said unto the Lord, "Increase our faith."

We know not the secret feelings from which this request sprung. Perhaps the hearts of the apostles failed within them, as they heard one weighty lesson after another fall from our Lord's lips. Perhaps the thought rose up in their minds, "Who is sufficient for these things? Who can receive such high doctrines? Who can follow such a lofty standard of practice?" These, however, are only conjectures. One thing, at any rate, is clear and plain. The request which they made was most deeply important—"Increase our faith."

Faith is the root of saving religion. "He that comes unto God must believe that He is, and that He is a rewarder of those who diligently seek Him." (Heb. 11:6.) It is the hand by which the soul lays hold on Jesus Christ, and is united to Him, and saved. It is the secret of all Christian comfort, and spiritual prosperity. According to a man's faith will be his peace, his hope, his strength, his courage, his decision, and his victory over the world. When the apostles made request about faith, they did wisely and well.

Faith is a grace which admits of degrees. It does not come to full strength and perfection as soon as it is planted in the heart by the Holy Spirit. There is "little" faith and "great" faith. There is "weak" faith and "strong" faith. Both are spoken of in the Scriptures. Both are to be seen in the experience of God's people. The more faith a Christian has the more happy, holy, and useful will he be. To promote the growth and progress of faith should be the daily prayer and endeavor of all who love life. When the apostles said, "increase our faith," they did well.

Have we any faith at all? This, after all, is the first question which the subject should raise in our hearts. Saving faith is not mere repetition of the creed, and saying, "I believe in God the Father—and in God the Son, and in God the Holy Spirit." Thousands are weekly using these words, who know nothing of real believing. The words of Paul are very solemn, "All men have not faith." (2 Thess. 3:2.) True faith is not natural to man. It comes down from heaven. It is the gift of God.

If we have any faith let us pray for more of it. It is a bad sign of a man's spiritual state when he is satisfied to live on old stock, and does not hunger and thirst after growth in grace. Let a prayer for more faith form part of our daily devotions. Let us covet earnestly the best gifts. We are not to despise "the day of small things" in a brother's soul, but we are not to be content with it in our own.

Let us notice, for another thing, in these verses, what a heavy blow our Lord gives to self-righteousness. He says to His apostles, "When you shall have done all these things which are commanded you, say we are unprofitable servants—we have done that which was our duty to do."

We are all naturally proud and self-righteous. We think far more highly of ourselves, our deserts, and our character, than we have any right to do. Self-righteousness is a subtle disease, which manifests itself in a hundred different ways. Most men can see it in other people. Few will allow its presence in themselves. Seldom will a man be found, however wicked, who does not secretly flatter himself that there is somebody else worse than he is. Seldom will a saint be found who is not at seasons tempted to be satisfied and pleased with himself. There is such a thing as a pride which wears the cloak of humility. There is not a heart upon earth which does not contain a piece of the Pharisee's character.

To give up self-righteousness is absolutely needful to salvation. He that desires to be saved must confess that there is no good thing in him, and that he has no merit, no goodness, no worthiness of his own. He must be willing to renounce his own righteousness, and to trust in the righteousness of another, even Christ the Lord. Once pardoned and forgiven, we must travel the daily journey of life under a deep conviction that we are "unprofitable servants." At our best we only do our duty, and have nothing to boast of. And even when we do our duty, it is not by our own power and might that we do it, but by the strength which is given to us from God. Claim upon God we have none. Right to expect anything from God we have none. Worthiness to deserve anything from God we have none. All that we have we have received. All that we are we owe to God's sovereign, distinguishing grace.

What is the true cause of self-righteousness? How is it that such a poor, weak, erring creature as man can ever dream of deserving anything at God's hands? It all arises from ignorance. The eyes of our understandings are naturally blinded. We see neither ourselves, nor our lives, nor God, nor the law of God, as we ought. Once let the light of grace shine into a man's heart, and the reign of self-righteousness is over. The roots of pride may remain, and often put forth bitter shoots. But the reign of pride is broken when the Spirit comes into the heart, and shows the man himself and God. The true Christian will never trust in his own goodness. He will say with Paul, "I am the chief of sinners." "God forbid that I should glory, save in the cross of our Lord Jesus Christ." (1 Tim. 1:15; Gal. 6:14.)

LUKE 17:11-19

TEN HEALED OF LEPROSY

And it came to pass, as they were on their way to Jerusalem, that he was passing along the borders of Samaria and Galilee. And as he entered into a certain village, there met him ten men that were lepers, who stood afar off: and they lifted up their voices, saying, Jesus, Master, have mercy on us. And when he saw them, he said unto them, Go and show yourselves unto the priests. And it came to pass, as they went, they were cleansed. And one of them, when he saw that he was healed, turned back, with a loud voice glorifying God; and he fell upon his face at his feet, giving him thanks: and he was a Samaritan. And Jesus answering said, Were not the ten cleansed? but where are the nine? Were there none found that returned to give glory to God, save this stranger? And he said unto him, Arise, and go thy way: thy faith hath made thee whole.

Let us mark, firstly, in this passage, how earnestly men can cry for help when they feel their need of it. We read that "as our Lord entered into a certain village there met him ten men that were lepers." It is difficult to conceive any condition more thoroughly miserable than that of men afflicted with leprosy. They were cast out from society. They were cut off from all communion with their fellows. The men described in the passage before us appear to have been truly sensible of their wretchedness. They "stood afar off;"—but they did not stand idly doing nothing. "They lifted up their voices and said, Jesus, Master, have mercy on us." They felt acutely the deplorable state of their bodies. They found words to express their feelings. They cried earnestly for relief when a chance of relief appeared in sight.

The conduct of the ten lepers is very instructive. It throws light on a most important subject in practical Christianity, which we can never understand too well. That subject is PRAYER.

How is it that many never pray at all? How is it that many others are content to repeat a form of words, but never pray with their hearts? How is it that dying men and women, with souls to be lost or saved, can know so little of real, hearty, business-like prayer? The answer to these questions is short and simple. The bulk of mankind have no sense of sin. They do not feel their spiritual disease. They are not conscious that they are lost, and guilty, and hanging over the brink of hell. When a man finds out his soul's ailment, he soon learns to pray. Like the leper, he finds words to express his need. He cries for help.

How is it, again, that many true believers often pray so coldly? What is the reason that their prayers are so feeble, and wandering, and lukewarm, as they frequently are? The answer once more is very plain. Their sense of need is not so deep as it ought to be. They are not truly alive to their own weakness and helplessness, and so they do not cry fervently for mercy and grace. Let us remember these things. Let us seek to have a constant and abiding sense of our real necessities. If saints could only see their souls as the ten afflicted lepers saw their bodies, they would pray far better than they do.

Let us mark, secondly, in these verses, how help meets men in the path of obedience. We are told that when the lepers cried to our Lord, He only replied, "Go show yourselves to the priests." He did not touch them and command their disease to depart. He prescribed no medicine, no washing, no use of outward material means. Yet healing power accompanied the words which He spoke. Relief met the afflicted company as soon as they obeyed His command. "It came to pass that as they went they were cleansed."

A fact like this is doubtless intended to teach us knowledge. It shows us the wisdom of simple, childlike obedience to every word which comes from the mouth of Christ. It does not become us to stand still, and reason, and doubt, when our Master's commands are plain and unmistakable. If the lepers had acted in this way, they would never have been healed. We must read the Scriptures diligently. We must try to pray. We must attend on the public means of grace. All these are duties which Christ requires at our hands, and to which, if we love life, we must attend, without asking vain and critical questions. It is just in the path of unhesitating obedience that

Christ will meet and bless us. "If any man will do His will he shall know of the doctrine." (John 7:17.)

Let us mark, lastly, in these verses, what a rare thing is thankfulness. We are told that of all the ten lepers whom Christ healed, there was only one who turned back and gave Him thanks. The words that fell from our Lord's lips upon this occasion are very solemn—"Were there not ten cleansed? But where are the nine?"

The lesson before us is humbling, heart-searching, and deeply instructive. The best of us are far too like the nine lepers. We are more ready to pray than to praise, and more disposed to ask God for what we have not, than to thank Him for what we have. Murmurings, and complainings, and discontent abound on every side of us. Few indeed are to be found who are not continually hiding their mercies under a bushel, and setting their needs and trials on a hill. These things ought not so to be. But all who know the church and the world must confess that they are true. The wide-spread thanklessness of Christians is the disgrace of our day. It is a plain proof of our little humility.

Let us pray for a daily thankful spirit. It is the spirit which God loves and delights to honor. David and Paul were eminently thankful men. It is the spirit which has marked all the brightest saints in every age of the church. McCheyne, and Bickersteth, and Haldane Stewart, were always full of praise. It is the spirit which is the very atmosphere of heaven. Angels and "just men made perfect" are always blessing God. It is the spirit which is the source of happiness on earth. If we would be anxious for nothing, we must make our requests known to God not only with prayer and supplication, but with thanksgiving. (Phil. 4:6.)

Above all, let us pray for a deeper sense of our own sinfulness, guilt, and undeserving. This, after all, is the true secret of a thankful spirit. It is the man who daily feels his debt to grace, and daily remembers that in reality he deserves nothing but hell—this is the man who will be daily blessing and praising God. Thankfulness is a flower which will never bloom well excepting upon a root of deep humility!

LUKE 17:20-25
THE KINGDOM OF GOD

And being asked by the Pharisees, when the kingdom of God cometh, he answered them and said, The kingdom of God cometh not with observation: neither shall they say, Lo, here! or, There! for lo, the kingdom of God is within you. And he said unto the disciples, The days will come, when ye shall desire to see one of the days of the Son of man, and ye shall not see it. And they shall say to you, Lo, there! Lo, here! go not away, nor follow after them: for as the lightning, when it lighteneth out of the one part under the heaven, shineth unto the other part under heaven; so shall the Son of man be in his day. But first must he suffer many things and be rejected of this generation.

We are taught, firstly, in this passage that the kingdom of God is utterly unlike the kingdoms of this world. The Lord Jesus tells the Pharisees that "it comes not with observation." He meant by this that its approach and presence were not to be marked by outward signs of dignity. Those who expected to observe anything of this kind would be disappointed. They would wait and watch for such a kingdom in vain, while the real kingdom would be in the midst of them without their knowing it. "Behold," He says, "the kingdom of God is within you."

The expression which our Lord here uses describes exactly the beginning of His spiritual kingdom. It began in a manger at Bethlehem, without the knowledge of the great, the rich, and the wise. It appeared suddenly in the temple at Jerusalem, and no one but Simeon and Anna recognized its King. It was received thirty years after by none but a few fishermen and publicans in Galilee. The rulers and Pharisees had no eyes to see it. The King came to His own, and His own received Him not. All this time the Jews professed to be waiting for the kingdom. But they were looking in the wrong direction. They were waiting for signs which they had no warrant for expecting. The kingdom of God was actually in the midst of them! Yet they could not see it!

The literal kingdom which Christ shall set up one day will begin in some respects very like His spiritual one. It will not be accompanied by the signs, and marks, and outward manifestations which many are expecting to see. It will not be ushered in by a period of universal peace and holiness. It will not be announced to the Church by such unmistakable warnings, that everybody will be ready for it, and prepared for its appearing. It shall come suddenly, unexpectedly, and without note of warning to the immense majority of mankind. The Simeons and Annas will be as few in the last day as they were at the beginning of the Gospel. The most shall awake one day, like men out of sleep, and find, to their surprise and dismay, that the kingdom of God is actually come.

We shall do well to lay these things to heart, and ponder them well. The vast majority of men are utterly deceived in their expectations with respect to the kingdom of God. They are waiting for signs which will never appear. They are looking for indications which they will never discover. They are dreaming of universal conversion. They are fancying that missionaries, and ministers, and schools, will change the face of the world before the end comes. Let us beware of such mistakes. Let us not sleep as do others. The kingdom of God will be upon men much sooner than many expect. "It comes not with observation."

We are taught, secondly, in this passage, that the second coming of Jesus Christ will be a very SUDDEN event. Our Lord describes this by a striking figure. He says, "For the Son of Man in his day will be like the lightning, which flashes and lights up the sky from one end to the other."

The second personal advent of Christ is the real fulfillment of these words. Of the precise day and hour of that advent we know nothing. But whenever it may take place, one thing at least is clear—it will come on the Church and the world suddenly, instantaneously, and without previous notice. The whole tenor of Scripture points this way. It shall be "in such an hour as you do not think." It shall come "as a thief in the night." (Matt. 24:44; 1 Thess. 5:2.)

This suddenness of Christ's second advent is a solemn thought. It ought to make us study a continual preparedness of mind. Our hearts' desire and endeavor should be to be always ready to meet our Lord. Our life's aim should be to do nothing, and say nothing, which could make us ashamed if Christ were suddenly to appear. "Blessed," says the apostle John, "is he who watches, and keeps his garments." (Rev. 16:15.) Those who denounce the doctrine of the second advent as speculative, fanciful, and unpractical, would do well to reconsider the subject. The doctrine was not so regarded in the days of the apostles. In their eyes patience, hope, diligence, moderation, personal holiness, were inseparably connected with an expectation of the Lord's return. Happy is the Christian who has learned to think with them! To be ever looking for the Lord's appearing is one of the best helps to a close walk with God.

We are taught, lastly, in this passage, that there are two personal comings of Christ revealed to us in Scripture. He was appointed to come the first time in weakness and humiliation, to suffer and to die. He was appointed to come the second time in power and great glory, to put down all enemies under His feet, and to reign. At the first coming He was to be "made sin for us," and to bear our sins upon the cross. At the second coming He was to appear without sin, for the complete salvation of His people. (2 Cor. 5:21; Heb. 9:28.) Of both these comings our Lord speaks expressly in the verses before us. Of the first He speaks when He says that the Son of Man "must suffer and be rejected." Of the second He speaks when He says the Son of Man "will be like the lightning, which flashes and lights up the sky from one end to the other."

To see these two comings of Christ distinctly is of great importance to a right understanding of Scripture. The disciples, and all the Jews of our Lord's time, appear to have seen only one personal advent. They expected a Messiah who would come to REIGN, but not one who would come to SUFFER. The majority of Christians, in like manner, appear to see only one personal advent. They believe that Christ came the first time to suffer. But they seem unable to understand that Christ is coming a second time to reign. Both parties have got hold of the truth, but neither, unhappily, has embraced the whole truth. Both are more or less in error, and the Christian's error is only second in importance to that of the Jew.

He that strives to be a well-instructed and established Christian, must keep steadily before his mind both the advents of Jesus Christ. Clear views of the subject are a great help to the profitable reading of the Bible. Without them we shall constantly find statements in prophecy which we can neither reconcile with other statements, nor yet explain away. Jesus coming in person the first time to suffer, and Jesus coming in person the second time to reign, are two landmarks of which we should never lose sight. We stand between the two. Let us believe that both are real and true.

LUKE 17:26-37

And as it came to pass in the days of Noah, even so shall it be also in the days of the Son of man. They ate, they drank, they married, they were given in marriage, until the day that Noah entered into the ark, and the flood came, and destroyed them all. Likewise even as it came to pass in the days of Lot; they ate, they drank, they bought, they sold, they planted, they builded; but in the day that Lot went out from Sodom it rained fire and brimstone from heaven, and destroyed them all: after the same manner shall it be in the day that the Son of man is revealed. In that day, he that shall be on the housetop, and his goods in the house, let him not go down to take them away: and let him that is in the field likewise not return back. Remember Lot's wife. Whosoever shall seek to gain his life shall lose it: but whosoever shall lose his life shall preserve it. I say unto you, In that night there shall be two men on one bed; the one shall be taken, and the other shall be left. There shall be two women grinding together; the one shall be taken, and the other shall be left. There shall be two men in the field; the one shall be taken, and the other shall be left. And they answering say unto him, Where, Lord? And he said unto them, Where the body is, thither will the eagles also be gathered together.

The subject of these verses is one of peculiar solemnity. It is the second advent of our Lord Jesus Christ. That great event, and the things immediately connected with it, are here described by our Lord's own lips.

We should observe, for one thing, in these verses, what a fearful picture our Lord gives of the state of the professing Church at His second coming. We are told that as it was in the "days of Noah," and in the "days of Lot," "so shall it be in the day when the Son of man is revealed." The character of those days we are not left to conjecture. We are told distinctly, that men were entirely taken up with eating, drinking, marrying, buying, selling, planting, building—and would attend to nothing else. The flood came at last in Noah's day, and drowned all except those who were in the ark. The fire fell from heaven at last in Lot's day, and destroyed all except Lot, his wife, and his daughters. And our Lord declares most plainly that like things will happen when He comes again at the end of the world. "When they shall say, Peace and safety; then sudden destruction comes upon them." (1 Thess. 5:3.)

It is hard to imagine a passage of Scripture which more completely over-throws the common notions that prevail among men about Christ's return. The world will not be converted when Jesus comes again. The earth will not be full of the knowledge of the Lord. The reign of peace will not have been established. The millennium will not have begun. These glorious things will come to pass after the second advent, but not before. If words have any meaning, the verses before us show that the earth will be found full of wickedness and worldliness in the day of Christ's appearing. The unbelievers and the unconverted will be found very many. The believers and the godly, as in the days of Noah and Lot, will be found very few.

Let us take heed to ourselves, and beware of the spirit of the world. It is not enough to do as others, and buy, and sell, and plant, and build, and eat, and drink, and marry, as if we were born for nothing else. Exclusive attention to these things may ruin us as thoroughly as open sin. We must come out from the world and be separate. We must dare to be singular. We must escape for our lives like Lot. We must flee to the ark like Noah. This alone is safety. Then, and then only, we shall be hid in the day of the Lord's anger, and avoid destruction when the Son of man is revealed. (Zeph. 2:3.)

We should observe, for another thing, in these verses, what a solemn warning our Lord gives us against unsound profession. He says to us, in immediate connection with the description of His second advent, "Remember Lot's wife."

Lot's wife went far in religious profession. She was the wife of a "righteous man." She was connected through him with Abraham, the father of the faithful. She fled with her husband from Sodom in the day when he escaped for his life by God's command. But Lot's wife was not really like her husband. Though she fled with him, she had left her heart behind her. She wilfully disobeyed the strict injunction which the angel had laid upon her. She looked back towards Sodom, and was at once struck dead. She was turned into a pillar of salt, and perished in her sins. "Remember" her, says our Lord—"Remember Lot's wife."

Lot's wife is meant to be a beacon and a warning to all professing Christians. It may be feared that many will be found like her in the day of Christ's second advent. There are many in the present day who go a certain length in religion. They conform to the outward ways of Christian relatives and friends. They speak the "language of Canaan." They use all the outward ordinances of religion. But all this time their souls are not right in the sight of God. The world is in their hearts, and their hearts are in the world. And by and bye, in the day of sifting, their unsoundness will be exposed to all the world. Their Christianity will prove rotten at the core. The case of Lot's wife will not stand alone.

Let us remember Lot's wife, and resolve to be real in our religion. Let us not profess to serve Christ for no higher motive than to please husbands, or wives, or masters, or ministers. A mere formal religion like this will never save our souls. Let us serve Christ for His own sake. Let us never rest until we have the true grace of God in our hearts, and have no desire to look back to the world.

We should observe, lastly, in these verses, what a dreadful separation there will be in the professing Church when Christ comes again. Our Lord describes this separation by a very striking picture. He says, "In that night there shall be two people in one bed; the one shall be taken, and the other shall be left. Two women shall be grinding together; the one shall be taken, and the other left."

The meaning of these expressions is clear and plain. The day of Christ's second advent shall be the day when good and evil, converted and unconverted, shall at length be divided into two distinct bodies. The visible Church shall no longer be a mixed body. The wheat and the tares shall no longer grow side by side. The good fish and the bad shall at length be sorted into two bodies. The angels shall come forth, and gather together the godly, that they may be rewarded; and leave the wicked behind to be punished.

"Converted or unconverted?" will be the only subject of enquiry. It will matter nothing that people have worked together, and slept together, and lived together for many years. They will be dealt with at last according to their religion. Those members of the family who have loved Christ, will be taken up to heaven; and those who have loved the world, will be cast down to hell. Converted and unconverted shall be separated for evermore when Jesus comes again.

Let us lay to heart these things. He that loves his relatives and friends is specially bound to consider them. If those whom he loves are true servants of Christ, let him know that he must cast in his lot with them, if he would not one day be parted from them forever. If those whom he loves are yet dead in trespasses and sins, let him know that he must work and pray for their conversion, lest he should be separated from them by and bye to all eternity. Life is the only time for such work. Life is fast ebbing away from us all. Partings, and separations, and the breaking up of families are at all times painful things. But all the separations that we see now are nothing compared to those which will ha seen when Christ comes again.

Chapter 18

And he spake a parable unto them to the end that they ought always to pray, and not to faint; saying, There was in a city a judge, who feared not God, and regarded not man: and there was a widow in that city; and she came oft unto him, saying, Avenge me of mine adversary. And he would not for a while: but afterward he said within himself, Though I fear not God, nor regard man; yet because this widow troubleth me, I will avenge her, lest she wear me out by her continual coming. And the Lord said, Hear what the unrighteous judge saith. And shall not God avenge his elect, that cry to him day and night, and yet he is longsuffering over them? I say unto you, that he will avenge them speedily. Nevertheless, when the Son of man cometh, shall he find faith on the earth?

The object of the parable before us, is explained by Christ Himself. To use the words of an old divine, "The key hangs at the door." "He spoke a parable to this end; that men ought always to pray, and not to give up." These words, be it remembered, are closely connected with the solemn doctrine of the second advent, with which the preceding chapter concludes. It is prayer without fainting, during the long weary intervals between the first and second advents, which Jesus is urging His disciples to keep up. In that interval we ourselves are standing. The subject therefore is one which ought to possess a special interest in our eyes.

These verses teach us firstly, the great importance of perseverance in prayer. Our Lord conveys this lesson by telling the story of a friendless widow, who obtained justice from a wicked magistrate, by dint of sheer importunity.

"Though I fear not God, nor regard man," said the unjust judge, "yet because this widow troubles me, I will see that she gets justice, lest by her continual coming she weary me." Our Lord Himself supplies the application of the parable—"And will not God bring about justice for his chosen ones, who cry out to him day and night? Will he keep putting them off?" If importunity obtains so much from a wicked man, how much more will it obtain for the children of God from the Righteous Judge, their Father in heaven!

The subject of PRAYER ought always to be interesting to Christians. Prayer is the very life-breath of true Christianity. Here it is that religion begins. Here it flourishes. Here it decays. Prayer is one of the first evidences of conversion. (Acts 9:11.) Neglect of prayer is the sure road to a fall. (Matt. 26:40, 41.) Whatever throws light on the subject of prayer is for our soul's health.

Let it then be engraved deeply in our minds, that it is far more easy to begin a habit of prayer than it is to keep it up. The fear of death—some temporary piercings of conscience—some excited feelings, may make a man begin praying, after a fashion. But to go on praying requires faith. We are apt to become weary, and to give way to the suggestion of Satan, that "it is of no use." And then comes the time when the parable before us ought to be carefully remembered. We must recollect that our Lord expressly told us "always to pray and not to faint."

Do we ever feel a secret inclination to hurry our prayers, or shorten our prayers, or become careless about our prayers, or omit our prayers altogether? Let us be sure, when we do, that it is a direct temptation from the devil. He is trying to sap and undermine the very citadel of our souls, and to cast us down to hell. Let as resist the temptation, and cast it behind our backs. Let us resolve to pray on steadily, patiently, perseveringly, and let us never doubt that it does us good. However long the answer may be in coming, still let us pray on. Whatever sacrifice and self-denial it may cost us, still let us pray on, "pray always"—"pray without ceasing"—and "continue in prayer." (1 Thess. 5:17. Coloss. 4:2.) Let us arm our minds with this parable, and while we live, whatever we make time for, let us make time for prayer.

These verses teach us, secondly, that God has an elect people upon earth, who are under His special care. The Lord Jesus declares that God will "avenge

His own elect, who cry day and night unto Him." "I tell you," He says, "that He will avenge them speedily."

Election is one of the deepest truths of Scripture. It is clearly and beautifully stated in the seventeenth Article of the Church of England. It is "the everlasting purpose of God, whereby, before the foundations of the world were laid, He has decreed by His counsel, secret to us, to deliver from curse and damnation, those whom He has chosen in Christ out of mankind, and to bring them by Christ to everlasting salvation." This testimony is true. This is "sound speech which cannot be condemned." (Titus 2:8.)

Election is a truth which should call forth praise and thanksgiving from all true Christians. Except God had chosen and called them, they would never have chosen and called on Him. Except He had chosen them of His own good pleasure, without respect to any goodness of theirs, there would never have been anything in them to make them worthy of His choice. The worldly and the carnal-minded may rail at the doctrine of election. The false professor may abuse it, and turn the "grace of God into lasciviousness." (Jude 4.) But the believer who knows his own heart will ever bless God for election. He will confess that without election there would be no salvation.

But what are the marks of election? By what tokens shall a man know whether he is one of God's elect? These marks are clearly laid down in Scripture. Election is inseparably connected with faith in Christ, and conformity to His image. (Rom. 8:29, 30.) It was when Paul saw the working "faith," and patient "hope," and laboring "love" of the Thessalonians, that he knew their "election of God." (1 Thess. 1:3, 4.) Above all, we have a plain mark, described by our Lord, in the passage before us. God's elect are a people who "cry unto Him night and day." They are essentially a praying people. No doubt there are many people whose prayers are formal and hypocritical. But one thing is very clear—a prayerless man must never be called one of God's elect. Let that never be forgotten.

These verses teach us, lastly, that true faith will be found very scarce at the end of the world. The Lord Jesus shows this, by asking a very solemn question, "When the Son of Man comes, shall He find faith on the earth?"

The question before us is a very humbling one. It shows the uselessness of expecting that all the world will be converted before Christ comes again. It shows the foolishness of supposing that all people are "good," and that though differing in outward matters, they are all right at heart, and all going to heaven. Such notions find no countenance in the text before us.

Where is the use, after all, of ignoring facts under our own eyes, facts in the world—facts in the churches—facts in the congregations we belong to—facts by our own doors and firesides? Where is faith to be seen? How many around us really believe what the Bible contains? How many live as if they believed that Christ died for them, and that there is a judgment, a heaven, and a hell? These are most painful and serious inquiries. But they demand and deserve an answer.

Have we faith ourselves? If we have, let us bless God for it. It is a great thing to believe all the Bible. It is matter for daily thankfulness if we feel our sins, and really trust in Jesus. We may be weak, frail, erring, short-coming sinners. But do we believe? That is the grand question. If we believe, we shall be saved. But he that believes not, shall not see life, and shall die in his sins. (John 3:36; 8:24.)

LUKE 18:9-14

PARABLE OF THE PHARISEE AND THE TAX COLLECTOR

And he spake also this parable unto certain who trusted in themselves that they were righteous, and set all others at nought: Two men went up into the temple to pray; the one a Pharisee, and the other a publican. The Pharisee stood and prayed thus with himself, God, I thank thee, that I am not as the rest of men, extortioners, unjust, adulterers, or even as this publican. I fast twice in the week; I give tithes of all that I get. But the publican, standing afar off, would not lift up so much as his eyes unto heaven, but smote his breast, saying, God, be thou merciful to me a sinner. I say unto you, This man went down to his house justified rather than the other: for every one that exalteth himself shall be humbled; but he that humbleth himself shall be exalted.

The parable we have now read is closely connected with the one which immediately precedes it. The parable of the persevering widow teaches the value of importunity in prayer. The parable of the Pharisee and tax-collector teaches the spirit which should pervade our prayers. The first parable encourages us to pray and faint not. The second parable reminds us how and in what manner we ought to pray. Both should be often pondered by every true Christian.

Let us notice, firstly, the sin against which our Lord Jesus Christ warns us in these verses. There is no difficulty in finding out this. Luke tells us expressly, that "He spoke this parable unto certain which trusted in themselves that they were righteous, and despised others." The sin which our Lord denounces is "self-righteousness."

We are all naturally self-righteous. It is the family-disease of all the children of Adam. From the highest to the lowest we think more highly of ourselves than we ought to do. We secretly flatter ourselves that we are not so bad as some, and that we have something to recommend us to the favor of God. "Most men will proclaim everyone his own goodness." (Prov. 20:6.) We forget the plain testimony of Scripture, "In many things we offend all." "There is not a just man upon earth, that does good and sins not"—"What is man that he should be clean, or he that is born of a woman that he should be righteous?" (James 3:2. Eccles. 7:20. Job 15:14.)

The true cure for self-righteousness is self-knowledge. Once let the eyes of our understanding be opened by the Spirit, and we shall talk no more of our own goodness. Once let us see what there is in our own hearts, and what the holy law of God requires, and self-conceit will die. We shall lay our hand on our mouths, and cry with the leper, "Unclean, unclean." (Levit. 13:45.)

Let us notice, secondly, in these verses, the prayer of the Pharisee, which our Lord condemns. We read that he said, "God, I thank you that I am not as other men are, extortioners, unjust, adulterers, or even as this tax-collector. I fast twice in the week. I give tithes of all I possess."

One great defect stands out on the face of this prayer—a defect so glaring that even a child might mark it. It exhibits no sense of sin and need. It contains no confession and no petition—no acknowledgment of guilt and emptiness—no supplication for mercy and grace. It is a mere boasting recital of fancied merits, accompanied by an uncharitable reflection on a brother sinner. It is a proud, high-minded profession, destitute alike of penitence, humility, and charity. In short, it hardly deserves to be called a prayer at all.

No state of soul can be conceived so dangerous as that of the Pharisee. Never are men's bodies in such desperate plight, as when disease and insensibility set in. Never are men's hearts in such a hopeless condition, as when they are not sensible of their own sins. He that would not make shipwreck on this rock, must beware of measuring himself by his neighbors. What does it signify that we are more moral than "other men?" We are all vile and imperfect in the sight of God. "If we contend with Him, we cannot answer him one in a thousand." (Job 9:3.) Let us remember this. In all our self-examination let us not try ourselves by comparison with the standard of men. Let us look at nothing but the requirements of God. He that acts on this principle will never be a Pharisee.

Let us notice, thirdly, in these verses, the prayer of the tax-collector, which our Lord commends. That prayer was in every respect the very opposite of that of the Pharisee. We read that he "stood afar off, and smote upon his breast, and said, God be merciful to me a sinner." Our Lord Himself stamps this short prayer with the seal of His approbation. He says, "I tell you, this man went down to his house justified rather than the other." The excellence of the Tax collector's prayer consists in five points, each of which deserves attention.

1. For one thing, it was a real petition. A prayer which only contains thanksgiving and profession, and asks nothing, is essentially defective. It may be suitable for an angel, but it is not suitable for a sinner.

2. For another thing, it was a direct personal prayer. The tax-collector did not speak of his neighbors, but himself. Vagueness and generality are the great defects of most men's religion. To get out of "we," and "our," and "us," into "I," and "my," and "me," is a great step toward heaven.

3. For another thing, it was a humble prayer—a prayer which put self in the right place. The tax-collector confessed plainly that he was a sinner. This is the very "A B C" of saving Christianity. We never begin to be good until we can feel and say that we are bad.

4. For another thing, it was a prayer in which mercy was the chief thing desired, and faith in God's covenant mercy, however weak, displayed. Mercy is the first thing we must ask for in the day we begin to pray. Mercy and grace must be the subject of our daily petitions at the throne of grace until the day we die.

5. Finally, the Tax-collector's prayer was one which came from his heart. He was deeply moved in uttering it. He smote upon his breast, like one who felt more than be could express. Such prayers are the prayers which are God's delight. A broken and a contrite heart He will not despise. (Psalm 51:17.)

Let these things sink down into our hearts. He that has learned to feel his sins has great reason to be thankful. We are never in the way of salvation until we know that we are lost, ruined, guilty, and helpless. Happy indeed is he who is not ashamed to sit by the side of the tax-collector! When our experience tallies with his, we may hope that we have found a place in the school of God.

Let us notice, lastly, in these verses, the high praise which our Lord bestows on humility. He says, "Every one that exalts himself shall be abased, and he that humbles himself shall be exalted."

The principle here laid down is so frequently found in the Bible, that it ought to be deeply engraved in our memories. Three times we find our Lord using the words before us in the Gospels, and on three distinct occasions. Humility, He would evidently impress upon us, is among the first and foremost graces of the Christian character. It was a leading grace in Abraham, Jacob, Moses, David, Job, Isaiah, and Daniel. It ought to be a leading grace in all who profess to serve Christ. All the Lord's people have not gifts or money. All are not called to preach, or write, or fill a prominent place in the church. But all are called to be humble. One grace at least should adorn the poorest and most unlearned believer. That grace is humility.

Let us leave the whole passage with a deep sense of the great encouragement it affords to all who feel their sins, and cry to God for mercy in Christ's name. Their sins may have been many and great. Their prayers may seem weak, faltering, unconnected, and poor. But let them remember the tax collector, and take courage. That same Jesus who commended his prayer is sitting at the right hand of God to receive sinners. Then let them hope and pray on.

LUKE 18:15-17

JESUS AND LITTLE CHILDREN

And they were bringing unto him also their babes, that he should touch them: but when the disciples saw it, they rebuked them. But Jesus called them unto him, saying, Suffer the little children to come unto me, and forbid them not: for to such belongeth the kingdom of God. Verily I say unto you, Whosoever shall not receive the kingdom of God as a little child, he shall in no wise enter therein.

Let us observe, for one thing, in this passage, how ignorantly people are apt to treat children, in the matter of their souls. We read that there were some who "brought their little children to Jesus so he could touch them and bless them, but the disciples told them not to bother him." They thought most probably that it was mere waste of their Master's time, and that little children could derive no benefit from being brought to Christ. They drew from our Lord a solemn rebuke. We read that "Jesus called them unto Him, and said, Allow the little children to come unto me, and forbid them not."

The ignorance of the disciples does not stand alone. On few subjects, perhaps, shall we find such strange opinions in the churches, as on the subject of the souls of children. Some think that children ought to be baptized, as a matter of course, and that if they die unbaptized they cannot be saved. Others think that children ought not to be baptized, but can give no satisfactory reason why they think so. Some think that all children are regenerate by virtue of their baptism. Others seem to think that children are incapable of receiving any grace, and that they ought not to be enrolled in the Church until they are grown up. Some think that children are naturally innocent, and would do no wickedness unless they learned it from others. Others think that it is no use to expect them to be converted when young, and that they must be treated as unbelievers until they come to years of discretion. All these opinions appear to be errors, in one direction or another. All are to be deprecated, for all lead to many painful mistakes.

We shall do well to get hold of some settled scriptural principles about the spiritual condition of children. To do so may save us much perplexity, and preserve us from grave false doctrine.

The souls of young children are evidently precious in God's sight. Both here and elsewhere there is plain proof that Christ cares for them no less than for grown-up people. The souls of young children are capable of receiving grace. They are born in sin, and without grace cannot be saved. There is nothing, either in the Bible or experience, to make us think that they cannot receive the Holy Spirit, and be justified, even from their earliest infancy. The baptism of young children seems agreeable to the general tenor of Scripture, and the mind of Christ in the passage before us. If Jewish children were not too young to be circumcised in the Old Testament dispensation, it is exceedingly hard to understand why Christian children should be too young to be baptized under the Gospel. Thousands of children, no doubt, receive no benefit from baptism. But the duty of baptizing them remains the same. The minds of young children are not unequal to receiving religious impressions. The readiness with which their minds receive the doctrines of the Gospel, and their consciences respond to them, is matter of fact well known to all who have anything to do with teaching. Last, but not least, the souls of children are capable of salvation, however young they may die. To suppose that Christ will admit them into His glorified Church, and yet maintain that He would not have them in His professing Church on earth, is an inconsistency which can never be explained.

These points deserve calm consideration. The subject is unquestionably difficult, and one on which good men disagree. But in every perplexity about it we shall find it good to return again and again to the passage before us. It throws a strong light on the position of children before God. It shows us in general terms the mind of Christ.

Let us observe, for another thing, in this passage, the strong declaration which our Lord Jesus Christ makes about little children. He says, "Of such is the kingdom of God."

The meaning of these words no doubt is a matter of dispute. That they were not meant to teach that children are born sinless and innocent, is abundantly clear from other parts of Scripture. "That which is born of the flesh is flesh." (John 3:6.) A threefold lesson is probably contained in our Lord's words. To that threefold lesson we shall do well to take heed.

"Like such as little children," all saints of God should strive to live. Their simple faith and dependence on others—their unworldliness and indifference to earthy treasures—their comparative humility, harmlessness, and freedom from deceit—are points in which they furnish believers with an excellent example. Happy is he who can draw near to Christ and the Bible in the spirit of a little child!

"Out of such as little children," the Church of God on earth ought to be constantly recruited. We should not be afraid to bring them to baptism even in their earliest infancy, and to dedicate them to Christ from the beginning of their days. Useless and formal as baptism often is, it is an ordinance appointed by Christ Himself. Those who use it with prayer and faith may confidently look for a blessing.

"Of such as little children," the kingdom of God in glory will be largely composed. The salvation of all who die in infancy may confidently be expected. Though sin has abounded, grace has much more abounded. (Rom. 5:20.) The number of those in the world who die before they "know good from evil" is exceedingly great. It is surely not too much to believe that a very large proportion of the glorified inhabitants of heaven will be found at length to be little children.

Let us leave the whole passage with a deep sense of the value of children's souls, and with a settled resolution to "put on the mind of Christ" in all our dealings with them. Let us regard children as a most important part of Christ's professing Church, and a part which the great Head of the Church does not like to see neglected. Let us train them from their earliest infancy in godly ways, and sow the seed of Scripture truth in their minds, with strong confidence that it will one day bear fruit.

Let us believe that they think more, and feel more, and consider more, than at first sight appears; and that the Spirit is often working in them, as really and truly as in older people. Above all, let us often name them before Christ in prayer, and ask Him to take them under His special charge. He never changes. He is always the same. He cared for boys and girls when He was upon earth. Let us not doubt that He cares for them at the right hand of God in heaven.

LUKE 18:18-27

THE RICH RULER

And a certain ruler asked him, saying, Good Teacher, what shall I do to inherit eternal life? And Jesus said unto him, Why callest thou me good? none is good, save one, even God. Thou knowest the commandments, Do not commit adultery, Do not kill, Do not steal, Do not bear false witness, Honor thy father and mother. And he said, All these things have I observed from my youth up. And when Jesus heard it, he said unto him, One thing thou lackest yet: sell all that thou hast, and distribute unto the poor, and thou shalt have treasure in heaven: and come, follow me. But when he heard these things, he became exceeding sorrowful; for he was very rich. And Jesus seeing him said, How hardly shall they that have riches enter into the kingdom of God! For it is easier for a camel to enter in through a needle's eye, than for a rich man to enter into the kingdom of God. And they that heard it said, Then who can be saved? But he said, The things which are impossible with men are possible with God.

The story we have now read is three times reported in the Gospels. Matthew, Mark and Luke were all moved by the Holy Spirit to record the history of the rich man who came to Christ. This fact should be noticed. It shows us that there are lessons before us which demand special attention. When God would impress on Peter his duty towards the Gentiles, He sent him a vision which was repeated "three times." (Acts 10:16.)

We learn, firstly, from these verses, to what lengths men may go in self-ignorance. We are told of "a certain ruler," who asked our Lord what he should "do to inherit eternal life." Our Lord knew the ruler's heart, and gave him the answer which was most likely to bring to light the real state of his soul. He reminds him of the ten commandments. He recites some of the principal requirements of the second table of the law. At once the spiritual blindness of the inquirer was detected. "All these," said the man, "I have kept from my youth up." An answer more full of darkness and self-ignorance it is impossible to conceive! He who made it could have known nothing rightly, either about himself, or God, or God's law.

Does the case of this rich ruler stand alone? Do we suppose there are none like him at the present day? If we do, we are greatly deceived. There are thousands, it may be feared, in all our congregations, who have not the least idea of the spiritual nature of God's law, and consequently know nothing of their own sinfulness. They do not see that God requires "truth in the inward parts," and that we may break commandments in our heart and thoughts, even when we do not break them in outward actions. (Psalm 51:6. Matt. 5:2128.) To be delivered from such blindness is one of the first things needful to our salvation. The eyes of our understandings must be enlightened by the Holy Spirit. (Ephes. 1:18.) We must learn to know ourselves. No man really taught of the Spirit will ever talk of having "kept all God's commandments from his youth." He will rather cry with Paul, "The law is spiritual, but I am carnal." "I know that in me dwells no good thing." (Rom. 7:14-18.)

We learn, secondly, from these verses, what harm one master-sin may do to a soul. The desires which the rich ruler expressed were right and good. He wanted "eternal life." There seemed at first sight no reason why he should not be taught the way of God, and become a disciple. But there was one thing, unhappily, which be loved better than "eternal life." That thing was his money. When invited by Christ, to give up all that he had on earth, and seek treasure in heaven, he had not faith to accept the invitation. The love of money was his master-sin.

Shipwrecks like this are sadly common in the Church of Christ. Few are the ministers who could not put their finger on many cases like that of the man before us. Many are ready to give up everything for Christ's sake, excepting one darling sin, and for the sake of that sin are lost for evermore. When Herod heard John the Baptist, he "heard him gladly and did many things." But there was one thing he could not do. He could not part with Herodias. That one thing cost Herod his soul. (Mark 6:20.)

There must be no reserve in our hearts, if we would receive anything at Christ's hands. We must be willing to part with anything, however dear it may be, if it stands between us and our salvation. We must be ready to cut off the right hand and pluck out the right eye, to make any sacrifice, and to break any idol. Life, we must remember, eternal life is at stake! One leak neglected, is enough to sink a mighty ship. One besetting sin, obstinately clung to, is enough to shut a soul out of heaven. The love of money, secretly nourished in the heart, is enough to bring a man, in other respects moral and irreproachable, down to the pit of hell.

We learn, thirdly, from these verses, how great is the difficulty of a rich man being saved. Our Lord declares this in the solemn comment which He makes on the ruler's case—"How hard it is for rich people to get into the Kingdom of God! It is easier for a camel to go through the eye of a needle than for a rich person to enter the Kingdom of God!"

The truth which our Lord lays down in this place, is one which we may see confirmed on every side. Our own eyes will tell us that grace and riches seldom go together. "Not many mighty, not many noble, are called." (1 Cor. 1:26.) It is plain matter of fact, that comparatively few rich men are to be found in the way of life. For one thing, riches incline their possessors to pride, self-will, self-indulgence, and love of the world. For another thing, the rich man is seldom dealt with faithfully about his soul. He is generally flattered and fawned upon. "The rich has many friends." (Prov. 14:20.) Few people have the courage to tell him the whole truth. His good points are grossly exaggerated. His bad points are glossed over, palliated, and excused. The result is, that while his heart is choked up with the things of the world, his eyes are blinded to his own real condition. What right have we to wonder is a rich man's salvation is a hard thing?

Let us beware of envying rich men and coveting their possessions. We little know what we might come to if our desires were granted. Money, which thousands are constantly wanting and longing for—money, which many make their god—money keeps myriads of souls out of heaven! "Those who will be rich fall into temptation and a snare." Happy is he who has learned to pray, "Give me neither poverty nor riches," and is really "content with such things as he has." (1 Tim. 6:9; Prov. 30:8; Heb. 13:5.)

We learn, lastly, from these verses, how mighty is the power of God's grace. We see this in the words which our Lord addressed to those who heard Him speaking of the rich man's danger. They said, "who then can be saved?" Our Lord's reply is broad and full—"The things which are impossible with men are possible with God." By grace a man may serve God and reach heaven in any condition of life.

The word of God contains many striking instances in illustration of this doctrine. Abraham, and David, and Hezekiah, and Jehoshaphat, and Josiah, and Job, and Daniel, were all great and rich. Yet they all served God and were saved. They all found grace sufficient for them, and overcame the temptations by which they were surrounded. Their Lord and Master still lives, and what He did for them He can do for others. He can give power to rich Christians to follow Christ in spite of their riches, as well as He did to rich Jews.

Let us beware of allowing ourselves to suppose that our own salvation is impossible, because of the hardness of our position. It is too often a suggestion of the devil and our own lazy hearts. We must not give way to it. It matters not where we live, so long as we are not following a sinful calling. It matters not what our income may be, whether we are burdened with riches, or pinched with poverty. Grace, and not place, is the hinge on which our salvation turns. Money will not keep us out of heaven if our hearts are right before God. Christ can make us more than conquerors. Christ can enable us to win our way through every difficulty. "I can do all things," said Paul, "through Christ who strengthens me." (Philip. 4:13.)

LUKE 18:28-34
JESUS PREDICTS HIS DEATH

And Peter said, Lo, we have left our own, and followed thee. And he said unto them, Verily I say unto you, There is no man that hath left house, or wife, or brethren, or parents, or children, for the kingdom of God's sake, who shall not receive manifold more in this time, and in the world to come eternal life.

And he took unto him the twelve, and said unto them, Behold, we go up to Jerusalem, and all the things that are written through the prophets shall be accomplished unto the Son of man. For he shall be delivered up unto the Gentiles, and shall be mocked, and shamefully treated, and spit upon: and they shall scourge and kill him: and the third day he shall rise again. And they understood none of these things; and this saying was hid from them, and they perceived not the things that were said.

Let us observe, firstly, in these verses, what a glorious and satisfying promise our Lord holds out to all believers who make sacrifices for His sake. He says, "There is no man that has left house, or parents, or brethren, or wife, or children, for the kingdom of God's sake, who shall not receive many times as much in this present time, and in the world to come life everlasting."

The promise before us is a very peculiar one. It does not refer to the believer's reward in another world, and the crown of glory which fades not away. It refers distinctly to the life that now is. It is spoken of "this present time."

The "many times as much" of the promise must evidently be taken in a spiritual sense. The meaning is, that the believer shall find in Christ a full equivalent for anything that he is obliged to give up for Christ's sake. He shall find such peace, and hope, and joy, and comfort, and rest, in communion with the Father and the Son, that his losses shall be more than counterbalanced by his gains. In short, the Lord Jesus Christ shall be more to him than property, or relatives, or friends.

The complete fulfillment of this wonderful promise has been often seen in the experience of God's saints. Hundreds could testify in every age of the church, that when they were obliged to give up everything for the kingdom of God's sake, their losses were amply supplied by Christ's grace. They were kept in perfect peace, staying their souls on Jesus. (Isaiah. 26:3.) They were enabled to glory in tribulation, and to take pleasure in infirmities, in reproaches, in necessities, in distresses for Christ's sake (Rom. 5:3. 2 Cor. 12:10.) They were enabled in the darkest hour to rejoice with joy unspeakable and full of glory, and to count it an honor to suffer shame for their Master's name. (1 Pet. 1:8. Acts 5:41.) The last day will show that in poverty and in exile—in prisons and before judgment seats—in the fire and under the sword—the words of Christ before us have repeatedly been made good. Friends have often proved faithless. Royal promises have often been broken. Riches have made themselves wings. But Christ's engagements have never been known to fail.

Let us grasp this promise firmly. Let us go forward in the way of life with a firm conviction that it is a promise which is the property of all God's people. Let us not give way to doubts and fears because of difficulties that cross our path. Let us press onward with a strong persuasion, that if we lose anything for Christ's sake, Christ will make it up to us even in this present world. What believers need is more daily practical faith in Christ's words. The well of living water is always near us, as we travel through the wilderness of this world. Yet for lack of faith we often fail to see it, and faint by the way. (Gen. 21:19.)

Let us observe, secondly, in these verses, the clear and plain prediction which our Lord makes about His own death. We see Him telling the disciples that He would be "delivered to the Gentiles, mocked, spitefully entreated, spitted on, scourged, and put to death."

The importance of our Lord's death appears in the frequency with which He foretold it, and referred to it during His life. He knew well that it was the principal end for which He came into the world. He was to give His life a ransom for many. He was to make His soul an offering for sin, and to bear our transgressions in His own body on the tree. He was to give His body and blood for the life of the world. Let us seek to be of the same mind with Christ in our estimate of His death. Let our principal thoughts about Jesus be inseparably bound up with His crucifixion. The corner-stone of all truth concerning Christ is this—that "While we were yet sinners, He died for us." (Rom. 5:8.)

The love of our Lord Jesus Christ towards sinners is strikingly shown in His steady purpose of heart to die for them. All through His life He knew that He was about to be crucified. There was nothing in His cross and passion which He did not foresee distinctly even to the minutest particular, long before it came upon Him. He tasted all the well-known bitterness of 'anticipated suffering'. Yet He never swerved from His path for a moment. He was straitened in spirit until He had finished the work He came to do. (Luke 12:50.) Such love passes knowledge. It is unspeakable—unsearchable. We may rest on that love without fear. If Christ so loved us before we thought of Him, He will surely not cease to love us after we have believed.

The calmness of our Lord Jesus Christ in the prospect of certain death ought to be a pattern to all His people. Like Him, let us drink the bitter cup which our Father gives us, without a murmur, and say, "not my will but yours be done." The man that has faith in the Lord Jesus has no reason to be afraid of the grave. "The sting of death is sin; and the strength of sin is the law. But thanks be to God, who gives us the victory through our Lord Jesus Christ." (1 Cor. 15:56, 57.) The grave is no longer what it once was. It is the place where the Lord lay. If the great Head of the body looked forward to the grave with calmness, much more may all His believing members. For them He has overcome death. The king of terrors at the worst is a conquered foe.

Let us observe, lastly, in these verses, the slowness of the disciples to understand Christ's death. We find that when our Lord described His coming sufferings, the disciples "didn't understand a thing he said. Its significance was hidden from them, and they failed to grasp what he was talking about." We read such passages as these, perhaps, with a mixture of pity and surprise. We wonder at the darkness and blindness of these Jews. We marvel that in the face of plain teaching, and in the light of plain types of the Mosaic law, the sufferings of Messiah should have been lost sight of in His glory, and His cross hidden behind His crown.

But are we not forgetting that the vicarious death of Christ has always been a stumbling-block and an offence to proud human nature? Do we not know that even now after Christ has arisen from the dead and ascended into glory, the doctrine of the cross is still foolishness to many, and that Christ's substitution for us on the cross is a truth which is often denied, rejected and refused? Before we wonder at these first weak disciples for not understanding our Lord's words about His death, we should do well to look around us. It may humble us to remember that thousands of so-called Christians neither understand nor value Christ's death at the present day.

Let us look well to our own hearts. We live in a day when false doctrines about Christ's death abound on every side. Let us see that Christ crucified is really the foundation of our own hopes, and that Christ's atoning death for sin is indeed the whole life of our souls. Let us beware of adding to Christ's sacrifice on the cross, as the Roman Catholic does. Its value was infinite. It admits of no addition. Let us beware of taking away from Christ's sacrifice, as the Socinian does. To suppose that the Son of God only died to leave us an example of self-denial, is to contradict a hundred plain texts of Scripture. Let us walk in the old paths. Let us say with Paul, "God forbid that I should glory, save in the cross of our Lord Jesus Christ." (Gal. 6:14.)

LUKE 18:35-43

THE BLIND BEGGAR

And it came to pass, as he drew nigh unto Jericho, a certain blind man sat by the way side begging: and hearing a multitude going by, he inquired what this meant. And they told him that Jesus of Nazareth passeth by. And he cried, saying, Jesus, thou son of David, have mercy on me. And they that went before rebuked him, that he should hold his peace: but he cried out the more a great deal, Thou son of David, have mercy on me. And Jesus stood, and commanded him to be brought unto him: and when he was come near, he asked him, What wilt thou that I should do unto thee? And he said, Lord, that I may receive my sight. And Jesus said unto him, Receive thy sight; thy faith hath made thee whole. And immediately he received his sight, and followed him, glorifying God: and all the people, when they saw it, gave praise unto God.

The miracle described in these verses is rich in instruction. It was one of the great works which witnessed that Christ was sent of the Father. (John 5:36.) But this is not all. It contains also some lively patterns of spiritual things which deserve attentive study.

We see, for one thing, in this passage, the importance of diligence in the use of means. We are told of "a certain blind man who sat by the wayside begging." He sought the place where his pitiful condition was most likely to attract notice. He did not sit lazily at home, and wait for relief to come to him. He placed himself by the road-side, in order that travelers might see him and give him help. The story before us shows the wisdom of his conduct. Sitting by the wayside, he heard that "Jesus was passing by." Hearing of Jesus he cried for mercy, and was restored to sight. Let us mark this well! If the blind man had not sat by the wayside that day, he might have remained blind to the hour of his death.

He that desires salvation should remember the example of this blind man. He must attend diligently on every means of grace. He must be found regularly in those places where the Lord Jesus is specially present. He must sit by the wayside, wherever the word is read and the Gospel preached, and God's people assemble together. To expect grace to be put into our hearts, if we sit idling at home on Sundays, and go to no place of worship, is presumption and not faith. It is true that "God will have mercy on whom He will have mercy;"-but it is no less true that He ordinarily has mercy on those who use means. It is true that Christ is sometimes "found of those who seek Him not;"—but it is also true that He is always found of those who really seek Him. The Sabbath breaker, the Bible-neglecter, and the prayerless man are forsaking their own mercies, and digging graves for their own souls. They are not sitting "by the wayside."

We see, for another thing, in this passage, an example of our duty in the matter of prayer. We are told that when this blind man heard that Jesus of Nazareth was passing by, he "cried, saying, Jesus, you Son of David, have mercy on me." We are told further, that when some rebuked him and bade him hold his peace, he would not be silenced. "He only cried so much the more." He felt his need, and found words to tell his story. He was not to be stopped by the rebukes of people who knew nothing of the misery of blindness. His sense of wretchedness made him go on crying. And his importunity was amply rewarded. He found what he sought. That very day he received sight.

What the blind man did on behalf of his bodily ailment, it is surely our bounden duty to do on behalf of our souls. Our need is far greater than his. The disease of sin is far more grievous than the lack of sight. The tongue that can find words to describe the necessities of the body, can surely find words to explain the needs of the soul. Let us begin praying if we never prayed yet. Let us pray more heartily and earnestly, if we have prayed in times past.

Jesus, the Son of David, is still passing by, and not far from every one of us. Let us cry to Him for mercy, and allow nothing to stop our crying. Let us not go down to the pit speechless and silent, without so much as a cry for help. None will be so excuseless at the last day as baptized men and women who never tried to pray.

We see, for another thing, in this passage, an encouraging instance of Christ's kindness and compassion. We are told that when the blind man continued crying for mercy, our Lord "stood and commanded him to be brought unto Him." He was going up to Jerusalem to die, and had weighty matters on His mind, but He found time to stop to speak kindly to this poor sufferer. Then Jesus asked the man, "What do you want me to do for you?" "Lord," he pleaded, "I want to see!" At once we are told, "Jesus said unto him, receive your sight; your faith has saved you." That faith perhaps was weak, and mixed with much imperfection. But it had made the man cry to Jesus, and go on crying in spite of rebukes. So coming with faith, our blessed Lord did not cast him out. The desire of his heart was granted, and "immediately he received sight."

Passages like these in the Gospels are intended for the special comfort of all who feel their sins and come to Christ for peace. Such people may be sensible of much infirmity in all their approaches to the Son of God. Their faith may be very feeble—their sins many and great—their prayers very poor and stammering—their motives far short of perfection. But after all, do they really come to Christ with their sins? Are they really willing to forsake all other confidence, and commit their souls to Christ's hands? If this be so, they may hope and not be afraid. That same Jesus still lives who heard the blind man's cry, and granted his request. He will never go back from His own words, "Him that comes to me, I will in no wise cast out." (John 6:37.)

We see, lastly, in this passage, a striking example of the conduct which becomes one who has received mercy from Christ. We are told that when the blind man was restored to sight, "he followed Jesus, glorifying God." He felt deeply grateful. He resolved to show his gratitude by becoming one of our Lord's followers and disciples. Pharisees might cavil at our Lord. Sadducees might sneer at His teaching. It mattered nothing to this new disciple. He had the witness in himself that Christ was a Master worth following. He could say, "I was blind, and now I see." (John 9:25.)

Grateful love is the true spring of real obedience to Christ! Men will never take up the cross and confess Jesus before the world, and live to Him, until they feel that they are indebted to Him for pardon, peace, and hope.

The ungodly are what they are, because they have no sense of sin, and no consciousness of being under any special obligation to Christ. The godly are what they are, because they love Him who first loved them, and washed them from sin in His own blood. Christ has healed them, and therefore they follow Christ.

Let us leave the passage with solemn self-inquiry. If we would know whether we have any part or lot in Christ, let us look at our lives. Whom do we follow? What are the great ends and objects for which we live? The man who has a real hope in Jesus, may always be known by the general bias of his life.

Chapter 19

A nd he entered and was passing through Jericho. And behold, a man called by name Zacchaeus; and he was a chief publican, and he was rich. And he sought to see Jesus who he was; and could not for the crowd, because he was little of stature. And he ran on before, and climbed up into a sycamore tree to see him: for he was to pass that way. And when Jesus came to the place, he looked up, and said unto him, Zacchaeus, make haste, and come down; for to-day I must abide at thy house. And he made haste, and came down, and received him joyfully. And when they saw it, they all murmured, saying, He is gone in to lodge with a man that is a sinner. And Zacchaeus stood, and said unto the Lord, Behold, Lord, the half of my goods I give to the poor; and if I have wrongfully exacted aught of any man, I restore fourfold. And Jesus said unto him, To-day is salvation come to this house, forasmuch as he also is a son of Abraham. For the Son of man came to seek and to save that which was lost.

These verses describe the conversion of a soul. Like the stories of Nicodemus, and the Samaritan woman, the story of Zacchaeus should be frequently studied by Christians. The Lord Jesus never changes. What He did for the man before us, He is able and willing to do for any one of ourselves.

We learn, firstly, from these verses, that no one is too bad to be saved, or beyond the power of Christ's grace. We are told of a wealthy tax-collector becoming a disciple of Christ. A more unlikely event we cannot well imagine! We see the "camel passing through the eye of a needle," and the "rich man entering the kingdom of God." We behold a plain proof that "all things are possible with God." We see a covetous tax-gatherer transformed into a liberal Christian!

The door of hope which the Gospel reveals to sinners, is very wide open. Let us leave it open as we find it Let us not attempt in narrow-minded ignorance, to shut it. We should never be afraid to maintain that Christ is "able to save to the uttermost," and that the vilest of sinners may be freely forgiven if they will only come to Him. We should offer the Gospel boldly to the worst and wickedest, and say, "There is hope. Only repent and believe. Though your sins be as scarlet they shall be as white as snow; though they be red like crimson they shall be as wool." (Isaiah. 1:18.) Such doctrine may seem to worldly people foolishness and licentiousness. But such doctrine is the Gospel of Him who saved Zacchaeus at Jericho. Hospitals discharge many cases as incurable. But there are no incurable cases under the Gospel. Any sinner may be healed, if he will only come to Christ.

We learn, secondly, from these verses, how little and insignificant are the things on which a soul's salvation often turns. We are told that Zacchaeus "sought to see who Jesus was; and could not, because he was little of stature." Curiosity, and nothing but curiosity, appears to have been the motive of his mind. That curiosity once roused, Zaccheus was determined to gratify it. Rather than not see Jesus he ran on before along the road, and "climbed up into a tree." Upon that little action, so far as man's eyes can see, there hinged the salvation of his soul. Our Lord stopped under the tree, and said When Jesus reached the spot, he looked up and said to him, "Zacchaeus, come down immediately. I must stay at your house today." From that very moment Zacchaeus was an altered man. That very night he lay down a Christian.

We must never "despise the day of small things." (Zech. 4:10.) We must never reckon anything little that concerns the soul. The ways by which the Holy Spirit leads men and women to Christ are wonderful and mysterious. He is often beginning in a heart a work which shall stand to eternity, when a looker-on observes nothing remarkable.

In every work there must be a beginning, and in spiritual work that beginning is often very small. Do we see a careless brother beginning to use means of grace, which in time past he neglected? Do we see him coming to Church and listening to the Gospel after a long course of Sabbath-breaking? When we see such things let us remember Zaccheus and be hopeful. Let us not look coldly on him because his motives are at present very poor and questionable. Let us believe that it is far better to hear the Gospel out of mere curiosity, than not to hear it at all. Our brother is with Zaccheus in the tree! For anything we know he may go further. Who can tell but that he may one day receive Christ joyfully?

We learn, thirdly, from these verses, Christ's free compassion towards sinners, and Christ's power to change hearts. A more striking instance than that before us it is impossible to conceive. Unasked, our Lord stops and speaks to Zaccheus. Unasked, He offers Himself to be a guest in the house of a sinner. Unasked, He sends into the heart of a tax-collector the renewing grace of the Spirit, and puts him that very day among the children of God. (Jerem. 3:19.)

It is impossible, with such a passage as this before as, to exalt too highly the grace of our Lord Jesus Christ. We cannot maintain too strongly that there is in Him an infinite readiness to receive, and an infinite ability to save sinners. Above all, we cannot hold too firmly that salvation is not of works, but of grace. If ever there was a soul sought and saved, without having done anything to deserve it, that soul was the soul of Zaccheus.

Let us grasp these doctrines firmly and never let them go. Their price is above rubies. Grace, free grace, is the only thought which gives men rest in a dying hour. Let us proclaim these doctrines confidently to everyone to whom we speak about spiritual things. Let us bid them come to Jesus Christ, just as they are, and not wait in the vain hope that they can make themselves fit and worthy to come. Not least, let us tell them that Jesus Christ waits for them, and would come and dwell in their poor sinful hearts, if they would only receive Him. "Behold," He says, "I stand at the door and knock; if any man hear my voice and open the door, I will come in to him and sup with him and he with me." (Rev. 3:20.)

We learn, lastly, from these verses, that converted sinners will always give evidence of their conversion. We are told that Zaccheus "stood, and said unto the Lord, the half of my goods I give unto the poor; and if I have taken anything from any man by false accusation, I restore him fourfold." There was reality in that speech. There was unmistakable proof that Zaccheus was a new creature. When a wealthy Christian begins to distribute his riches, and an extortioner begins to make restitution, we may well believe that old things have passed away, and all things become new. (2 Cor. 5:17.) There was decision in that speech. "I give," says Zaccheus—"I restore." He does not speak of future intentions. He does not say, "I will," but "I do." Freely pardoned, and raised from death to life, Zaccheus felt that he could not begin too soon to show whose he was and whom he served.

He that desires to give proof that he is a believer, should walk in the steps of Zaccheus. Like him, let him thoroughly renounce the sins which have formerly most easily beset him. Like him, let him follow the Christian graces which he has formerly most habitually neglected. In any case a believer should so live that all may know that he is a believer. Faith that does not purify the heart and life, is not faith at all. Grace that cannot be seen, like light—and tasted, like salt, is not grace, but hypocrisy. The man who professes to know Christ and trust Him, while he cleaves to sin and the world, is going down to hell with a lie in his right hand. The heart that has really tasted the grace of Christ, will instinctively hate sin.

Let us turn from the whole passage with the last verse ringing in our ears-"The Son of man came to seek and save that which is lost." It is as a Savior, more than as a Judge, that Christ desires to be known. Let us see that we know Him as such. Let us take heed that our souls are saved. Once saved and converted, we shall say, "What shall I render to the Lord for all His benefits?" (Psalm 116:12.) Once saved, we shall not complain that self-denial, like that of Zaccheus, is a grievous requirement.

LUKE 19:11-27

PARABLE OF THE TEN MINAS

And as they heard these things, he added and spake a parable, because he was nigh to Jerusalem, and because they supposed that the kingdom of God was immediately to appear. He said therefore, A certain nobleman went into a far country, to receive for himself a kingdom, and to return. And he called ten servants of his, and gave them ten pounds, and said unto them, Trade ye herewith till I come. But his citizens hated him, and sent an ambassage after him, saying, We will not that this man reign over us. And it came to pass, when he was come back again, having received the kingdom, that he commanded these servants, unto whom he had given the money, to be called to him, that he might know what they had gained by trading. And the first came before him, saying, Lord, thy pound hath made ten pounds more. And he said unto him, Well done, thou good servant: because thou wast found faithful in a very little, have thou authority over ten cities. And the second came, saying, Thy pound, Lord, hath made five pounds. And he said unto him also, Be thou also over five cities. And another came, saying, Lord, behold, here is thy pound, which I kept laid up in a napkin: for I feared thee, because thou art an austere man: thou takest up that which thou layedst not down, and reapest that which thou didst not sow. He saith unto him, Out of thine own mouth will I judge thee, thou wicked servant. Thou knewest that I am an austere man, taking up that which I laid not down, and reaping that which I did not sow; then wherefore gavest thou not my money into the bank, and I at my coming should have required it with interest? And he said unto them that stood by, Take away from him the pound, and give it unto him that hath the ten pounds. And they said unto him, Lord, he hath ten pounds. I say unto you, that unto every one that hath shall be given; but from him that hath not, even that which he hath shall be taken away from him. But these mine enemies, that would not that I should reign over them, bring hither, and slay them before me.

The occasion of our Lord speaking the parable before us, is clear and plain. It was intended to correct the false expectations of the disciples on the subject of Christ's kingdom. It was a prophetical sketch of things present and things to come, which ought to raise solemn thoughts in the minds of all professing Christians.

We see, for one thing, in this parable, the present position of our Lord Jesus Christ. He is compared to "a certain nobleman, who went into a far country, to receive for himself a kingdom, and to return."

When the Lord Jesus left the world, He ascended up into heaven as a conqueror, leading captivity captive. He is there sitting at the right hand of God, doing the work of a High Priest for His believing people, and ever making intercession for them. But He will not sit there always. He will come forth from the holy of holies to bless His people. He will come again with power and glory to put down every enemy under His feet, and to set up His universal kingdom on earth. At present "we see not all things put under Him." The devil is the "prince of this world." (Heb. 2:8; John 14:30.) But the present state of things shall be changed one day. When Christ returns, the kingdoms of the world shall become His.

Let these things sink down into our minds. In all our thoughts about Christ, let us never forget His second advent. It is well to know that He lived for us, and died for us, and rose again for us, and intercedes for us. But it is also well to know that He is soon coming again.

We see, for another thing, in this parable, the present position of all professing Christians. Our Lord compares them to servants who have been left in charge of money by an absent master, with strict directions to use that money well. They are to "occupy until He comes."

The countless privileges which Christians enjoy, compared to the heathen, are "pounds" given to them by Christ, for which they must one day give account. We shall not stand side by side in the judgment day with the African and Chinese, who never heard of the Bible, the Trinity, and the crucifixion. The most of us, it may be feared, have little idea of the extent of our responsibility. To whomsoever much is given, of them much will be required.

Are we "occupying?" Are we living like men who know to whom they are indebted, and to whom they must one day give account? This is the only life which is worthy of a reasonable being. The best answer we can give to those who invite us to plunge into worldliness and frivolity, is the Master's commandment which is before us. Let us tell them that we cannot consent, because we look for the coming of the Lord. We would gladly be found "occupying" when He comes.

We see, for another thing, in this parable, the certain reckoning which awaits all professing Christians. We are told that when the master returned, he "commanded his servants to be called, that he might know how much every man had gained."

There is a day coming when the Lord Jesus Christ shall judge His people, and give to every one according to His works. The course of this world shall not always go on as it does now. Disorder, confusion, false profession, and unpunished sin, shall not always cover the face of the earth. The great white throne shall be set up. The Judge of all shall sit upon it. The dead shall be raised from their graves. The living shall all be summoned to the bar. The books shall be opened. High and low, rich and poor, gentle and simple, all shall at length give account to God, and shall all receive an eternal sentence.

Let the thought of this judgment exercise an influence on our hearts and lives. Let us wait patiently when we see wickedness triumphing in the earth. The time is short. There is one who sees and notes down all that the ungodly are doing. "There be higher than they." (Eccles. 5:8.) Above all, let us live under an abiding sense, that we shall stand one day at the judgment seat of Christ. Let us "judge ourselves," that we be not condemned of the Lord. It is a weighty saying of James, "So speak, and so do, as those who shall be judged by the law of liberty." (1 Cor. 11:31. James 2:12.)

We see, for another thing, in this parable, the certain reward of all true Christians. Our Lord tells us that those who are found to have been faithful servants shall receive honor and dignity. Each shall receive a reward proportioned to his diligence. One shall be placed "over ten cities," and another "over five."

The people of God receive little apparent recompense in this present time. Their names are often cast out as evil. They enter the kingdom of God through much tribulation. Their good things are not in this world. The gain of godliness does not consist in earthly rewards, but in inward peace, and hope, and joy in believing. But they shall have an abundant recompense one day. They shall receive wages far exceeding anything they have done for Christ. They shall find, to their amazement, that for everything they have done and borne for their Master, their Master will pay them a hundred-fold.

Let us often look forward to the good things which are yet to come. The "sufferings of this present time are not worthy to be compared with the glory which shall be revealed." (Rom. 8:18.) Let the thought of that glory cheer us in every time of need, and sustain us in every dark hour. Many, no doubt, are "the afflictions of the righteous." One great receipt for bearing them patiently is to "have respect, like Moses, to the recompense of the reward." (Psalm 34:19. Heb. 11:26.)

We see, lastly, in this parable, the certain exposure of all unfaithful Christians at the last day. We are told of one servant who had done nothing with his master's money, but had laid it up in a piece of cloth. We are told of his useless arguments in his own defense, and of his final ruin, for not using the knowledge which he confessedly possessed. There can be no mistake as to the people he represents. He represents the whole company of the ungodly; and his ruin represents their miserable end in the judgment day.

Let us never forget the end to which all ungodly people are coming. Sooner or later, the unbeliever and the impenitent will be put to shame before the whole world, stripped of the means of grace and hope of glory, and cast down to hell. There will be no escape at the last day. False profession and formality will fail to abide the fire of God's judgment. Grace, and grace alone, shall stand. Men will discover at last, that there is such a thing as "the wrath of the Lamb." The excuses with which so many content their consciences now, shall prove unavailing at the bar of Christ. The most ignorant shall find that they had knowledge enough to be their condemnation. The possessors of buried talents and misused privileges will discover at last that it would have been good for them never to have been born.

These are solemn things. Who shall stand in the great day when the Master requires an account of "His pounds?" The words of Peter will form a fitting conclusion to the whole parable, "Seeing that you look for such things, be diligent that you may be found of Him in peace, without spot, and blameless." (2 Pet. 3:14.)

LUKE 19:28-40

And when he had thus spoken, he went on before, going up to Jerusalem. And it came to pass, when he drew nigh unto Bethphage and Bethany, at the mount that is called Olivet, he sent two of the disciples, saying, Go your way into the village over against you; in which as ye enter ye shall find a colt tied, whereon no man ever yet sat: loose him, and bring him. And if any one ask you, Why do ye loose him? thus shall ye say, The Lord hath need of him. And they that were sent went away, and found even as he had said unto them. And as they were loosing the colt, the owners thereof said unto them, Why loose ye the colt? And they said, The Lord hath need of him. And they brought him to Jesus: and they threw their garments upon the colt, and set Jesus thereon. And as he went, they spread their garments in the way. And as he was now drawing nigh, even at the descent of the mount of Olives, the whole multitude of the disciples began to rejoice and praise God with a loud voice for all the mighty works which they had seen; saying, Blessed is the King that cometh in the name of the Lord: peace in heaven, and glory in the highest. And some of the Pharisees from the multitude said unto him, Teacher, rebuke thy disciples. And he answered and said, I tell you that, if these shall hold their peace, the stones will cry out.

Let us mark, for one thing, in these verses, the perfect knowledge of our Lord Jesus Christ. We see Him sending two of His disciples to a village, and telling them that they would find at the entrance of it, "a colt tied, whereon yet never man sat." We see Him describing what they would see and hear, with as much confidence as if the whole transaction had been previously arranged. In short, He speaks like one to whom all things were naked and open, like one whose eyes were in every place—like one who knew things unseen as well as things seen.

An attentive reader will observe the same thing in other parts of the Gospel. We are told in one place that "He knew the thoughts" of His enemies. We are told in another, that "He knew what was in man." We are told in another, that "He knew from the beginning who they were that believed not and who should betray Him." (Luke 6:8; John 2:25; John 6:64.) Knowledge like this is the peculiar attribute of God. Passages like these are meant to remind us, that "the man Christ Jesus" is not only man. He is also "God blessed forever." (Rom. 9:5.)

The thought of Christ's perfect knowledge should alarm sinners and awaken them to repentance. The great Head of the Church knows them and all their doings. The Judge of all sees them continually, and marks down all their ways. There is "no darkness where the workers of iniquity can hide themselves." (Job 34:22.) If they go into the secret chamber the eyes of Christ are there. If they privately scheme villainy and plot wickedness, Christ knows it and observes it. If they speak secretly against the righteous, Christ hears. They may deceive men all their life long, but they cannot deceive Christ. A day comes when God "will judge the secrets of men by Jesus Christ, according to the Gospel." (Rom. 2:16.)

The thought of Christ's perfect knowledge should comfort all true-hearted Christians, and quicken them to increased diligence in good works. The Master's eye is always upon them. He knows where they dwell, and what are their daily trials, and who are their companions. There is not a word in their mouths, or a thought in their hearts, but Jesus knows it altogether. Let them take courage when they are slandered, misunderstood, and misrepresented by the world. It matters nothing so long as they can say, "You, Lord, who know all things, know that I love you." (John 21:17.) Let them walk on steadily in the narrow way, and not turn aside to the right hand or the left. When sinners entice them, and weak brethren say, "Spare yourself," let them reply, "My Master is looking at me. I desire to live and move as in the sight of Christ."

Let us mark, for another thing, in this passage, the public visibility of our Lord's last entry into Jerusalem. We are told of His riding in on an donkey, like a king visiting his capital, or a conqueror returning in triumph to his native land. We read of a "multitude of disciples" surrounding Him as He rode into the city, "rejoicing and praising God with a loud voice." The whole history is strikingly unlike the general tenor of our Lord's life. On other occasions, we see Him withdrawing from public observation, retiring into the wilderness, charging those whom He healed to tell no man what was done. On the present occasion all is changed. Reserve is completely thrown aside. He seems to court public notice. He appears desirous that all should see Him, and should mark, note, and observe what He did.

The reasons of our Lord's conduct at this crisis of His ministry, at first sight, may appear hard to discover. On calm reflection they are clear and plain. He knew that the time had come when He was to die for sinners on the cross. His work as the great Prophet, so far as His earthly ministry was concerned, was almost finished and completed. His work as the sacrifice for sin and substitute for sinners, remained to be accomplished. Before giving Himself up as a sacrifice, He desired to draw the attention of the whole Jewish nation to Himself. The Lamb of God was about to be slain. The great sin-offering was about to be killed. It was fit that the eyes of all Israel should be fixed upon Him. This great thing was not to be done in a corner.

Forever let us bless God that the death of our Lord Jesus Christ was so widely known and so public an event. Had He been suddenly stoned in some popular tumult, or privately beheaded like John the Baptist in prison, there never would have been lacking Jewish and Gentile unbelievers, who would have denied that the Son of God had died at all. The wisdom of God so ordered events that such a denial was rendered impossible. Whatever men may think of the doctrine of Christ's atoning death, they can never deny the fact that Christ died. Publicly He rode into Jerusalem a few days before His death. Publicly He was seen and heard in the city until the day that He was betrayed. Publicly He was brought before the High Priests and Pilate, and condemned. Publicly He was led forth to Calvary, and nailed to the cross. The corner-stone and crowning-event in our Lord's ministry was His death for sinners. Of all the events of His ministry, that death was the one most public, and the one witnessed by the greatest number of Jews. And that death was the "life of the world." (John 6:51.)

Let us leave the whole passage with the cheering reflection, that the joy of Christ's disciples at His entry into Jerusalem, when He came to be crucified, will prove as nothing compared to the joy of His people when He comes again to reign. That first joy was soon broken off and exchanged for sorrow and bitter tears. The second joy shall be a joy for evermore. That first joy was often interrupted by the bitter sneers of enemies, who were plotting mischief. The second joy shall be liable to no such crude interruptions. Not a word shall be said against the King when He comes to Jerusalem the second time. "Before Him every knee shall bow, and every tongue confess that He is Lord." (Phil. 2:11.)

LUKE 19:41-48

JESUS WEEPING OVER JERUSALEM

And when he drew nigh, he saw the city and wept over it, saying, If thou hadst known in this day, even thou, the things which belong unto peace! but now they are hid from thine eyes. For the days shall come upon thee, when thine enemies shall cast up a bank about thee, and compass thee round, and keep thee in on every side, and shall dash thee to the ground, and thy children within thee; and they shall not leave in thee one stone upon another; because thou knewest not the time of thy visitation. And he entered into the temple, and began to cast out them that sold, saying unto them, It is written, And my house shall be a house of prayer: but ye have made it a den of robbers. And he was teaching daily in the temple. But the chief priests and the scribes and the principal men of the people sought to destroy him: and they could not find what they might do; for the people all hung upon him, listening.

We learn, firstly, from these verses, how great is the tenderness and compassion of Christ towards sinners. We are told that when He came near Jerusalem for the last time, "He beheld the city and wept over it." He knew well the character of the inhabitants of Jerusalem. Their cruelty, their self-righteousness, their stubbornness, their obstinate prejudice against the truth, their pride of heart were not hidden from Him. He knew well what they were going to do to Himself within a very few days—His unjust judgment, His delivery to the Gentiles, His sufferings, His crucifixion, were all spread out distinctly before His mind's eye. And yet knowing all this, our Lord pitied Jerusalem! "He beheld the city and wept over it."

We err greatly if we suppose that Christ cares for none but His own believing people. He cares for all. His heart is wide enough to take an interest in all mankind. His compassion extends to every man, woman, and child on earth. He has a love of 'general pity' for the man who is going on still in wickedness, as well as a love of 'special affection' for the sheep who hear His voice and follow Him. He is not willing that any should perish, but that all should come to repentance. Hardened sinners are fond of making excuses for their conduct. But they will never be able to say that Christ was not merciful, and was not ready to save.

We know but little of true Christianity, if we do not feel a deep concern about the souls of unconverted people. A lazy indifference about the spiritual state of others, may doubtless save us much trouble. To care nothing whether our neighbors are going to heaven or hell, is no doubt the way of the world. But a man of this spirit is very unlike David, who said, "rivers of waters run down my eyes, because men keep not your law." He is very unlike Paul, who said, "I have great heaviness and continual sorrow of heart for my brethren." (Psalm 119:136; Rom. 9:2.) Above all, he is very unlike Christ. If Christ felt tenderly about wicked people, the disciples of Christ ought to feel likewise.

We learn, secondly, from these verses, that there is a religious ignorance which is sinful and blameworthy. We read that our Lord denounced judgments on Jerusalem, "because she knew not the time of her visitation." She might have known that the times of Messiah had fully come, and that Jesus of Nazareth was the Messiah. But she would not know. Her rulers were wilfully ignorant. They would not calmly examine evidences, and impartially consider great plain facts. Her people would not see "the signs of the times." Therefore judgment was soon to come upon Jerusalem to the uttermost. Her willful ignorance left her without excuse.

The principle laid down by our Lord in this place is deeply important. It contradicts an opinion which is very common in the world. It teaches distinctly that all ignorance is not excusable, and that when men might know truth, but refuse to know it, their guilt is very great in the sight of God. There is a degree of knowledge for which all are responsible, and if from indolence or prejudice we do not attain that knowledge, the lack of it will ruin our souls.

Let us impress this great principle deeply on our own hearts. Let us urge it diligently on others, when we speak to them about religion. Let us not flatter ourselves that ignorance will excuse everyone who dies in ignorance, and that he will be pardoned because he knew no better! Did he live up to the light he had? Did he use every means for attaining knowledge? Did he honestly employ every help within his reach, and search industriously after wisdom? These are grave questions. If a man cannot answer them, he will certainly be condemned in the judgment day. A willful ignorance will never be allowed as a plea in a man's favor. On the contrary, it will rather add to his guilt.

We learn, thirdly, from these verses, that God is sometimes pleased to give men special opportunities and invitations. We are told by our Lord, that Jerusalem "knew not the day of her visitation." Jerusalem had a special season of mercy and privilege. The Son of God Himself visited her. The mightiest miracles that man had ever seen were wrought around her. The most wonderful preaching that ever was heard was preached within her walls. The days of our Lord's ministry were days of the clearest calls to repentance and faith that ever any city received. They were calls so marked, peculiar, and unlike any previous calls Jerusalem had received, that it seemed impossible they should be disregarded. But they were disregarded! And our Lord declares that this disregard was one of Jerusalem's principal sins.

The subject before us is a deep and mysterious one. It requires careful stating and delicate handling, lest we should make one scripture contradict another. There seems no doubt that churches, nations, and even individuals are sometimes visited with special manifestations of God's presence, and that their neglect of such manifestations is the turning point in their spiritual ruin. Why this should take place in some cases and not in others we cannot tell. Facts, plain facts in history and biography, appear to prove that it is so. The last day will probably show the world, that there were seasons in the lives of many who died in sin, when God drew very near to them, when conscience was peculiarly alive, when there seemed but a step between them and salvation. Those seasons will probably prove to have been what our Lord calls their "day of visitation." The neglect of such seasons will probably be at last, one of the heaviest charges against their souls.

Deep as the subject is, it should teach men one practical lesson. That lesson is the immense importance of not stifling convictions, and not quenching the workings of conscience. He that resists the voice of conscience may be throwing away his last chance of salvation. That warning voice may be God's "day of visitation." The neglect of it may fill up the measure of a man's iniquity, and provoke God to let him alone forever.

We learn, lastly, from these verses, how much Christ disapproves of the profanation of holy things. We read that He cast the buyers and sellers out of the temple, and told them that they had made God's house "a den of thieves." He knew how formal and ignorant the ministers of the temple were. He knew how soon the temple and its services were to be destroyed, the veil to be rent, and the priesthood to be ended. But He would have us know that a reverence is due to every place where God is worshiped. The reverence He claimed for the temple, was not for the temple as the house of sacrifice, but as "the house of prayer."

Let us remember this conduct and language of our Lord, whenever we go to a place of public worship. Christian churches no doubt are not like the Jewish temples. They have neither altars, priesthood, sacrifices, nor symbolical furniture. But they are places where God's word is read, where Christ is present, and where the Holy Spirit works on souls. These facts ought to make us grave, reverent, solemn and decorous, whenever we enter them. The man who behaves as carelessly in a church as he would in an inn, or a private dwelling, has yet much to learn. He has not the "mind of Christ."

Chapter 20

LUKE 20:1-8

THE AUTHORITY OF JESUS QUESTIONED

*A*nd *it came to pass, on one of the days, as he was teaching the people in the temple, and preaching the gospel, there came upon him the chief priests and the scribes with the elders; and they spake, saying unto him, Tell us: By what authority doest thou these things? or who is he that gave thee this authority? And he answered and said unto them, I also will ask you a question; and tell me: The baptism of John, was it from heaven, or from men? And they reasoned with themselves, saying, If we shall say, From heaven; he will say, Why did ye not believe him? But if we shall say, From men; all the people will stone us: for they are persuaded that John was a prophet. And they answered, that they knew not whence it was. And Jesus said unto them, Neither tell I you by what authority I do these things.*

Let us notice, firstly, in this passage, the demand which the chief Priests and scribes made upon our Lord. "Tell us," they said, "by what authority you do these things? and who gave you this authority?"

The spirit which prompted this demand is too evident to be mistaken. These men hated and envied Christ. They saw His influence increasing. They saw their own power waning. They resolved, if possible, to stop the progress of this new teacher; and the point on which they made their assault was His authority. His mighty works they ought to have examined. His teaching they ought, in all fairness, to have compared with their own Scriptures. But they refused to take either one course or the other. They preferred to call in question His commission.

Every true-hearted Christian who tries to do good in the world, must make up his mind to be treated like his Master. He must never be surprised to find, that the self-righteous and the worldly-minded dislike His ways. The lawfulness of his proceedings will be constantly called in question. He will be regarded as meddlesome, disorderly, and self-conceited, a pestilent fellow, and a troubler of Israel. (Acts 24:5; 1 Kings 18:17.) Scripture-readers, district-visitors, layagents, and unordained missionaries, are specially liable to meet with such treatment. And worst of all they will often meet with enemies, where they ought to find friends.

Let all who are attacked by the world for trying to do good, take comfort in the thought that they are only drinking of the cup which Christ drank. Their Master in heaven sympathizes with them. Let them work on patiently, and believe that, if they are faithful, their work will speak for itself. The world's opposition is sure to attend every really good work. If the servants of Christ are to cease from every movement which the world calls in question, they will soon come to an entire stand-still. If we are to wait until the world approves our plans, and is satisfied with the propriety of our efforts, we shall never do anything on earth.

Let us notice, secondly, in this passage, the manner in which our Lord speaks of John the Baptist's ministry. He refers those who questioned His authority, to John's constant and unvarying testimony to Himself. "Ought they not to remember how John had spoken of Him as the Lamb of God—as One whose shoe-latchets he was not worthy to bear—as One who had the fan in His hand, and had the Spirit without measure? Ought they not to recollect that they and all Jerusalem had gone out to John's baptism, and confessed that John was a prophet? Yet John had always told them plainly that Christ was the Messiah! Surely, if they were honest they would not come now to demand His authority. If they really believed John to be a prophet sent from God, they were bound to believe that Jesus was the Christ."

It may reasonably be doubted whether the importance of John the Baptist's ministry is generally understood by Christians. The brightness of our Lord's history overshadows the history of His forerunner, and the result is that John's baptism and preaching do not receive the attention which they deserve. Yet it should never be forgotten, that the ministry of the Baptist was the only New Testament ministry foretold in the Old Testament, excepting that of Christ. It was a ministry which produced an immense effect on the Jewish mind and aroused the expectation of Israel from one end of Palestine to the other. Above all, it was a ministry which made the Jews without excuse in their rejection of Christ, when Christ appeared. They could not say that they were taken by surprise when our Lord began to preach. Their minds had been thoroughly prepared for His appearing. To see the full sinfulness of the Jews, and the entire justice of the judgments which came on them after crucifying our Lord, we must remember the ministry of John the Baptist.

However little man may esteem the work of faithful ministers there is One in heaven who sees it, and keeps account of all their labor. However little their proceedings may be understood, and however much they may be slandered and misrepresented, the Lord Jesus Christ writes all their doings in His book. He lives who testified to the importance of John the Baptist's ministry when John was dead and buried. He will yet testify to the toil of every one of His faithful servants at the last day. In the world they may have tribulation and disappointment. But they are not forgotten by Christ.

Let us notice, lastly, in this passage, the falsehood of which our Lord's enemies were guilty. In reply to our Lord's question whether John's baptism was from heaven or of men, "they answered that they did not know." This was a downright untruth. They could have told, but they would not. They knew that if they said what they really believed they would condemn themselves. If they confessed that John was a prophet sent from God, they would be guilty of a gross inconsistency in not believing his testimony about Christ.

Falsehoods like this, it may be feared, are only too common among unconverted men. Thousands will say anything rather than acknowledge themselves to be in the wrong. Lying is just one of the sins to which the human heart is most naturally inclined, and one of the commonest sins in the world. Gehazi, Ananias, and Sapphira have more followers and imitators than Peter and Paul. The number of lies which are constantly told by men, to save their own credit, and to cover over their own wickedness, is probably far greater than we are aware.

The true servant of Christ will do well to remember these things as he travels through this world. He must not believe all he hears, and especially in the matter of religion. He must not suppose that unconverted men really believe in their own hearts all that they say. They often feel more than they appear to feel. They often say things against religion and religious people, which they secretly know to be untrue. They often know the Gospel is true, but have not the courage to confess it. They often know the Christians life is right, but are too proud to say so. The chief priests and scribes are not the only people who deal dishonestly in religion, and say what they know to be false. Then let the servant of Christ go patiently on his way. Those who are now his enemies, will one day confess that he was right, though they used to cry loudly that he was wrong.

LUKE 20:9-19

THE PARABLE OF THE TENANTS

And he began to speak unto the people this parable: A man planted a vineyard, and let it out to husbandmen, and went into another country for a long time. And at the season he sent unto the husbandmen a servant, that they should give him of the fruit of the vineyard: but the husbandmen beat him, and sent him away empty. And he sent yet another servant: and him also they beat, and handled him shamefully, and sent him away empty. And he sent yet a third: and him also they wounded, and cast him forth. And the lord of the vineyard said, What shall I do? I will send my beloved son; it may be they will reverence him. But when the husbandmen saw him, they reasoned one with another, saying, This is the heir; let us kill him, that the inheritance may be ours. And they cast him forth out of the vineyard, and killed him. What therefore will the lord of the vineyard do unto them? He will come and destroy these husbandmen, and will give the vineyard unto others. And when they heard it, they said, God forbid. But he looked upon them, and said, What then is this that is written, The stone which the builders rejected, The same was made the head of the corner? Every one that falleth on that stone shall be broken to pieces; but on whomsoever it shall fall, it will scatter him as dust. And the scribes and the chief priests sought to lay hands on him in that very hour; and they feared the people: for they perceived that he spake this parable against them.

The parable we have now read, is one of the very few which are recorded more than once by the Gospel writers. Matthew, Mark, and Luke, all give it at full length. This three-fold repetition is alone sufficient to point out the importance of its contents.

The parable, no doubt, was specially intended for the Jews to whom it was addressed. But we must not confine its application to them. It contains lessons which should be remembered in all churches of Christ as long as the world stands.

In the first place, the parable shows us the deep corruption of human nature. The conduct of the wicked "farmers" is a vivid representation of man's dealings with God. It is a faithful picture of the history of the Jewish church. In spite of privileges, such as no nation ever had, in the face of warnings such as no people ever received, the Jews rebelled against God's lawful authority, refused to give Him His rightful dues, rejected the counsel of His prophets, and at length crucified His only-begotten Son.

It is a no less faithful picture of the history of all the Gentile churches. Called as they were out of heathen darkness by infinite mercy, they have done nothing worthy of the vocation with which they were called. On the contrary, they have allowed false doctrines and wicked practices to spring up rankly among them, and have crucified Christ afresh. It is a mournful fact that in hardness, unbelief, superstition, and self-righteousness—the Christian churches, as a whole, are little better than the Jewish church of our Lord's time. Both are described with painful correctness in the story of the wicked farmers. In both we may point to countless privileges misused, and countless warnings despised.

Let us often pray that we may thoroughly understand the sinfulness of man's heart. Few of us, it may be feared, have the least conception of the strength and virulence of the spiritual disease with which we are born. Few entirely realize that "the carnal mind is enmity against God," and that unconverted human nature, if it had the power, would cast its Maker down from His throne. The behavior of the farmers before us, whatever we may please to think, is only a picture of what every natural man would do to God, if he only could. To see these things is of great importance. Christ is never fully valued, until sin is clearly seen. We must know the depth and malignity of our disease, in order to appreciate the great Physician.

In the second place, this parable shows us the amazing patience and patience of God. The conduct of the "owner of the vineyard" is a vivid representation of God's dealings with man. It is a faithful picture of His merciful dealings with the Jewish church. Prophet after prophet was sent to warn Israel of his danger. Message after message was repeatedly sent, notwithstanding insults and injuries heaped on the messengers.

It is a no less faithful picture of His gracious treatment of the Gentile churches. For eighteen hundred years He has suffered their hurtful manners. They have repeatedly tried Him by false doctrines, superstitions, and contempt of His word, Yet He has repeatedly granted them seasons of refreshing, raised up for them holy ministers and mighty reformers, and not cut them off, notwithstanding all their persecutions. The churches of Christ have no right to boast. They are debtors to God for innumerable mercies, no less than the Jews were in our Lord's time. They have not been dealt with according to their sins, nor rewarded according to their iniquities.

We should learn to be more thankful for God's mercy. We have probably little idea of the extent of our obligations to it, and of the number of gracious messages which the Lord of the vineyard is constantly sending to our souls. The last day will unfold to our wondering eyes a long list of unacknowledged kindnesses, of which while we lived we took no notice.

Mercy we shall find was indeed God's darling attribute. "He delights in mercy." (Micah 7:18.) Mercies before conversion, mercies after conversion, mercies at every step of their journey on earth, will be revealed to the minds of saved saints, and make them ashamed of their own thanklessness. Sparing mercies, providential mercies, mercies in the way of warnings, mercies in the way of sudden visitations, will all be set forth in order before the minds of lost sinners, and confound them by the exhibition of their own hardness and unbelief. We shall all find that God was often speaking to us when we did not hear, and sending us messages which we did not regard. Few texts will be brought out so prominently at the last day as that of Peter—"The Lord is patient toward us, not willing that any should perish." (2 Peter 3:9.)

In the last place, this parable shows us the severity of God's judgments when they fall on obstinate sinners. The punishment of the wicked farmers is a vivid representation of God's final dealings with such as go on still in wickedness. At the time when our Lord spoke this parable, it was a prophetical picture of the approaching ruin of the Jewish church and nation. The vineyard of the Lord in the land of Israel, was about to be taken from its unfaithful tenants. Jerusalem was to be destroyed. The temple was to be burned. The Jews were to be scattered over the earth.

At the present time, it may be feared, it is a mournful picture of things yet to come on the Gentile churches in the latter days. The judgments of God will yet fall on unbelieving Christians, as they fell on unbelieving Jews. The solemn warning of Paul to the Romans will yet receive an accomplishment—"If you continue not in God's goodness, you also shall be cut off." (Rom. 11:22.)

We must never flatter ourselves that God cannot be angry. He is indeed a God of infinite grace and compassion. But it is also written, that He is "a consuming fire." (Heb. 12:29.) His spirit will not always strive with men. (Gen. 6:3.) There will be a day when His patience will come to an end, and when He will arise to dreadfully judge the earth. Happy will they be who are found hidden in the ark, in the day of the Lord's anger! Of all wrath, none can be conceived so dreadful as "the wrath of the Lamb." The man on whom the "stone cut out without hands" falls at His second coming, will indeed be crushed to powder. (Dan. 2:34, 35.)

Do we know these things, and do we live up to our knowledge? The chief priests and elders, we are told, "perceived that this parable was spoken against them." But they were too proud to repent, and too hardened to turn from their sins. Let us beware of doing likewise.

LUKE 20:20-26

PAYING TAXES TO CAESAR

And they watched him, and sent forth spies, who feigned themselves to be righteous, that they might take hold of his speech, so as to deliver him up to the rule and to the authority of the governor. And they asked him, saying, Teacher, we know that thou sayest and teachest rightly, and acceptest not the person of any, but of a truth teachest the way of God: Is it lawful for us to give tribute unto Caesar, or not? But he perceived their craftiness, and said unto them, Show me a denarius. Whose image and superscription hath it? And they said, Caesar's. And he said unto them, Then render unto Caesar the things that are Caesar's, and unto God the things that are God's. And they were not able to take hold of the saying before the people: and they marvelled at his answer, and held their peace.

Let us mark, for one thing, in this passage, the cloak of goodness under which some of our Lord's enemies approached Him. We read that they "sent forth spies, who pretended to be honest men." We read further that they attempted to trick Him by flattering words—"Teacher, we know that you speak and teach what is right and are not influenced by what others think. You sincerely teach the ways of God." These words sounded well. An ignorant bystander would have said, "These are sincere inquirers after truth!" But all was hollow and unreal. It was the wolf putting on the sheep's clothing, under the vain idea of deceiving the shepherd. "Their words were smoother than butter," yet there was "war in their hearts." (Psalm 55:21.)

The true servant of Christ must expect to meet people of this description, as long as the world stands. There never will be lacking those, who from selfish or sinister motives will profess with their lips to love Christ, while in heart they deny Him. There will always be some, who "by good words and fair speeches," will attempt to deceive the heart of the simple. The union of "burning lips and a wicked heart," is far from uncommon. There are probably few congregations which do not contain some of those whom Solomon likens to "potsherds, covered with silver dross." (Rom. 16:18. Prov. 26:23.)

He that would not be often deceived in this wicked world, must carefully remember these things. We must exercise a wise caution as we travel through life, and not play the part of the "simple who believes every word." (Prov. 14:15.) We must not lightly put confidence in every new religious volunteer, nor hastily take it for granted that all people are good who talk like good men. Such caution at first sight may appear narrow-minded and uncharitable. But the longer we live the more shall we find that it is needful. We shall discover by experience that all is not gold that glitters, and all are not true Christians who make a loud profession of Christianity. The language of Christianity is precisely that part of religion which a false Christian finds it most easy to attain. The walk of a man's daily life, and not the talk of his lips, is the only safe test of his character.

Let us mark, for another thing, in these verses, the consummate wisdom of our Lord's answer to His enemies. We read that a most difficult and subtle question was proposed to Him for solution. "Is it lawful to pay taxes to Caesar or not?" It was a question eminently calculated to entangle anyone who attempted to answer it. If our Lord had replied that it was not lawful to pay tribute to Caesar, He would have been accused to Pilate as a rebel against the Roman power. If our Lord had replied that it was lawful to pay tribute to Caesar, He would have been denounced to the people as regardless of the rights and privileges of the Jewish nation. An answer which would not involve our Lord in difficulties, seemed at first sight impossible to be found. But He who is truly called "the wisdom of God," found an answer which silenced His adversaries. He bade them show Him a Roman coin. He asked them whose image and superscription was on that Roman coin? "They answered and said, Caesar's." At once our Lord made that Roman coin the groundwork of a reply, at which even His enemies were obliged to marvel. "Render," He said, "unto Caesar the things which be Caesar's, and unto God the things which be God's."

They were to "render to CAESAR the things which were Caesar's." Their own lips had just confessed that Caesar had a certain temporal authority over them. They used the money which Caesar had coined. It was a lawful tender between man and man. They probably had no objection to receive gifts and payments in Roman coin. They must not therefore pretend to say that all payments to Caesar were unlawful. By their own admission he exercised some dominion over them. Let them obey that dominion in all temporal things. If they did not refuse to use Caesar's coin, let them not refuse to pay Caesar's temporal dues.

They were to "render to GOD the things which were God's." There were many dues which God required at their hands which they might easily pay, if they were inclined. Honor, love, obedience, faith, fear, prayer, spiritual worship, were payments to God which they might daily make, and payments with which the Roman government did not interfere. They could not say that Caesar made such payments impossible. Let them see to it that they gave to God His dues in spiritual things, as well as to Caesar his dues in temporal things. There was no necessity for collision between the demands of their temporal and their heavenly sovereign. In temporal things, let them obey the powers, under whose authority they allowed themselves to be. In spiritual things let them do as their forefathers had done, and obey God.

The principles laid down by our Lord in this well-known sentence are deeply instructive. Well would it have been for the peace of the world, if they had been more carefully weighed and more wisely applied!

The attempts of the civil power in some countries to control men's consciences by intolerant interference, and the attempts of the church in other countries to interfere with the action of the civil power, have repeatedly led to strifes, wars, rebellions, and social disorder. The injuries which the cause of true religion has received from morbid scrupulosity on one side; and servile compliance to state demands on the other, have been neither few nor small. Happy is he who has attained to a sound mind on the whole subject! To distinguish rightly between the things of Caesar, and the things of God, and to pay to each their real dues regularly, habitually, and cheerfully, is a great help towards a quiet and peaceable life.

Let us often pray that we may have wisdom from above, in order to answer rightly, when perplexing questions are put to us. The servant of Christ must expect a portion like his Master. He must count it no strange thing, if the wicked and worldly-minded endeavor to "entangle him in his talk," and to provoke him to speak unadvisedly with his lips. In order to be prepared for such occasions let him often ask the Lord Jesus for the gift of sound wisdom and a discreet tongue. In the presence of those who watch for our halting, it is a great thing to know what to say and how to say it, when to be silent, and when to speak. Blessed be God, He who silenced the chief priests and scribes by His wise answers, still lives to help His people and has all power to help them. But He loves to be entreated.

LUKE 20:27-40
RESURRECTION AND MARRIAGE

And there came to him certain of the Sadducees, they that say that there is no resurrection; and they asked him, saying, Teacher, Moses wrote unto us, that if a man's brother die, having a wife, and he be childless, his brother should take the wife, and raise up seed unto his brother. There were therefore seven brethren: and the first took a wife, and died childless; and the second: and the third took her; and likewise the seven also left no children, and died. Afterward the woman also died. In the resurrection therefore whose wife of them shall she be? for the seven had her to wife. And Jesus said unto them, The sons of this world marry, and are given in marriage: but they that are accounted worthy to attain to that world, and the resurrection from the dead, neither marry, nor are given in marriage: for neither can they die any more: for they are equal unto the angels; and are sons of God, being sons of the resurrection. But that the dead are raised, even Moses showed, in the place concerning the Bush, when he calleth the Lord the God of Abraham, and the God of Isaac, and the God of Jacob. Now he is not the God of the dead, but of the living: for all live unto him.

And certain of the scribes answering said, Teacher, thou hast well said. For they durst not any more ask him any question.

We see in these verses what an old thing unbelief is. We are told that "there came to our Lord certain of the Sadducees, who deny that there is any resurrection." Even in the Jewish Church, the Church of Abraham, and Isaac, and Jacob, the Church of Moses, and Samuel, and David, and the prophets- we find that there were bold, avowed, unblushing skeptics. If infidelity like this existed among God's peculiar? If these things existed in a green tree, what must have been the condition of the dry?

We must never be surprised when we hear of infidels, deists, heretics and free-thinkers rising up in the Church, and drawing away disciples after them. We must not count it a rare and a strange thing. It is only one among many proofs that man is a fallen and corrupt being. Since the day when the devil said to Eve "you shall not surely die," and Eve believed him, there never has been wanting a constant succession of forms of unbelief. There is nothing new about any of the modern theories of infidelity. There is not one of those who is not an old disease under a new name. They are all mushrooms which spring up spontaneously in the hot-bed of human nature. It is not in reality an astonishing thing that there should rise up so many who call in question the truth of the Bible. The marvel is rather, that in a fallen world the sect of the Sadducees should be so small.

Let us take comfort in the thought that in the long run of years the truth will always prevail. Its advocates may often be feeble, and their arguments very weak. But there is an inherent strength in the cause itself which keeps it alive. Bold infidels like Porphyry, and Julian, and Hobbes, and Hume, and Voltaire, and Paine arise from time to time and make a stir in the world. But they produce no lasting impression. They pass away like the Sadducees and go to their own place. The great evidences of Christianity remain like the Pyramids, unshaken and unmoved. The "gates of hell" shall never prevail against Christ's truth. (Matt. 16:18.)

We see, secondly, in these verses, what a favorite weapon of skeptics is a 'supposed case'. We are told that the Sadducees brought to our Lord a difficulty arising out of the case of a woman who had married seven brothers in succession. They professed a desire to know "whose wife of the seven" the woman would be in the resurrection. The intention of the inquiry is clear and plain. They wished to pour contempt on the whole doctrine of a life to come. The case itself is one which we cannot suppose had really arisen. It seems the highest probability that it was a story invented for the occasion, in order to raise a difficulty and found an argument.

Reasoning of this kind will often meet us, if we are thrown into company with people of a skeptical turn of mind. Some imaginary difficulty or complication, and that connected probably with some fancied state of things in the world to come, will often prove the stronghold of an unbeliever. "He cannot understand it! He cannot reconcile it! It seems to him revolting and absurd! It offends his common sense!"—Such is the language which is often used.

Reasoning of this kind should never shake us for a moment. For one thing, we have nothing to do with 'supposed and imaginary cases'. It will be time enough to discuss them when they really arise. Enough for us to talk and argue about facts as they are. For another thing, it is mere waste of time to speculate about difficulties connected with a state of existence in a world to come. We know so little of anything beyond the visible world around us, that we are very poor judges of what is possible or not possible in the unseen world. A thousand things beyond the grave must necessarily be unintelligible to us at present. In the meantime it is our wisdom to wait patiently. What we don't know now, we shall know hereafter.

We see, thirdly, in these verses, something of the true character of the saints' existence in the world to come. We read that our Lord said to the

Pharisees, "But that is not the way it will be in the age to come. For those worthy of being raised from the dead won't be married then. And they will never die again. In these respects they are like angels. They are children of God raised up to new life."

Two things are abundantly clear from this description, respecting the saints in glory. For one thing, their happiness is not a carnal happiness, but a spiritual one. "They neither marry nor are given in marriage." The glorified body shall be very unlike what it is now. It shall no longer be a clog and a hindrance to the believer's better nature. It shall be a fit habitation for a glorified soul. For another thing, their happiness shall he eternal. "They can die no more." No births shall be needed, to supply the constant waste caused by death. Weakness, and sickness, and disease, and infirmity, shall be no more at all. The curse shall be clean removed. Death himself shall die.

The nature of what we call "heaven" is a subject which should often engage our thoughts. Few subjects in religion are so calculated to show the utter folly of unconverted men, and the dreadful danger in which they stand. A heaven where all the joy is spiritual, would surely be no heaven to an unconverted soul! Few subjects are so likely to cheer and animate the mind of a true Christian. The holiness and spiritual-mindedness which he follows after in this life will be the very atmosphere of his eternal abode. The cares of family relationships shall no longer distract his mind. The fear of death shall no longer bring him into bondage. Then let him press on and bear his cross patiently. Heaven will make amends for all.

We see, lastly, in these verses, the antiquity of belief in a resurrection. Our Lord shows that it was the belief of Moses. "That the dead are raised, even Moses showed at the burning bush."

Faith in a resurrection and a life to come has been to universal belief of all God's people from the beginning of the world. Abel, and Enoch, and Noah, and Abraham and all the Patriarchs, were men who looked forward to a better inheritance than they had here below. "They looked for a city which had foundations." "They desired a better country, that is, a heavenly one." (Heb. 11:10-16.)

Let us anchor our own souls firmly on this great foundation truth, "that we shall all rise again." Whatever ancient or modern Sadducees may say, let us believe firmly that we are not made like the beasts that perish, and that there shall be "a resurrection of the dead, both of the just and unjust." (Acts 24:15.) The recollection of this truth will cheer us in the day of trial, and comfort us in the hour of death. We shall feel that though earthly prosperity fail us, there is a life to come where there is no change. We shall feel that though worms destroy our body, yet in the flesh we shall see God. (Job 19:26.) We shall not lie always in the grave. Our God is "not a God of the dead, but of the living."

LUKE 20:41-47

WHOSE SON IS CHRIST

And he said unto them, How say they that the Christ is David's son? For David himself saith in the book of Psalms, The Lord said unto my Lord, Sit thou on my right hand, Till I make thine enemies the footstool of thy feet. David therefore calleth him Lord, and how is he his son? And in the hearing of all the people he said unto his disciples, Beware of the scribes, who desire to walk in long robes, and love salutations in the marketplaces, and chief seats in the synagogues, and chief places at feasts; who devour widows' houses, and for a pretence make long prayers: these shall receive greater condemnation.

Let us observe in this passage, what striking testimony to Christ's divinity the book of Psalms contains. We read that after patiently replying to the attacks of His enemies, our Lord in turn propounds a question to them. He asks them to explain an expression in the hundred and tenth Psalm, where David speaks of the Messiah as his Lord. To this question the Scribes could find no answer. They did not see the mighty truth, that Messiah was to be God as well as man, and that while as man He was to be David's son, as God He was to be David's Lord. Their ignorance of Scripture was thus exposed before all the people. Professing themselves to be instructors of others and possessors of the key of knowledge, they were proved unable to explain what their own Scriptures contained. We may well believe that of all the defeats which our Lord's malicious enemies met with, none galled them more than this. Nothing so abashes the pride of man, as to be publicly proved ignorant of that which he fancies is his own peculiar department of knowledge.

We have probably little idea how much deep truth is contained in the book of Psalms. No part of the Bible perhaps is better known in the letter, and none so little understood in the spirit. We err greatly if we suppose that it is nothing but a record of David's feelings, of David's experience, David's praises, and David's prayers. The hand that held the pen was generally David's. But the subject matter was often something far deeper and higher than the history of the son of Jesse.

The book of Psalms, in a word, is a book full of Christ—Christ suffering—Christ in humiliation—Christ dying—Christ rising again—Christ coming the second time—Christ reigning over all. Both the advents are here—the advent in suffering to bear the cross—the advent in power to wear the crown. Both the kingdoms are here—the kingdom of grace, during which the elect are gathered—the kingdom of glory, when every tongue shall confess that Jesus is Lord. Let us always read the Psalms with a peculiar reverence. Let us say to ourselves as we read, "A greater than David is here."

The remark now made, applies more or less to all the Bible. There is a fullness about the whole Book, which is a strong proof of its inspiration. The more we read it, the more it will seem to contain. All other books become threadbare, if they are constantly read. Their weak points, and their shallowness become every year more apparent. The Bible alone seems broader, and deeper, and fuller, the oftener it is studied. We have no need to look for allegorical and mystical meanings. The fresh truths that will constantly spring up before our eyes, are simple, plain, and clear. Of such truths the Bible is an inexhaustible mine. Nothing can account for this, but the great fact, that the Bible is the word, not of man, but of God.

Let us observe, secondly, in this passage, how abominable is hypocrisy in the eyes of Christ. We are told that in the presence of all the people He said unto His disciples-"Beware of these teachers of religious law! For they love to parade in flowing robes and to have everyone bow to them as they walk in the marketplaces. And how they love the seats of honor in the synagogues and at banquets. But they shamelessly cheat widows out of their property, and then, to cover up the kind of people they really are, they make long prayers in public."

This was a bold and remarkable warning. It was a public denunciation, we must remember, of men who "sat in Moses' seat," and were the recognized teachers of the Jewish people. It teaches us clearly that there may be times when the sins of people in high religious places make it a positive duty to protest publicly against them. It shows us that it is possible to speak out, and yet not to "speak evil of dignities."

No sin seems to be regarded by Christ as more sinful than hypocrisy. None certainly drew forth from His lips such frequent, strong, and withering condemnation, during the whole course of His ministry. He was ever full of mercy and compassion for the chief of sinners. "Fury was not in Him" when He saw Zaccheus, the penitent thief, Matthew the tax-collector, Saul the persecutor, and the woman in Simon's house. But when He saw Scribes and Pharisees wearing a mere cloak of religion, and pretending to great outward sanctity, while their hearts were full of wickedness, His righteous soul seems to have been full of indignation. Eight times in one chapter (Matt. 23.) we find Him saying, "Woe unto you, Scribes and Pharisees, hypocrites."

Let us not forget that the Lord Jesus never changes. He is the same yesterday, and today, and forever. Whatever else we are in religion let us be true. However feeble on faith, and hope, and love, and obedience may be, let us see to it that they are real, genuine, and sincere. Let us abhor the very idea of play-acting and mask-wearing in our Christianity. At any rate let us be thorough. It is a striking fact that the very first piece of armor which Paul recommends to the Christian soldier is "truth." "Stand therefore," he says, "having your loins girt about with truth." (Eph. 6:14.)

Let us observe, lastly, in this passage, that there will be degrees of condemnation and misery in hell. The words of our Lord are distinct and express. He says of those who live and die hypocrites, "these shall receive greater damnation."

The subject opened up in these words is a deeply painful one. The reality and eternity of future punishment are among the great foundation truths of revealed religion, which it is hard to think upon without a shudder. But it is well to have all that the Bible teaches about heaven and hell firmly fixed on our minds. The Bible teaches distinctly that there will be degrees of glory in heaven. It teaches with no less distinctness, both here and elsewhere, that there will be degrees of misery in hell.

Who, after all, are those who will finally receive condemnation? This is the practical point that concerns us most. All who will not come to Christ—all who know not God and obey not the Gospel—all who refuse to repent, and go on still in wickedness, all such will be finally condemned. They will reap according as they have sown. God wills not their eternal ruin. But if they will not hear His voice, they must die in their sins. But who among those who are condemned will receive the heaviest condemnation? It will not fall on heathens who never heard the truth. It will not fall on ignorant and neglected Englishmen, for whose souls, however sunk in profligacy, no man cared. It will fall on those who had great light and knowledge, but made no proper use of it. It will fall on those who professed great sanctity and religiousness, but in reality clung to their sins. In one word, the hypocrite will have the lowest place in hell. These are dreadful things. But they are true.

Chapter 21

LUKE 21:1-4

THE WIDOW'S OFFERING

*A*nd he looked up, and saw the rich men that were casting their gifts into the treasury. And he saw a certain poor widow casting in thither two mites. And he said, Of a truth I say unto you, This poor widow cast in more than they all: for all these did of their superfluity cast in unto the gifts; but she of her want did cast in all the living that she had.

We learn, for one thing, from these verses, how keenly our Lord Jesus Christ observes the things that are done upon earth. We read that "He looked up and saw the rich men casting their gifts into the treasury. And He saw also a certain poor widow casting in two pennies." We might well suppose that our Lord's mind at this season would have been wholly occupied with the things immediately before Him. His betrayal, His unjust judgment, His cross, His passion, His death, were all close at hand; and He knew it. The approaching destruction of the temple, the scattering of the Jews, the long period of time before His second advent, were all things which were spread before His mind like a picture. It was but a few moments ago he spoke of them. And yet at a time like this we find Him taking note of all that is going on around Him! He thinks it not beneath Him to observe the conduct of a "certain poor widow."

Let us remember, that the Lord Jesus never changes. The thing that we read of in the passage before us is the thing that is going on all over the world. "The eyes of the Lord are in every place." (Prov. 15:3.) Nothing is too little to

374 | J.C. RYLE

escape His observation. No act is too trifling to be noted down in the book of His remembrance. The same hand that formed the sun, moon, and stars, was the hand that formed the tongue of the gnat and the wing of the fly with perfect wisdom. The same eye that sees the council-chambers of kings and emperors, is the eye that notices all that goes on in the laborer's cottage. "All things are naked and opened to the eyes of Him with whom we have to do." (Heb. 4:13.) He measures littleness and greatness by a very different measure from the measure of man. Events in our own daily life, to which we attach no importance, are often very grave and serious matters in Christ's sight. Actions and deeds in the weekly history of a poor man, which the great of this world think trivial and contemptible, are often registered as weighty and important in Christ's books. He lives who marked the gift of one "poor widow" as attentively as the gifts of many "rich men."

Let the believer of low degree take comfort in this mighty truth. Let him remember daily that his Master in heaven takes account of everything that is done on earth, and that the lives of cottagers are noticed by Him as much as the lives of kings. The acts of a poor believer have as much dignity about them as the acts of a prince. The little contributions to religious objects which the laborer makes out of his scanty earnings, are as much valued in God's sight as a ten thousand dollar check from a noble. To know this thoroughly is one great secret of contentment. To feel that Christ looks at what a man is, and not at what a man has, will help to preserve us from envious and murmuring thoughts. Happy is he who has learned to say with David, "I am poor and needy; but the Lord thinks upon me." (Psalm 40:17.)

We learn, for another thing, from these verses, who they are whom Christ reckons most liberal in giving money to religious purposes. We read that He said of her who cast in two mites into the treasury, "She has cast in more than all the others. All these of their abundance have cast in unto the offerings of God—but she, out of her poverty has cast in all that she had to live on." These words teach us that Christ looks at something more than the mere amount of men's gifts in measuring their liberality. He looks at the proportion which their gifts bear to their property. He looks at the degree of self-denial which their giving entails upon them. He would have us know that some people appear to give much to religious purposes who in God's sight give very little, and that some appear to give very little who in God's sight give very much.

The subject before us is peculiarly heart-searching. On no point perhaps do professing Christians come short so much as in the matter of giving money to God's cause. Thousands, it may be feared, know nothing whatever of "giving" as a Christian duty. The little giving that there is, is confined entirely to a select few in the churches. Even among those who give, it may be boldly asserted, that the poor generally give far more in proportion to their means than the rich. These are plain facts which cannot be denied. The experience of all who collect for religious societies and Christian charities, will testify that they are correct and true.

Let us judge ourselves in this matter of giving, that we may not be judged and condemned at the great day. Let it be a settled principle with us to watch against stinginess, and whatever else we do with our money, to give regularly and habitually to the cause of God. Let us remember, that although Christ's work does not depend on our money, yet Christ is pleased to test the reality of our grace by allowing us to help Him. If we cannot find it in our hearts to give anything to Christ's cause, we may well doubt the reality of our faith and charity. Let us recollect that our use of the money God has given us, will have to be accounted for at the last day. The "Judge of all" will be He who noticed the widow's mite. Our incomes and expenditures will be brought to light before an assembled world. If we prove in that day to have been rich toward ourselves, but poor toward God, it would be good if we had never been born. Not least, let us look round the world and ask where are the men that were ever ruined by liberal giving to godly purposes, and who ever found himself really poorer by lending to the Lord? We shall find that the words of Solomon are strictly true—"There is one that scatters and yet increases; and there is one that withholds more than is fit, and it tends to poverty." (Prov. 11:24.)

Finally, let us pray for rich men, who as yet know nothing of the luxury of "giving," that their riches may not be their ruin. Hundreds of charitable and religious movements are standing still continually for lack of funds. Great and effectual doors are open to the church of Christ for doing good all over the world, but for lack of money few can be sent to enter in by them. Let us pray for the Holy Spirit to come down on all our congregations, and to teach all our worshipers what to do with their money. Of all people on earth, none ought to be such liberal givers as Christians. All that they have, they owe to the free gift of God. Christ, the Holy Spirit, the Gospel, the Bible, the means of grace, the hope of glory, all are undeserved, incomparable gifts, which millions of heathen never heard of. The possessors of such gifts ought surely to be "ready to distribute" and "willing to give." A giving Savior ought to have giving disciples. Freely we have received—freely we ought to give. (1 Tim. 6:18; Matt. 10:8.)

LUKE 21:5-9

SIGNS OF THE END OF THE AGE

And as some spake of the temple, how it was adorned with goodly stones and offerings, he said, As for these things which ye behold, the days will come, in which there shall not be left here one stone upon another, that shall not be thrown down. And they asked him, saying, Teacher, when therefore shall these things be? and what shall be the sign when these things are about to come to pass? And he said, Take heed that ye be not led astray: for many shall come in my name, saying, I am he; and, The time is at hand: go ye not after them. And when ye shall hear of wars and tumults, be not terrified: for these things must needs come to pass first; but the end is not immediately.

Let us notice in this passage, our Lord Jesus Christ's words about the temple at Jerusalem. We read that some spoke of it, "how it was adorned with beautiful stones and gifts." They praised it for its outward beauty. They admired its size, its architectural grandeur, and its costly decorations. But they met with no response from our Lord. We read that he said, "As for these things which you behold, the days will come in the which there shall not be left one stone upon another that shall not be thrown down."

These words were a striking prophecy. How strange and startling they must have sounded to Jewish ears, an English mind can hardly conceive. They were spoken of a building which every Israelite regarded with almost idolatrous veneration. They were spoken of a building which contained the ark, the holy of holies, and the symbolical furniture formed on a pattern given by God Himself. They were spoken of a building associated with most of the principal names in Jewish history; with David, Solomon, Hezekiah, Josiah, Isaiah, Jeremiah, Ezra, and Nehemiah. They were spoken of a building toward which every devout Jew turned his face in every quarter of the world, when he offered up his daily prayers. (1 Kings 8:44; Jonah 2:4; Dan. 6:10.)

But they were words spoken advisedly. They were spoken in order to teach us the mighty truth that the true glory of a place of worship does not consist in outward ornaments. "The Lord sees not as man sees." (1 Sam. 16:7.) Man looks at the outward appearance of a building. The Lord looks for spiritual worship, and the presence of the Holy Spirit. In the temple at

Jerusalem these things were utterly lacking, and therefore Jesus Christ could take no pleasure in it.

Professing Christians will do well to remember our Lord's words in the present day. It is fit and right beyond doubt that buildings set apart for Christian worship, should be worthy of the purpose for which they are used. Whatever is done for Christ ought to be well done. The house in which the Gospel is preached, and the Word of God read, and prayer offered up, ought to lack nothing that can make it lovely and substantial.

But let it never be forgotten that the material part of a Christian Church is by far the least important part of it. The fairest combinations of marble, and stone and wood, and painted glass, are worthless in God's sight, unless there is truth in the pulpit and grace in the congregation. The dens and caves in which the early Christians used to meet, were probably far more beautiful in the eyes of Christ than the noblest cathedral that was ever reared by man. The temple in which the Lord Jesus delights most, is a broken and contrite heart, renewed by the Holy Spirit.

Let us notice for another thing in this passage, our Lord Jesus Christ's solemn warning against deception. His striking words about the temple drew from His disciples an important question—"Master, when shall these things be? and what sign will there be, when these things shall come to pass?" Our Lord's reply to that question was long and full. And it began with a pointed caution, "Take heed that you be not deceived."

The position which this caution occupies is very remarkable. It stands in the forefront of a prophecy of vast extent and universal importance to all Christians—a prophecy reaching from the day in which it was delivered, to the day of the second advent—a prophecy revealing matters of the most tremendous interest both to Jews and Gentiles—and a prophecy of which a large portion remains to be fulfilled. And the very first sentence of this wondrous prophecy is a caution against deception, "Take heed that you be not deceived."

The necessity of this caution has been continually proved in the history of the Church of Christ. On no subject perhaps have divines made so many mistakes as in the interpretation of unfulfilled prophecy. On no subject have they shown so completely the weakness of man's intellect, and confirmed so thoroughly the words of Paul, "We see through a glass darkly—we know in part." (1 Cor. 13:12.) Dogmatism, positiveness, controversial bitterness, obstinacy in maintaining untenable positions, rash assertions and specula- tions, have too often brought discredit on the whole subject of the prophetical Scriptures, and caused the enemies of Christianity to blaspheme. There are only too many books on prophetical interpretation, on the titlepages of which might be justly written, "Who is this that darkens counsel by words without knowledge?"

Let us learn from our Lord's warning words to pray for a humble, teachable spirit, whenever we open the pages of unfulfilled prophecy. Here, if anywhere, we need the heart of a little child, and the prayer" open my eyes." (Psalm 119:18.) Let us beware, on the one side, of that lazy indifference which turns away from all prophetical Scripture, on account of its difficulties. Let us beware, on the other side, of that dogmatical and arrogant spirit, which makes men forget that they are students, and talk as confidently as if they were prophets themselves. Above all, let us read prophetical Scripture with a thorough conviction that the study carries with it a blessing, and that more light may be expected on it every year. The promise remains in full force, "Blessed is he that reads." At the time of the end, the vision shall be unsealed. (Rev. 13; Dan. 12:9.)

LUKE 21:10-19

Then said he unto them, Nation shall rise against nation, and kingdom against kingdom; and there shall be great earthquakes, and in divers places famines and pestilences; and there shall be terrors and great signs from heaven. But before all these things, they shall lay their hands on you, and shall persecute you, delivering you up to the synagogues and prisons, bringing you before kings and governors for my name's sake. It shall turn out unto you for a testimony. Settle it therefore in your hearts, not to meditate beforehand how to answer: for I will give you a mouth and wisdom, which all your adversaries shall not be able to withstand or to gainsay. But ye shall be delivered up even by parents, and brethren, and kinsfolk, and friends; and some of you shall they cause to be put to death. And ye shall be hated of all men for my name's sake. And not a hair of your head shall perish. In your patience ye shall win your souls.

We should notice, for one thing, in this passage, Christ's prediction concerning the nations of the world. He says, "Nation shall rise against nation, and kingdom against kingdom—and great earthquakes shall be in diverse places, and famines and pestilences—and fearful sights, and great signs shall there be from heaven."

These words no doubt received a partial fulfillment in the days when Jerusalem was taken by the Romans, and the Jews were led into captivity. It was a season of unparalleled desolation to Judea, and the countries round about Judea. The last days of the Jewish dispensation were wound up by a struggle which for bloodshed, misery, and tribulation, has never been equaled since the world began.

But the words before us have yet to receive a more complete accomplishment. They describe the time which shall immediately precede the second advent of Jesus Christ. The "time of the end" shall be a time of war, and not of universal peace. The Christian dispensation shall pass away like the Jewish one, amid wars, tumults, and desolation, amid a general crash of empires and kingdoms, such as the eyes of man have never yet seen.

A thorough understanding of these things is of great importance to our souls. Nothing is so calculated to chill the heart and dampen the faith of a Christian as indulgence in unscriptural expectations. Let us dismiss from our minds the vain idea that nations will ever give up wars entirely, before Jesus Christ comes again. So long as the devil is the prince of this world, and the hearts of the many are unconverted, so long there must be strife and fighting. There will be no universal peace before the second advent of the Prince of peace. Then, and then only, men shall "learn war no more." (Isaiah 2:4.)

Let us cease to expect that missionaries and ministers will ever convert the world, and teach all mankind to love one another. They will do nothing of the kind. They were never intended to do it. They will call out a witnessing people who shall serve Christ in every land, but they will do no more. The bulk of mankind will always refuse to obey the Gospel. The nations will always go on quarreling, wrangling, and fighting. The last days of the earth shall be its worst days. The last war shall be the most fearful and terrible war that ever desolated the earth.

The duty of the true Christian is clear and plain. Whatever others do, he must give all diligence to make his own calling and election sure. While other are occupied in national conflicts and political speculations, he must steadily seek first the kingdom of God. So doing he shall feel his feet upon a rock when the foundations of the earth are out of course, and the kingdoms of this earth are going to ruin. He shall be like Noah, safe within the ark. He shall be "hidden in the day of the Lord's anger." (Zeph. 2:3.)

We should notice, for another thing, in this passage, Christ's prediction concerning His own disciples. He does not prophesy smooth things, and promise them an uninterrupted course of temporal comfort. He says that they shall be "persecuted," put in "prison," "brought before kings and rulers," "betrayed," "put to death," and "hated of all men for His name's sake."

The words of this prophecy were doubtless intended to apply to every age of the Church of Christ. They began to be fulfilled in the days of the apostles. The book of Acts supplies us with many an instance of their fulfillment. They have been repeatedly fulfilled during the last eighteen hundred years. Wherever there have been disciples of Christ, there has always been more or less persecution. They will yet receive a more full accomplishment before the end comes. The last tribulation will probably be marked by special violence and bitterness. It will be a "great tribulation." (Rev. 7:14.)

Let it be a settled principle in our minds that the true Christian must always enter the kingdom of God "through much tribulation." (Acts 14:22.) His best things are yet to come. This world is not our home. If we are faithful and decided servants of Christ, the world will certainly hate us, as it hated our Master. In one way or another grace will always be persecuted. No consistency of conduct, however faultless, no kindness and amiability of character, however striking, will exempt a believer from the world's dislike, so long as he lives. It is foolish to be surprised at this. It is mere waste of time to murmur at it. It is a part of the cross, and we must bear it patiently. The children of Cain will hate the children of Abel, as long as the earth continues. "Marvel not, my brethren," says John, "if the world hates you." "If you were of the world," says our Lord, "the world would love his own; but because you are not of the world, but I have chosen you out of the world, therefore the world hates you." (1 John 3:13; John 15:18, 19.)

We should notice, lastly, in this passage, Christ's gracious promise to His disciples. He says, "but not a hair of your head shall perish." Our blessed Lord knew well the hearts of His disciples. He saw that the prophecy He had just spoken might well make them faint. He supplies them with a cheering word of encouragement—"Not a hair of your head shall perish."

The promise before us is wide and comprehensive, and one which is the property of all believers in every age. A literal interpretation of it is clearly impossible. It cannot apply to the bodies of disciples. To say that would be contradictory to the notorious fact that James and other of the apostles died violent deaths. A figurative interpretation must evidently be placed upon the words. They form a great proverbial saying. They teach us that whatever sufferings a disciple of Christ may go through, his best things can never be injured. His life is hidden with Christ in God. His treasure in heaven can never be touched. His soul is beyond the reach of harm. Even his vile body shall be raised again, and made like his Savior's glorious body at the last day.

If we know anything of true religion let us lean back on the words of the glorious promises in every time of need. If we believe in Christ, let us rest in the comfortable thought that Christ has pledged His word that we shall not perish. We may lose much by serving Christ, but we shall never lose our souls. The world may deprive a believer of property, friends, country, home, liberty, health, and life. It has done so in innumerable cases from the days of Stephen to the present time. The roll of the noble army of martyrs is a very long one. But one thing the world cannot do to any believer. It cannot deprive him of his interest in Christ's love. It cannot break the union between Christ and his soul. Surely it is worthwhile to be a thorough-going believer! "I am persuaded," says Paul, "that neither death, nor life, nor angels, nor principalities, nor powers, nor things present, nor things to come, nor height, nor depth, nor any other creature shall be able to separate me from the love of God, which is in Christ Jesus our Lord." (Rom. 8:38-39.)

LUKE 21:20-24

THE DESTRUCTION OF JERUSALEM

But when ye see Jerusalem compassed with armies, then know that her desolation is at hand. Then let them that are in Judaea flee unto the mountains; and let them that are in the midst of her depart out; and let not them that are in the country enter therein. For these are days of vengeance, that all things which are written may be fulfilled. Woe unto them that are with child and to them that give suck in those days! for there shall be great distress upon the land, and wrath unto this people. And they shall fall by the edge of the sword, and shall be led captive into all the nations: and Jerusalem shall be trodden down of the Gentiles, until the times of the Gentiles be fulfilled.

The subject of the verses before us is the taking of Jerusalem by the Romans. It was fit and right that this great event, which wound up the Old Testament dispensation, should be specially described by our Lord's mouth. It was fitting that the last days of that holy city, which had been the seat of God's presence for so many centuries, should receive a special notice in the greatest prophecy which was ever delivered to the Church.

We should mark in this passage, our Lord Jesus Christ's perfect knowledge. He gives us a fearful picture of the miseries which were coming on

Jerusalem. Forty years before the armies of Titus encompassed the city, the dreadful circumstances which would attend the siege are minutely described. The distress of weak and helpless women—the slaughter of myriads of Jews—the final scattering of Israel in captivity among all nations—the treading down of the holy city by the Gentiles for eighteen hundred years, are things which our Lord narrates with as much particularity as if He saw them with His own eyes.

Foreknowledge like this is a special attribute of God. Of ourselves we "know not what a day may bring forth." (Prov. 27:1.) To say what will happen to any city or kingdom in forty years from the present time, is far beyond the power of man. The words in Isaiah are very solemn—"I am God, and there is none like me, declaring the end from the beginning, and from ancient times the things that are not yet done." (Isa. 46:10.) He who could speak with authority of things to come, as our Lord did in this place, must have been very God as well as very man.

The true Christian should continually keep in mind this perfect knowledge of Christ. Past things, present things, and things to come, are all naked and open to the eyes of Him with whom we have to do. The recollection of the sins of youth may well make us humble. The sense of present weakness may make us anxious. The fear of trials yet to come may make our hearts faint. But it is a strong consolation to think that Christ knows all. For past, present, and future things we may safely trust Him. Nothing can ever happen to us that Christ has not known long ago.

We should mark, secondly, in this passage, our Lord's words about flight in time of danger. He says respecting the days preceding the siege of Jerusalem, "Then let those who are in Judea flee to the mountains; and let those who are in the midst of it depart out; and let not those who are in the countries enter thereunto."

The lesson of these words is very instructive. They teach us plainly that there is nothing cowardly or unworthy of a Christian in endeavoring to escape from danger. There is nothing unbecoming our high vocation in a diligent use of means in order to secure our safety. To meet death patiently and courageously, if it comes on us in the path of God's providence, is a duty incumbent on every believer. But to court death and suffering, and rush needlessly into danger, is the part of the fanatic and enthusiast, not of the wise disciple of Christ. It is those who use all means which God has placed within their reach, who may confidently expect God's protection. There is a wide difference between presumption and faith.

We should mark, thirdly, in this passage, our Lord's words about vengeance. He says, with reference to the siege of Jerusalem, "These are the days of vengeance (punishment), that all things which are written may be fulfilled."

There is something peculiarly dreadful in this expression. It shows us that the sins of the Jewish nation had been long noted down in the book of God's remembrance. The Jews by their unbelief and impenitence, had been treasuring up wrath against themselves for many hundred years. The anger of God, like a pent-up river, had been silently accumulating for ages. The fearful tribulation which attended the siege of Jerusalem, would only be the outburst of a thunderstorm which had been gradually gathering since the days of the kings. It would only be the fall of a sword which had been long hanging over Israel's head.

The lesson of the expression is one which we shall do well to lay to heart. We must never allow ourselves to suppose that the conduct of wicked men or nations is not observed by God. All is seen, and all is known; and a reckoning day will certainly arrive at last. It is a mighty truth of Scripture, that "God requires that which is past." (Eccles. 3:15.) In the days of Abraham "the iniquity of the Amorites was not yet full," and four hundred years passed away before they were punished. Yet punishment came at last, when Joshua and the twelve tribes of Israel took possession of Canaan. God's "sentence against an evil work" is not always executed speedily, but it does not follow that it will not be executed at all. The wicked may flourish for many years "like a green bay-tree," but his latter end will be that his sin will find him out. (Gen. 15:16; Eccles. 8:11; Psalm 37:35.)

We should mark, lastly, in this passage, our Lord's words about the times of the Gentiles. We read that He said, "Jerusalem shall be trodden down by the Gentiles, until the times of the Gentiles be fulfilled."

A fixed period is here foretold, during which Jerusalem was to be given over into the hands of Gentile rulers, and the Jews were to have no dominion over their ancient city. A fixed period is likewise foretold which was to be the time of the Gentiles' visitation, the time during which they were to enjoy privileges, and occupy a position something like that of Israel in ancient days. Both periods are one day to end. Jerusalem is to be once more restored to its ancient inhabitants. The Gentiles, because of their hardness and unbelief, are to be stripped of their privileges and endure the just judgments of God. But the times of the Gentiles are not yet run out. We ourselves are living within them at the present day.

The subject before us is a very affecting one, and ought to raise within us great searchings of heart. While the nations of Europe are absorbed in political conflicts and worldly business, the sands in their hour-glass are ebbing away. While Governments are disputing about secular things, and Parliaments can hardly condescend to find a place for religion in their discussions, their days are numbered in the sight of God. Yet a few years, and "the times of the Gentiles will be fulfilled." Their day of visitation will be past and gone. Their misused privileges will be taken away. The judgments of God shall fall on them. They shall be cast aside as vessels in which God has no pleasure. Their dominion shall crumble away, and their vaunted institutions shall fall to pieces. The Jews shall be restored. The Lord Jesus shall come again in power and great glory. The kingdoms of this world shall become the kingdoms of our God and of His Christ, and the "times of the Gentiles" shall come to an end.

Happy is he who knows these things and lives the life of faith in the Son of God! He is the man, and he only, who is ready for the great things coming on the earth, and the appearing of the Lord Jesus Christ. The kingdom to which he belongs, is the only kingdom which shall never be destroyed. The King whom he serves, is the only King whose dominion shall never be taken away. (Dan 2:44; 7:14.)

LUKE 21:25-33
THE SECOND COMING OF CHRIST

And there shall be signs in sun and moon and stars; and upon the earth distress of nations, in perplexity for the roaring of the sea and the billows; men fainting for fear, and for expectation of the things which are coming on the world: for the powers of the heavens shall be shaken. And then shall they see the Son of man coming in a cloud with power and great glory. But when these things begin to come to pass, look up, and lift up your heads; because your redemption draweth nigh.

And he spake to them a parable: Behold the fig tree, and all the trees: when they now shoot forth, ye see it and know of your own selves that the summer is now nigh. Even so ye also, when ye see these things coming to pass, know ye that the kingdom of God is nigh. Verily I say unto you, This generation shall not pass away, till all things be accomplished. Heaven and earth shall pass away: but my words shall not pass away.

The subject of this portion of our Lord's great prophecy is His own second coming to judge the world. The strong expressions of the passage appear inapplicable to any event less important than this. To confine the words before us, to the taking of Jerusalem by the Romans, in an unnatural straining of Scripture language.

We see, firstly, in this passage, how terrible will be the circumstances accompanying the second advent of Christ. Our Lord tells us that "there will be signs in the sun, moon and stars. On the earth, nations will be in anguish and perplexity at the roaring and tossing of the sea. Men will faint from terror, apprehensive of what is coming on the world, for the heavenly bodies will be shaken. At that time they will see the Son of Man coming in a cloud with power and great glory."

This is a singularly dreadful picture. It may not be easy perhaps to attach a precise meaning to every part of it. One thing however, is abundantly plain. The second coming of Christ will be attended by everything which can make it alarming to the senses and heart of man. If the giving of the law at Sinai was so terrible that even Moses said, "I exceedingly fear and quake," the return of Christ when He comes to earth in power and great glory shall be much more terrible. If the hardy Roman soldiers "became as dead men," when an angel rolled the stone away and Christ rose again, how much greater will the terror be when Christ shall return to judge the world. No wonder that Paul said, "Knowing the terrors of the Lord we persuade men." (Heb. 12:21; Matt. 28:4; 2 Cor. 5:11.)

The thoughtless and impenitent man may well tremble when he hears of this second advent of Christ. What will he do when worldly business is suddenly stopped and the precious things of the world are made worthless? What will he do when the graves on every side are opening, and the trumpet is summoning men to judgment? What will he do when that same Jesus whose Gospel he has so shamefully neglected shall appear in the clouds of heaven, and put down every enemy under His feet? Surely he will call on the rocks to fall on him and on the hills to cover him. (Hosea 10:8.) But he will call in vain for help, if he has never called on Christ before. Happy will they be in that day who have fled beforehand from the wrath to come, and been washed in the blood of the Lamb!

We see, secondly, in this passage, how complete will be the security of true Christians at the second advent of Christ. We read that our Lord said to His disciples, "When these things begin to come to pass, then look up, and lift up your heads; for your redemption draws near."

386 | J.C. RYLE

However terrible the signs of Christ's second coming may be to the impenitent, they need not strike terror into the heart of the true believer. They ought rather to fill him with joy. They ought to remind him that his complete deliverance from sin, the world and the devil, is close at hand, and that he shall soon bid an eternal farewell to sickness, sorrow, death and temptation. The very day when the unconverted man shall lose everything, shall be the day when the believer shall enter on his eternal reward. The very hour when the worldly man's hopes shall perish, shall be the hour when the believer's hope shall be exchanged for joyful certainty and full possession.

The servant of God should often look forward to Christ's second advent. He will find the thought of that day a cordial to sustain him under all the trials and persecutions of this present life. "Yet a little while," let him remember, "and he that shall come will come and will not tarry." The words of Isaiah shall be fulfilled, "The Lord God shall wipe away tears from off all faces; and the rebuke of his people shall be taken away from off all the earth." One sure receipt for a patient spirit is to expect little from this world, and to be ever "waiting for the coming of our Lord Jesus Christ." (Heb. 10:37. Isaiah. 25:8. 1 Cor. 1:7.)

We see, thirdly, in this passage, how needful it is to watch the signs of the times in the prospect of the second advent of Christ. Our Lord teaches this lesson by a parable—"Notice the fig tree, or any other tree. When the leaves come out, you know without being told that summer is near. Just so, when you see the events I've described taking place, you can be sure that the Kingdom of God is near." The disciples ignorantly supposed that Messiah's kingdom would be ushered in by universal peace. Our Lord, on the contrary, tells those who the signs which shall immediately precede it shall be wars, confusions, perplexity, and distress.

The general duty which these words should teach us is very plain. We are to observe carefully the public events of the times in which we live. We are not to be absorbed in politics, but we are to mark political events. We are not to turn prophets ourselves, but we are to study diligently the signs of our times. So doing, the day of Christ will not come upon us entirely unawares.

Are there any signs in our own day? Are there any circumstances in the world around us which specially demand the believer's attention? Beyond doubt there are very many. The drying up of the Turkish empire—the revival of the Romish church—the awakened desire of the Protestant churches to preach the Gospel to the heathen—the general interest in the state of the Jews—the universal shaking of governments and established institutions—the rise and progress of the subtlest forms of infidelity—all, all are signs peculiar to our day. All should make us remember our Lord's words about the fig-tree. All should make us think of the text, "Behold, I come quickly." (Rev. 22:7.)

We see, lastly, in this passage, how certain it is that all our Lord's predictions about the second advent will be fulfilled. Our Lord speaks as if He foresaw the unbelief and incredulity of man on this mighty subject. He knew how ready people would be to say "Improbable! impossible! The world will always go on as it has done." He arms His disciples against the infection of this skeptical spirit by a very solemn saying. "Heaven and earth shall pass away—but my words shall not pass away."

We shall do well to remember this saying, whenever we are thrown into the company of those who sneer at unfulfilled prophecy. The sneers of unbelievers must not be allowed to shake our faith. If God has said a thing He will certainly bring it to pass, and the probability or possibility of it are matters which need not trouble us for a moment. That Christ should come again in power to judge the world and reign, is not half so improbable as it was that Christ should come to suffer and die. If He came the first time, much more may we expect that He will come the second time. If he came to be nailed to the cross, much more may we expect that He will come in glory and wear the crown. He has said it, and He will do it. "His words shall not pass away."

Let us turn from the study of these verses with a deep conviction that the second advent of Christ is one of the leading truths of Christianity. Let the Christ in whom we believe be not only the Christ who suffered on Calvary, but the Christ who is coming again in person to judge the earth.

LUKE 21:34-38

WATCH AND PRAY

But take heed to yourselves, lest haply your hearts be overcharged with surfeiting, and drunkenness, and cares of this life, and that day come on you suddenly as a snare: for so shall it come upon all them that dwell on the face of all the earth. But watch ye at every season, making supplication, that ye may prevail to escape all these things that shall come to pass, and to stand before the Son of man. And every day he was teaching in the temple; and every night he went out, and lodged in the mount that is called Olivet. And all the people came early in the morning to him in the temple, to hear him.

These verses form the practical conclusion of our Lord Jesus Christ's great prophetical discourse. They supply a striking answer to those who condemn the study of unfulfilled prophecy as speculative and unprofitable. It would be difficult to find a passage more practical, direct, plain, and heart-searching than that which is now before our eyes.

Let us learn from these verses, the spiritual danger to which even the holiest believers are exposed in this world. Our Lord says to His disciples, "Watch out! Don't let me find you living in careless ease and drunkenness, and filled with the worries of this life. Don't let that day catch you unaware, as in a trap." These words are exceedingly startling. They were not addressed to carnalminded Pharisees, or skeptical Sadducees, or worldly Herodians. They were addressed to Peter, James, and John, and the whole company of the Apostles. They were addressed to men who had given up everything for Christ's sake, and had proved the reality of their faith by loving obedience and steady adhesion to their Master. Yet even to them our Lord holds out the peril of surfeiting, and drunkenness, and worldliness! Even to them He says, "Watch out!"

The exhortation before us should teach us the immense importance of humility. There is no sin so great but a great saint may fall into it. There is no saint so great but he may fall into a great sin. Noah escaped the pollutions of the world before the flood; and yet he was afterwards overtaken by drunkenness. Abraham was the father of the faithful; and yet through unbelief he said falsely that Sarah was his sister. Lot did not take part in the horrible wickedness of Sodom; and yet he afterwards fell into foul sin in the cave. Moses was the meekest man on earth; and yet he so lost self-control that he spoke angrily and unadvisedly. David was a man after God's own heart; and yet he plunged into most heinous adultery. These examples are all deeply instructive. They all show the wisdom of our Lord's warning in the passage before us. They teach us to be "clothed with humility." "Let him that thinks he stands, take heed lest he fall." (1 Pet. 5:5; 1 Cor. 10:12.)

The exhortation before us should teach us furthermore the great importance of an unworldly spirit. The "cares of this life" are placed side by side with surfeiting and drunkenness. Excess in eating and drinking is not the only excess which injures the soul. There is an excessive anxiety about the innocent things of this life, which is just as ruinous to our spiritual prosperity, and just as poisonous to the inner man. Never, never let us forget that we may make spiritual shipwreck on lawful things, as really and truly as on open vices. Happy is he who has learned to hold the things of this world with a loose hand, and to believe that seeking first the kingdom of God, "all other things shall be added to him!" (Matt. 6:33.)

Let us learn secondly from these verses, the exceeding suddenness of our Lord's second coming. We read that "as a trap shall it come on all those who dwell on the face of the whole earth." As a trap falling suddenly on an animal, and catching it in a moment—as the lightning flash shining suddenly in heaven, before the thunder is heard—as a thief coming suddenly in the night, and not giving notice that he will come—so sudden, so instantaneous will the second advent of the Son of man be.

The precise date of our Lord Jesus Christ's return to this world has been purposely withheld from us by God. "Of that day and hour knows no man." On one point however all the teaching of Scripture about it is clear and unmistakable. Whenever it shall take place, it shall be a most sudden and unexpected event. The business of the world shall be going on as usual. As in the days of Sodom, and the days before the flood, men shall be "eating and drinking, marrying and given in marriage." Few, even among true believers, shall be found completely alive to the great fact, and living in a state of thorough expectation. In a moment, in the twinkling of an eye, the whole course of the world shall be stopped. The King of kings shall appear. The dead shall be raised. The living shall be changed. Unbelief shall wither away. Truth shall be known by myriads too late. The world with all its trifles and shadows shall be thrust aside. Eternity with all its dreadful realities shall begin. All this shall begin at once, without notice, without warning, without note of preparation. "As a trap shall it come on the face of the whole earth."

The servant of God must surely see that there is only one state of mind which becomes the man who believes these things. That state is one of perpetual preparedness to meet Christ. The Gospel does not call on us to retire from earthly callings, or neglect the duties of our stations. It does not bid us retire into hermitages, or live the life of a monk or a nun. But it does bid us to live like men who expect their Lord to return. Repentance toward God, faith toward our Lord Jesus Christ, and holiness of conversation, are the only true habitual preparedness required. The Christian who knows these things by experience, is the man who is always ready to meet his Lord.

Let us learn, lastly, from these verses, the special duties of believers in the prospect of the second advent of Christ. Our Lord sums up these duties under two great heads. One of these two is watchfulness. The other is prayer. "Watch therefore," He says, "and pray always." We are to "watch." We are to live on our guard like men in an enemy's country. We are to remember that evil is about us, and near us, and in us—that we have to contend daily with a treacherous heart, an ensnaring world, and a busy devil. Remembering this, we must put on the whole armor of God, and beware of spiritual drowsiness. "Let us not sleep as do others," says Paul, "but let us watch and be sober." (1 Thess. 5:6.)

We are to "pray always." We are to keep up a constant habit of real, businesslike prayer. We are to speak with God daily, and hold daily communion with Him about our souls. We are to pray specially for grace to lay aside every weight, and to cast away everything which may interfere with readiness to meet our Lord. Above all, we are to watch our habits of devotion with a godly jealousy, and to beware of hurrying over or shortening our prayers.

Let us leave the whole passage with a hearty determination, by God's help, to action what we have been reading. If we believe that Christ is coming again, let us get ready to meet Him. "If we know there things, happy are we if we do them." (John 13:17.)

Chapter 22

LUKE 22:1-13

THE LAST SUPPER

Now the feast of unleavened bread drew nigh, which is called the Passover. And the chief priests and the scribes sought how they might put him to death; for they feared the people. And Satan entered into Judas who was called Iscariot, being of the number of the twelve. And he went away, and communed with the chief priests and captains, how he might deliver him unto them. And they were glad, and covenanted to give him money. And he consented, and sought opportunity to deliver him unto them in the absence of the multitude.

And the day of unleavened bread came, on which the passover must be sacrificed. And he sent Peter and John, saying, Go and make ready for us the passover, that we may eat. And they said unto him, Where wilt thou that we make ready? And he said unto them, Behold, when ye are entered into the city, there shall meet you a man bearing a pitcher of water; follow him into the house whereinto he goeth. And ye shall say unto the master of the house, The Teacher saith unto thee, Where is the guestchamber, where I shall eat the passover with my disciples? And he will show you a large upper room furnished: there make ready. And they went, and found as he had said unto them: and they made ready the passover.

The chapter which opens with these verses, begins Luke's account of our Lord's sufferings and death. No part of the Gospels is so important as this. The death of Christ was the life of the world. No part of our Lord's history is so fully given by all the gospel writers as this. Only two of them describe the circumstances of Christ's birth. All four dwell minutely on Christ's death. And of all the four, no one supplies us with such full and interesting details as Luke.

We see, firstly, in these verses, that high offices in the church do not preserve the holders of them from great blindness and sin. We read that "the chief priests and scribes sought how they might kill Jesus."

The first step in putting Christ to death, was taken by the religious teachers of the Jewish nation. The very men who ought to have welcomed the Messiah, were the men who conspired to kill Him. The very pastors who ought to have rejoiced at the appearing of the Lamb of God, had the chief hand in slaying Him. They sat in Moses' seat. They claimed to be "guides of the blind," and "lights of those who were in darkness." (Rom. 2:19.) They belonged to the tribe of Levi. They were, most of them, in direct succession and descent from Aaron. Yet they were the very men who crucified the Lord of glory! With all their boasted knowledge, they were far more ignorant than the few Galilean fishermen who followed Christ.

Let us beware of attaching an excessive importance to ministers of religion because of their office. Ordination and office confer no exemption from error. The greatest heresies have been sown, and the greatest practical abuses introduced into the church by ordained men. Respect is undoubtedly due to high official position. Order and discipline ought not to be forgotten. The teaching and counsel of regularly appointed teachers ought not to be lightly refused. But there are limits beyond which we must not go. We must never allow the blind to lead us into the ditch. We must never allow modern chief priests and scribes to make us crucify Christ afresh. We must test all teachers by the unerring rule of the Word of God. It matters little who says a thing in religion—but it matters greatly what it is that is said. Is it scriptural? Is it true? This is the only question. "To the law and to the testimony—if they speak not according to this word, it is because there is no light in them." (Isaiah 8:20.)

We see, secondly, in these verses, how far men may fall after making a high profession. We read that the second step toward our Lord's crucifixion, was the treachery of one of the twelve apostles—"Then entered Satan into Judas Iscariot, being of the number of the twelve." These words are peculiarly dreadful. To be tempted by Satan is bad enough. To be sifted, buffeted, led captive by him is truly terrible. But when Satan "enters into a man," and dwells in him, the man becomes indeed a child of hell.

Judas Iscariot ought to be a standing beacon to the church of Christ. This man, be it remembered, was one of our Lord's chosen apostles. He followed our Lord during the whole course of His ministry. He forsook all for Christ's sake. He heard Christ preach and saw Christ's miracles. He preached himself. He spoke like the other apostles. There was nothing about him to distinguish him from Peter, James, and John. He was never suspected of being unsound at heart. And yet this man turns out at length a hypocrite, betrays his Master, helps his enemies to deliver Him up to death, and dies himself "the son of perdition." (John 17:12.) These are fearful things. But they are true.

Let the recollection of Judas Iscariot constrain every professing, Christian to pray much for humility. Let us often say, "Search me, O God, and know my heart—try me, and know my thoughts." (Psalm. 139:23.) At best we have but a faint conception of the deceitfulness of our hearts. The lengths to which men may go in religion, and yet be without grace, is far greater than we suppose.

We see, thirdly, in these verses, the enormous power of the love of money. We are told that when Judas went to the chief priests and offered to betray his Master, they "agreed to give him money." That little sentence reveals the secret of this wretched man's fall. He was fond of money, He had doubtless heard our Lord's solemn warning, "Take heed and beware of covetousness." (Luke 12:15.) But he had either forgotten it, or given it no heed. Covetousness was the rock on which he made shipwreck. Covetousness was the ruin of his soul.

We need not wonder that Paul called the love of money "the root of all evil." (1 Tim. 6:10.) The history of the church is full of mournful proofs, that it is one of the choicest weapons of Satan for corrupting and spoiling professors of religion. Gehazi, Ananias and Sapphira are names which naturally occur to our minds. But of all proofs, there is none so melancholy as the one before us. For money a chosen apostle sold the best and most loving of Masters! For money Judas Iscariot betrayed Christ!

Let us watch and pray against the love of money. It is a subtle disease, and often far nearer to us than we suppose. A poor man is just as liable to it as a rich man. It is possible to love money without having it, and it is possible to have it without loving it. Let us be "content with such things as we have." (Heb. 13:5.) We never know what we might do if we became suddenly rich. It is a striking fact, that there is only one prayer in all the Book of Proverbs, and that one of the three petitions in that prayer, is the wise request—"Give me neither poverty nor riches." (Prov. 30:8.)

We see, lastly, in these verses, the close connection between our Lord Jesus Christ's death and the Feast of the Passover. Four times we are reminded here that the evening before His crucifixion was the time of the great Jewish feast. It was "the day when the Passover lamb must be killed."

We cannot doubt that the time of our Lord's crucifixion was overruled by God. His perfect wisdom and controlling power arranged that the Lamb of God should die, at the very time when the passover-lamb was being slain. The death of Christ was the fulfillment of the passover. He was the true sacrifice to which every passover-lamb had been pointing for 1500 years. What the death of the lamb had been to Israel in Egypt, His death was to be to sinners all over the world. The safety which the blood of the passover-lamb had provided for Israel, His blood was to provide far more abundantly for all that believed in Him.

Let us never forget the sacrificial character of Christ's death. Let us reject with abhorrence the modern notion that it was nothing more than a mighty instance of self-sacrifice and self-denial. It was this no doubt—but it was something far higher, deeper, and more important than this. It was a propitiation for the sins of the world. It was an atonement for man's transgression. It was the killing of the true passover Lamb, through whose death destruction is warded off from sinners believing on Him. "Christ our passover Lamb," says Paul, "is sacrificed for us." (1 Cor. 5:7.) Let us grasp that truth firmly, and never let it go.

LUKE 22:14-23
THE LAST SUPPER

And when the hour was come, he sat down, and the apostles with him. And he said unto them, With desire I have desired to eat this passover with you before I suffer: for I say unto you, I shall not eat it, until it be fulfilled in the kingdom of God. And he received a cup, and when he had given thanks, he said, Take this, and divide it among yourselves: for I say unto you, I shall not drink from henceforth of the fruit of the vine, until the kingdom of God shall come. And he took bread, and when he had given thanks, he brake it, and gave to them, saying, This is my body which is given for you: this do in remembrance of me. And the cup in like manner after supper, saying, This cup is the new covenant in my blood, even that which is poured out for you.

But behold, the hand of him that betrayeth me is with me on the table. For the Son of man indeed goeth, as it hath been determined: but woe unto that man through whom he is betrayed! And they began to question among themselves, which of them it was that should do this thing.

These verses contain Luke's account of the institution of the Lord's supper. It is a passage which every true Christian will always read with deep interest. How astonishing it seems that an ordinance, so beautifully simple at its first appointment, should have been obscured and mystified by man's inventions! What a painful proof it is of human corruption, that some of the bitterest controversies which have disturbed the Church, have been concerning the table of the Lord. Great indeed is the ingenuity of man, in perverting God's gifts! The ordinance that should have been for his wealth is too often made an occasion of falling.

We should notice, for one thing in these verses, that the principal object of the Lord's supper was to remind Christians of Christ's death for sinners. In appointing the Lord's supper, Jesus distinctly tells His disciples that they were to do what they did, "in remembrance of him." In one word, the Lord's supper is not a sacrifice. It is eminently a commemorative ordinance.

The bread that the believer eats, at the Lord's table, is intended to remind him of Christ's body given to death on the cross for his sins. The wine that he drinks is intended to remind him of Christ's blood shed to make atonement for his transgressions. The whole ordinance was meant to keep fresh in his memory the sacrifice of Christ on the cross, and the satisfaction which that sacrifice made for the sin of the world. The two elements of bread and wine were intended to preach Christ crucified as our substitute under lively emblems. They were to be a visible sermon, appealing to the believer's senses, and teaching the old foundation-truth of the Gospel, that Christ's death on the cross is the life of man's soul.

We shall do well to keep steadily in view this simple view of the Lord's supper. That a special blessing is attached to a worthy use of it, as well to the worthy use of every ordinance appointed by Christ, there is of course no doubt. But that there is any other means by which Christians can eat Christ's body, and drink Christ's blood excepting by faith, we must always steadily deny. He that comes to the Lord's table with faith in Christ, may confidently expect to have his faith increased by receiving the bread and wine. But he that comes without faith has no right to expect a blessing. Empty he comes to the ordinance and empty he will go away.

The less mystery and obscurity we attach to the Lord's supper, the better will it be for our souls. We should reject with abhorrence the unscriptural notion that there is any oblation or sacrifice in it—that the substance of the bread and wine is at all changed—or that the mere formal act of receiving the sacrament can do any good to the soul.

We should cling firmly to the great principle laid down at its institution, that it is eminently a commemorative ordinance, and that reception of it without faith and a thankful remembrance of Christ's death can do us no good. The words of the Church Catechism are wise and true—"It was ordained for the continual remembrance of the sacrifice of the death of Christ." The declaration of the Articles is clear and distinct—"The means whereby the body of Christ is received and taken in the supper, is faith." The exhortation of the Prayer-Book points out the only way in which we can feed on Christ—"Feed on Him in your hearts by faith with thanksgiving." Last, but not least, the caution of the Homily is most instructive—"Let us take heed, lest of the memory it be made a sacrifice."

We should notice, for another thing, in these verses, that the observance of the Lord's Supper is a duty binding on all true Christians. The words of our Lord on this point are direct and emphatic—"Do this in remembrance of me." To suppose, as some do, that these words are only an injunction to the apostles and all ministers to administer the Lord's Supper to others, is a thoroughly unsatisfactory interpretation. The obvious sense of the words is a general precept to all disciples.

The command before us is overlooked to a fearful extent. Myriads of members of Christian churches never go to the Lord's table. They would be ashamed perhaps to be known as open breakers of the ten commandments. Yet they are not ashamed of breaking a plain command of Christ! They appear to think there is no great sin in not being communicants. They seem utterly unconscious that if they had lived in the days of the apostles they would not have been reckoned Christians at all.

The subject no doubt is one on which we must beware of mistakes. It is not, of course, to be desired that every baptized person should receive the Lord's Supper as a mere matter of form. It is an ordinance which was intended for the living, and not for the dead in sins. But when we see vast numbers of church-goers never going to the Lord's table, and no way ashamed of their neglect of the sacrament, it is clear that there is something very wrong in the state of the churches. It is a sign either of wide-spread ignorance, or of callous indifference to a divine precept. When such multitudes of baptized people habitually break a command of Christ, we cannot doubt that Christ is displeased.

What are we doing ourselves? This, after all, is the point that concerns us. Do we stay away from the Lord's Supper under a vague notion that there is no great necessity for receiving it? If we hold such an opinion, the sooner we give it up the better. A plain precept of God's own Son is not to be trifled with in this way. Do we stay away from the Lord's Supper because we are not fit to be communicants? If we do, let us thoroughly understand that we are not fit to die. Unfit for the Lord's table, we are unfit for heaven, and unprepared for the judgment day, and not ready to meet God! Surely this is a most serious state of things. But the words before us are clear and explicit. Christ gives us a plain command. If we wilfully disobey it, we are in danger of ruining our souls. If we are not fit to obey it, we ought to repent without delay.

Let us notice, lastly, WHO were the communicants at the first appointment of the Lord's Supper. They were not all holy. They were not all believers. Luke informs us that the traitor, Judas Iscariot, was one of them. The words of our Lord admit of no other fair interpretation. "Behold," He says, "the hand of him that betrays me is with me on the table."

The lesson of these words is deeply important. They show us that we must not regard all communicants as true believers and sincere servants of Christ. The evil and good will be found side by side even at the Lord's Supper. No discipline can possibly prevent it. They show us furthermore that it is foolish to stay away from the Lord's Supper because some communicants are unconverted, or to leave a church because some of its members are unsound. The wheat and the tares will grow together until the harvest. Our Lord himself tolerated a Judas at the first communion that ever took place. The servant of God must not pretend to be more exclusive than his Master. Let him see to his own heart, and leave others to answer for themselves to God.

And now, if we are not communicants, let us ask ourselves, as we leave this passage, "Why are we not? What satisfactory reason can we possibly give for neglecting a plain command of Christ?" May we never rest, until we have looked this inquiry in the face! If we are communicants, let us take heed that we receive the sacrament worthily. "The sacraments have a wholesome effect and operation in those only, who worthily receive them." Let us often enquire whether we repent, and believe, and strive to live holy lives.

So living we need not be afraid, to eat of that bread and drink of that cup, which the Lord has commanded to be received.

LUKE 22:24-30

WHO IS THE GREATEST?

And there arose also a contention among them, which of them was accounted to be greatest. And he said unto them, The kings of the Gentiles have lordship over them; and they that have authority over them are called Benefactors. But ye shall not be so: but he that is the greater among you, let him become as the younger; and he that is chief, as he that doth serve. For which is greater, he that sitteth at meat, or he that serveth? is not he that sitteth at meat? but I am in the midst of you as he that serveth. But ye are they that have continued with me in my temptations; and I appoint unto you a kingdom, even as my Father appointed unto me, that ye may eat and drink at my table in my kingdom; and ye shall sit on thrones judging the twelve tribes of Israel.

Let us observe, in this passage, how firmly pride and love of preeminence can stick to the hearts of Christian men. We are told that "There was a dispute among the disciples, as to which of them should be considered the greatest." The strife was one which had been rebuked by our Lord on a former occasion. The ordinance which the disciples had just been receiving, and the circumstances under which they were assembled, made the strife peculiarly inappropriate. And yet at this very season, the last quiet time they could spend with their Master before His death, this little flock begins a dispute, as to who should be the greatest! Such is the heart of man, ever weak, ever deceitful, ever ready, even at its best times, to turn aside to what is evil.

The sin before us is a very old one. Ambition, self-esteem, and self-conceit lie deep at the bottom of all men's hearts, and often in the hearts where they are least suspected. Thousands imagine that they are humble, who cannot bear to see an equal more honored and favored than themselves. Few indeed can be found who rejoice heartily in a neighbor's promotion over their own heads. The quantity of envy and jealousy in the world is a glaring proof of the prevalence of pride. Men would not envy a brother's advancement if they had not a secret thought that their own merit was greater than his.

Let us live on our guard against this sore disease, if we make any profession of serving Christ. The harm that it has done to the Church of Christ is far beyond calculation. Let us learn to take pleasure in the prosperity of others, and to be content with the lowest place for ourselves. The rule given to the Philippians should be often before our eyes—"In lowliness of mind let each esteem others better than themselves." The example of John the Baptist is a bright instance of the spirit at which we should aim. He said of our Lord, "He must increase, but I must decrease." (Phil. 2:3; John 3:30.)

Let us observe, secondly, in this passage, the striking account which our Lord gives of true Christian greatness. He tells His disciples that the worldly standard of greatness was the exercise of 'lordship and authority'. "But you," He says, "shall not be so. He that is greatest among you, let him be as the younger; and he that is chief, as he that serves." And then He enforces this principle by the mighty fact of His own example—"I am among you as he that serves."

Usefulness in the world and Church—a humble readiness to do anything, and put our hands to any good work—a cheerful willingness to fill any post, however lowly, and discharge any office, however unpleasant, if we can only promote happiness and holiness on earth—these are the true tests of Christian greatness. The hero in Christ's army is not the man who has rank, and title, and dignity, and chariots and horsemen, and fifty men to run before him. It is the man who looks not on his own things, but the things of others. It is the man who is kind to all, tender to all, thoughtful for all, with a hand to help all, and a heart to feel for all. It is the man who spends and is spent to make the vice and misery of the world less, to bind up the broken-hearted, to befriend the friendless, to cheer the sorrowful, to enlighten the ignorant, and to raise the poor. This is the truly great man in the eyes of God. The world may ridicule his labors and deny the sincerity of his motives. But while the world is sneering, God is pleased. This is the man who is walking most closely in the steps of Christ.

Let us follow after greatness of this sort, if we desire to prove ourselves Christ's servants. Let us not be content with clear head-knowledge, and loud lip-profession, and keen insight into controversy, and fervent zeal for the interests of our own party. Let us see that we minister to the needs of a sin burdened world, and do good to bodies and souls. Blessed be God! the greatness which Christ commended is within the reach of all. All have not learning, or gifts, or money. But all can minister to the happiness of those around them, by passive or by active graces. All can be useful, and all can be kind. There is a grand reality in constant kindness. It makes the men of the world think.

Let us observe, thirdly, in this passage, our Lord's gracious commendation of His disciples. He said to them, "You have remained true to me in my time of trial." There is something very striking in these words of praise. We know the weakness and infirmity of our Lord's disciples during the whole period of His earthly ministry. We find Him frequently reproving their ignorance and lack of faith. He knew full well that within a few hours they were all going to forsake Him. But here we find Him graciously dwelling on one good point in their conduct, and holding it up to the perpetual notice of His Church. They had been faithful to their Master, notwithstanding all their faults. Their hearts had been right, whatever had been their mistakes. They had clung to Him in the day of His humiliation, when the great and noble were against Him. They had "remained true to Him in His time of trial."

Let us rest our souls on the comfortable thought that the mind of Christ is always the same. If we are true believers, let us know that He looks at our graces more than at our faults, that He pities our infirmities, and that He will not deal with us according to our sins. Never had a master such poor, weak servants as believers are to Christ—but never had servants such a compassionate and tender Master as Christ is to believers! Surely we cannot love Him too well. We may come short in many things. We may fail in knowledge and courage, and faith, and patience. We may stumble many times. But one thing let us always do. Let us love the Lord Jesus with heart, and soul, and mind, and strength. Whatever others do, let us "remain true to Him," and cleave to Him with purpose of heart. Happy is he who can say with Peter, however humbled and ashamed, "Lord, you know that I love you." (John 21:15.)

Let us observe, lastly, what a glorious promise our Lord holds out to His faithful disciples. He says, "I appoint unto you a kingdom, as my Father has appointed unto me; that you may eat and drink at my table in my kingdom, and sit on thrones judging the twelve tribes of Israel."

These words were our Lord's parting legacy to His little flock. He knew that in a few hours His ministry among them would be ended. He winds it up by a wonderful declaration of good things laid up in store for them. We may not perhaps see the full meaning of every part of the promise. Enough for us to know that our Lord promised His eleven faithful ones—glory, honor, and rewards, far exceeding anything they had done for Him. They had gone a little way with Him, like Barzillai with David, and done a little for Him. He assures them that they shall have in another world a recompense worthy of a king.

Let us leave the whole passage with the cheering thought that the wages which Christ will give to his believing people will be far out of proportion to anything they have done for Him. Their tears will be found in His bottle. Their least desires to do good will be found recorded. Their weakest efforts to glorify Him sill be found written in His book of remembrance. Not a cup of cold water shall miss its reward.

LUKE 22:31-38

SIMON PETER

Simon, Simon, behold, Satan asked to have you, that he might sift you as wheat: but I made supplication for thee, that thy faith fail not; and do thou, when once thou hast turned again, establish thy brethren. And he said unto him, Lord, with thee I am ready to go both to prison and to death. And he said, I tell thee, Peter, the cock shall not crow this day, until thou shalt thrice deny that thou knowest me. And he said unto them, When I sent you forth without purse, and wallet, and shoes, lacked ye anything? And they said, Nothing. And he said unto them, But now, he that hath a purse, let him take it, and likewise a wallet; and he that hath none, let him sell his cloak, and buy a sword. For I say unto you, that this which is written must be fulfilled in me, And he was reckoned with transgressors: for that which concerneth me hath fulfilment. And they said, Lord, behold, here are two swords. And he said unto them, It is enough.

We learn, from these verses, what a fearful enemy the devil is to believers. We read that "the Lord said, Simon, Simon, Satan has desired to have you, that he may sift you as wheat." He was near Christ's flock, though they saw him not. He was longing to accomplish their ruin, though they knew it not. The wolf does not crave the blood of the lamb more than the devil desires the destruction of souls.

The personality, activity, and power of the devil are not sufficiently thought of by Christians. This is he who brought sin into the world at the beginning, by tempting Eve. This is he who is described in the book of Job as "going to and fro in the earth, and walking up and down in it." This is he whom our Lord calls "the prince of this world," a "murderer," and a "liar." This is he whom Peter compares to a "roaring lion, seeking whom he may devour." This is he whom John speaks of as "the accuser of the brethren." This is he who is ever working evil in the churches of Christ, catching away good seed from the hearts of hearers, sowing tares amid the wheat, stirring up persecutions, suggesting false doctrines, and fomenting divisions. The world is a snare to the believer. The flesh is a burden and a clog. But there is no enemy so dangerous as that restless, invisible, experienced enemy, the devil.

If we believe the Bible, let us not be ashamed to believe that there is a devil. It is an dreadful proof of the hardness and blindness of unconverted men, that they can jest and speak lightly of Satan.

If we profess to have any real religion, let us be on our guard against the devil's devices. The enemy who overthrew David and Peter, and assaulted Christ Himself, is not an enemy to be despised. He is very subtle. He has studied the heart of man for six thousand years. He can approach us under the garb of an "angel of light." We have need to watch and pray, and put on the whole armor of God. It is a blessed promise, that if we resist him he will flee from us. It is a still more blessed thought, that when the Lord comes, He will bruise Satan under our feet, and bind him in chains. (James 4:7; Rom. 16:20.)

We learn, secondly, in these verses, one great secret of a believer's perseverance in the faith. We read that our Lord said to Peter, "I have prayed for you that your faith fail not." It was owing to Christ's intercession that Peter did not entirely fall away.

The continued existence of grace in a believer's heart is a great standing miracle. His enemies are so mighty, and his strength is so small—the world is so full of snares, and his heart is so weak—that it seems at first sight impossible for him to reach heaven. The passage before us explains his safety. He has a mighty Friend at the right hand of God, whoever lives to make intercession for him. There is a watchful Advocate, who is daily pleading for him, seeing all his daily necessities, and obtaining daily supplies of mercy and grace for his soul. His grace never altogether dies, because Christ always lives to intercede. (Heb. 7:25.)

If we are true Christians, we shall find it essential to our comfort in religion to have clear views of Christ's priestly office and intercession. Christ lives, and therefore our faith shall not fail. Let us beware of regarding Jesus only as one who died for us. Let us never forget that He is alive for evermore. Paul bids us specially remember that He is risen again, and is at the right hand of God, and also makes intercession for us. (Rom. 8:34.) The work that He does for His people is not yet over. He is still appearing in the presence of God for them, and doing for their souls what He did for Peter. His present life for them is just as important as His death on the cross eighteen hundred years ago. Christ lives, and therefore true Christians "shall live also."

We learn, thirdly, from these verses, the duty incumbent on all believers who receive special mercies from Christ. We read that our Lord said to Peter, "So when you have repented and turned to me again, strengthen and build up your brothers." It is one of God's peculiar attributes, that He can bring good out of evil. He can cause the weaknesses and infirmities of some members of His Church to work together for the benefit of the whole body of His people. He can make the fall of a disciple the means of fitting him to be the strengthener and upholder of others.

Have we ever fallen, and by Christ's mercy been raised to newness of life? Then surely we are just the men who ought to deal gently with our brethren. We should tell them from our own experience what an evil and bitter thing is sin. We should caution them against trifling with temptation. We should warn them against pride, and presumption, and neglect of prayer. We should tell them of Christ's grace and compassion, if they have fallen. Above all, we should deal with them humbly and meekly, remembering what we ourselves have gone through

Well would it be for the Church of Christ, if Christians were more ready to good works of this kind! There are only too many believers who in discussion add nothing to their brethren. They seem to have no Savior to tell of, and no story of grace to report. They chill the hearts of those they meet, rather than warm them. They weaken rather than strengthen. These things ought not so to be. The words of the apostle ought to sink down into our minds, "Having received mercy, we faint not. We believe, and therefore we speak." (2 Cor. 4:1, 13.)

We learn, lastly, from these verses, that the servant of Christ ought to use all reasonable means in doing his Master's work. We read that our Lord said to His disciples, "He that has a purse, let him take it, and likewise his bag; and he that has no sword, let him sell his garment and buy one."

It is safest to take these remarkable words in a proverbial sense. They apply to the whole period of time between our Lord's first and second advents. Until our Lord comes again, believers are to make a diligent use of all the faculties which God has implanted in them. They are not to expect miracles to be worked, in order to save them trouble. They are not to expect bread to fall into their mouths, if they will not work for it. They are not to expect difficulties to be surmounted, and enemies to be overcome, if they will not wrestle, and struggle and take pains. They are to remember that it is "the hand of the diligent which makes rich." (Prov. 10:4.)

We shall do well to lay to heart our Lord's words in this place, and to act habitually on the principle which they contain. Let us labor, and toil, and give, and speak, and act, and write for Christ, as if all depended on our exertions. And yet let us never forget that success depends entirely on God's blessing! To expect success by our own "purse" and "sword" is pride and self-righteousness. But to expect success without the "purse and sword" is presumption and fanaticism. Let us do as Jacob did when he met his brother Esau. He used all innocent means to conciliate and appease him. But when he had done all, he spent all night in prayer. (Gen. 32:1-24.)

LUKE 22:39-46

JESUS PRAYS ON THE MOUNT OF OLIVES

And he came out, and went, as his custom was, unto the mount of Olives; and the disciples also followed him. And when he was at the place, he said unto them, Pray that ye enter not into temptation. And he was parted from them about a stone's cast; and he kneeled down and prayed, saying, Father, if thou be willing, remove this cup from me: nevertheless not my will, but thine, be done. And there appeared unto him an angel from heaven, strengthening him. And being in an agony he prayed more earnestly; and his sweat became as it were great drops of blood falling down upon the ground. And when he rose up from his prayer, he came unto the disciples, and found them sleeping for sorrow, and said unto them, Why sleep ye? rise and pray, that ye enter not into temptation.

The verses before us contain Luke's account of our Lord's agony in the garden. It is a passage of Scripture which we should always approach with peculiar reverence. The history which it records is one of the "deep things of God." While we read it, the words of Exodus should come across our minds, "Put off your shoes from off your feet; the place whereon you stands is holy ground." (Exod. 3:5.)

We see, firstly, in this passage, an example of what believers ought to do in time of trouble. The great Head of the Church Himself supplies the pattern. We are told that when He came to the Mount of Olives, the night before He was crucified, "He knelt down and prayed."

It is a striking fact, that both the Old and New Testaments give one and the same receipt for bearing trouble. What does the book of Psalms say? "Call upon me in the time of trouble—I will deliver you." (Psalm 50:15.) What does the apostle James say? "Is any afflicted? let him pray." (James v. 13.) Prayer is the remedy which Jacob used, when he feared his brother Esau. Prayer is the remedy which Job used when property and children were suddenly taken from him. Prayer is the remedy which Hezekiah used when Sennacherib's threatening letter arrived. And prayer is the remedy which the Son of God Himself was not ashamed to use in the days of His flesh. In the hour of His mysterious agony He "prayed."

Let us take care that we use our Master's remedy, if we want comfort in affliction. Whatever other means of relief we use, let us pray. The first Friend we should turn to ought to be God. The first message we should send ought to be to the throne of grace. No depression of spirits must prevent us. No crushing weight of sorrow must make us speechless. It is a prime device of Satan, to supply the afflicted man with false reasons for keeping silence before God. Let us beware of the temptation to brood sullenly over our wounds. If we can say nothing else, we can say, "I am oppressed—undertake for me." (Isaiah. 38:14.)

We see, secondly, in these verses, what kind of prayers a believer ought to make to God in time of trouble. Once more the Lord Jesus Himself affords a model to His people. We are told that He said, "Father, if you are willing, remove this cup from me—nevertheless, not my will, but yours be done." He who spoke these words, we must remember, had two distinct natures in one Person. He had a human will as well as a divine. When He said, "Not my will be done," He meant that will which He had as a man, with a body, flesh and blood, like our own.

The language used by our blessed Master in this place shows exactly what should be the spirit of a believer's prayer in his distress. Like Jesus, he should tell his desires openly to his heavenly Father, and spread His wishes unreservedly before Him. But like Jesus, he should do it all with an entire submission of will to the will of God. He should never forget that there may be wise and good reasons for His affliction. He should carefully qualify every petition for the removal of crosses with the saving clause, "If you are willing." He should wind up all with the meek confession, "Not my will, but yours be done."

Submission of will like this is one of the brightest graces which can adorn the Christian character. It is one which a child of God ought to aim at in everything, if he desires to be like Christ. But at no time is such submission of will so needful as in the day of sorrow, and in nothing does it shine so brightly as in a believer's prayers for relief. He who can say from his heart, when a bitter cup is before him, "Not my will, but yours be done," has reached a high position in the school of God.

We see, thirdly, in these verses, an example of the exceeding guilt and sinfulness of sin. We are meant to learn this in Christ's agony and bloody sweat, and all the mysterious distress of body and mind which the passage describes. The lesson at first sight may not be clear to a careless reader of the Bible. But the lesson is there.

How can we account for the deep agony which our Lord underwent in the garden? What reason can we assign for the intense suffering, both mental and bodily, which He manifestly endured? There is only one satisfactory answer. It was caused by the burden of a world's imputed sin, which then began to press upon Him in a peculiar manner. He had undertaken to be "sin for us"—to be "made a curse for us"—and to allow our iniquities to be laid on Himself. (2 Cor. 5:21; Gal. 3:13; Isaiah. 53:6.) It was the enormous weight of these iniquities which made Him suffer agony. It was the sense of a world's guilt pressing Him down which made even the eternal Son of God sweat great drops of blood, and called from Him "strong crying and tears." The cause of Christ's agony was man's sin. (Heb. 5:7.)

We must beware jealously of the modern notion that our blessed Lord's life and death were nothing more than a great example of self-sacrifice. Such a notion throws darkness and confusion over the whole Gospel. It dishonors the Lord Jesus, and represents Him as less resigned in the day of death than many a modern martyr. We must cling firmly to the old doctrine that Christ was "bearing our sins," both in the garden and on the cross. No other doctrine can ever explain the passage before us, or satisfy the conscience of guilty man.

Would we see the sinfulness of sin in its true colors? Would we learn to hate sin with a godly hatred? Would we know something of the intense misery of souls in hell? Would we understand something of the unspeakable love of Christ? Would we comprehend Christ's ability to sympathize with those that are in trouble? Then let the agony in the garden come often into our minds. The depth of that agony may give us some idea of our debt to Christ.

We see, lastly, in these verses, an example of the feebleness of the best of saints. We are told that while our Lord was in agony, His disciples fell asleep. In spite of a plain injunction to pray, and a plain warning against temptation the flesh overcame the spirit. While Christ was sweating great drops of blood, His apostles slept!

Passages like these are very instructive. We ought to thank God that they have been written for our learning. They are meant to teach us humility. When apostles can behave in this way, the Christian who thinks he stands should take heed lest he fall. They are meant to reconcile believers to death, and make them long for that glorious body which they will have when Christ returns. Then, and not until then, shall we be able to wait upon God without bodily weariness, and to serve Him day and night in His temple.

LUKE 22:47-53

JESUS ARRESTED

While he yet spake, behold, a multitude, and he that was called Judas, one of the twelve, went before them; and he drew near unto Jesus to kiss him. But Jesus said unto him, Judas, betrayest thou the Son of man with a kiss? And when they that were about him saw what would follow, they said, Lord, shall we smite with the sword? And a certain one of them smote the servant of the high priest, and struck off his right ear. But Jesus answered and said, Suffer ye them thus far. And he touched his ear, and healed him. And Jesus said unto the chief priests, and captains of the temple, and elders, that were come against him, Are ye come out, as against a robber, with swords and staves? When I was daily with you in the temple, ye stretched not forth your hands against me: but this is your hour, and the power of darkness.

We should learn, for one thing, from these verses, that the worst and most wicked acts may be done under a show of love to Christ. We read that when the traitor Judas brought the enemies of Christ to take Him, he betrayed Him "with a kiss." He made a pretense of affection and respect, at the very moment when he was about to deliver his Master into the hands of his deadliest enemies.

Conduct like this, unhappily, is not without its parallels. The pages of history record many an instance of enormous wickedness wrought out and perfected under the garb of religion. The name of God has too often been pressed into the service of persecution, treachery, and crime. When Jezebel would have Naboth killed, she ordered a "fast to be proclaimed," and false witnesses to accuse him of "blaspheming God and the king." (1 Kings 21:9-10.) When Count de Montfort led a crusade against the Albigenses, he ordered them to be murdered and pillaged, as an act of service to Christ's Church. When the Spanish Inquisition tortured and burned suspected heretics, they justified their abominable dealings by a profession of zeal for God's truth. The false apostle Judas Iscariot has never lacked successors and imitators. There have always been men ready to betray Christ with a kiss, and willing to deliver the Gospel to its enemies under a show of respect.

Conduct like this, we need not doubt, is utterly abominable in the sight of God. To injure the cause of religion under any circumstances is a great sin, but to injure it while we pretend to show kindness is the blackest of crimes. To betray Christ at any time is the very height of wickedness, but to betray Him with a kiss, proves a man to have become a very child of hell.

We should learn, for another thing, from these verses, that it is much easier to fight a little for Christ, than to endure hardness and go to prison and death for His sake. We read that when our Lord's enemies drew near to take Him, one of His disciples "smote the servant of the high priest, and cut off his right ear." Yet the zeal of that disciple was very short-lived. His courage soon died away. The fear of man overcame him. By and bye when our Lord was led away prisoner, he was led away alone. The disciple who was so ready to fight and smite with the sword, had actually forsaken his Master and fled!

The lesson before us is deeply instructive. To suffer patiently for Christ is far more difficult than to work actively. To sit still and endure calmly, is far more hard than to stir about and take part in the battle. 'Crusaders' will always be found more numerous than 'Martyrs'. The passive graces of religion are far more rare and precious than the active graces. Work for Christ may be done from many spurious motives—from excitement, from emulation, from party spirit, or from love of praise. Suffering for Christ will seldom be endured from any but one motive. That motive is the grace of God.

We shall do well to remember these things in forming our estimate of the comparative grace of professing Christians. We err greatly if we suppose that those who do public work, and preach, and speak, and write, and fill the eyes of the Church, are those who are most honorable in God's sight. Such men are often far less esteemed by Him than some poor unknown believer, who has been lying for years on his back, enduring pain without a murmur. Their public efforts perhaps will prove at last to have brought less glory to Christ than his patience, and to have done less good than his prayers.

The grand test of grace is patient suffering. "I will show Saul," said the Lord Jesus, "what great things he shall suffer for my name." (Acts 9:16.) Peter, we may be sure, did far less good when he drew his sword and cut off a man's ear, than he did when be stood calmly before the council as a prisoner, and said, "We cannot but speak the things which we have seen and heard." (Acts 4:20.)

We should learn, lastly, from these verses, that the time during which evil is permitted to triumph is fixed and limited by God. We read that our Lord said to His enemies when they took Him, "This is your hour and the power of darkness."

The sovereignty of God over everything done upon earth is absolute and complete. The hands of the wicked are bound until He allows them to work. They can do nothing without His permission. But this is not all. The hands of the wicked cannot stir one moment before God allows them to begin, and cannot stir one moment after God commands them to stop. The very worst of Satan's instruments are 'working in chains'. The devil could not touch Job's property or person until God allowed him. He could not prevent Job's prosperity returning, when God's designs on Job were accomplished. Our Lord's enemies could not take and slay him, until the appointed "hour" of His weakness arrived. Nor yet could they prevent His rising again, when the hour came in which He was declared the Son of God with power, by His resurrection from the dead. (Rom. 1:4.) When He was led forth to Calvary, it was "their hour." When He rose victorious from the grave, it was His.

The verses before us throw light on the history of believers in ages gone by, from the time of the apostles down to the present day. They have often been severely oppressed and persecuted, but the hand of their enemies has never been allowed entirely to prevail. The "hour" of their trials has generally been succeeded by a season of light. The triumph of their enemies has never been entire and complete. They have had their "hour," but they have had no more. After the persecution about Stephen, came the conversion of Paul. After the martyrdom of John Huss, came the German Reformation. After the Marian persecution, came the establishment of English Protestantism. The longest night has had its morning. The sharpest winters have been followed by spring. The heaviest storms have been changed for blue sky.

Let us take comfort in these words of our Lord, in looking forward to our own future lives. If we are followers of Christ, we shall have an "hour" of trial, and it may be a long hour too. But we may rest assured that the darkness shall not last one moment longer than God sees fit for us. In His good time it shall vanish away. "At evening time there shall be light."

Finally, let us take comfort in these words of our Lord, in looking forward to the future history of the Church and the world. Clouds and darkness may gather round the ark of God. Persecutions and tribulations may assail the people of God. The last days of the Church and world will probably be their worst days. But the "hour" of trial, however grievous, will have an end. Even at the worst we may boldly say, "The night is far spent and the day is at hand." (Rom. 13:12.)

LUKE 22:54-62
PETER DISOWNS JESUS

And they seized him, and led him away, and brought him into the high priest's house. But Peter followed afar off. And when they had kindled a fire in the midst of the court, and had sat down together, Peter sat in the midst of them. And a certain maid seeing him as he sat in the light of the fire, and looking stedfastly upon him, said, This man also was with him. But he denied, saying, Woman, I know him not. And after a little while another saw him, and said, Thou also art one of them. But Peter said, Man, I am not. And after the space of about one hour another confidently affirmed, saying, Of a truth this man also was with him; for he is a Galilaean. But Peter said, Man, I know not what thou sayest. And immediately, while he yet spake, the cock crew. And the Lord turned, and looked upon Peter. And Peter remembered the word of the Lord, how that he said unto him, Before the cock crow this day thou shalt deny me thrice. And he went out, and wept bitterly.

The verses we have now read describe the fall of the apostle Peter. It is a passage which is deeply humbling to the pride of man, but singularly instructive to true Christians. The fall of Peter has been a beacon to the Church, and has probably preserved myriads of souls from destruction. It is a passage which supplies strong proof that the Bible is inspired and Christianity is from God. If the Christian religion had been the invention of uninspired men, its first historians would never have told us that one of the chief apostles denied his Master three times.

The story of Peter's fall teaches us, firstly, how small and gradual are the steps by which men may go down into great sins. The various steps in Peter's fall are clearly marked out by the Gospel-writers. They ought always to be observed in reading this part of the apostle's history. The first step was proud self-confidence. Though all men denied Christ, yet he never would! He was ready to go with Him both to prison and to death! The second step was indolent neglect of prayer. When his Master told him to pray, lest he should enter into temptation, he gave way to drowsiness, and was found asleep. The third step was vacillating indecision. When the enemies of Christ came upon Him, Peter first fought, then ran away, then turned again, and finally "followed afar off." The fourth step was mingling with bad company. He went into the high priest's house and sat among the servants by the fire, trying to conceal his religion, and hearing and seeing all manner of evil. The fifth and last step was the natural consequence of the preceding four. He was overwhelmed with fear when suddenly charged with being a disciple. The snare was round his neck. He could not escape. He plunged deeper into error than ever. He denied his blessed Master three times. The mischief, be it remembered, had been done before. The denial was only the disease coming to a head.

Let us beware of the beginnings of backsliding, however small. We never know what we may come to, if we once leave the king's high-way. The professing Christian who begins to say of any sin or evil habit, "it is but a little one," is in imminent danger. He is sowing seeds in his heart, which will one day spring up and bear bitter fruit. It is a homely saying, that "if men take care of the pence the pounds will take care of themselves." We may borrow a good spiritual lesson from the saying. The Christian who keeps his heart diligently in little things shall be kept from great falls.

The story of Peter's fall teaches us, secondly, how very far a believer may backslide.

In order to see this lesson clearly, the whole circumstances of Peter's case ought to be fully weighed. He was a chosen apostle of Christ. He had enjoyed greater spiritual privileges than most men in the world. He had just received the Lord's supper. He had just heard that wonderful discourse recorded in the fourteenth, fifteenth, and sixteenth chapters of John. He had been most plainly warned of his own danger. He had boasted most loudly that he was ready for anything that might come upon him. And yet this very man denies his gracious Master, and that repeatedly and after intervals giving him space for reflection. He denies Him once, twice, and three times!

The best and highest believer is a poor weak creature, even at his best times. Whether he knows it or not, he carries within him an almost boundless capacity of wickedness, however fair and decent his outward conduct may seem. There is no enormity of sin into which he may not run, if he does not watch and pray, and if the grace of God does not hold him up. When we read the falls of Noah, Lot, and Peter, we only read what might possibly befall any of ourselves. Let us never presume. Let us never indulge in high thoughts about our own strength, or look down upon others. Whatever else we pray for, let us daily pray that we may "walk humbly with God." (Micah 6:8.)

The story of Peter's fall teaches us, thirdly, the infinite mercy of our Lord Jesus Christ. This is a lesson which is brought out most forcibly by a fact which is only recorded in Luke's Gospel. We are told that when Peter denied Christ the third time, and the rooster crowed, "the Lord turned and looked straight at Peter."

Those words are deeply touching! Surrounded by blood-thirsty and insulting enemies, in the full anticipation of horrible outrages, an unjust trial, and a painful death, the Lord Jesus yet found time to think kindly of His poor erring disciple. Even then He would have Peter know, that He did not forget him. Sorrowfully no doubt, but not angrily, He "turned and looked straight at Peter." There was a deep meaning in that look. It was a sermon which Peter never forgot.

The love of Christ toward His people, is a deep well which has no bottom. Let us never measure it by comparison with any kind of love of man or woman. It exceeds all other love, as far as the sun exceeds the rush light. There is about it a mine of compassion, and patience, and readiness to forgive sin, of whose riches we have but a faint conception. Let us not be afraid to trust that love, when we first feel our sins. Let us never be afraid to go on trusting it after we have once believed. No man need despair, however far he may have fallen, if he will only repent and turn to Christ. If the heart of Jesus was so gracious when He was a prisoner in the judgment hall, we surely need not think it is less gracious, when He sits in glory at the right hand of God.

The story of Peter's fall teaches us, lastly, how bitter sin is to believers, when they have fallen into it and discovered their fall.

This is a lesson which stands out plainly on the face of the verses before us. We are told that when Peter remembered the warning he had received, and saw how far he had fallen, "he went out and wept bitterly." He found out by experience the truth of Jeremiah's words, "It is an evil thing and a bitter that you have forsaken the Lord." (Jer. 2:19.) He felt keenly the truth of Solomon's saying, "The backslider in heart shall be filled with his own ways." (Prov. 14:14.) No doubt he could have said with Job, "I abhor myself, and repent in dust and ashes." (Job 42:6.)

Sorrow like this, let us always remember, is an inseparable companion of true repentance. Here lies the grand distinction between "repentance unto salvation," and unavailing remorse. Remorse can make a man miserable, like Judas Iscariot, but it can do no more. It does not lead him to God. Repentance makes a man's heart soft and his conscience tender, and shows itself in real turning to a Father in heaven. The falls of a graceless professor are falls from which there is no rising again. But the fall of a true saint always ends in deep contrition, self-abasement, and amendment of life.

Let us take heed, before we leave this passage, that we always make a right use of Peter's fall. Let us never make it an excuse for sin. Let us learn from his sad experience, to watch and pray, lest we fall into temptation. If we do fall, let us believe that there is hope for us as there was for him. But above all, let us remember, that if we fall as Peter fell, we must repent as Peter repented, or else we shall never be saved.

LUKE 22:63-71

And the men that held Jesus mocked him, and beat him. And they blindfolded him, and asked him, saying, Prophesy: who is he that struck thee? And many other things spake they against him, reviling him. And as soon as it was day, the assembly of the elders of the people was gathered together, both chief priests and scribes; and they led him away into their council, saying, If thou art the Christ, tell us. But he said unto them, If I tell you, ye will not believe: and if I ask you, ye will not answer. But from henceforth shall the Son of man be seated at the right hand of the power of God. And they all said, Art thou then the Son of God? And he said unto them, Ye say that I am. And they said, What further need have we of witness? for we ourselves have heard from his own mouth.

We should notice, firstly, in these verses, the shameful treatment that our Lord Jesus Christ underwent at the hands of His enemies. We read that the men who held Him, "mocked" Him, "smote" Him, "blindfolded" Him, and "struck Him on the face." It was not enough to have taken a prisoner a person of most blameless and charitable life. They must needs add insult to injury.

Conduct like this shows the desperate corruption of human nature. The excesses of savage malice to which unconverted men will sometimes go, and the fierce delight with which they will sometimes trample on the most holy and the most pure, almost justify the strong saying of an old divine, that "man left to himself is half-beast and half-devil." He hates God and all who bear anything of God's image about them. "The carnal mind is enmity against God." (Rom. 8:7.) We have probably a very faint idea of what the world would become, if it were not for the constant restraint that God mercifully puts upon evil. It is not too much to say that if unconverted men had their own way entirely, the earth would soon be little better than a hell.

Our Lord's calm submission to insults like those here described, shows the depth of His love towards sinners. Had He so willed, He could have stopped the insolence of His enemies in a moment. He who could cast out devils with a word, could have summoned legions of angels to His side, and scattered those wretched tools of Satan to the winds. But our Lord's heart was set on the great work he had come on earth to do. He had undertaken to purchase our redemption by His own humiliation, and He did not flinch from paying the uttermost farthing of the price. He had undertaken to drink the bitter cup of vicarious suffering to save sinners, and "for the joy set before Him He despised the shame," and drank the cup to the very dregs. (Heb. 12:2.)

Patience like that which our blessed Lord exhibited on this occasion should teach His professing people a mighty lesson. We should forbear all murmuring and complaining, and irritation of spirit, when we are ill-treated by the world. What are the occasional insults to which we have to submit compared to the insults which were heaped on our Master? Yet "when He was reviled He reviled not again. When He suffered He threatened not." He left us an example that we should walk in His steps. Let us go and do likewise. (1 Peter 2:21-23.)

We should notice, secondly, in these verses, the striking prophecy which our Lord delivers about His own coming glory. He says to His insulting enemies, "Hereafter shall the Son of man sit on the right hand of the power of God." Did they find fault with His lowly appearance, and want a glorious Messiah? They would see Him in glory one day. Did they think He was weak, powerless, and contemptible, because at present there was no outward majesty about Him? They would behold Him one day in the most honorable position in heaven, fulfilling the well-known prophecy of Daniel, with all judgment committed to His hands. (Dan. 7:9, 10.)

Let us take heed that the future glory of Christ forms a part of our creed, as much as Christ's cross and passion. Let it be a first principle in our religion, that the same Jesus who was mocked, despised, and crucified, is He who has now "all power in heaven and earth and will one day come again in His Father's glory with all His angels."

We see but half the truth if we see nothing but the cross and the first advent. It is essential to our own comfort to see also the second advent, and the crown. That same Jesus who stood before the bar of the high priest and of Pilate, will one day sit upon a throne of glory and summon all His enemies to appear before Him. Happy is that Christian who keeps steadily before his mind that word "hereafter!" Now in this present time believers must be content to take part in their Master's sufferings and with Him to be weak. "Hereafter" they shall share in His glory, and with Him be strong. Now like their Lord they must not be surprised if they are mocked, despised, and disbelieved. "Hereafter" they shall sit with Him on the right hand of God.

We should notice, lastly, in these verses, what a full and bold confession our Lord makes of His own Messiahship and divinity. We read that in answer to this question of His enemies, "Then you claim you are the Son of God?" Jesus replied, "You are right in saying that I am." The meaning of this short sentence may not be clear at first sight to an English reader. It signifies in other words, "You speak the truth. I am, as you say, the Son of God."

Our Lord's confession deprived His enemies of all excuse for unbelief. The Jews can never plead that our Lord left their forefathers in ignorance of His mission, and kept them in doubt and suspense. Here we see our Lord telling them plainly who he was, and telling them in words which would convey even more to a Jewish mind than they do to ours. And yet the confession had not the least good effect upon the Jews! Their hearts were hardened by prejudice. Their minds were darkened by judicial blindness. The veil was over the eyes of their inward man. They heard our Lord's confession unmoved, and only plunged deeper into the most dreadful sin.

The bold confession of our Master upon this occasion, is intended to be an example to all His believing people. Like Him, we must not shrink from speaking out when occasion requires our testimony. The fear of man, and the presence of a multitude must not make us hold our peace. (Job 31:34.) We need not blow a trumpet before us, and go out of our way, to proclaim our own religion. Opportunities are sure to occur in the daily path of duty, when, like Paul on board ship, we may show "whose we are and whom we serve." (Acts 27:23.) At such opportunities, if we have the mind of Christ, let us not be afraid to show our colors. A confessing Master loves bold, uncompromising, and confessing disciples. Those who honor Him by an outspoken, courageous testimony, He will honor, because they are walking in His steps. "Whoever," He says, "shall confess me before men, him will I confess before my Father who is in heaven." (Matt. 10:32.)

Chapter 23

And the whole company of them rose up, and brought him before Pilate. And they began to accuse him, saying, We found this man perverting our nation, and forbidding to give tribute to Caesar, and saying that he himself is Christ a king. And Pilate asked him, saying, Art thou the King of the Jews? And he answered him and said, Thou sayest. And Pilate said unto the chief priests and the multitudes, I find no fault in this man. But they were the more urgent, saying, He stirreth up the people, teaching throughout all Judaea, and beginning from Galilee even unto this place. But when Pilate heard it, he asked whether the man were a Galilaean. And when he knew that he was of Herod's jurisdiction, he sent him unto Herod, who himself also was at Jerusalem in these days. Now when Herod saw Jesus, he was exceeding glad: for he was of a long time desirous to see him, because he had heard concerning him; and he hoped to see some miracle done by him. And he questioned him in many words; but he answered him nothing. And the chief priests and the scribes stood, vehemently accusing him. And Herod with his soldiers set him at nought, and mocked him, and arraying him in gorgeous apparel sent him back to Pilate. And Herod and Pilate became friends with each other that very day: for before they were at enmity between themselves.

Let us observe, for one thing, in this passage, what false accusations were laid to our Lord Jesus Christ's charge. We are told that the Jews accused Him of "subverting the nation, forbidding to give tribute to Caesar, and stirring up the people." In all this indictment, we know, there was not a word of truth. It was nothing but an ingenious attempt to enlist the feeling of a Roman governor against our Lord.

False witness and slander are two favorite weapons of the devil. He was a liar from the beginning, and is still the father of lies. (John 8:44.) When he finds that he cannot stop God's work, his next device is to blacken the character of God's servants, and to destroy the value of their testimony. With this weapon he assaulted David—"False witnesses," he says, "did rise against me—they laid to my charge things that I knew not." With this weapon he assaulted the prophets. Elijah was a "troubler of Israel!" Jeremiah was a man who "sought not the welfare of the people but the hurt!" (Psalm 35:11; 1 Kings 18:17; Jer. 38:4.) With this weapon he assaulted the apostles. They were "pestilent fellows," and men who "turned the world upside down." (Acts 24:5; 17:6.) With this weapon he assaulted our Lord all through His ministry. He stirred up his agents to call Him a gluttonous man and a drunkard, a Samaritan and a devil. (Luke 7:34; John 8:48.) And here, in the verses before us, we find him plying his old weapon to the very last. Jesus is arraigned before Pilate upon charges which are utterly untrue.

The servant of Christ must never be surprised if he has to drink of the same cup with his Lord. When He who was holy, harmless, and undefiled, was foully slandered, who can expect to escape? "If they called the master of the house Beelzebub, how much more will they call them of his household?" (Matt. 10:25.) Nothing is too bad to be reported against a saint. Perfect innocence is no fence against enormous lying, calumny, and misrepresentation. The most blameless character will not secure us against false tongues. We must bear the trial patiently. It is part of the cross of Christ. We must sit still, lean back on God's promises, and believe that in the long run truth will prevail. "Rest in the Lord," says David, "and wait patiently for Him." "He shall bring forth your righteousness as the light, and your judgment as the noonday." (Psalm 37:6, 7.)

Let us observe, for another thing, in this passage, the strange and mingled motives which influence the hearts of unconverted great men. We are told that when our Lord was sent by Pilate to Herod, king of Galilee, "Herod was exceeding glad; for he was desirous to see him of a long season, because he had heard many things of him; and he hoped to see some miracles done by him."

These words are remarkable. Herod was a sensual, worldly man, the murderer of John the Baptist—a man living in foul adultery with his brother's wife. Such a man, we might have supposed, would have had no desire to see Christ. But Herod had an uneasy conscience. The blood of God's murdered saints, no doubt, rose often before his eyes, and destroyed his peace. The fame of our Lord's preaching and miracles had penetrated even into his court. It was said that another witness against sin had risen up, who was even more faithful and bold than John the Baptist; and who confirmed his teaching by works which even the power of kings could not perform. These rumors made Herod restless and uncomfortable. No wonder that his curiosity was stirred, and he "desired to see Christ."

It may be feared that there are many great and rich men like Herod in every age of the church, men without God, without faith, and living only for themselves. They generally live in an atmosphere of their own—flattered, fawned upon, and never told the truth about their souls—haughty, tyrannical, and knowing no will but their own. Yet even these men are sometimes conscience-stricken and afraid.

God raises up some bold witness against their sins, whose testimony reaches their ears. At once their curiosity is stirred. They feel "found out," and are ill at ease. They flutter round his ministry, like the moth round the candle, and seem unable to keep away from it, even while they do not obey it. They praise his talents and openly profess their admiration of his power. But they never get any further. Like Herod, their conscience produces within them a morbid curiosity to see and hear God's witnesses. But, like Herod, their heart is linked to the world by chains of iron. Tossed to and fro by storms of lust or ungovernable passions, they are never at rest while they live, and after all their fitful struggles of conscience, they die at length in their sins. This is a painful history. But it is the history of many rich men's souls.

Let us learn from Herod's case to PITY great men. With all their greatness and apparent splendor, they are often thoroughly miserable within. Silks and satins and official robes, often cover hearts which are utter strangers to peace. That man knows not what he is wishing, who wishes to be a rich man. Let us PRAY for rich men, as well as pity them. They carry weight in the race for eternal life. If they are saved, it can only be by the greatest miracles of God's grace. Our Lord's words are very solemn, "It is easier for a camel to go through the eye of a needle than for a rich man to enter the kingdom of God." (Matt. 19:24.)

Let us observe, finally, in this passage, how easily and readily, unconverted men can agree in disliking Christ. We are told that when Pilate sent our Lord a prisoner to Herod, "the same day Pilate and Herod were made friends together; for before they were at enmity between themselves." We know not the cause of their enmity. It was probably some petty quarrel, such as will arise among great as well as small. But whatever the cause of enmity, it was laid aside when a common object of contempt, fear, or hatred was brought before them. Whatever else they disagreed about, Pilate and Herod could agree to despise and persecute Christ.

The incident before us is a striking emblem of a state of things which may always be seen in the world. Men of the most discordant opinions can unite in opposing truth. Teachers of the most opposite doctrines can make common cause in fighting against the Gospel. In the days of our Lord, the Pharisees and the Sadducees might be seen combining their forces to entrap Jesus of Nazareth and put Him to death. In our own times we sometimes see Romanists and Socinians—infidels and idolaters—worldly pleasure-lovers and bigoted ascetics—the friends of so-called liberal views and the most determined opponents of all changes—all ranked together against evangelical religion. One common hatred binds them together. They hate the cross of Christ. To use the words of the apostles in the Acts—"Against your holy child Jesus, whom you have anointed, both Herod and Pontius Pilate, with the Gentiles, and the people of Israel, are gathered together." (Acts 4:27.) All hate each other very much, but all hate Christ much more.

The true Christian must not count the enmity of the world a strange thing. He must not marvel, if like Paul at Rome, he finds the way of life, a "way everywhere spoken against," and if all around him agree in disliking his religion. (Acts 28:22.) If he expects that by any concession he can win the favor of man, he will be greatly deceived. Let not his heart be troubled. He must wait for the praise of God. The saying of his Master should often come across his mind—"If you were of the world, the world would love his own; but because you are not of the world, but I have chosen you out of the world, therefore the world hates you." (John 15:19.)

LUKE 23:13-25

And Pilate called together the chief priests and the rulers and the people, and said unto them, Ye brought unto me this man, as one that perverteth the people: and behold, I having examined him before you, found no fault in this man touching those things whereof ye accuse him: no, nor yet Herod: for he sent him back unto us; and behold, nothing worthy of death hath been done by him. I will therefore chastise him, and release him. Now he must needs release unto them at the feast one prisoner. But they cried out all together, saying, Away with this man, and release unto us Barabbas: — one who for a certain insurrection made in the city, and for murder, was cast into prison. And Pilate spake unto them again, desiring to release Jesus; but they shouted, saying, Crucify, crucify him. And he said unto them the third time, Why, what evil hath this man done? I have found no cause of death in him: I will therefore chastise him and release him. But they were urgent with loud voices, asking that he might be crucified. And their voices prevailed. And Pilate gave sentence that what they asked for should be done. And he released him that for insurrection and murder had been cast into prison, whom they asked for; but Jesus he delivered up to their will.

We should observe, for one thing, in this passage, what striking testimony was borne to our Lord Jesus Christ's perfect innocence by His judges.

We are told that Pilate said to the Jews, "You have brought this man unto me as one that subverts the people—and behold I, having examined him before you, have found no fault in this man concerning those things whereof you accuse him—no, nor yet Herod." The Roman and the Galilean governors were both of one mind. Both agreed in pronouncing our Lord not guilty of the things laid to His charge.

There was a peculiar fitness in this public declaration of Christ's innocence. Our Lord, we must remember, was about to be offered up as a sacrifice for our sins. It was fit and right that those who examined Him should formally pronounce Him a guiltless and blameless person. It was fit and right that the Lamb of God should be found by those who slew Him "a Lamb without blemish and without spot." (1 Pet. 1:19.) The over-ruling hand of God so ordered the events of His trial, that even when His enemies were judges, they could find no fault and prove nothing against Him.

The circumstance before us may seem of trifling moment to a careless Bible reader. It ought however to commend itself to the heart of every well instructed Christian. We ought to be daily thankful that our great Substitute was in all respects perfect, and that our Surety was a complete and faultless Surety. What child of man can count the number of his sins? We leave undone things we should do; and do things we ought not to do, every day we live. But this must be our comfort, that Christ the Righteous has undertaken to stand in our place, to pay the debt we all owe, and to fulfill the law we have all broken. He did fulfill that law completely. He satisfied all its demands. He accomplished all its requirements. He was the second Adam, who had "clean hands and a pure heart," and could therefore enter with boldness into God's holy hill. (Psalm 24:4.) He is the righteousness of all sinners who believe in Him. (Rom. 10:4.) In Him all believers are counted perfect fulfillers of the law. The eyes of a holy God behold them in Christ, clothed with Christ's perfect righteousness. For Christ's sake God can now say of the believer, "I find in him no fault at all."

Let us learn for another thing, in this passage, how thoroughly the Jews took on themselves the whole responsibility of our Lord Jesus Christ's death. We are told that when Pilate was "willing to release Jesus," the Jews "cried, saying, crucify him, crucify him!" Again, we are told that "with loud shouts they insistently demanded that he be crucified, and their shouts prevailed." This fact in the history of our Lord's passion deserves particular notice. It shows the strict accuracy of the words of the apostles in after times, when speaking of Christ's death. They speak of it as the act of the Jewish nation, and not of the Romans. "You killed the Prince of life," says Peter to the Jews at Jerusalem. "You slew and hanged him on a tree." (Acts 3:15; 5:30.) "The Jews have both killed the Lord Jesus and their own prophets," says Paul to the Thessalonians. (1 Thess. 2:15.) So long as the world stands the fact before us is a memorial of man's natural hatred against God. When the Son of God came down to earth and dwelt among His own chosen people, they despised Him, rejected Him, and slew Him.

The fearful responsibility which the Jews took on themselves in the matter of our Lord's death was not forgotten by God. The righteous blood which they shed has been crying against them as a people for eighteen hundred years. Scattered all over the earth, wanderers among the nations, without a land, without a government, without a home, the Jews show to this day that their own words have been terribly fulfilled. The blood of their slain Messiah "is upon them and upon their children." They are a standing warning to the world that it is a fearful thing to reject the Lord Christ, and that the nation which speaks stoutly against God, must not be surprised if God deals with it according to its words. Marvelous indeed is the thought that there is mercy in store for Israel, notwithstanding all its sins and unbelief! The nation which pierced and slew Him, shall yet look to Him by faith and be restored to favor. (Zech. 12:10.)

We should observe, lastly, in this passage, the remarkable circumstances connected with the release of Barabbas. We are told that Pilate "released Barabbas, the man in prison for insurrection and murder. But he delivered Jesus over to them to do as they wished." Two people were before him, and he must needs release one of the two. The one was a sinner against God and man, a malefactor stained with many crimes. The other was the holy, harmless, and undefiled Son of God, in whom there was no fault at all. And yet Pilate condemns the innocent prisoner and acquits the guilty! He orders Barabbas to be set free, and delivers Jesus to be crucified.

The circumstance before us is very instructive. It shows the bitter malice of the Jews against our Lord. To use the words of Peter, "They denied the holy one and the just, and desired a murderer to be granted to them." (Acts 3:14.) It shows the deep humiliation to which our Lord submitted, in order to procure our redemption. He allowed Himself to be reckoned lighter in the balance than a murderer, and to be counted more guilty than the chief of sinners!

But there is a deeper meaning yet beneath the circumstance before us, which we must not fail to observe. The whole transaction is a lively emblem of that wondrous exchange that takes place between Christ and the sinner, when a sinner is justified in the sight of God. Christ has been made "sin for us who knew no sin, that we might be made the righteousness of God in Him." (2 Cor. 5:21.) Christ the innocent has been reckoned guilty before God, that we the guilty might be reckoned innocent, and be set free from condemnation.

If we are true Christians, let us daily lean our souls on the comfortable thought that Christ has really been our Substitute, and has been punished in our stead. Let us freely confess that, like Barabbas, we deserve death, judgment, and hell. But let us cling firmly to the glorious truth that a sinless Savior has suffered in our stead, and that believing in Him the guilty may go free.

LUKE 23:26-38

THE CRUCIFIXION

And when they led him away, they laid hold upon one Simon of Cyrene, coming from the country, and laid on him the cross, to bear it after Jesus. And there followed him a great multitude of the people, and of women who bewailed and lamented him. But Jesus turning unto them said, Daughters of Jerusalem, weep not for me, but weep for yourselves, and for your children. For behold, the days are coming, in which they shall say, Blessed are the barren, and the wombs that never bare, and the breasts that never gave suck. Then shall they begin to say to the mountains, Fall on us; and to the hills, Cover us. For if they do these things in the green tree, what shall be done in the dry?

And there were also two others, malefactors, led with him to be put to death. And when they came unto the place which is called The skull, there they crucified him, and the malefactors, one on the right hand and the other on the left. And Jesus said, Father, forgive them; for they know not what they do. And parting his garments among them, they cast lots. And the people stood beholding. And the rulers also scoffed at him, saying, He saved others; let him save himself, if this is the Christ of God, his chosen. And the soldiers also mocked him, coming to him, offering him vinegar, and saying, If thou art the King of the Jews, save thyself. And there was also a superscription over him, THIS IS THE KING OF THE JEWS.

We ought to notice, in this passage, our Lord's words of prophetical warning. We read that He said to the women who followed Him, as He was being led away to Calvary, "Daughters of Jerusalem, don't weep for me, but weep for yourselves and for your children. For the days are coming when they will say, "Fortunate indeed are the women who are childless, the wombs that have not borne a child and the breasts that have never nursed."

These words must have sounded peculiarly terrible to the ears of a Jewish woman. To her it was always a disgrace to be childless. The idea of a time coming when it would be a blessing to have no children, must have been a new and fearsome thought to her mind. And yet within fifty years this prediction of Christ was literally fulfilled! The siege of Jerusalem by the Roman army under Titus, brought down on all the inhabitants of the city the most horrible sufferings from famine and pestilence that can be conceived. Women are reported to have actually eaten their own children during the siege for lack of food. Upon none did the last judgments sent upon the Jewish nation fall so heavily as upon the wives, the mothers, and the little children.

Let us beware of supposing that the Lord Jesus holds out to man nothing but mercy, pardon, love, and forgiveness. Beyond all doubt He is plenteous in mercy. There is mercy with Him like a mighty stream. He "delights in mercy." But we must never forget that there is justice with Him as well as mercy. There are judgments preparing for the impenitent and the unbelieving. There is wrath revealed in the Gospel for those who harden themselves in wickedness. The same cloud which was bright to Israel was dark to the Egyptians. The same Lord Jesus who invites the laboring and heavy-laden to come to Him and rest, declares most plainly that unless a man repents he will perish, and that he who believes not shall be damned. (Luke 13:3; Mark 16:16.)

The same Savior who now holds out His hands to the disobedient and gainsaying, will come one day in flaming fire, taking vengeance on those that know not God and obey not the Gospel. (2 Thess. 1:8.) Let these things sink down into our hearts. Christ is indeed most gracious. But the day of grace must come to an end at last. An unbelieving world will find at length, as Jerusalem did, that there is judgment with God as well as mercy. No wrath will fall so heavily as that which has been long accumulating and heaping up.

We ought to notice, for another thing, in this passage, our Lord's words of gracious intercession. We read that when He was crucified, His first words were, "Father, forgive them, for they know not what they do." His own racking agony of body did not make Him forget others. The first of His seven sayings on the cross was a prayer for the souls of His murderers. His prophetical office He had just exhibited by a remarkable prediction. His kingly office He was about to exhibit soon by opening the door of paradise to the penitent thief. His priestly office He now exhibited by interceding for those who crucified Him. "Father," He said, "forgive them."

The fruits of this wonderful prayer will never be fully seen until the day when the books are opened, and the secrets of all hearts are revealed. We have probably not the least idea how many of the conversions to God at Jerusalem which took place during the first six months after the crucifixion, were the direct reply to this marvelous prayer. Perhaps this prayer was the first step towards the penitent thief's repentance. Perhaps it was one means of affecting the centurion, who declared our Lord "a righteous man," and the people who "smote their breasts and returned." Perhaps the three thousand converted on the day of Pentecost, foremost, it may be at one time among our Lord's murderers, owed their conversion to this very prayer. The day will declare it. There is nothing secret that shall not be revealed. This only we know, that "the Father hears the Son always." (John 11:42.) We may be sure that this wondrous prayer was heard.

Let us see in our Lord's intercession for those who crucified Him, one more proof of Christ's infinite love to sinners. The Lord Jesus is indeed most pitiful, most compassionate, most gracious. None are too wicked for Him to care for. None are too far gone in sin for his almighty heart to take interest about their souls. He wept over unbelieving Jerusalem. He heard the prayer of the dying thief. He stopped under the tree to call the tax-collector Zaccheus. He came down from heaven to turn the heart of the persecutor Saul. He found time to pray for His murderers even on the cross. Love like this is a love that passes knowledge. The vilest of sinners have no cause to be afraid of applying to a Savior like this. If we want warrant and encouragement to repent and believe, the passage before us surely supplies enough.

Finally, let us see in our Lord's intercession a striking example of the spirit which should reign in the hearts of all His people. Like Him, let us return good for evil, and blessing for cursing. Like Him, let us pray for those who evil entreat us and persecute us. The pride of our hearts may often rebel against the idea. The fashion of this world may call it foolish to behave in such a way. But let us never be ashamed to imitate our divine Master. The man who prays for his enemies shows the mind that was in Christ, and will have his reward.

LUKE 23:39-43

THE DYING THIEF

And one of the malefactors that were hanged railed on him, saying, Art not thou the Christ? save thyself and us. But the other answered, and rebuking him said, Dost thou not even fear God, seeing thou art in the same condemnation? And we indeed justly; for we receive the due reward of our deeds: but this man hath done nothing amiss. And he said, Jesus, remember me when thou comest in thy kingdom. And he said unto him, Verily I say unto thee, To-day shalt thou be with me in Paradise.

The verses we have now read deserve to be printed in letters of gold. They have probably been the salvation of myriads of souls. Multitudes will thank God to all eternity that the Bible contains this story of the penitent thief.

We see, firstly, in the history before us, the sovereignty of God in saving sinners. We are told that two malefactors were crucified together with our Lord, one on His right hand and the other on His left. Both were equally near to Christ. Both saw and heard all that happened, during the six hours that He hung on the cross. Both were dying men, and suffering acute pain. Both were alike wicked sinners, and needed forgiveness. Yet one died in his sins, as he had lived, hardened, impenitent, and unbelieving. The other repented, believed, cried to Jesus for mercy, and was saved.

A fact like this should teach us humility. We cannot account for it. We can only say, "Even so, Father, for so it seems good in your sight." (Matt. 11:26.) How it is that under precisely the same circumstances one man is converted and another remains dead in sins—why the very same sermon is heard by one man with complete indifference and sends another home to pray and seek Christ—why the same Gospel is hidden to one and revealed to another, all these are questions which we cannot possibly answer. We only know that it is so, and that it is useless to deny it.

Our own duty is clear and plain. We are to make a diligent use of all the means which God has appointed for the good of souls. There is no necessity that any one should be lost. There is no such a thing as decreed damnation in the Bible. The offers of the Gospel are wide, free and general. "In all our doings," says the 17th Article, "that will of God is to be followed, which we have expressly declared to us in the word of God." God's sovereignty was never meant to destroy man's responsibility. One thief was saved that no sinner might despair, but only one, that no sinner might presume.

We see secondly in this history, the unvarying character of repentance unto salvation. This is a point in the penitent thief's story which is fearfully overlooked. Thousands look at the broad fact that he was saved in the hour of death, and look no further. They do not look at the distinct and well-defined evidences of repentance which fell from his lips before he died. Those evidences deserve our closest attention.

The first notable step in the thief's repentance was his concern about his companion's wickedness in reviling Christ. "Do you not fear God," he said, "seeing you are in the same condemnation."

The second step was a full acknowledgment of his own sin. "We indeed are just in condemnation. We receive the due reward of our deeds."

The third step was an open confession of Christ's innocence. "This man has done nothing amiss."

The fourth step was faith in Jesus Christ's power and will to save him. He turned to a crucified sufferer, and called Him "Lord," and declared his belief that He had a kingdom.

The fifth step was prayer. He cried to Jesus when he was hanging on the cross, and asked Him even then to think upon his soul.

The sixth and last step was humility. He begged to be "remembered" by our Lord. He mentions no great thing. Enough for him if he is remembered by Christ.

These six points should always be remembered in connection with the penitent thief. His time was very short for giving proof of his conversion. But it was time well used. Few dying people have ever left behind them such good evidences as were left by this man.

Let us beware of a repentance without evidences. Thousands, it may be feared, are every year going out of the world with a lie in their right hand. They fancy they will be saved because the thief was saved in the hour of death. They forget that if they would be saved as he was, they must repent as he repented. The shorter a man's time is, the better must be the use he makes of it. The nearer he is to death, when he first begins to think, the clearer must be the evidence he leaves behind. Nothing, it may be safely laid down as a general rule, nothing is so thoroughly unsatisfactory as a death-bed repentance.

We see, thirdly, in this history, the amazing power and willingness of Christ to save sinners. It is written that He is "able to save to the uttermost." (Heb. 7:25.) If we search the Bible through, from Genesis to Revelation, we shall never find a more striking proof of Christ's power and mercy than the salvation of the penitent thief.

The time when the thief was saved was the hour of our Lord's greatest weakness. He was hanging in agony on the cross. Yet even then He heard and granted a sinner's petition, and opened to him the gate of life. Surely this was "power!"

The man whom our Lord saved was a wicked sinner at the point of death, with nothing in his past life to recommend him, and nothing notable in his present position but a humble prayer. Yet even he was plucked like a brand from the burning. Surely this was "mercy."

Do we want proof that salvation is of grace and not of works? We have it in the case before us. The dying thief was nailed hand and foot to the cross. He could do literally nothing for his own soul. Yet even he through Christ's infinite grace was saved. No one ever received such a strong assurance of his own forgiveness as this man.

Do we want proof that sacraments and ordinances are not absolutely needful to salvation, and that men may be saved without them when they cannot be had? We have it in the case before us. The dying thief was never baptized, belonged to no visible church, and never received the Lord's supper. But he repented and believed, and therefore he was saved.

Let these things sink down into our hearts. Christ never changes. The way of salvation is always one and the same. He lives who saved the penitent thief. There is hope for the vilest sinner, if he will only repent and believe.

We see, lastly, in the history before us, how near a dying believer is to rest and glory. We read that our Lord said to the malefactor in reply to his prayer, "Today shall you be with me in paradise."

That word "today" contains a body of divinity. It tells us that the very moment a believer dies, his soul is in happiness and in safe keeping. His full redemption is not yet come. His perfect bliss will not begin before the resurrection morning. But there is no mysterious delay, no season of suspense, no purgatory, between his death and a state of reward. In the day that he breathes his last he goes to Paradise. In the hour that he departs he is with Christ. (Phil 1:23.)

Let us remember these things, when our believing friends fall asleep in Christ. We must not sorrow for them as those who have no hope. While we are sorrowing they are rejoicing. While we are putting on our mourning, and weeping at their funerals, they are safe and happy with their Lord. Above all, let us remember these things, if we are true Christians, in looking forward to our own deaths. To die is a solemn thing. But if we die in the Lord, we need not doubt that our death will be gain.

LUKE 23:44-49

JESUS' DEATH

And it was now about the sixth hour, and a darkness came over the whole land until the ninth hour, the sun's light failing: and the veil of the temple was rent in the midst. And Jesus, crying with a loud voice, said, Father, into thy hands I commend my spirit: and having said this, he gave up the ghost. And when the centurion saw what was done, he glorified God, saying, Certainly this was a righteous man. And all the multitudes that came together to this sight, when they beheld the things that were done, returned smiting their breasts. And all his acquaintance, and the women that followed with him from Galilee, stood afar off, seeing these things.

Let us observe in these verses, the miraculous SIGNS which accompanied our Lord's death on the cross. We are told that there was "a darkness over all the earth" for three hours. "The sun was darkened and the curtain of the temple was torn in two."

It was fit and right that the attention of all around Jerusalem should be arrested in a marked way, when the great sacrifice for sin was being offered, and the Son of God was dying. There were signs and wonders wrought in the sight of all Israel, when the law was given on Sinai. There were signs and wonders in like manner when the atoning blood of Christ was shed on Calvary. There was a sign for an unbelieving world. The darkness at mid-day was a miracle which would compel men to think. There was a sign for the professing Church and the ministers of the temple. The tearing of the curtain which hung between the holy place and the holy of holies, was a miracle which would strike awe into the heart of every priest and Levite in Jewry.

Signs like these, on special occasions, let us remember, are a part of God's ways in dealing with man. He knows the desperate stupidity and unbelief of human nature. He sees it necessary to arouse our attention by miraculous works, when He brings in a new dispensation. He thus compels men to open their eyes whether they will or not, and to hear His voice for a little season. He has done so frequently in the days that are past. He did so when He gave the law. He did so in the passage before us when He brought in the Gospel. He will do so once more when Christ comes again the second time. He will show a sneering, unbelieving world that He can suspend the laws of nature at His pleasure, and alter the framework of creation as easily as He called the earth into being. He will yet fulfill His words, "Yet once more, I will shake not the earth only, but also the heavens." "The moon shall be confounded, and the sun ashamed, when the Lord of hosts shall reign in mount Zion." (Heb. 12:26; Isaiah 24:23.)

Let us observe, secondly, in these verses, the remarkable WORDS which our Lord spoke when He died. We read that "When he had cried with a loud voice, he said, Father, into your hands I commend my spirit—and having said thus, he gave up the spirit."

There is a depth of meaning, no doubt, in these words which we have no line to fathom. There was something mysterious about our Lord's death, which made it unlike the death of any mere man. He who spoke the words before us, we must carefully remember, was God as well as man. His divine and human nature were inseparably united. His divine nature of course could not die. He says Himself; "I lay down my life, that I might take it again. No man takes it from me, but I lay it down of myself. I have power to lay it down, and I have power to take it again." (John 10:17, 18.) Christ died, not as we die when our hour is come—not because He was compelled and could not help dying-but voluntarily, and of His own free will.

There is a sense, however, in which our Lord's words supply a lesson to all true Christians. They show us the manner in which death should be met by all God's children. They afford an example which every believer should strive to follow. Like our Master, we should not be afraid to confront the king of terrors. We should regard him as a vanquished enemy, whose sting has been taken away by Christ's death. We should think of him as a foe who can hurt the body for a little season, but after that has no more that he can do. We should await his approaches with calmness and patience, and believe that when flesh fails our soul will be in good keeping. This was the mind of dying Stephen; "Lord Jesus," he said, "receive my spirit." This was the mind of Paul the aged, when the time of his departure was at hand. He says, "I know whom I have believed, and am persuaded that He is able to keep that which I have committed to him against that day." (Acts 7:59; 2 Tim. 1:12.) Happy indeed are those who have a last end like this!

Let us observe, lastly, in these verses, the power of conscience in the case of the centurion and the people who saw Christ die. We are told that the centurion "praised God, saying, Certainly this was a righteous man." We are told that the people who had come together to the sight, "smote their breasts and went away."

We know not exactly the nature of the feelings here described. We know not the extent to which they went, or the after-fruit which they brought forth. One thing, at all events, is clear. The Roman officer felt convinced that he had been superintending an unrighteous action, and crucifying an innocent person. The gazing crowd were pierced to the heart by a sense of having aided, countenanced, and abetted a grievous wrong. Both Jew and Gentile left Calvary that evening heavy-hearted, self-condemned, and ill at ease.

Great indeed is the power of conscience! Mighty is the influence which it is able to exercise on the hearts of men! It can strike terror into the minds of monarchs on their thrones. It can make multitudes tremble and shake before a few bold friends of truth, like a flock of sheep. Blind and mistaken as conscience often is, unable to convert man or lead him to Christ, it is still a most blessed part of man's constitution, and the best friend in the congregation that the preacher of the Gospel has. No wonder that Paul says, "By manifestation of the truth we commend ourselves to every man's conscience." (2 Cor. 4:2.)

He that desires inward peace must beware of quarreling with his conscience. Let him rather use it well, guard it jealously, hear what it has to say, and reckon it his friend. Above all, let him pray daily that his conscience may be enlightened by the Holy Spirit, and cleansed by the blood of Christ. The words of John are very significant—"If our heart condemns us not, then have we confidence toward God." (1 John 3:21.) That man is doing well who can say, "I exercise myself to have a conscience void of offence toward God and toward man." (Acts 24:16.)

LUKE 23:50-56
JESUS' BURIAL

And behold, a man named Joseph, who was a councillor, a good and righteous man 51(he had not consented to their counsel and deed), a man of Arimathaea, a city of the Jews, who was looking for the kingdom of God: this man went to Pilate, and asked for the body of Jesus. And he took it down, and wrapped it in a linen cloth, and laid him in a tomb that was hewn in stone, where never man had yet lain. And it was the day of the Preparation, and the sabbath drew on. And the women, who had come with him out of Galilee, followed after, and beheld the tomb, and how his body was laid. And they returned, and prepared spices and ointments. And on the sabbath they rested according to the commandment.

We see from these verses that Christ has some disciples of whom little is known. We are told of one Joseph, "a good man and a just"—a man who "had not consented to the counsel" of those who condemned our Lord—a man who "himself waited for the kingdom of God. This man went boldly to Pilate after the crucifixion, begged the body of Jesus, "took it down" from the cross, and "laid it in a tomb."

We know nothing of Joseph excepting what is here told us. In no part of the Acts or Epistles do we find any mention of his name. At no former period of our Lord's ministry does he ever come forward. His reason for not openly joining the disciples before, we cannot explain. But here, at the eleventh hour, this man is not afraid to show himself one of our Lord's friends. At the very time when the apostles had forsaken Jesus, Joseph is not ashamed to show his love and respect. Others had confessed Him while He was living and doing miracles. It was reserved for Joseph to confess Him when He was dead.

The history of Joseph is full of instruction and encouragement. It shows us that Christ has friends of whom the Church knows little or nothing, friends who profess less than some do, but friends who in real love and affection are second to none. It shows us, above all, that events may bring out grace in quarters where at present we do not expect it; and that the cause of Christ may prove one day to have many supporters, of whose existence we are at present not aware. These are they whom David calls "hidden ones," and Solomon compares to a "lily among thorns." (Psalm 83:3; Cant. 2:2.)

Let us learn from the case of Joseph of Arimathaea, to be charitable and hopeful in our judgments. All is not barren in this world, when our eyes perhaps see nothing. There may be some latent sparks of light when all appears dark. Little plants of spiritual life may be existing in some remote Romish, or Greek, or Armenian congregations, which the Father Himself has planted. Grains of true faith may be lying hid in some neglected English parish, which have been placed there by God. There were seven thousand true worshipers in Israel of whom Elijah knew nothing. The day of judgment will bring forward men who seemed last, and place them among the first. (1 Kings 19:18.)

We see secondly, from these verses, the reality of Christ's death. This is a fact which is placed beyond dispute, by the circumstances related about His burial. Those who took His body from the cross and wrapped it in linen, could not have been deceived. Their own senses must have been witnesses to the fact, that He whom they handled was a corpse. Their own hands and eyes must have told them, that He whom they laid in Joseph's sepulcher was not alive but dead.

The importance of the fact before us is far greater than a careless reader supposes. If Christ did not really die, there would be an end of all the comfort of the Gospel. Nothing short of His death could have paid man's debt to God. His incarnation, and sermons, and parables, and miracles, and sinless obedience to the law, would have availed nothing, if He had not died. The penalty threatened to the first Adam was death eternal in hell. If the second Adam had not really and actually died in our stead, as well as taught us truth, the original penalty would have continued in full force against Adam and all his children. It was the life-blood of Christ which was to save our souls.

Forever let us bless God that our great Redeemer's death is a fact beyond all dispute. The centurion who stood by the cross, the friends who took out the nails, and laid the body in the grave, the women who stood by and beheld, the priests who sealed up the grave, the soldiers who guarded the sepulcher, all, all are witnesses that Jesus actually was dead. The great sacrifice was really offered. The life of the Lamb was actually taken away. The penalty due to sin has actually been discharged by our Divine Substitute. Sinners believing in Jesus may hope and not be afraid. In themselves they are guilty. But Christ has died for the ungodly; and their debt is now completely paid.

We see, lastly, in these verses, the respect paid by Christ's disciples to the fourth commandment. We are told that the women who had prepared spices and ointment to anoint our Lord's body, "rested the Sabbath Day, according to the commandment."

This little fact is a strong indirect argument in reply to those who tell us that Christ abolished the fourth commandment. Neither here nor elsewhere do we find anything to warrant any such conclusion. We see our Lord frequently denouncing the man-made traditions of the Jews about Sabbath observance. We see Him purifying the blessed day from superstitious and unscriptural opinions. We see Him maintaining firmly that works of necessity and works of mercy were not breaches of the fourth commandment.

But nowhere do we find Him teaching that the Sabbath was not to be kept at all. And here, in the verse before us, we find His disciples as scrupulous as any about the duty of keeping holy a Sabbath Day. Surely they could never have been taught by their Master that the fourth commandment was not intended to be binding on Christians.

Let us cling firmly to the old doctrine that the Sabbath is not a mere Jewish institution, but a day which was meant for man from the beginning, and which was intended to be honored by Christians quite as much as by Jews. Let us not doubt that the Apostles were taught by our Lord to change the day from the last day of the week to the first, although mercifully checked from publicly proclaiming the change, in order to avoid giving offence to Israel. Above all, let us regard the Sabbath as an institution of primary importance to man's soul, and contend earnestly for its preservation among us in all its integrity. It is good for body, mind and soul. It is good for the nation which observes it, and for the church which gives it honor. It is but a few steps from "no Sabbath" to "no God." The man who would make the Sabbath a day for business and pleasure, is an enemy to the best interests of his fellow-creatures. The man who supposes that a believer ought to be so spiritual as not to need the separation of one day in the week from the rest, can know but little of the human heart, or the requirements of our position in an ensnaring and evil world.

Chapter 24

But on the first day of the week, at early dawn, they came unto the tomb, bringing the spices which they had prepared. And they found the stone rolled away from the tomb. And they entered in, and found not the body of the Lord Jesus. And it came to pass, while they were perplexed thereabout, behold, two men stood by them in dazzling apparel: and as they were affrighted and bowed down their faces to the earth, they said unto them, Why seek ye the living among the dead? He is not here, but is risen: remember how he spake unto you when he was yet in Galilee, saying that the Son of man must be delivered up into the hands of sinful men, and be crucified, and the third day rise again. And they remembered his words, and returned from the tomb, and told all these things to the eleven, and to all the rest. Now they were Mary Magdalene, and Joanna, and Mary the mother of James: and the other women with them told these things unto the apostles. And these words appeared in their sight as idle talk; and they disbelieved them. But Peter arose, and ran unto the tomb; and stooping and looking in, he seeth the linen cloths by themselves; and he departed to his home, wondering at that which was come to pass.

The resurrection of Christ is one of the great foundation-stones of the Christian religion. In practical importance it is second only to the crucifixion. The chapter we have now begun directs our mind to the evidence of the resurrection. It contains unanswerable proof that Jesus not only died, but rose again.

We see, in the verses before us, the reality of Christ's resurrection. We read, that upon "the first day of the week" certain women came to the tomb in which the body of Jesus had been laid, in order to anoint Him. But when they came to the place, "they found the stone rolled away. And they entered in and found not the body of the Lord Jesus."

This simple fact is the starting-point in the history of the resurrection of Christ. On Friday morning His body was safe in the tomb. On Sabbath morning His body was gone. By whose hands had it been taken away? Who had removed it? Not surely the priests and scribes and other enemies of Christ! If they had had Christ's body to show in disproof of His resurrection, they would gladly have shown it. Not the apostles and other disciples of our Lord! They were far too much frightened and dispirited to attempt such an action, and the more so when they had nothing to gain by it. One explanation, and one only, can meet the circumstance of the case. That explanation is the one supplied by the angels in the verse before us. Christ "had risen" from the grave. To seek Him in the sepulcher was seeking "the living among the dead." He had risen again, and was soon seen alive and conversing in the body by many credible witnesses.

The fact of our Lord's resurrection rests on evidence which no infidel can ever explain away. It is confirmed by testimony of every kind, sort, and description. The plain unvarnished story which the Gospel writers tell about it, is one that cannot be overthrown. The more the account they give is examined, the more inexplicable will the event appear, unless we accept it as true. If we choose to deny the truth of their account we may deny everything in the world. It is not so certain that Julius Caesar once lived, as it is that Christ rose again.

Let us cling firmly to the resurrection of Christ, as one of the pillars of the Gospel. It ought to produce in our minds a settled conviction of the truth of Christianity. Our faith does not depend merely on a set of texts and doctrines. It is founded on a mighty historical fact which the skeptic has never been able to overturn. It ought to assure us of the certainty of the resurrection of our own bodies after death. If our Master has risen from the grave, we need not doubt that His disciples shall rise again at the last day.

Above all it ought to fill our hearts with a joyful sense of the fullness of Gospel salvation. Who is he that shall condemn us? Our Great Surety has not only died for us but risen again. (Rom. 8:34.) He has gone to prison for us, and come forth triumphantly after atoning for our sins. The payment He made for us has been accepted. The work of satisfaction has been perfectly accomplished. No wonder that Peter exclaims, "Blessed be the God and Father of our Lord Jesus Christ, who according to His abundant mercy, has begotten us again to a living hope by the resurrection of Jesus Christ from the dead." (1 Pet. 1:3.)

We see, secondly, in the verses before us, how dull the memory of the disciples was about some of our Lord's teachings. We are told that the angels who appeared to the women, reminded them of their Master's words in Galilee, foretelling His own crucifixion and resurrection. And then we read, "They remembered his words." They had heard them, but made no use of them. Now after many days they call them to mind.

This dulness of memory is a common spiritual disease among believers. It prevails as widely now as it did in the days of the first disciples. It is one among many proofs of our fallen and corrupt condition. Even after men have been renewed by the Holy Spirit, their readiness to forget the promises and precepts of the Gospel is continually bringing them into trouble. They hear many things which they ought to store up in their hearts, but seem to forget as fast as they hear. And then, perhaps after many days, affliction brings them up before their recollection, and at once it flashes across their minds that they heard them long ago! They find that they had heard, but heard in vain.

The true cure for a dull memory in religion, is to get deeper love toward Christ, and affections more thoroughly set on things above. We do not readily forget the things we love, and the objects which we keep continually under our eyes. The names of our parents and children are always remembered. The face of the husband or wife we love is engraved on the tablets of our hearts. The more our affections are engaged in Christ's service, the more easy shall we find it to remember Christ's words. The words of the apostle ought to be carefully pondered—"We ought to give the more earnest heed to the things which we have heard, lest at any time we should let them slip." (Heb. 2:1.)

We see, lastly, how slow of belief the first disciples were on the subject of Christ's resurrection. We read that when the women returned from the sepulcher and told the things they had heard from the angels to the eleven apostles, "their words seemed to them idle tales, and they believed them not." In spite of the plainest declarations from their Master's own lips that He would rise again the third day—in spite of the distinct testimony of five or six credible witnesses that the sepulcher was empty, and that angels had told them He was risen—in spite of the manifest impossibility of accounting for the empty tomb on any other supposition than that of a miraculous resurrection—in spite of all this, these eleven faithless ones would not believe!

Perhaps we marvel at their unbelief. No doubt it seems at first sight most senseless, most unreasonable, most provoking, most unaccountable. But shall we not do well to look at home? Do we not see around us in the Christian Churches a mass of unbelief far more unreasonable and far more blame-worthy than that of the apostles? Do we not see, after eighteen centuries of additional proofs that Christ has risen from the dead, a general lack of faith which is truly deplorable? Do we not see myriads of professing Christians who seem not to believe that Jesus died and rose again, and is coming to judge the world? These are painful questions. Strong faith is indeed a rare thing. No wonder that our Lord said, "When the Son of man comes, shall He find faith on the earth?" (Luke 18:8.)

Finally, let us admire the wisdom of God, which can bring great good out of seeming evil. The unbelief of the apostles is one of the strongest indirect evidences that Jesus rose from the dead. If the disciples were at first so backward to believe our Lord's resurrection, and were at last so thoroughly persuaded of its truth that they preached it everywhere, Christ must have risen indeed. The first preachers were men who were convinced in spite of themselves, and in spite of determined, obstinate unwillingness to believe. If the apostles at last believed, the resurrection must be true.

LUKE 24:13-35

And behold, two of them were going that very day to a village named Emmaus, which was threescore furlongs from Jerusalem. And they communed with each other of all these things which had happened. And it came to pass, while they communed and questioned together, that Jesus himself drew near, and went with them. But their eyes were holden that they should not know him. And he said unto them, What communications are these that ye have one with another, as ye walk? And they stood still, looking sad. And one of them, named Cleopas, answering said unto him, Dost thou alone sojourn in Jerusalem and not know the things which are come to pass there in these days? And he said unto them, What things? And they said unto him, The things concerning Jesus the Nazarene, who was a prophet mighty in deed and word before God and all the people: and how the chief priests and our rulers delivered him up to be condemned to death, and crucified him. But we hoped that it was he who should redeem Israel. Yea and besides all this, it is now the third day since these things came to pass. Moreover certain women of our company amazed us, having been early at the tomb; and when they found not his body, they came, saying, that they had also seen a vision of angels, who said that he was alive. And certain of them that were with us went to the tomb, and found it even so as the women had said: but him they saw not. And he said unto them, O foolish men, and slow of heart to believe in all that the prophets have spoken! Behooved it not the Christ to suffer these things, and to enter into his glory? And beginning from Moses and from all the prophets, he interpreted to them in all the scriptures the things concerning himself. And they drew nigh unto the village, whither they were going: and he made as though he would go further. And they constrained him, saying, Abide with us; for it is toward evening, and the day is now far spent. And he went in to abide with them. And it came to pass, when he had sat down with them to meat, he took the bread and blessed; and breaking it he gave to them. And their eyes were opened, and they knew him; and he vanished out of their sight. And they said one to another, Was not our heart burning within us, while he spake to us in the way, while he opened to us the scriptures? And they rose up that very hour, and returned to Jerusalem, and found the eleven gathered together, and them that were with them, saying, The Lord is risen indeed, and hath appeared to Simon. And they rehearsed the things that happened in the way, and how he was known of them in the breaking of the bread.

The history contained in these verses is not found in any other Gospel but that of Luke. Of all the eleven appearances of Christ after His resurrection, none perhaps is so interesting as the one described in this passage.

Let us mark, in these verses, what encouragement there is to believers to speak to one another about Christ. We are told of two disciples walking together to Emmaus, and talking of their Master's crucifixion. And then come the remarkable words, "While they communed together and reasoned, Jesus Himself drew near, and went with them."

Conference on spiritual subjects is a most important means of grace. As iron sharpens iron, so does exchange of thoughts with brethren sharpen a believer's soul. It brings down a special blessing on all who make a practice of it. The striking words of Malachi were meant for the Church in every age -"Then those who feared the Lord spoke often one to another—and the Lord hearkened, and heard it, and a book of remembrance was written before him for those who feared the Lord, and that thought upon His name. And they shall be mine says the Lord, in that day when I make up my jewels." (Mal. 3:16, 17.)

What do we know ourselves of spiritual conversation with other Christians? Perhaps we read our Bibles, and pray in private, and use public means of grace. It is all well, very well. But if we stop short here we neglect a great privilege and have yet much to learn. We ought to "consider one another to provoke to love and good works." We ought to "exhort" and "edify one another." (Heb. 10:24; 1 Thess. 5:11.) Have we no time for spiritual conversation? Let us think again. The quantity of time wasted on frivolous, trifling, and unprofitable talk, is fearfully great. Do we find nothing to say on spiritual subjects? Do we feel tongue-tied and speechless on the things of Christ? Surely if this is the case, there must be something wrong within. A heart right in the sight of God will generally find words. "Out of the abundance of the heart the mouth speaks." (Matt. 12:34.)

Let us learn a lesson from the two travelers to Emmaus. Let us speak of Jesus, when we are sitting in our houses and when we are walking by the way, whenever we can find a disciple to speak to. (Deut. 6:7.) If we believe we are journeying to a heaven where Christ will be the central object of every mind, let us begin to learn the manners of heaven, while we are yet upon earth. So doing we shall often have One with us whom our eyes will not see, but One who will make our hearts "burn within us" by blessing the conversation.

Let us mark, secondly, in these verses, how weak and imperfect was the knowledge of some of our Lord's disciples. We are told that the two disciples confessed frankly that their expectations had been disappointed by the crucifixion of Christ. "We had hoped," said they, "that it had been He who would have redeemed Israel." A temporal redemption of the Jews by a conqueror appears to have been the redemption which they looked for. A spiritual redemption by a sacrificial death was an idea which their minds could not thoroughly take in.

Ignorance like this, at first sight, is truly astounding. We cannot be surprised at the sharp rebuke which fell from our Lord's lips, "how foolish you are, and slow of heart to believe." Yet ignorance like this is deeply instructive. It shows us how little cause we have to wonder at the spiritual darkness which obscures the minds of careless Christians. Myriads around us are just as ignorant of the meaning of Christ's sufferings as these travelers to Emmaus. As long as the world stands the cross will seem foolishness to natural man.

Let us bless God that there may be true grace hidden under much intellectual ignorance. Clear and accurate knowledge is a most useful thing, but it is not absolutely needful to salvation, and may even be possessed without grace. A deep sense of sin, a humble willingness to be saved in God's way, a teachable readiness to give up our own prejudices when a more excellent way is shown, these are the principal things. These things the two disciples possessed, and therefore our Lord "went with them" and guided them into all truth.

Let us mark, thirdly, in these verses, how full the Old Testament is of Christ. We are told that our Lord began "with Moses and all the prophets, and expounded in all the Scriptures the things concerning himself."

How shall we explain these words? In what way did our Lord show "things concerning himself," in every part of the Old Testament field? The answer to these questions is short and simple. Christ was the substance of every Old Testament sacrifice, ordained in the law of Moses. Christ was the true Deliverer and King, of whom all the judges and deliverers in Jewish history were types. Christ was the coming Prophet greater than Moses, whose glorious advent filled the pages of prophets. Christ was the true seed of the woman who was to bruise the serpent's head—the true seed in whom all nations were to be blessed—the true Shiloh to whom the people were to be gathered, the true scape-goat—the true bronze serpent—the true Lamb to which every daily offering pointed—the true High Priest of whom every descendant of Aaron was a figure. These things, or something like them, we need not doubt, were some of the things which our Lord expounded in the way to Emmaus.

Let it be a settled principle in our minds, in reading the Bible, that Christ is the central sun of the whole book. So long as we keep Him in view, we shall never greatly err in our search for spiritual knowledge. Once losing sight of Christ, we shall find the whole Bible dark and full of difficulty. The key of Bible knowledge is Jesus Christ.

Let us mark, finally, in these verses, how much Christ loves to be entreated by His people. We are told, that when the disciples drew near to Emmaus, our Lord "made as though he would have gone further." He desired to see if they were weary of His conversation. But it was not so. "They constrained Him, saying, abide with us—for it is toward evening, and the day is far spent. And He went in to tarry with them."

Cases like this are not uncommon in Scripture. Our Lord sees it good for us to prove our love, by withholding mercies until we ask for them. He does not always force His gifts upon us, unsought and unsolicited. He loves to draw out our desires, and to compel us to exercise our spiritual affections, by waiting for our prayers. He dealt so with Jacob at Peniel. "Let me go," He said, "for the day breaks." And then came the noble declaration from Jacob's lips, "I will not let you go except you bless me." (Gen. 32:26.) The story of the Canaanitish mother, the story of the healing of two blind men at Jericho, the story of the nobleman at Capernaum, the parables of the unjust judge and friend at midnight, are all meant to teach the same lesson. All show that our Lord loves to be entreated, and likes importunity.

Let us act on this principle in all our prayers, if we know anything of praying. Let us ask much, and ask often, and lose nothing for lack of asking. Let us not be like the Jewish king who smote three times on the ground, and then stopped his hand. (2 Kings 13:18.) Let us rather remember the words of David's Psalm, "Open your mouth wide and I will fill it." (Psalm. 81:10.) It is the man who puts a holy constraint on Christ in prayer, who enjoys much of Christ's manifested presence.

LUKE 24:36-43

JESUS APPEARS TO THE DISCIPLES

And as they spake these things, he himself stood in the midst of them, and saith unto them, Peace be unto you. But they were terrified and affrighted, and supposed that they beheld a spirit. And he said unto them, Why are ye troubled? and wherefore do questionings arise in your heart? See my hands and my feet, that it is I myself: handle me, and see; for a spirit hath not flesh and bones, as ye behold me having. And when he had said this, he showed them his hands and his feet. And while they still disbelieved for joy, and wondered, he said unto them, Have ye here anything to eat? And they gave him a piece of a broiled fish. And he took it, and ate before them.

We should observe in this passage the singularly gracious words with which our Lord introduced Himself to His disciples after His resurrection. We read that He suddenly stood in the midst of them and said, "Peace be unto you."

This was a wonderful saying when we consider the men to whom it was addressed. It was addressed to eleven disciples, who three days before had shamefully forsaken their Master and fled. They had broken their promises. They had forgotten their professions of readiness to die for their faith. They had been scattered, "every man to his own," and left their Master to die alone. One of them had even denied Him three times. All of them had proved backsliders and cowards. And yet behold the return which their Master makes to His disciples! Not a word of rebuke is spoken. Not a single sharp saying falls from His lips. Calmly and quietly He appears in the midst of them, and begins by speaking of peace. "Peace be unto you!"

We see, in this touching saying, one more proof that the love of Christ "passes knowledge." It is His glory to pass over a transgression. He "delights in mercy." He is far more willing to forgive than men are to be forgiven, and far more ready to pardon than men are to be pardoned. There is in His almighty heart an infinite willingness to put away man's transgressions. Though our sins have been as scarlet He is ever ready to make them as white as snow, to blot them out, to cast them behind His back, to bury them in the depths of the sea, to remember them no more. All these are scriptural phrases intended to convey the same great truth. The natural man is continually stumbling at them, and refusing to understand them. At this we need not wonder. Free, full, and undeserved forgiveness to the very uttermost is not the manner of man. But it is the manner of Christ.

Where is the sinner, however great his sins, who need be afraid of beginning to apply to such a Savior as this? In the hand of Jesus there is mercy enough and to spare. Where is the backslider, however far he may have fallen, who need be afraid of returning? "Fury is not in Christ." (Isaiah. 27:4.) He is willing to raise and restore the very worst. Where is the saint who ought not to love such a Savior, and to pay Him willingly a holy obedience? There is forgiveness with Him, that He may be feared. (Psalm 130:4.) Where is the professing Christian who ought not to be forgiving toward his brethren? The disciples of a Savior whose words were so full of peace, ought to be peaceable, gentle, and easy to be entreated. (Coloss. 3:13.)

We should observe, for another thing, in this passage, our Lord's marvelous condescension to the infirmity of His disciples. We read that when His disciples were terrified at His appearance, and could not believe that it was Himself, He said, "Behold my hands and feet—touch me and see."

Our Lord might fairly have commanded His disciples to believe that He had risen. He might justly have said "Where is your faith? Why do you not believe my resurrection, when you see me with your own eyes?" But He does not do so. He stoops even lower than this. He appeals to the bodily senses of the eleven. He bids them touch Him with their own hands, and satisfy themselves that He was a material being, and not a ghost or spirit.

A mighty principle is contained in this circumstance, which we shall do well to store up in our hearts. Our Lord permits us to use our senses in testing a fact or an assertion in religion. Things ABOVE our reason we must expect to find in Christianity. But things CONTRARY to reason, and contradictory to our own senses, our Lord would have us know, we are not meant to believe. A doctrine, so-called, which contradicts our senses, is not a doctrine which came from Him who bade the eleven touch His hands and His feet.

Let us remember this principle in dealing with the Romish doctrine of a change in the bread and wine at the Lord's Supper. There is no such change at all. Our own eyes and our own tongues tell us that the bread is bread and the wine is wine, after consecration as well as before. Our Lord never requires us to believe that which is contrary to our senses. The doctrine of transubstantiation is therefore false and unscriptural.

Let us remember this principle in dealing with the Romish doctrine of baptismal regeneration. There is no inseparable connection between baptism and the new birth of man's heart. Our own eyes and senses tell us that myriads of baptized people have not the Spirit of God, are utterly without grace, and are servants of the devil and the world. Our Lord never requires us to believe that which is contrary to our senses. The doctrine that regeneration invariably accompanies baptism is therefore undeserving of credit. It is mere antinomianism to say that there is grace where no grace is to be seen.

A mighty practical lesson is involved in our Lord's dealing with the disciples, which we shall do well to remember. That lesson is the duty of dealing gently with weak disciples, and teaching them as they are able to bear. Like our Lord, we must be forbearing and patient. Like our Lord, we must condescend to the feebleness of some men's faith, and treat them as tenderly as little children, in order to bring them into the right way. We must not cast off men because they do not see everything at once. We must not despise the humblest and most childish means, if we can only persuade men to believe. Such dealing may require much patience. But he who cannot condescend to deal thus with the young, the ignorant, and the uneducated, has not the mind of Christ. Well would it be for all believers, if they would remember Paul's words more frequently, "To the weak became I as weak, that I might gain the weak." (1 Cor 9:22.)

LUKE 24:44-49

And he said unto them, These are my words which I spake unto you, while I was yet with you, that all things must needs be fulfilled, which are written in the law of Moses, and the prophets, and the psalms, concerning me. Then opened he their mind, that they might understand the scriptures; and he said unto them, Thus it is written, that the Christ should suffer, and rise again from the dead the third day; and that repentance and remission of sins should be preached in his name unto all the nations, beginning from Jerusalem. Ye are witnesses of these things. And behold, I send forth the promise of my Father upon you: but tarry ye in the city, until ye be clothed with power from on high.

Let us observe, firstly, in these verses, the gift which our Lord bestowed on His disciples immediately before He left the world. We read that He "opened their understanding that they might understand the Scriptures."

We must not misapprehend these words. We are not to suppose that the disciples knew nothing about the Old Testament up to this time, and that the Bible is a book which no ordinary person can expect to comprehend. We are simply to understand that Jesus showed His disciples the full meaning of many passages which had hitherto been hidden from their eyes. Above all, He showed the true interpretation of many prophetical passages concerning the Messiah.

We all need a like enlightenment of our understandings. "The natural man receives not the things of the Spirit of God; for they are foolishness unto him; neither can he know them, because they are spiritually discerned." (1 Cor. 2:14.) Pride, and prejudice, and love of the world blind our intellects, and throw a veil over the eyes of our minds in the reading of the Scriptures. We see the words, but do not thoroughly understand them until we are taught from above.

He that desires to read his Bible with profit, must first ask the Lord Jesus to open the eyes of his understanding by the Holy Spirit. Human commentaries are useful in their way. The help of good and learned men is not to be despised. But there is no commentary to be compared with the teaching of Christ. A humble and prayerful spirit will find a thousand things in the Bible, which the proud, self-conceited student will utterly fail to discern.

Let us observe secondly in these verses, the remarkable manner in which the Lord Jesus speaks of His own death on the cross. He does not speak of it as a misfortune, or as a thing to be lamented, but as a necessity. He says, "The Messiah must suffer, and rise again the third day."

The death of Christ was necessary to our salvation. His flesh and blood offered in sacrifice on the cross were "the life of the world." (John 6:51.) Without the death of Christ, so far as we can see, God's law could never have been satisfied—sin could never have been pardoned—man could never have been justified before God—and God could never have shown mercy to man. The cross of Christ was the solution of a mighty difficulty. It untied a vast knot. It enabled God to be "just, and yet the justifier" of the ungodly.

(Rom. 3:26.) It enabled man to draw near to God with boldness, and to feel that though a sinner he might have hope. Christ by suffering as a Substitute in our stead, the just for the unjust, has made a way by which we can draw near to God. We may freely acknowledge that in ourselves we are guilty and deserve death. But we may boldly plead, that One has died for us, and that for His sake, believing on Him, we claim life and acquittal.

Let us ever glory in the cross of Christ. Let us regard it as the source of all our hopes, and the foundation of all our peace. Ignorance and unbelief may see nothing in the sufferings of Calvary but the cruel martyrdom of an innocent person. Faith will look far deeper. Faith will see in the death of Jesus the payment of man's enormous debt to God, and the complete salvation of all who believe.

Let us observe, thirdly, in these verses, what were the first truths which the Lord Jesus bade His disciples preach after He left the world. We read that "repentance and forgiveness of sins" were to be preached in His name among all nations.

"Repentance and forgiveness of sins" are the first things which ought to be pressed on the attention of every man, woman, and child throughout the world. All ought to be told the necessity of repentance. All are by nature desperately wicked. Without repentance and conversion, none can enter the kingdom of God. All ought to be told God's readiness to forgive every one who believes on Christ. All are by nature guilty and condemned. But any one may obtain by faith in Jesus, free, full, and immediate pardon. All, not least, ought to be continually reminded, that repentance and forgiveness of sins are inseparably linked together. Not that our repentance can purchase our pardon. Pardon is the free gift of God to the believer in Christ. But still it remains true, that an impenitent man, is an unforgiven man.

He that desires to be a true Christian, must be experimentally acquainted with repentance and remission of sins. These are the principal things in saving religion. To belong to a pure Church, and hear the Gospel, and receive the sacraments, are great privileges. But are we converted? Are we justified? If not, we are dead before God. Happy is that Christian who keeps these two points continually before his eyes! Repentance and forgiveness are not mere elementary truths, and milk for babes. The highest standard of sanctity is nothing more than a continual growth in practical knowledge of these two points. The brightest saint is the man who has the most heart-searching sense of his own sinfulness, and the liveliest sense of his own complete acceptance in Christ.

Let us observe, fourthly, what was the first place at which the disciples were to begin preaching. They were to begin "at Jerusalem."

This is a striking fact, and one full of instruction. It teaches us that none are to be reckoned too wicked for salvation to be offered to them, and that no degree of spiritual disease is beyond the reach of the Gospel remedy. Jerusalem was the wickedest city on earth when our Lord left the world. It was a city which had stoned the prophets and killed those whom God sent to call it to repentance. It was a city full of pride, unbelief, self-righteousness, and desperate hardness of heart. It was a city which had just crowned all its transgressions by crucifying the Lord of glory. And yet Jerusalem was the place at which the first proclamation of repentance and pardon was to be made. The command of Christ was plain—"Begin at Jerusalem."

We see in these wondrous words, the length, and breadth, and depth, and height of Christ's compassion toward sinners. We must never despair of any one being saved, however bad and profligate he may have been. We must open the door of repentance to the chief of sinners. We must not be afraid to invite the worst of men to repent, believe, and live. It is the glory of our Great Physician, that He can heal incurable cases. The things that seem impossible to men are possible with Christ.

Let us observe, lastly, the peculiar position which believers, and especially ministers, are meant to occupy in this world. Our Lord defines it in one expressive word. He says, "You are witnesses."

If we are true disciples of Christ, we must bear a continual testimony in the midst of an evil world. We must testify to the truth of our Master's Gospel—the graciousness of our Master's heart—the happiness of our Master's service—the excellence of our Master's rules of life, and the enormous danger and wickedness of the ways of the world. Such testimony will doubtless bring down upon us the displeasure of man. The world will hate us, as it did our Master, because we "testify of it, that its works are evil." (John 7:7.) Such testimony will doubtless be believed by few comparatively, and will be thought by many offensive and extreme. But the duty of a witness is to bear his testimony, whether he is believed or not. If we bear a faithful testimony, we have done our duty, although, like Noah and Elijah, and Jeremiah, we stand almost alone.

What do we know of this witnessing character? What kind of testimony do we bear? What evidence do we give that we are disciples of a crucified Savior, and, like Him, are "not of the world?" (John 17:14.) What marks do we show of belonging to Him who said, "I came that I should bear witness unto the truth?" (John 18:37.) Happy is he who can give a satisfactory answer to these questions, and whose life declares plainly that he" seeks a country." (Heb. 11:14.)

LUKE 24:50-53

And he led them out until they were over against Bethany: and he lifted up his hands, and blessed them. And it came to pass, while he blessed them, he parted from them, and was carried up into heaven. And they worshipped him, and returned to Jerusalem with great joy: and were continually in the temple, blessing God.

These verses are the winding up of Luke's history of our Lord's ministry. They form a suitable conclusion to a Gospel, which in touching tenderness and full exhibition of Christ's grace, stands first among the four records of the things which Jesus did and taught. (Acts 1:1.)

Let us notice, firstly, in this passage, the remarkable manner in which our Lord left His disciples. We read that "He lifted up His hands and blessed them. And it came to pass, while He blessed them, He was parted from them." In one word, He left them when in the very act of blessing.

We cannot for a moment doubt that there was a meaning in this circumstance. It was intended to remind the disciples of all that Jesus had brought with Him when He came into the world. It was intended to assure them of what He would yet do, after He left the world. He came on earth to bless and not to curse, and blessing He departed. He came in love and not in anger, and in love He went away. He came not as a condemning judge, but as a compassionate Friend, and as a Friend He returned to His Father. He had been a Savior full of blessings to His little flock while He had been with them. He would be a Savior full of blessings to them, He would have them know, even after He was taken away.

Forever let our souls lean on the gracious heart of Christ, if we know anything of true religion. We shall never find a heart more tender, more loving, more patient, more compassionate, and more kind. To talk of the Virgin Mary as being more compassionate than Christ is a proof of miserable ignorance. To flee to the saints for comfort, when we may flee to Christ, is an act of mingled stupidity and blasphemy, and a robbery of Christ's crown. Gracious was our Lord Jesus while He lived among His weak disciples, gracious in the very season of His agony on the cross, gracious when He rose again and gathered His scattered sheep around Him—gracious in the manner of His departure from this world. It was a departure in the very act of blessing! Gracious, we may be assured He is at the right hand of God. He is the same yesterday, today, and forever—a Savior ever ready to bless abounding in blessings.

Let us notice, secondly, in this passage, the place to which our Lord went when He left the world. We read that "He was carried up into heaven."

The full meaning of these words we cannot of course comprehend. It would be easy to ask questions about the exact residence of Christ's glorified body, which the wisest theologian could never answer. We muse not waste our time in unedifying speculations, or "intrude into things unseen." (Col. 2:18.) Let it suffice us to know that our Lord Jesus Christ is gone into the presence of God on behalf of all who believe on Him, as a Forerunner and a High Priest. (Heb. 6:20. John 14:2.)

As a Forerunner, Jesus has gone into heaven to prepare a place for all His members. Our great Head has taken possession of a glorious inheritance in behalf of His mystical body, and holds it as an elder brother and trustee, until the day comes when His body shall be perfected. As a High Priest, Jesus has gone into heaven to intercede for all who believe on Him. There in the holy of holies He presents on their behalf the merit of His own sacrifice, and obtains for them daily supplies of mercy and grace. The grand secret of the perseverance of saints is Christ's appearance for them in heaven. They have an everlasting Advocate with the Father, and therefore they are never cast away. (Heb. 9:24. 1 John 2:1.)

A day will come when Jesus shall return from heaven, in like manner as He went. He will not always abide within the holy of holies. He will come forth, like the Jewish high priest, to bless the people, to gather His saints together, and to restore all things. (Lev. 9:23. Acts 3:21.) For that day let us wait, and long, and pray. Christ dying on the cross for sinners—Christ living in heaven to intercede—Christ coming again in glory, are three great objects which ought to stand out prominently before the eyes of every true Christian.

Let us notice, lastly, in this passage, the feelings of our Lord's disciples when He finally left them and was carried up into heaven. We read that "they returned to Jerusalem with great joy, and were continually in the temple, praising and blessing God."

How shall we account for these joyful feelings? How shall we explain the singular fact, that this little company of weak disciples, left, for the first time, like orphans, in the midst of an angry world, was not cast down, but was full of joy? The answer to these questions is short and simple. The disciples rejoiced, because now for the first time they saw all things clearly about their Master. The veil was removed from their eyes. The darkness had at length passed away. The meaning of Christ's humiliation and low estate—the meaning of His mysterious agony, and cross, and passion—the meaning of His being Messiah and yet a sufferer—the meaning of His being crucified, and yet being Son of God—all, all was at length unraveled and made plain. They saw it all. They understood it all. Their doubts were removed. Their stumbling blocks were taken away. Now at last they possessed clear knowledge, and possessing clear knowledge felt unmingled joy.

Let it be a settled principle with us, that the little degree of joy which many believers feel arises often from lack of knowledge. Weak faith and inconsistent practice are doubtless two great reasons why many of God's children enjoy so little peace. But it may well be suspected that dim and indistinct views of the Gospel are the true cause of many a believer's discomfort. When the Lord Jesus is not clearly known and understood, it must needs follow that there is little "joy in the Lord."

Let us leave the Gospel of Luke with a settled purpose of heart to seek more spiritual knowledge every year we live. Let us search the Scriptures more deeply and pray over them more heartily. Too many believers only scratch the surface of Scripture, and know nothing of digging down into its hidden treasures. Let the word dwell in us more richly. Let us read our Bibles more diligently. So doing we shall taste more of joy and peace in believing, and shall know what it is to be "continually praising and blessing God."

Made in the USA
Coppell, TX
10 November 2019

11190620R00252